The Emerging Field
Of Personal Relationships

The Emerging Field Of Personal Relationships

Edited by

Robin Gilmour
Steve Duck

University of Lancaster
Lancaster, England

LAWRENCE ERLBAUM ASSOCIATES, PUBLISHERS
1986   Hillsdale, New Jersey   London

Lawrence Erlbaum Associates, Inc., Publishers
365 Broadway
Hillsdale, New Jersey 07642

Library of Congress Cataloging in Publication Data
Main entry under title:

The Emerging field of personal relationships.

Bibliography: p.
Includes indexes.
1. Interpersonal relations—Congresses. I. Gilmour,
Robin. II. Duck, Steve.
HM132.E54 1986   302.3′4   85-27454
ISBN 0–89859–547–9

Printed in the United States of America
10 9 8 7 6 5 4 3 2 1

Contents

PART IV. DISORDER AND REPAIR OF RELATIONSHIPS

PART V.   SUMMARY AND PERSPECTIVE

Contributors

MICHAEL ARGYLE, Institute of Experimental Psychology, Oxford University, South Parks Road, Oxford, England.

GRAZIA ATTILI, Instituto di Psicologia del CNR, via dei Monti Tiburtini 509, 00157 Roma, Italy.

LESLIE A. BAXTER, Department of Communications, Lewis & Clark College, Portland, OR 97219, U.S.A.

ELLEN BERSCHEID, Department of Psychology, University of Minnesota, Minneapolis, MN 55455, U.S.A.

ROBERT G. BRINGLE, Department of Psychology, Purdue University, Indianapolis, IN 47907, U.S.A.

BRAM BUUNK, Department of Social Psychology, University of Nijmegen, 6500 HE Nijmegen, The Netherlands.

ANN C. CROUTER, Individual and Family Studies, Pennsylvania State University, University Park, State College, PA 16802, U.S.A.

STEVE DUCK, Department of Psychology, Fylde College, University of Lancaster, Lancaster, England.

JANET FARRELL, Department of Psychology, University of Denver, Denver, CO 80112, U.S.A.

KATHRYN S. GALVIN, Department of Psychology, Texas Tech University, Lubbock TX 79409, U.S.A.

NETTIE N. GARNICK, Department of Psychology, Texas Tech University, Lubbock, TX 79409, U.S.A.

ROBIN GILMOUR, Department of Psychology, Fylde College, University of Lancaster, Lancaster, England.

GERALD P. GINSBURG, Department of Sociology, University of Nevada, Reno, NV 89557, U.S.A.

JOHN H. HARVEY, Department of Psychology, Texas Tech University, Lubbock, TX 79409, U.S.A.

ROBERT A. HINDE, MRC Unit on the Development and Integration of Behaviour, University of Cambridge, Maddingley, Cambridge, England.

TED L. HUSTON, Division of Child Development and Family Relations, Mary Gearing Hall, University of Texas, Austin, TX 78712, U.S.A.

HEATHER G. HUSZTI, Department of Psychology, Texas Tech University, Lubbock, TX 79409, U.S.A.

JENNY DE JONG-GIERVELD, Subjfaculteit de Sociaal-Kulturele Wetenschappen Afdeling Methoden en Technieken, Vrije Universiteit, Amsterdam, The Netherlands.

HAROLD H. KELLEY, Department of Psychology, University of California, Los Angeles, CA 90024, U.S.A.

BARRY MCCARTHY, School of Psychology, Lancashire Polytechnic, Corporation Street, Preston, England.

SUSAN M. MCHALE, Individual and Family Studies, Pennsylvania State University, University Park, State College, PA 16802, U.S.A.

HOWARD J. MARKMAN, Department of Psychology, University of Denver, Denver, CO 80112, U.S.A.

DOROTHY MIELL, Department of Psychology, Open University, Milton Keynes, England.

HARRY T. REIS, Department of Psychology, The University of Rochester, River Station, Rochester, NY 14627, U.S.A.

HARRIET K. A. SANTS, MRC Unit on the Development and Integration of Behaviour, University of Cambridge, Maddingley, Cambridge, England.

JOAN STEVENSON-HINDE, MRC Unit on the Development and Integration of Behaviour, University of Cambridge, Maddingley, Cambridge, England.

MARGARET S. STROEBE, Psychologisches Institut, Universität Tübingen, Friedrichstrasse 21, D-74 Tübingen, West Germany.

WOLFGANG STROEBE, Psychologisches Institut, Universität Tübingen, Friedrichstrasse 21, D-74 Tübingen, Germany.

ANN L. WEBER, Department of Psychology, University of North Carolina, Asheville, NC 28814, U.S.A.

WILLIAM W. WILMOT, Department of Interpersonal Communication, University of Montana, Missoula, MT, U.S.A.

Preface

This book is the result of the first International Conference on Personal Relationships held in Madison, Wisconsin, in 1982. The conference itself was a significant event in publicly bringing together major figures whose work was starting to define the new area of personal relationships. We would like to think also, that the conference played an important part in helping to formally establish personal relationships as a distinctive and vital area in its own right.

Certainly before and since that time, there has been a growing wealth of publications attesting to the emergence and health of this new science, but the Madison conference had a special contribution to make through its clear public statement to colleagues in the social sciences: that this is a viable new field.

While this book came out of the Madison conference, it is not merely "proceedings" of the conference: instead, it represents selected highlights of that conference. It is different, too, in that the chapters here are *based on* contributions to the conference rather than simply being printed versions of the spoken papers given. Thus the various chapters have been rewritten and edited accordingly. In some cases, the conference presentation was used just as a starting point so that the chapter finally presented here is very different from the paper given at the conference. The overall aim was to avoid a transcript and to produce a properly constituted volume.

There are two somewhat different kinds of contributions. Some chapters are based on the more extensive papers from invited speakers; whereas others derive from the rather briefer competitive paper sessions. Thus, there is a combination of broader, more discursive coverage of the field as in the chapters by Kelley, Argyle, Ginsburg, Hinde, Stroebe, Berscheid, Huston, and Harvey, and more specific presentation of important recent research in the chapters by McCarthy,

Reis, Baxter and Wilmot, Duck and Miell, Attili, Sants, Bringle and Buunk, de Jong-Gierveld, and Farrell and Markman. The chapters are arranged to follow the structure of the conference program, with major opening and closing discussions covering the whole field by Kelley and Berscheid, respectively, and the rest of the chapters grouped under the headings of "Depiction and Taxonomy of Relationships," "Development and Growth of Relationships," and "Disorder and Repair of Relationships." The result is by no means a comprehensive treatment of the field, but we hope (as the book's title suggests) that the book highlights significant issues in personal relationship research as well as some excellent examples of the ways in which issues and problems are being tackled. Finally, just as good research should not merely record phenomena but should have some practical function, so we hope that this volume will not only act as a record, however valuable, of the Madison conference but will also have some effect on the future development of the field of personal relationships by indicating its value and potential.

At this point, we acknowledge all the hidden assistance that inevitably goes into compiling a work such as this one. More specifically, we want to thank all the participants who made the Madison conference such an exciting and enjoyable, as well as an important, event. Nearer home, particular thanks go to our invaluable departmental secretaries—Margaret Gill, Hazel Satterthwaite, Sylvia Sumner, and Sheila Whalley—whose abilities to cope with outrageous demands never fail to surprise and gratify us. Finally—and certainly not least—Robert Hinde has been an inspiration not only to the whole field but also more personally, and for that our special thanks are due.

Robin Gilmour
Steve Duck

INTRODUCTION AND OVERVIEW

1 Personal Relationships: Their Nature and Significance

Harold H. Kelley
University of California, Los Angeles

This chapter describes the present status of the field of "personal relationships," emphasizes some of the important facts in which research on personal relationships is anchored, and highlights some of the issues the field faces. Consequently, I briefly summarize (1) the significance of the Madison Conference, (2) the significance of personal relationships, (3) the nature of what I think personal relationships are, and (4) scientific versus popular thought about personal relationships. Each of these topics relates to the others, so ideally they should be developed all at once. However, the linear structure of verbal communication requires that they be taken up in some order and I have chosen the one above.

THE SIGNIFICANCE OF THE MADISON CONFERENCE

The Conference dealt with important practical psychological and social problems (such as loneliness, alternative life styles, and sexual satisfaction) and raised crucial scientific questions about such phenomena as social roles, power, social motivation, and perception. However, I believe that this was more than just another exciting conference; I believe that we participated in one of several collective activities by which a new field of science is being formed. We took part in the emergence of a new science—the science of interpersonal relationships.

I refer to "several collective activities" of which this Conference was one. The other activities that can be viewed as contributing to this new science are well known but worth mentioning here. A partial listing would include a number of recent publications such as Swensen's textbook, *Interpersonal Relations*

(1973), Huston's edited volume *Foundations of Interpersonal Attraction* (1974), Duck's volume on *Theory and Practice in Interpersonal Attraction* (1977a), Levinger and Raush's edited volume on *Close Relationships* (1977), Triandis' book, *Interpersonal Behavior* (1977), Burgess and Huston's collection on exchange theories and relationship development (1979), the recent Duck and Gilmour series entitled *Personal Relationships* (1981a, 1981b, 1981c, and Duck, 1982), and Robert Hinde's important overview, *Towards Understanding Relationships* (1979). These are some of the recent works that take relationships as their focal topic, draw together a variety of facts about them, and try to develop systematic understandings—not of individuals but of *relationships*. In doing this, these works typically draw on literatures from diverse disciplines and specialties. The writings are, of course, deeply rooted in the literature on the family that has developed over many years within sociology and, within social work, in the field of family and marital counseling. Within psychology, there has recently been important research in the specialities of clinical and developmental psychology—research on marital relations, parent–child interaction, and most recently, peer relations among children. The most remarkable advances within both of these specialities have been made through research in which actual, natural interaction has been closely observed and analyzed statistically in order to identify patternings of interaction. This is illustrated by the research on family interaction by Patterson (1982) and others at Oregon, the work reported by Gottman in his book *Marital Interaction* (1979b), and the studies of mother–infant interaction by Ainsworth and Bell (1969), Brazelton, Koslowski, and Main (1974), Bruner (1975), Kaye (1977), and many others.

The recent focus on interpersonal relations is also partly rooted in social psychology. Here, the interest derives in the first place from the tradition of attitudes and attitude measurement. About 10 years ago, the work on interpersonal attraction shifted from the study of positive attitudes between strangers to the study of people in love, as illustrated by Rubin's development of the "love scale" (1970, 1973) and Berscheid and Walster's research on passionate love (1974). A second origin within social psychology has been the small group field from which there have been extensions to interpersonal relations of ideas about cooperation, competition, and conflict resolution, as in Kressel and Deutsch's writings on divorce (1977), and Kelley and Thibaut on *Interpersonal Relations* (1978). Finally, various ideas in cognitive social psychology have been brought to bear on personal relationships, as in Walster's research on equity (e.g., Walster, Walster, & Traupmann, 1978), which is an offshoot of cognitive dissonance theory, and in the emphasis in my *Personal Relationships* book (Kelley, 1979) on attributional processes and conflicts. Along with these more theory-based efforts, there are a number of research areas that derive from current social concerns and practical issues, such as loneliness (Peplau & Perlman, 1982), female and male interaction (Henley, 1977), and so-called "alternative" forms of relationships such as cohabitation and homosexual relations (Peplau and Gordon, 1983).

From this brief list, we can see that our field draws its ideas and data from a broad range of behavioral science disciplines and specialties. Also, as the title of our Conference suggests, our field can accurately be described as an international one.

These developments—within sociology, social work, clinical and developmental psychology, and social psychology—have led some of us to believe that it is now desirable to have personal relationships recognized as a special field. During recent years, a group of us have been reviewing and organizing the field with this goal in mind. Our work has culminated in a volume entitled *Close Relationships* (Kelley, Berscheid, Christensen, Harvey, Huston, Levinger, McClintock, Peplau, & Peterson, 1983). One of the purposes of this book is to make a case for "close relationships" as a field of specialization within psychology, coordinate with, say, developmental, perception, or personality. We regard a focus on close relationships as an important and basic one for psychology, and we see coordinated work on relationships as a meaningful way to restore contact among certain areas of psychology, such as clinical, developmental, personality, and social, that presently are much too compartmentalized.

Not incompatible with that goal is the more ambitious one of establishing "interpersonal relationships" as a field of science coordinate with its parent disciplines sociology and psychology. It is some of the implications of that goal that I now wish to highlight.

By asserting that the field of interpersonal relations is emerging as a new science, we imply first that the phenomena of personal relationships are *unique*. The phenomena of relationships are distinctive from those studied in neighboring domains of science. To simplify our consideration of this matter, let us fit personal relationships into the hierarchy of science at a location between the sciences concerned with society, on the one hand, and those concerned with the person, on the other hand, as suggested in Fig. 1.1. When we describe relationship phenomena as *unique*, we mean that they consist of processes and properties not found at the levels studied by the sciences of society or the sciences of the person. The interaction patterns, the conflict resolution styles, the informal normative controls, the reward and cost sharing agreements, the shared views of the world, etc. that characterize a relationship are not phenomena of either its constituent individuals or its social environment.

The reason for this distinctiveness of relationship phenomena is found in the configuration of causal connections shown in Fig. 1.1. The personal relationship is (1) affected by personal and societal factors, but it also (2) has its own internal dynamics (the arrows within the relationship) and (3) affects both the personal and the social levels (arrows directed outward from the relationship). Thus, a marriage is affected by the needs and abilities of the two spouses, but it also affects them. There is dynamic interaction between the two persons that changes those properties or modifies their expression. Young lovers are affected by their social environment (e.g., their in-laws), but at the same time, depending on the influence they have on each other in their interaction, they modify the way their social environment acts on them.

From this we see that personal relationships are not the mere creatures of their personal and social milieus. By virtue of their internal dynamics and their feedback effects on the external personal and social factors, personal relationships manifest a distinctive level of phenomena. Relationship phenomena are, in principle, no more explained by society and persons than social and personal phenomena are explained by relationships.

From these observations, it follows that the field of personal relationships is not simply a marginal field, standing at the borders or at the intersection of several parent fields. It is a separate field in its own right, with its own set of phenomena and issues.

Second, when we consider personal relationships as a new science, we imply that *it is needed by the other, neighboring sciences.* This implication reflects our belief that the phenomena we study play an important causal role in relation to those investigated in other disciplines. As the causal arrows in Fig. 1.1 show, not only are relationships not simply the creatures of social and personal factors, they importantly affect those factors. Psychological structures and processes are partly determined by personal relationships. Similarly, social structure and process are partly determined by personal relationships. Consequently, knowledge of the phenomena of relationships is essential to a full understanding of how both individuals and social organizations develop, function, and change.

Figure 1.1 is not meant to suggest that all the causal linkage between society and person is by way of personal relationships. However, it does suggest that the most important society–person linkages are mediated by relationships. An important implication of this view is that understanding how society affects the person or how the person affects society requires that we understand the internal dynamics of personal relationships. For example, during economic depression, the ways in which people's changing needs or levels of frustration affect their communities depends on the specific interaction processes within families and peer groups. It is these processes—the discussion, the joint decisions, the shared interpretations of the situation—that greatly affect how people will attempt to gain and use various economic resources, whether and how they will vote, whether and how they will take to the streets in public demonstrations, and so on. Similarly, the effects on each person of major social changes (the "downward" arrows in Figure 1.1) depend on the relevant interaction within his/her personal relationships. With loss of employment, the degree to which a person experiences physical and mental symptoms depends on specific features of interaction with family and friends, such as the causal interpretations they provide, their material and moral support, and the problem solutions they offer and facilitate.

To repeat, the understanding of both person-to-society and society-to-person causal links requires our investigating the details of the mediating links provided by the interaction within personal relationships.

There is a third implication of our thinking of "personal relationships" as a new field of science: *There are systematic laws to be discovered that apply over a variety of specific types of relationships.* Many different relationships qualify as "personal" relations, for example, those between lovers, those in marriage and cohabitation arrangements, those within families between parents and children, between brothers and sisters, and between relatives and kinfolk, those between close friends in school, those at work between close co-workers, and so on. At one level, a conference on personal relationships consists of a loose collection of researchers and practitioners interested in various particular types of relationships. However, at a more basic level, and implied in our thinking of ourselves as forming a new science, we are a group of workers involved in the highly cooperative activity of identifying the phenomena and laws that *cut across* these various kinds of relationships. These are the general phenomena and the broad principles of formation, development, power, dependence, conflict, coordination, and so on that can be observed in many or all personal relations.

THE SIGNIFICANCE OF PERSONAL RELATIONSHIPS

Much of the foregoing discussion suggests the significance of personal relationships. In Fig. 1.1, the diagram of the personal relation as its stands between society and person is one characterization of its significance. The personal relationship is shown to form part of the causal interface whereby society affects the individual and the individual, in turn, affects society. This general view of the significance of personal relationships is easily accepted. It is a readily observable fact that individuals exist in and take part in society primarily in clusters or small groups. A drive through any community, a visit to the market, a Sunday afternoon stroll in the park, a TV news report on a refugee camp—all of these experiences and many more show us that people live, work, buy, relax, migrate, go to war, and survive catastrophes in small tight-knit groups, primarily families. These personally interrelated clusters are the primary units out of which social organizations are constructed and by which social processes are carried.

However, there are some crucial qualitative and quantitative distinctions we have to make. First, we must determine, for various specific types of relationships, the precise roles they play in this mediation. In what respects and to what degrees does a particular type of relationship affect the individual, as compared with, say, the direct connections between social organizations and individuals of the sort provided by school teachers, social workers, or the mass media? And in what ways do personal relationships mediate even these "direct" connections, for example, highlighting, interpreting, and evaluating the informa-

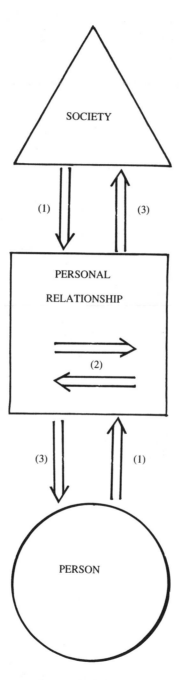

FIG. 1.1. The phenomena of personal relationships located relative to the phenomena of society and person.

tion from the TV news by discussing it within the family circle? This kind of question calls to mind the line of research that goes back to the pioneering work of Katz and Lazarsfeld (1955) on mass media versus personal influence and that extends to Ward, Wackman, and Wortella's 1977 book, *How Children Learn to Buy.*

Second, there are some quantitative aspects of the personal relationship mediation that require careful analysis. These quantitative aspects are more readily seen if we expand our society–relationship–person diagram to reflect differences between the levels in their numerosity. Each social organization includes a number of relationships and each relationship includes a number of persons. Several different aggregation or combination problems are then involved. There is the problem of how effects to and from the different relationships linked to a given social organization are aggregated or combined across relationships, and there is the parallel problem for each of the personal relationships of how the effects to and from its different members are aggregated or combined across the members. In addition, there are further temporal aggregation problems that crosscut those mentioned here. These problems have to do with the cumulative impact of each causal link over time. And, of course, the picture is further complicated if we take account of the different types of personal relationships that link a given social organization to a given population of individuals, there again being problems of their combined or aggregate effects.

One or more of these facets of aggregate or cumulative effects enters into all of our significant generalizations about personal relationships. To illustrate these aggregation problems, let us consider a community church, the various families that constitute its congregation, and the many members of these families. From the church's perspective, the personal relationships are significant because through their respective cumulative effects on their members, effects achieved through consistent patterns of interaction, most or all of each family's members may develop religious practices and behaviors that support the church. Furthermore, it is important for the church that these effects be achieved with some uniformity across the various families. Thus, each family unit must have a marked cumulative impact on its children and this impact becomes important at the social level insofar as it is replicated over a large number of families. Similar analysis can be made of the manner in which families link their members to the welfare system, adolescent gangs link their members to the criminal justice system, dating relationships link their members to the popular music culture, and married couples link their members to the world of work.

Personal relationships gain their significance from their cumulative effects. From the perspective of the individual, relationships provide interaction that occurs over a considerable period of time and is characterized by frequent and intense experiences. If the frequent and intense events of any stable personal relationship are consistently patterned, it has great psychological significance for the development and stability or change of the individuals. From the perspective of society, personal relationships are important not only for their effectiveness in shaping individual propensities but for the uniformity with which large numbers of similar relationships do so. Personal relations are significant to society, then, insofar as there are many relationships of a certain type and there is uniformity among those of that type in their effects on their members and environments.

To summarize, from both a psychological and a social perspective, the significance of personal relationships derives from their cumulative, aggregate effects. Relationships are common, they are often of long duration, they exercise strong and generally consistent influence, they are numerous within each type, and they often exhibit uniformity within type.

It is perhaps not too digressive here to point out that this conception of the significance of personal relationships has important implications for our research designs. To properly reflect their significance—to document, assess, or describe their aggregate consequences—our research must, as a collective enterprise, span the variations over which the cumulative effects occur. From the psychological perspective, this requires longitudinal study of the consistency, over time and over persons, of the linkages between each personal relationship and its members. From the social perspective, longitudinal study is also necessary, with a dual focus on (1) consistency versus trends in each personal relationship's links to various institutions and (2) uniformities across different relationships of a given type.

THE NATURE OF PERSONAL RELATIONSHIPS

The preceding discussion has implied much about what personal relationships are, but now that matter will be considered directly. The characterization here of the "personal relationship" is derived from a particular theory and I will attempt to demonstrate its merits. However, other investigators will propose alternative characterizations.

The present notion is implicit in the interdependence theory of Kelley and Thibaut (1978) and was made explicit in *Personal Relationships* (Kelley, 1979). The basic idea is simple. Personal relationships are first of all *close,* and then, derivative from that closeness, they are *personal.* This might be described as the "two-level hypothesis" about personal relations. They exist at two interrelated levels of interdependence, as described in Fig. 1.2. At what we refer to as the *given* level, the persons are interdependent in outcomes that are direct and concrete, and they control these outcomes through the specific behaviors they enact. The given level of interdependence is illustrated by the ways in which each person's gratifications depend on the compliments, gifts, information, services, and companionship the other provides. At the *dispositional* level, the persons are interdependent in symbolic outcomes and they control these outcomes by the interpersonal attitudes and traits they express. The dispositional

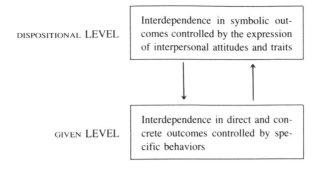

Fig. 1.2. The characterization of the personal relationship in terms of two interlinked levels of interdependence.

level of interdependence is illustrated by the ways in which each person's outcomes depend on the love, concern, fairness, assertiveness, and other dispositions that the partner displays. This is not merely a distinction between two broad classes of satisfaction and dissatisfaction that exist within interpersonal relationships: It is a theory about the basis of that distinction and about the dynamic processes it implies. Thus, as Fig. 1.2 suggests, these two levels of interdependence are interlinked in systematic ways: the upper level being derivative from the lower one and the lower one being governed by the upper one.

In asserting that personal relationships are "close," I follow the definition of Kelley et al. (1983): Close relationships are ones in which persons affect each other frequently, strongly, in diverse ways, and over considerable periods of time. In interdependence theory, closely related persons are highly interdependent over a considerable span of time.

Closeness of a relationship is no guarantee of its being free of problems. A relationship can have high interdependence and yet have problems of conflict of interest, problems of inequality in degrees and areas of dependence (and derivative problems of power and control), and problems stemming from different patterns of interdependence (i.e., problems of exchange versus problems of coordination). These conditions make it desirable, indeed, often necessary, for the closely related persons to work on the issues of what attitudes and qualities each person can be counted on to display within the relationship. As the individuals face and work on these issues, as they become concerned about and negotiate some sort of understanding about the attitudes and traits each will dependably exhibit in the relationship, it becomes a "personal" one. The individuals become interdependent not only in the specific behaviors they enact but in the interpersonal dispositions they display toward each other. In the dictionary sense of "personal," the members of a personal relationship interact with each other as particular persons, not in generalized ways or as they might with other persons. Their specific behaviors have a personal significance, pertaining to their respective individual motives and characteristics. Their actions are directed to each person as an individual, and not in relation to his/her rank, office, or other formal attributes.

As already noted, the dispositional level derives from the problems of interdependence at the given level. Through experience with interdependence and through practical and moral training, each individual learns to pay attention to the consequences of interaction for other persons as well as for self. In close relationships, the person learns the advantages of becoming responsive to the partner's outcomes and of putting one's behavior partly under the control of those outcomes. Becoming responsive to the partner's outcomes involves being prosocial in some instances (e.g., fair, considerate, responsible), but egoistic and even antisocial in other instances (e.g., competitive, coercive, preemptive). Each of these tendencies has its occasional advantages, depending on the opportunities and problems in the given interdependence and the similar or dissimilar tendencies of a particular partner. Thus, attitudes such as considerateness, fairness, assertiveness, and submissiveness are learned, partly as strategies for gaining good given outcomes and partly as internalized values. As moderately stable dispositions directed toward a particular partner, these attitudes are enormously important to that partner, providing the basic assumptions on which the relationship proceeds and from which its problems are resolved.

This characterization of the personal relationship, which is at once a definition (interdependence at both the given and the dispositional levels) and a theory about personal relationships, is consistent with many phenomena observed in them and has a number of implications for their analysis. Four of these implications are described as follows.

First, the events in a personal relationship are evaluated on a dual basis. Their affective consequences derive partly from the specific rewards and costs they entail but also partly from what the events reveal about each person's underlying dispositions. This idea is consistent both with common sense and with evidence from research on couples' satisfaction and dissatisfaction. The birthday gift a husband brings his wife pleases or displeases her partly on the basis of its intrinsic merits and partly on the basis of the love and thoughtfulness she sees as lying behind it. Research shows that partners have complaints and praise both about specific behaviors and about traits and attitudes (Kelley, 1979). The results of Walster and her colleagues' research on equity (Walster, Walster, & Traupmann, 1978) are consistent with a dual basis of evaluation: satisfaction with a relationship depends partly on the quality of one's own outcomes in it and partly on how equitable the relationship is seen to be.

This dual evaluation of events is not unique to personal relationships. It also exists, for example, in achievement settings when a teacher evaluates a student partly on the basis of concrete performance and partly on the basis of the effort seen to lie behind it. An unexamined derivation from the dual basis idea is that there may be inconsistencies between the two kinds of feelings about a relationship. Thus, with good given but poor dispositional outcomes, a relationship may be experienced as practical but unfulfilling. Most of one's needs for concrete rewards are satisfied, but something is missing because the attitudes oneself and/or the partner express are not satisfactory. This may be contrasted with a relationship experienced as fulfilling, with, say, much expression of love and a mutually satisfying nurturant-succorant arrangement, but not practical, due to poor concrete outcomes.

Second, conflict in personal relationships often revolves around the correct causal interpretation to place on behavior. The two-level conception implies that conflict will often escalate from concrete matters to questions of the attitudes or traits revealed by disagreeable behavior. This implication is consistent with current evidence on attributional conflict within personal relationships. Disagreement about the causes of behavior is most common and extreme when one partner does something the other one does not like. The common form of the escalation process is also consistent with attributional conflict. A specific issue is expanded and generalized, becoming linked to other real or imagined injuries and forming the basis for charges about the poor attitudes or undesirable traits possessed by the partner. The importance that closely related persons attach to each other's dispositions also appears in treatment settings, being reflected in the emphasis with which distressed couples state their attributions and in their resistance to dealing with their problems wholly at the level of specific behaviors without getting at what they understand to be the true (i.e., dispositional) causes of their difficulties.

Third, theoretical analysis of the patterns of interdependence at the given level reveals the major properties and problems of relationships and suggests the common scenarios of interaction. The two-level conception of the personal relationship asserts that the given level of interdependence is basic to the entire structure, the dispositonal being derivative from it. To the extent that an entire relation can be described by a particular pattern, this conception implies that variations in the patterns of interdependence at the given level will correspond to the properties that differentiate *among* actual relationships. Furthermore, to the extent that relationships are complex and encompass a variety of different problems, variations in patterns of given interdependence will correspond to the different problems found *within* relationships. The evidence bearing on this implication of the theory is too complicated to present here, but some of it is in Kelley and Thibaut (1978) and Kelley (1979). To outline it briefly, we use the 2 × 2 outcome matrix as our means of describing the given level of interdependence. Theoretical analysis of 2 × 2 matrices reveals four features with respect to which they can be distinguished: the degree of interdependence, the mutuality or equality of dependence, the commonality versus conflict of interest, and dependence based on individual versus joint action (technically, Fate Control versus Behavior Control). The first three of these features correspond to dimensions found by Wish, Deutsch, and Kaplan (1976) to empirically distinguish among relationships: intensity versus superficiality, equality versus inequality, and cooperative versus competitive. The fourth theoretical feature (Fate Control versus Behavior Control) appears to be a distinction between two types of problem, exchange versus coordination problems, both of which are found in most relationships. A variety of kinds of evidence can be found to demonstrate that these two types of situation can be (and are) distinguished within relationships. Among the more interesting of these is Turiel's evidence that two types of interpersonal transgression occur among preschool children on the playground, the two types being readily distinguished both by observers and by the children themselves. One type reflects a failure in an exchange situation, one child harming or failing to benefit another. The other type reflects a failure in a coordination situation, one child failing to follow the rules governing the coordination of joint activities. These two situations have different rules associated with them and preschoolers learn early to distinguish between the absolute nature of the rules governing the first, "moral" situation and the arbitrariness of the rules governing the second, "conventional" situation. Corresponding to these differences between absolute moral rules and arbitrary conventional rules, the scenarios of interaction following the two types of transgression are different. For example, communication to the transgressor in the case of a moral transgression emphasizes the harm done to the victim and how it feels to be a victim. Communication following a conventional transgression points out how the behavior creates a disorder or mess (Nucci & Turiel, 1978).

This last point illustrates an idea mentioned earlier, that the scenario of interaction between people is determined by the nature of the interdependence between them. In general, the nature of the particular problem they face determines what they may have conflict about and the kinds of rules they are likely to invoke in order to resolve the conflict. The theory suggests that interaction processes may be broadly characterized as involving exchange processes or coordination processes. The first type includes promises and threats, giving and taking, etc. The second includes initiative-taking preemptiveness or leadership versus waiting for others to act and following their lead. In each case, as Deutsch demonstrated some years ago (1949), the quality of communication (its degree, openness, candor, and acceptance) depends on the degree of conflict versus commonality of interest. And each of these interaction features is given a special skew by inequalities between the partners in their respective degrees of dependence on the continuation of the relationship.

These remarks about the structure of interdependence and its relevance for the problems and processes observed in a relationship pertain to the science of relationships, per se. They exemplify the kind of phenomena that must be thought about and studied in our new science. These remarks illustrate the fact that our analysis must be conducted at the relationship level, as we focus on relationship structures and processes.

Fourth, theoretical analysis of the patterns of interdependence at the given level reveals the major features of interpersonal dispositions. This point relates to the interface between a science of relationships and that of individual psychology. It illustrates an important way in which the study of personal relationships can contribute to a solution of some of psychology's problems.

According to the two-level conception of the personal relationship, interpersonal dispositions—interpersonal traits and attitudes—evolve out of the problems existing at the given level of interdependence. Were there not conflicts of interest at the given level, were there not problems of unequal dependence and power, were there not exchange and coordination problems to be solved, there would be no need for the domain of interpersonal dispositions ever to come into existence. In a world of high but bland interdependence (interdependence without problems), such dispositions as love, dominance, and competitiveness would have no meaning. This being so, the two-level conception implies that the patterns of given interdependence should reveal the major features of interpersonal dispositions—what they are and how they are interrelated. This means, of course, that our analysis of personal relationships will be of value to the field of personality research as it works on social and interpersonal motivation. This is an obvious conclusion, perhaps, but I believe its importance will be very great when the details are finally worked out. I anticipate that our analysis of personal relations will reveal what the domain of interpersonal dispositions includes, how the various dispositions are to be assessed, and how they are interrelated (i.e., their factorial or hierarchical structure).

How are interpersonal dispositions revealed in interaction? Here we get into complex problems of attribution and self-presentation that are highly technical and not yet fully worked out. However, the general idea is easily explained. Any particular pattern of given interdependence lends itself to a number of different scenarios of interaction. For example, the well-known Prisoner's Dilemma game is a simple exchange pattern in which self-interest works against developing the exchange process. This pattern lends itself to cooperative interaction, competition, scenarios of trust building followed by double cross, scenarios of unrelieved distrust and defensiveness, and so on. The popularity of this given pattern as a research tool derives precisely from this fact, that it makes possible a variety of scenarios. Not all interdependence patterns are this productive of scenario variation, but any pattern can support some variety of interactions.

Now we come to the heart of the matter. From among these scenarios made possible by a particular *given* pattern of interdependence, *the specific scenario generated by a particular pair of persons reveals their interpersonal dispositions.* Once again, this is a part of common sense, as in the aphorism, "It's not whether you win or lose; it's how you play the game." However, when applied to a detailed analysis of interdependence, this is a powerful principle. The notion that a person's attitudes are revealed by how the person "plays the game" can be conceptualized in terms of *what game,* other than the given one, *the person appears to be playing.* The person who behaves "as if" the situation were something different from what it is specified to be thereby reveals an interpersonal disposition—an attitude toward the particular partner or a general way of relating to others.

Consequently, the key notion is that interpersonal dispositions are revealed in "as if" behavior: The person acts as if the given situation were some other situation. This notion provides the systematic link suggested above—the link between properties of patterns of interdependence and the features of interpersonal dispositions. The way the person "shifts" or "transforms" the terms of the relationship reveals interpersonal attitudes and traits. From this, it follows that *all* the dispositions that can be displayed and the ways in which they can be displayed are specified by the ways in which situations differ from each other. In other words, there is a close correspondence between the properties of interdependence and the features of interpersonal dispositions. Dispositions can vary only in ways analogous to the properties, say, of 2×2 outcome matrices, that is, only in ways relevant to degree of dependence, equality versus inequality of dependence, commonality versus conflict of interest, and control of outcomes through individual versus joint action.

Only a beginning has been made in studying this implication of the two-level theory. I can report some success in using the "as if" or transformation notion to generate a set of brief scenarios that seem to provide a good coverage of the domain of interpersonal trait terms that Wiggins (1979) has identified empirically. In other words, the "vocabulary" for the expression of traits that is provided by a person's treating a given situation "as if" it were a different one— that vocabulary seems to be fairly adequate. It is both comprehensive, covering the range of traits Wiggins identifies, and moderately informative, enabling distinctions to be made among Wiggins' categories of traits. This conclusion must necessarily be tentative, because the last word has not been said either on the side of the theoretical analysis or on the side of the empirical delineation of interpersonal traits. My recent developments in the theoretical description of interdependence, which move beyond the 2×2 outcome matrix, lead me to suspect that although Wiggins' data capture the main features of interpersonal motivation, they overlook many specific aspects.

Whatever the upshot of this particular issue, its importance here is in illustrating the way in which research on personal relationships can and will contribute to the identification and resolution of key problems in psychology, particularly those in the areas of personality and motivation. Social motives have no meaning or existence apart from social interdependence. Social motives develop out of individual motives as the latter are activated and acted upon in interpersonal contexts. To understand these matters, we must, of course, familiarize ourselves with the relevant thought and research within individual psychology. However, we must be aware of how that knowledge may be limited or otherwise flawed as a consequence of its being developed largely from the perspective of the isolated individual. We must be sensitive, then, to the contributions that, working from a relationship perspective, we can make to the understanding of social motives, cognition, and personality.

Admittedly, these last two points have not been explained fully, but perhaps the gist of them will be clear. Hopefully, the reader will understand what the development of interdependence theory is moving toward: a set of three interrelated taxonomies. The first is a theoretically generated taxonomy of interdependence *situations,* which will specify the varieties of situations in which people find themselves when they come into close association. From that taxonomy will be derived two further interrelated taxonomies, one of interpersonal *dispositions* (one might say a taxonomy of rules for cognition and action in interpersonal situations) and another of interaction *scenarios,* that is, sequences of social interaction.

SCIENTIFIC VERSUS POPULAR THOUGHT ABOUT PERSONAL RELATIONSHIPS

This final point was suggested to me by the topics listed in the program of the Conference. Some of the titles seemed directed to a scientific audience. At least they used the abstract language typical of science—the language of "cognition," "process," "norms," "decision making," "interdependence," and so on. Other titles were cast in terms that might be more understandable to a popular audience and they seemed to pose questions in which a popular audience might be interested. I realize these titles may not reflect real differences, but merely different tastes or skills in packaging research projects. However, this variation once again raised for me the perplexing question of the relation between these two domains in which we inevitably find ourselves enmeshed—the domain of scientific concepts, "jargon," and analysis, and the domain of popular thought, everyday language, and homely aphorisms.

It is obvious that there exists a great deal of popular knowledge about and interest in the phenomena that we investigate. This is true to some degree for any science, especially during its early development. However, it is probably more characteristic of our science than of any other. The reason is that the phenomena we study, in our science of interpersonal relations, are quite observable and salient in everyday life (for the most part), are very important to common people, and, consequently, are the subject of their continual speculation and discussion.

These circumstances create problems for us, inasmuch as we are regularly in the position both to draw on common knowledge and to contribute to it. How are we properly to do these two things? I offer here no definitive answers, merely some thoughts on the matter. My hunch is that the issues of *using* and *contributing* to common knowledge are not separable ones, and that if we become clearer about our use of common knowledge, then some of the problems in presenting our work to the public will be lessened.

There is no doubt in my mind that popular knowledge about personal relationships contains useful information. In its concepts, beliefs, and theories, popular thought deserves our attention. This is so not merely because common people (ourselves included) often act on the basis of their common knowledge, but also because of the kernels of truth common thought contains. Its usefulness is often challenged on the grounds that common knowledge contains many internal contradictions. However, I believe that this simply reflects the fact that "generalization" in common knowledge usually omits specification of necessary qualifying conditions. It is part of our job, although it may not seem a very glamorous one, to identify and specify those qualifications.

More generally, I suggest that on the scale that ranges from microanalysis to macroanalysis, popular knowledge is usually pitched at a rather narrow, intermediate band. On one hand, it overlooks details: It fails to see the details of microprocesses that underlie everyday appearances. On the other hand, it fails to comprehend the "big picture": It views things narrowly without taking account of contingencies and context. Given these limitations, our collective efforts must enable us to expand the range of levels at which contact is made with relationship phenomena. Some of us must study the details of process and detect the fine-grain, underlying structure that escapes ordinary notice. Others of us must study the broad social and personal contexts that provide the "ground" against which relationships are experienced as "figure." Both the micro- and macroanalysis will enable us to account for variations in process that otherwise appear as inconsistencies or contradictions.

Realistically, then, much of what we learn consists of refinements on and systematization of common knowledge, rather than revelations or discoveries. We will provide conceptual distinctions that refine and depart from common usage (and will therefore appear to outsiders as needless jargon). We will account for shifts in the correlation between two focal variables by identifying other variables in the causal system. We will provide process descriptions of what people commonly observe and also of what they fail to observe. We will provide precise quantitative characterizations of what people already know in a general and vague way. More generally, we will provide a systematic account of the origins, interconnections, and arrangements of many, many facts, every single one of which may be represented in some nook or cranny of popular knowledge.

It is difficult to explain, in simple terms, why such refinement or systematic accounting is useful. We are haunted by the thought that we should be making great discoveries, that we should be finding out facts that will surprise our colleagues, our aunts, our neighbors, or the press. Instead, we often find ourselves embarrassed by the feeling (or the criticism) that we are merely showing something to be true that everyone already knows to be true.

One reaction to this embarrassment is to parade out what William Bevan recently referred to as our "two-headed calves." Referring to the Convention of the American Psychological Association, Bevan suggested that to bolster psychology's deteriorating public image, we should "minimize publicity—especially at the annual convention—of psychology's 'two-headed' calves, those aspects of psychology that are sensational, odd, or unusual" (1982b, p. 1). He illustrates these by referring to sex and drugs. Bevan's proposal has as much relevance for our field as for any area within psychology. However, I think it would be foolish for us to attempt to distinguish the two-headed from the more normal calves in our field, and we certainly cannot entertain any censorship in the presentation of our work, even if self-imposed. On the other hand, we must somehow learn to explain our enterprise in realistic terms and to avoid feeling inadequate about lack of "discoveries" and communicating to the public only the odd and the sensational.

As I have suggested, it is essential that we understand the relation of our work to popular thought and the bases in that relationship of our ambivalence about trying to explain to the public the nature and goals of our science. To exhibit our products only when we have two-headed calves to show is to provide a seriously distorted picture of our enterprise. To feel guilty about not discovering things that astound and perplex popular thought is to distort the motivations behind our enterprise. Instead, we must have a conception of the purposes, means, and time span of our science that frees us from these sorts of distorting impulses. For me, that conception includes the goal of a systematic structure of knowledge about relationships the value of which will lie primarily in its comprehensiveness and interconnectedness rather than in any of its particular pieces.

DEPICTION AND TAXONOMY OF RELATIONSHIPS

2 The Skills, Rules, and Goals of Relationships

Michael Argyle
University of Oxford

INTRODUCTION

There are a variety of reasons for studying relationships, some theoretical, some practical. The work presented at the Madison Conference stemmed mainly from the latter, from a concern to understanding how we could cope better with relationship problems and how we might help others who had difficulty in making friends or establishing or maintaining intimate relationships. An interest in *social situations* emerged for similar reasons—people experience difficulty in coping with particular situations, like parties, committees, and so on.

Given this practical concern, it soon became apparent that merely analysing relationships or situations in terms of dimensions, like friendly-hostile, although interesting, was not particularly useful, and a means was developed of analysing situations into their main component features such as rules, goals, repertoire, etc. (Argyle, Furnham, & Graham, 1981). The value of the latter approach is best illustrated by using the analogy of games: If you want to play a game you need to know the goals, how to win, the detailed rules, the moves allowed, and so on. Much the same is true of situations and relationships—the rules and other features are functional in that they facilitate the attainment of common goals, rather in the same way that, for example, the rule of the road (keeping to the left or right) makes it easier to travel without collisions.

RULES

Rules are defined here as "behaviour which members of a group believe should or should not, or may be, performed in some situation or range of situations."

Rules form one of the main features in our conceptual model of situations and of relationships and are regarded as the means by which the behaviour of interactors in a social situation is coordinated so that goals can be attained. Rules in this sense can be distinguished from "norms," which are often used by social psychologists to refer to modal behaviour (i.e., what most people do; sometimes most people break the rules). Rules can also be distinguished from "conventions," which refer to arbitrary customs such as fashion in clothes. It is a rule in cricket that the batsman should use a bat (rather than, say, a tennis racquet), but a convention that he should wear white trousers.

Rules often sound restrictive—do this and don't do that. These restrictions often bring obvious benefits—for example, driving on a certain side of the road, or not talking during concerts. But rules do far more that this—they make whole realms of behaviour possible. According to Twining and Miers (1976):

> Using language, playing games, courting, getting married, reasoning in mathematics, making decisions in committees, buying and selling a house, passing sentences on a person convicted of crime and even fighting a war are all to a large extent rule-governed activities [p. 57].

It is possible to find out about rules by asking people how they would react to hypothetical instances of rule breaking, or more directly by simply asking people whether a certain rule applies (Price & Bouffard, 1974). Another method is to interview members of a group about acceptable forms of behaviour: Marsh, Rosser, and Harré (1978) interviewed football hooligans about how to "put the boot in" and allied matters, and found that a number of rules were stated more or less directly by informants: for example, it was not acceptable to injure members of the opposing gang though it was desirable to frighten them.

The theory we propose is simply this: Rules are created and changed in order that situational goals can be attained. It is a familiar psychological principle that an individual person or animal will discover routes to desired goals, either by trial and error or by other forms of problem solving. We are now proposing an extension to this principle: *Groups* of people will find routes to their goals, and these routes will be collective solutions, including the necessary coordination of some behaviours and the exclusion of other behaviours by means of rules. Unless such coordination is achieved group goals will not be attained: Thus Harris (1975) offered an explanation of the Indian rules protecting cows in terms of the value of cow dung as fertiliser and fuel, of oxen for pulling farm implements, and so on.

Llewellyn (1962) has also proposed a functional theory of rules, in this case the rules of social groups. He suggested that the needs met by rules are the avoidance of conflicts within the group, the settling of disputes when they arise, the adjustment of the behaviour and expectations of members when the circumstances of the group change, and the regulation of decision making.

We predict then that there would be universal rules that meet the common requirements of all social situations, such as preventing withdrawal and aggression, and making communication possible, and that there would be other rules that meet the requirements of paricular kinds of situations—coordinating behaviour so that goals may be attained, guarding against temptations, and helping with common difficulties.

Argyle, Graham, Campbell, and White (1979) did two studies altogether using 75 subjects, 25 situations, and 124 possible rules, elicited in pilot interviews. They first predicted that there would be universal rules, and a cluster analysis did produce a cluster that consisted of the rules that applied to most situations such as being polite and not embarrassing others. We also expected rules that would apply to groups of similar situations: A second cluster emerged which, for example, applied to formal situations.

We now turn to the rules of relationships. Rules of marriage and descent are regarded as functional by anthropologists: For example, exogamy creates links between different families. In our own society there appear to be definite rules about behaviour towards close kin—one should keep in touch and provide help when it is needed (Blood, 1972). In a study with overseas collaborators (Argyle, Henderson, Bond, Iizuka, & Contarello, in press) we examined rules for a wide range of relationships. From pilot interviews and other sources we compiled 33 rules that might apply to any relationship, and for each of 22 relationships we devised 5 to 10 additional rules that might apply to that particular relationship. The sample was divided into 3, and each group rated the 40 or so rules for 7 or 8 relationships. In the British sample there were 180 subjects, each relationship scale being completed by 60 subjects in two sex groups and two age groups. This was a fairly modest N. but the subjects were carefully drawn from similar sections of the population within each age and sex group. Two-ended scales were used since it was anticipated that some rules like "should show affection in public" would apply in opposite directions for different relationships.

Again we expected that there would be a number of universal rules. Table 2.1 shows the rules that were most widely endorsed, and the number of situations to which each were thought to apply. The rules have been divided into four types, which emerged from factor analyses and on theoretical grounds. The three most widely endorsed rules were: should respect other's privacy, should keep confidences, and should look the other in the eye during conversation.

We predicted that relationships would be grouped into intimate and less intimate in respect of the rules that apply, and a cluster analysis of the 22 relationships using only the 33 common rules supported this. Out of 33 common rules, 26 were endorsed significantly more strongly for one cluster of relationships than for the other. Rules proscribing the expression of personal feelings, attitudes and affection—behaviours that maintain interpersonal distance—tend to be endorsed in the nonintimate cluster, while the opposite of these rules is endorsed for the intimate cluster.

TABLE 2.1
General Rules

	Number of Relationships
Exchange	
22. Should seek to repay debts, favours or compliments, no matter how small	13
33. Should be emotionally supportive	10
Intimacy	
32. Should look the other person in the eye during conversation	21
1. Should address the other by their first name	11
30. Should share news of success with the other person	10
Coordination	
31. Should respect the other's privacy	22
20. Should not engage in sexual activity with the other	14
Third party	
19. Should keep confidences	21
17. Should not criticize the other person publicly	13
18. Should stand up for the other person in their absence	12

We also predicted that specific rules operate in particular relationships to avoid potential sources of conflict that would disrupt that particular relationship, and the following results bear on this:

1. A common danger is in an unsuitable relationship. We found that rules forbidding sexual behaviour were most strongly endorsed for parents, parents-in-law, and adolescent children.

2. Some sociobiologists like Alexander (1979) have argued that exchange theory does not apply to kin, for whom altruism and selfish gene theories are more appropriate. We expected, therefore, that rules about equitable exchange would apply less to family members, but this was not the case.

3. We found that for all the work relationships (teacher, repairman, etc.), there were a number of specific rules directly related to the task, and that these were endorsed more strongly than the 33 general rules.

This study has now been replicated in Hong Kong, Japan, and Italy, with 993 subjects in all. Some of the main differences are these:

England. More rules endorsed, greatest emphasis on repaying debts and favours, and standing up for people in their absence. This is the only country in which joking and teasing is thought to be desirable, in a number of relationships.

Hong Kong. Many rules endorsed. Greatest emphasis on respecting privacy.

Japan. Strong on avoiding public criticism, weak on keeping confidences and standing up for others in their absence. Sex proscribed in nearly all relationships.

Italy. Sex is not proscribed for many relationships nor is public criticism. Relationships with in-laws and dating partners are less intimate.

Finally, we have taken a closer look at the rule for friendship. Are all of the endorsed rules important and does breaking them lead to a weakening of the relationship? Eighty-six subjects reported their behaviour in 27 role-related areas for a current and a lapsed friendship and indicated which friendships were "good" and "poor." One hundred and fifty-six subjects rated the rules for the extent to which breaking them had been responsible for the breakup of a particular friendship. We now had four criteria for friendship rules, (1) endorsed as rules by the original sample, (2) rule was kept more for current than for lapsed friends, and (3) rule was more for a good than a poor friend, (4) rule was rated as an important cause of the breakup by over 20% of the second sample. Six of the 27 rules passed on all four criteria. In addition, 3 more rules passed on three criteria, but did not affect the *quality* of friendship. Four rules were endorsed and blamed for the breakup by a large percentage of subjects but failed to discriminate between current and lapsed friends, perhaps because they are universal rules, kept to some extent in all relationships. These rules are given in Table 2.2.

We can see that exchange and third-party rules are the most important, and that it is third-party rules that are commonly broken by friends. Intimacy rules are of least importance; although behaviours do discriminate between current and lapsed friends, they are better interpreted as consequences or signs of friendship than as causes of it (Argyle & Henderson, 1984).

TABLE 2.2
Rules of Friendship

Exchange
13.[a] Seek to repay debts, favours, or compliments, no matter how small
17.   Share news of success with the other
20.   Show emotional support
25.   Volunteer help in time of need
27.   Strive to make him/her happy while in each other's company

Intimacy
24.   Trust and confide in each other

Coordination
18.[b] Respect privacy
21.[a] Don't nag

Third party
10.[b] Don't criticise other in public
11.   Stand up for the other person in their absence
12.[b] Keep confidences
23.[a] Be tolerant of each other's friends
26.   Don't be jealous or critical of other relationships

---

[a]Do not affect quality of friendship.
[b]Frequently broken by friends and blamed for breakup.

GOALS

A number of social psychologists, like Lewin and more recently Pervin (1983), have found goals a useful concept. Palys (1979) has devised a method of sampling individual goals or "projects" by "beeping" subjects at random times; at these points they fill in scales about the activity in which they are engaged. And we have been influenced by developments of exchange theory, which directed us to the study of the benefits received by those who seek or stay in situations and relationships, and the interdependence of participants on one another in this respect.

Our first study was on the goals of social situations. We assumed that people enter social situations because they are motivated to do so, that is they expect to be able to attain certain goals, which in turn lead to the satisfaction of needs or other drives. Situations have presumably developed as cultural institutions because they satisfy needs in this way. A person is often motivated to pursue more than one goal, in which case the two motives may come into conflict, or they may be compatible with one another. When two or more people enter a social situation, they are attracted to it by their particular combination of motives. The combination of the important goals of each person, and the relations between them, intrapersonal and interpersonal, we call the "goal structure" of the situation. In our analysis of situations in terms of their basic features, we consider that the goal structure is the most basic feature, and that all the other features can be explained in terms of the goals and goal structure.

Graham, Argyle, and Furnham (1980) carried out three studies of the goals of each participant in common social situations. A total of 133 subjects rated the importance of 21 goals in eight situations. Principal components analyses were carried out for each situation separately, and rather similar factors appeared: own physical well-being, social acceptance, and task goals specific to the situation.

We also asked subjects to rate the extent to which each goal was instrumental to, independent of, or interfered with other goals on a five-point scale. This showed the amount of conflict versus instrumentality, and other scales elicited the direction of such relationships. Links between goals both within and between persons were found, so that in the case of nurse and patient, for example, the nurse's goal of looking after the patient leads to patient's well-being, but it is in conflict with the nurse's own well-being—she might become ill herself. We think that this is potentially a powerful method for exploring the conflicts and instrumental links between goals; it is perhaps limited to the goals that subjects are willing to admit to, although in the present study a number of fairly basic and biological goals were reported.

We have tried to use the same method to tease out the goal structure of long-term relationships like marriage and friendship (Argyle & Furnham, 1983). Here we did find goal factors and goal structures for relationships, but these did not have the clear and simple structures which we obtained for situations. Instead of three factors, there were six or seven, with very large numbers of linkages, and subjects found the linkage scales difficult to use. Argyle and Furnham (1983) therefore adopted a rather different approach; from various sources we drew up lists of 15 common goals or sources of satisfaction, and 15 common sources of conflict, which could apply to a wide range of relationships. Fifty-two subjects rated the amount of satisfaction and conflict that they experienced in nine different relationships. A principal components analysis of the satisfaction scores produced three orthogonal factors. Factor I, which takes up the most variance, consists of a variety of sources of satisfaction, based on advice, property, money, and joint work. It is difficult to summarise these elements in a single label, but this factor might be called "Instrumental Reward." Factor II is easier to label and can be interpreted as "Emotional Support." Factor III can be called "Shared Interests."

Similarly a principal components analysis was computed for the 15 sources of conflict, followed by varimax rotation. This yielded two orthogonal factors. Factor I, which accounts for 51% of the variance, is based on many kinds of conflict, but particularly the kinds of conflict found in more intimate relationships, and we call it "Emotional Conflict." Factor II is based primarily on problems with the other's behaviour and is called "Criticism."

We thought that there might be a universal source of satisfaction with relationships. One reason for expecting this is from the evidence that one relationship can substitute for another; for example, studies by Shanas and Townsend (1968) show that siblings, children, friends, and spouses are interchangeable to some extent. Of our three factors, Factor III, shared interests and doing things together, is high for all relationships except neighbour while the scale with the highest score throughout was "respecting each other's privacy."

We were particularly interested in conflict, and its relationship to satisfaction. Braiker and Kelley (1979) suggested that a closer relationship and deeper commitment often requires working through, rather than avoiding conflicts. Scanzoni (1979) similarly argues that at a greater level of interdependence conflict is more likely, but that its resolution will lead to a higher level of rewards; hostility may occur, but only if it is believed that the other is committed to the relationship, and that it may help to resolve the conflict. All this goes contrary to the common-sense view that conflict is a wholly negative feature of relationships. Recent research on marriage has found that there are two independent factors here. For example Jacob, Feiring, and Anderson (1980) found a factor of warmth, understanding, and involvement and an independent factor of indifference and uninvolvement. Gilford and Bengtson (1979), on the other hand, found a positive factor of number of shared activities and a negative factor of frequency of negative affective interaction. We found that arguing is one of the most characteristic marital activities. We also found that satisfaction and conflict were positively correlated *across* relationships ($r = .57$), and that there were small positive correlations *within* a number of relationships.

It was expected that satisfaction and conflict would vary with the power and status of the other. Previous findings are rather contradictory here. On one hand, one's superior is found to be a major source of social support and job satisfaction (Payne, 1980). On the other hand, Wish et al. (1976) found this was a very superficial relationship. We expected that supervisors would be seen as an important source of instrumental, rather than expressive, reward and that the level of conflict would be high. Overall satisfaction was similar for work superior and work associate. However, work superior was higher on Instrumental Reward (Factor 1). Conflict was somewhat higher for work superior (1.77 versus 1.61, $p < .05$), and this was especially so for Criticism (Factor II) but also for Emotional Conflict (Factor I). On this factor, conflict for work superior was second only to spouse. From general principles of exchange theory, the more powerful person in a relationship would be expected to get a better balance of rewards over costs, corresponding to their satisfactions and conflicts. The only relationship with a clear power difference on our list was that of work superior, so we predicted a lower conflict/satisfaction ratio with work superior compared with work associate. The ratio of conflict to satisfaction was greater for work superiors (0.75) than for work associates (0.67) ($p < .05$) (Argyle and Furnham, 1983).

Exchange theory also led us to expect a lower balance of satisfactions over conflicts in the less voluntary relationships, such as at work, with neighbours, and certain kin—where the relationship has to be maintained whether it is rewarding or not. We therefore took the average of all satisfaction and conflict scores, and looked at the ratios of conflict/satisfaction, finding that there was a significant difference between the two kinds of relationships, with more voluntary relationships showing a higher balance of satisfaction over conflicts than the less voluntary ones.

In addition, we predicted and found a number of age and sex effects. For example, females derived more satisfaction from giving and receiving emotional support and had closer relationships with their friends and sisters. Younger subjects had more conflict in all relationships, giving some support to the idea that conflicts have to be worked through. Young women derived a lot of satisfaction from their sisters but also had a lot of conflict with them.

RELATIONSHIPS ANALYSED IN TERMS OF ACTIVITIES

Argyle and Furnham (1982) did a study in which 60 subjects, in four age and sex groups, were asked how often they had engaged in 26 relationships, with others in 7 different relationships during the previous month. One of the analyses extracted the most characteristic activities for each relationship by calculating the relative frequencies for each (Table 2.3). The table shows, for example, that the most characteristic activity with spouse was watching TV. (Later research by has shown that being in bed together is even more characteristic.) Factor analysis of

TABLE 2.3
Situations and Activities *Most* Chosen for Certain Relationships
(Ratios to Mean Frequency for All Relationships)

Spouse *Mean Ratio 1.64*		*Work Colleague, Liked, Same Status* *Mean Ratio 1.11*		*Friend, Similar Age* *Mean Ratio 1.26*	
Situations Above This Ratio		*Situations Above This Ratio*		*Situations Above This Ratio*	
Watch TV	2.61	Attend lecture	2.11	Dancing	2.00
Do domestic jobs together	2.48	Work together on joint task	1.56	Tennis	1.67
Play chess or other indoor game	2.31	Together in a committee	1.55	Sherry party	1.63
Go for a walk	2.28	Morning coffee, tea	1.50	Joint leisure	1.63
Go shopping	2.15	Casual chat, telling jokes	1.35	Pub	1.60
Play tennis, squash	2.03	One helps the other	1.31	Intimate conversation	1.52
Informal meal together	1.93			Walk	1.50
Intimate conversation Have argument, disagreement	1.92 1.84				

the data produced a general intimacy factor, based on items such as intimate conversation, informal meals, and watching TV. Spouse was by far the highest on this factor, friends intermediate, work mates lowest.

INTERPRETATION OF CERTAIN RELATIONSHIPS

To see whether our findings throw new light on particular relationships, let us look at a number of different kinds of relationships.

Friendship

This is the most familiar and most studied relationship, and I will compare some of the others with it. However, it does have some special features. First, there is a characteristic range of activities: It can readily be seen that friends talk, eat and drink, and engage in joint leisure activities, and in another study we found that talking, while eating or drinking, was a very typical activity. Second, friendship is the most important relationship for certain age groups such as adolescents and students, who may see their immediate friends for 3 hours a day, and sometimes have a few more hours on the telephone as well.

One very interesting sex difference is that female friends talk and make intimate disclosures, male friends *do* things together. Sources of satisfaction are Shared Interests—doing things together—and Emotional Support, but friends are low on Instrumental Reward. We and others have also found that friends provide much less help than kin do: Friends *are* a source of social support in buffering the effects of stress but are rarely the main source.

Friends are voluntary and often temporary (unlike kin); friendship seems to be dependent on exchange of rewards—but rewards of a special sort: these are not the Instrumental Rewards of work relations and marriage, or the serious help provided by kin, but rewards derived primarily from talk and leisure, simply enjoying each other's company.

Marriage

The differences between marriage and friendship can be illustrated by some of our studies. First, the shared activities are totally different. Second, marriage is a much more intense relationship, as our study of levels of satisfaction showed; the greatest difference from friends was on the Instrumental Reward factor. The other part of that study showed that the spouse was also the greatest source of conflict; while the activities study showed that arguing is one of the most characteristic marital activities. Indeed, other studies have found that most married couples have arguments, even rows, once a day for the unhappily married, once a week for the happily married (Burgess, 1981). Stark and McEvoy (1970) found that physical violence occurs and is regarded as acceptable in 25% of marriages, yet several surveys have found that about 70% of couples say they are happily married at the highest point of a seven-point satisfaction scale.

It is not difficult to see why there should be so much conflict in marriage— living at very close quarters, having satisfactions depend on joint and coordinated activities, the spouses usually having rather different roles and spheres of activity. What is interesting is that all this conflict is compatible with a high level of satisfaction.

What is the source of this intense marital bond? Traditional theory says that the main biological function of marriage is the production care and socialization of children; however, according to several recent American studies, married couples are actually happier before and after they have children in the home (Walker, 1977). Sex may also be considered to be the main root of marital attachment: Couples who have more sexual satisfaction are more happily married, although it is not clear which causes which, and living together among the young often does not lead to any more permanent attachment. Exchange theory suggests that there is a *broader* exchange of rewards in marital happiness—sex, companionship, income, housekeeping, etc.

There are several other processes that may contribute to the marital bond. (1) Regularly engaging in joint activities that are satisfying, for which the other is necessary, makes the other valued. As stated, male friends *do* things together (e.g., playing squash); this may be the male form of bonding. (2) Talking regularly and discussing personal problems leads to a shared cognitive world.

Female friends talk a lot: perhaps this is the female form of bonding. (3) Shared property, children, friends etc. comprise a social and physical environment that supports the relationship. (4) Shared emotional experiences, surviving trials and tribulations, may be a special source of attachment. (5) A shared past or a shared identity makes the other part of the self-image as shown by answers to questions like, "Who am I?" "I am X's husband (or wife)." It would be useful, however, to know which of these processes is most important, because this would have implications for how to strengthen or repair a marriage.

Marriage is the greatest source of social support (see Table 2.4) and has immense benefits for physical health, mental health, and general well-being, as many studies have shown (e.g., Lynch, 1977). The sixth figure in the "single" column means, for example, that single men are 4.1 more times as likely than

TABLE 2.4
The Effects of Marriage (Ratios to Married)

		Single	Widowed	Separated/Divorced	
1. Total death rate		1.50	1.70	1.90	
2. Suicide	M	1.88	5.41	4.29	
	F	1.25	2.00	3.50	
				Div.	*Sep.*
3. Prison	M	8.6	7.0	15.5	17.9
	F	2.0	2.0	9.0	5.0
				(Lynch, 1977)	
4. Psychiatric inpatients	M	4.10	2.92	14.0	
	F	2.65	1.87	7.25	
				Sep.	*Div.*
5. Psychiatric outpatients	M	2.92	1.27	9.62	4.95
	F	1.76	0.68	6.70	3.83
				(Bloom et al., 1978)	
6. Heart disease (death by)	M	1.35	1.55	2.05	
	F	1.16	1.50	1.41	
				(Lynch op. cit.)	
				Sep./Div.	*Married + Children*
7. Happiness	M	.61	.71	.50	.93
	F	.67	.70	.50	.82
				(Campbell et al., 1976)	

married men to be mental hospital in-patients. Could the explanation of these results be that only people who are happy and well get married? The other direction of causation is more important as is shown by (1) the fact that all the nonmarried statuses have higher rates of illness, and (2) married people, or those with other kinds of social support, are made less ill by stressful life events (e.g., Brown & Harris, 1978). On the other hand, the processes involved are not clear: one element is that married people, and others receiving social support, smoke and drink less and may get a better diet. There is a striking sex difference, too, in the benefits of marriage—men get more of these benefits than women. I think that the most likely explanation of this is that women *provide* more social support than men, especially in working-class couples (Komarovsky, 1964).

Kin

Kinship has been rather neglected by psychologists, although it is the main form of relationship for most of the world, especially in Africa and Asia, and accounts for 50% of the strongest ties outside the home for most of us (Wellman, 1979). In terms of satisfaction scores, we found that kin are similar to friends, but there are important differences. The activities are different—with friends it is joint leisure and common interests, with kin it is helping with the shopping, baby sitting, and keeping up with the family news. Most people live with kin, or very near to them, or both. Kin are asked for and are willing to provide major help—over money, accommodation, looking after children when ill, for example, while this does not happen with friends, as Adams (1967) was the first to show. Whereas help is provided in both directions, there is a considerable imbalance at any particular point in time. For example, adult children do more for their elderly parents than vice versa (Hill, 1970). Frequency of contact between parents and adult children does not decline at all over time, while frequency of contact with siblings follows a flat U-shaped curve, with a small increase in the later years (Leigh, 1982). This last point is interesting—it shows that kinship is a very long-lasting relationship, and it shows that kinship can, to some extent, act as a substitute for marriage. The widowed are much more likely than those still married to see frequently, or live with, a sibling or one of their own children. Kin are particularly important in old age; most letters, telephone calls, and social encounters are, then, with children and sibs.

What is the explanation for the attachments between kin, which survive for so many years and lead to such a strong sense of obligation and willingness to provide help?

1. Could it be due to the process of exchange of rewards, which is so important for friends and spouses? There certainly is some exchange of rewards, and this probably affects the preference for one sibling over another. On the other

hand, the fact that rewards are so imbalanced for years on end rather goes against this explanation.

2. The virtually permanent attachments between primary kin could be due to some kind of imprinting or conditioning in early childhood. Infants become closely attached to parents and other members of the family in early life, they spend several years together in great intimacy, and are very emotionally involved with one another. It is interesting that favourite cousins are those who were also childhood companions (Blood, 1972).

3. Some sociobiologists have argued that exchange theory does not apply to kin and that kin are concerned with one another because they want their own genes to prosper, and so are willing to help those who are most closely related to themselves.

Hewstone, Argyle, and Furnham (1982) used a version of the Bristol matrices for studying such strategies as Self-favouritism, Altruism, Fairness, and Maximum Joint Profit. Forty subjects were chosen who had a spouse, a child between 10 and 15, a friend, and a work mate. They were asked to say how they would divide a sum of money between themself and each of these others. We found that subjects were least selfish and most fair with spouse, followed by child, friend, and work mate. Women were more generous than men.

WORK RELATIONSHIPS

There are quite a variety of work relationships—with work mates, colleagues, superiors, subordinates, clients, and rivals or other opponents. In our sources of satisfaction study work relations came out very low, although least low on Instrumental Reward. Supervisor was a source of conflict second only to spouse—but without the satisfactions due to spouse. We found that the *activities* shared with work mates consist, of course, of working together, plus the various social events at work—morning coffee, jokes and gossip, and so on.

There is often quite of lot of conflict at work. A major cause of this is the social structure. Managers and shop stewards, salespeople from rival firms, personnel and production, and many other different groups are often on opposite sides. These are relationships that have to be maintained, although they are unlikely to lead to close attachments. Co-workers are sometimes competing for promotion, or other benefits, or may have conflicting views about policy. This, however, may be combined with quite strong attachment. Supervisors and subordinates can be in quite strong conflict, as the Argyle and Furnham (1983) study found. Nevertheless people at work on the whole get on fairly smoothly, perhaps because their relationships are supported, even enforced, by the working organisation and the incentive system. People want to earn their living, keep their jobs, and do well; the others are instrumental to this. This perhaps explains why individuals can get on perfectly well with members of other racial groups or social classes at work but not outside work.

There are probably a range of work relationships, and we have carried out a study to test this:

1. Some people at work become friends in the usual sense (i.e., they are seen outside work and invited home). It has been found that 25% of friends are made in this way, although this is more common in closed communities.

2. Some co-workers are chosen for their company at coffee breaks and other social events at work, for jokes and games, gossip, and chat but are rarely seen outside the work place. They are not quite friends in the usual sense but fulfill the same functions except that their company, help, and social support takes place at work rather than at leisure.

3. Many of the people who we see at work we collaborate with perfectly smoothly, help and are helped by them, enjoy working with them, but we have no particular attachment to them, and we would not bother to say goodbye if we left for another job. This covers the majority of work contacts and includes most of those with people from different social classes or racial groups.

4. A few individuals at work we find difficult to deal with, or actively dislike, yet we have to sustain the relationship. We may find them difficult because they are disturbed or aggressive personalities (or because we are!), or as a result of conflict within the organisation. Furnham and I found that we see these people in short and formal encounters (e.g., at committee meetings, sometimes at morning coffee). (Henderson and Argyle, 1985).

In terms of exchange theory, our type (1) is like regular friendship—the other is found rewarding inside and outside work: in (2) he or she is rewarding in the work setting only, including help and social support at work; in (3) the level of reward is minimal and mainly derived from the task, and in (4) costs are greater than rewards, but the incentives provided by the organisation compel a certain level of cooperation.

THE SOCIAL SKILLS OF MAINTAINING RELATIONSHIPS

I have shown that relationships are good for people, and that the disruption of relationships is often distressing and bad for health. Clients for social skills training and marital therapy would often like to be able to cope with their relationships better. Here I shall discuss two sets of relationship skills—marriage, and the provision of social support.

Marital Skills

The most sophisticated procedures at the moment are those developed in the United States by Jacobson and Margolin (1979) and others, known as Behavioral Marital Therapy, with the following main components:

1. *Increasing rewardingness* (following Exchange Theory); identifying rewarding behaviour for the partners, starting caring days once a week, on which 8 to 20 such acts are performed—a flower, a kiss, a compliment, a special meal, etc.

2. *Training in communication skills.* The partners are trained in verbal disclosure of feelings, thoughts and intentions, nonverbal expression of emotions, and to be assertive rather than aggressive.

3. *Teaching negotiation and problem-solving skills.* This includes training in contracts (example of a contract: *he* agrees to take her out on two nights a week; *she* agrees to sex games of his choice one night a week) and dealing with problems in an open, flexible, and constructive manner.

Some of the research which I have reported suggests a number of ways in which this kind of therapy could be augmented:

1. *Keep to the rules.* The rules that we have located so far for marriage in Britain are shown in Table 2.5, and we are currently engaged in research to find out which of these rules actually affect marital harmony.

2. *Engage in bonding activities.* The following ones may be important, although more verification is needed: do more things together, and things that lead to important goals; talk more, disclose more; establish more joint social contacts, more shared physical environment; take part in stressful and emotionally arousing experiences (e.g., take an exciting vacation trip).

3. *Analysis of interaction sequences.* Studies of interaction in distressed and happy marriages, which I have not discussed here, suggest what to look out for. Marital friction may be due to reciprocation of negative acts, repeated buildup to rows of a certain pattern, failures of nonverbal communication, particular failures in the negotiation process, and so on. It would then be possible to give normal social skills training but with the couple as the unit.

Social Support Skills

One of the main benefits produced by relationships is in the form of ''social support,'' which sustains the health and mental health of those supported in the face of stressful life events. It has been found that men are worse at providing it then are women, especially working-class men. But exactly how does one provide social support? There appear to be several components:

TABLE 2.5
Rules for Marriage

For Husbands, the 10 Most Important Rules Were (in the following order)

1. Should look after the family when the wife is unwell
2. Should be emotionally supportive
3. Should show an interest in the wife's daily activities
4. Should create a harmonious home atmosphere
5. Should share news of success
6. Should be faithful
7. Should address the other person by first name
8. Should give birthday cards and presents
9. Should respect the other's privacy
10. Should be tolerant of the other

For Wives, the 10 Most Important Rules Were

1. Should be emotionally supportive
2. Should be faithful
3. Should share news of success
4. Should respect the other's privacy
5. Should not discuss that which is said in confidence with the other person
6. Should indulge in sexual activity
7. Should stand up for the other person in their absence
8. Should create a harmonious home atmosphere
9. Should address the other person by first name
10. Should give birthday cards and presents

1. Tangible help: with cooking, shopping, child care, etc., which tend to be female skills; this is important for those recovering from serious illnesses but not for buffering work stress.

2. Listening and talking: acting as a confidant, listening to self-disclosures, offering advice. This requires quite sophisticated social skills, similar to counselling—listening sympathetically without criticizing, perhaps offering needed but unwelcome advice.

3. Emotional help. If Schachter's ideas are even partly correct, it follows that adopting a calm and positive mood may reduce the other's anxiety or depression. Displaying signs of affection for them may have similar effects; this requires the skills of controlling nonverbal signals.

4. Help with self-esteem. Those who are ill or otherwise in need of help are likely to feel inadequate, and social support can help them to feel valued.

5. Network support. Men in particular need to feel integrated into a network of shared activities and mutual obligations (Gottlieb, 1981).

CONCLUSIONS

I have tried to show that by studying the goals, rules, and other features of particular relationships we can start to map out the special properties of each one, and this enables us to make suggestions about training and therapy for marriage and other relationships. It has even more far-reaching implications—it is even possible that we could modify or create completely new relationships, as has already happened in the case of situations. To aid our analysis, several theories are useful—exchange theory and functionalism for example; however, one significant problem that does emerge is that each of the relationships I have discussed turns out to have more complex properties than any of these theories had envisaged.

3 The Structural Analysis of Primary Relationships

G. P. Ginsburg
University of Nevada, Reno

INTRODUCTION

This chapter is a conceptual rather than a conventional review of the literature and statement of a theory and suggests certain shifts in emphasis in research on primary relationships. In general, there has been too much emphasis on mental processes as causal mechanisms and insufficient attention to the nature of real relationships, the contexts in which they occur, and what people actually do to maintain them. The relative emphasis on unobservable mental processes has allowed the continued use of what Duncan and Fiske (1977) call "external variable" designs, in which we experimentally manipulate one or more external variables, observe the "outcome" behaviours, and infer the processes by which the outcome must have been generated—processes that presumably are hidden in the mind and have to be inferred. Examples of putatively causal mental processes include causality and responsibility attributions, fairness and equity judgments, the workings of "identity images" (Schlenker, 1980, 1982, 1985), and "role identities" (McCall & Simmons, 1978, 1982). It is not that these concepts are implausible or incorrect but that they refer to hidden, mental phenomena or causes, and that that putative location—in the mind—relieves us of the investigative responsibility of discovering whether and how people actually do such things. A primary relationship is a *social* fact, an entity of social interdependencies that exists over an extended time period and has its own emergent qualities (Hinde, 1979). One basic step in coming to understand primary relationships is to determine how it is that people know that a particular relationship exists and what it is like. After all, within a given culture it ordinarily is not necessary to step into the minds of a young couple in love to know that they are a young couple in love; nor are the members of that pair dipping continually into their own minds or their partners' minds to infer their states—even though they have the capacity to do so and might *on occasion* do it. The quality of what they are doing, and the implications that their actions have for the future, are contained in the situated performances themselves, and that is where we should direct more of our investigative attention. That is, we should increase our efforts to discover the social and interactional states and processes that constitute primary relationships and the social and interactional processes by which they are maintained and regulated.

Efforts of this form will entail certain shifts in emphasis. Some of the shifts concern the kind of inferences we draw from our work, while other shifts concern what we look at and how we go about looking at it. When taken together, the shifts in emphasis will focus more attention on what actually goes on in the initiation and maintenance of specific types of primary relationships at specific points in the careers of these relationships, with somewhat less effort devoted to building models of the mind. This state of affairs, I believe, will facilitate our conceptualisation of various types of relationships—and it may even enhance our understanding of the mind.

SOCIAL AND CULTURAL CATEGORIES OF PRIMARY RELATIONSHIPS

Most contemporary work—theoretical and empirical—has focused on voluntary, heterosexual, primary relationships, based on attraction, usually among young, unmarried or recently married, childless people, generally of middle-class origin and often in college or university. Furthermore, they are almost always members of advanced, technological societies, usually North American or Western European. A number of writers expressed concern over the obviously narrow nature of this population (e.g., Backman, 1981, 1982; Berscheid, 1985; Hinde, 1979) and questioned whether universal principles of relationship can be constructed on such a presumably biased data base. Their basic concern—that of generalisability of findings—is well taken; and a close examination reveals other issues that bear not only on generalisability but on internal validity as well. Discussing these points will make them clearer.

For example, heterosexual, attraction-based relationships among young North American and Western European adults are negotiable, involve roughly equal power, and allow relatively free entry and exit (cf. Backman, 1982). But clearly, there are forms of close relationships that do not have all of those characteristics; kin relations are one example, stepkin another (Chester, 1983). Our understandings may have limited applicability to those other sorts of relationships; and the existence of such features in attraction-based relationships may well reflect cultural specifications, economic opportunities and individual mobility rather than necessities of that kind of relationship.

Furthermore, the attraction-based relationships seem to carry an imperative for continued growth and orderly progress (Backman, 1982), but that imperative for orderly progress from casual acquaintance through deep intimacy may well be a reflection of culture and history (Gergen & Gergen, 1981); it may be relevant primarily to twentieth-century industrial and technological societies. The requirement of orderly progression does make sense to those of us from the United States as does the apparent "imperative for continued growth"—it does seem reasonable that if a relationship doesn't continue to grow, it will stagnate and eventually crumble. But the metaphor of growth versus stagnation merely reflects the fact that both we and the people we study are members of the same culture, a culture in which "progress," "growth," and "success" are basic social and economic values.

In fact, a French journalist (Roussy de Sales, 1938) who knew the United States very well was so struck by this blend of success striving and close relationships that he wrote: "The prevailing concept of love . . . is similar to the idea of democracy. It is fine in theory . . . but it does not work, and the Americans feel that something should be done about it . . . (The) constant effort to make things work perfectly and the conviction that they can be made to . . . is the great national preoccupation," and—he went on to say—it is applied to love as to anything else. Any maladjustments or deviations from the ideal state should be fixable, and if they can't be fixed, the relationship is dissolved or the participants live with considerable dissatisfaction. This pervasion of close, primary relationships by the theme of success is not a necessary feature of such relationships, but it was a striking feature of American close relationships when Roussy de Sales wrote of it in 1938; and I suspect he would write a similar article today. It is not a question of whether many relationships do grow and progress; instead, it is a question of whether all relationships *have to* in order to remain viable.

A similar point can be made regarding theories of the development and maintenance of relationships. Developing and maintaining a relationship is often conceptualised in terms of expected and experienced rewards and costs. Changes—or expected changes—in the ratio of rewards to costs are tied to progression and deterioration of the relationship. (See Berscheid, 1985, for an excellent summary of the common themes of major psychological and social psychologically oriented theories of relationship development.) But these common themes reflect, again, a concern with attraction-based relationships with a potential for high and intense intimacy; and they also reflect a model of people who are reflective, rational, and oriented toward outcomes, with an interest in the returns on their investments. In essence, they are economic decision makers. Such a conception once more reflects a cultural bias. On the other hand, this is not to say that the model is wrong—people often do display or report just such a mode of thought in the regulation of their relationships (although perhaps more commonly in secondary than primary relationships). But their mode of thought and the model that reflects it are grounded in the practices and values of the time, place, and culture in which they are both located, and neither is necessarily universal.

The fact that both the phenomena and the theories of relationship are culturally grounded has three implications, one of which is obvious and the others less so. First, even within a culture, there will be different types of relationships with different natures. Whether we will find the same lawful regularities across them is an empirical question. Second, to the extent that there are differences in the nature of relationships across type or time or place or culture, the site of operation of the principles by which we understand human relationships is not restricted to either the biology or the psychology of the members of the species, both of which I presume to be universal and relatively unchanging. Instead, the site of operation of those principles is likely to be our cultures and societies— which do vary from each other. That is, although the biology of our species may predispose us to certain types of interpersonal arrangements and certainly provides us with the capacity to learn and to develop flexible and adaptive interpersonal strategies, it generally does not specify the content of the strategies or the substantive form of the arrangements. The contents and forms, in their wide varieties, are more likely to be specified by the cultures and societies in which our species exists. Therefore, when we discover differences in the nature of relationships across time or place or culture or type, the explanation of those differences is likely to lie more directly in the culture and society of the people involved than in the biology and psychology of the species. A similar argument can be made regarding such basic psychological processes as perception and learning. This suggests that much of the research to date on primary relationships may actually be revealing not the role of the mind in the regulation of relationships, but the role of society (a closely related argument is developed by Backman, 1985).

This leads to a third implication: The theoretical mechanisms postulated for the initiation and regulation of relationships are more likely to be systematic statements of the intelligibility rules of the culture than they are systematic statements of psychological mechanisms or processes. That is, they are likely to be statements of the cultural grounds on which an action performed within a relationship is to be understood as intelligible, as making sense. They are likely to be systems of accounting for actions (Backman, 1976; Harre & Secord, 1972; Harvey, Weber, Galvin, Huysti, & Gamick, this volume; Scott & Lyman, 1968). This does not mean that people's actions in relationships are not guided by such rules as equity; on the contrary, people may frequently employ those rules in making a decision or choosing an action. However, the making a decision or choosing an action would be a complex, discrete act that would contain the exercise of such a rule as equity as part of the act and not as a cause of it.

For example, Weiner and his colleagues (Weiner, Graham, & Chandler, 1982) reported recently that personal accounts by subjects about incidents in which they had experienced anger, guilt, or pity were compatible with hypotheses linking those affects to the "causal dimensions" of locus and controllability. According to the accounts, pity usually was felt on observing another person in a negative state due to uncontrollable conditions, while guilt was experienced when the subject had produced a negative consequence through a personally controllable act. Weiner and his colleagues interpreted the data in terms of the different sorts of "causal thoughts eliciting the affects of pity, anger, and guilt." However, the data also can be interpreted—and more directly and straightforwardly so—as a specification of the circumstances under which the experience of such emotions is intelligible and warranted. This interpretation is based on the argument that we routinely learn the sensible conditions for the experience and even the active production of emotions (Averill, 1979; Sabini & Silver, 1982), and what we have learned should be reflected in the accounts we give of emotional episodes.

Smith (1982) published an interesting and potentially important version of this argument in the *Journal for the Theory of Social Behaviour*. He persuasively argues that Fishbein's model (Fishbein & Ajzen, 1975) of intentional behaviour is a codification of rules for making intelligible attitude statements. That is, Smith argues that the model, rather than describing the causation of a behaviour, actually is a claim for the existence of a rule that specifies the characteristics that an attitude statement must have to be intelligible. For example, if a person were to express the attitude that a performance of a particular action would be good or worthwhile and that relevant others would view the action as good and proper, a subsequent statement of intention by that person *not* to perform the action would be unintelligible without further explanation.

Data that reflect the operation of principles of equity also can be interpreted as reflections of cultural rules of intelligibility. And equity models can be seen as attempts at systematic codification of those rules. To the extent that the actions of subjects imply the operation of such rules, it is reasonable to infer that those people have the capacity or resources to use those rules on occasion, but not that the rules operate as continuous causal processes inherent in the thinking, planning, and doing of all individuals. Viewing the data as accounts by which actions are made intelligible forces us to specify the conditions under which such accounting performances enter into our activities, including our planning, as discrete actions. But, more importantly, an account conception of our data about relationships emphasises the cultural grounding of our knowledge by construing the data as reflecting cultural rules that guide the intelligibility of statements about primary relationships and of people's activities within them.

In summary, attention has been drawn to the important cultural grounding of both our theories of personal relationships and the actual phenomena of those relationships. In particular, some of the theoretical mechanisms proposed as causal generators of interpersonal transactions are likely to be systematic statements of cultural criteria for giving intelligible accounts of action, shared by investigators and actors alike. Similarly shared by observers and observed is the culturally grounded assumption of growth and progress in personal relationships, an assumption that pertains especially to the population whose relationships we generally study—young, Western, middle class, heterosexual and so on, as noted earlier. Our understanding of close relationships is necessarily limited by our selective emphasis on a particular sort of relationship in a particular sort of cultural milieu, especially since we are members of the same culture as the people under observation and therefore unwittingly share many of the same background assumptions.

Another feature that characterises the relationships ordinarily studied and that has ramifications for our understanding of them is their "primary" nature. That is, research has focused virtually exclusively on primary relationships—on such pair relations as husband and wife, or two friends, or an uncle and a nephew, rather than a dentist and patient or a lawyer and client. Two aspects of this focus are worthy of note. First, it is the dyad that is the object of study, rather than larger and more complex systems of interdependency. Thus, the set of relationships constituting a nuclear family is not the focus; instead, each of the dyadic relationships within that family becomes a focus, with the remaining relationships serving as part of the context of the focal relationship. This apparent oversimplification of interpersonal ties is justified, however, and need not bias our understanding of close relationships. The justification derives from the second aspect of the focus on primary relationships, specifically, in primary pair relationships, the solidarity of the pair is a prime feature, in contrast to secondary relations, such as lawyer and client, in which the arrangement is characterised largely by the role relationship. A primary relationship necessarily is restricted to a dyad, although any person can participate in a number of primary relationships. A young mother, for example, can have primary relationships with her infant, her older child, her husband, each of her parents, and so on; but one cannot talk of her relationship (singular) to her husband and children without implying a qualitatively different conception of "relationship," since the solidarity of her tie with each of those people necessarily is substantively different from the solidarities entailed by her ties to the others (see McCall & Simmons, 1978, 1982, for detailed discussions of primary relationships).

Therefore, the focus on primary pair relationships is legitimate and nonbiasing, given the interest in close personal relationships and with the important provision that other relationships are taken into account as part of the context. The issue of context is discussed later in the chapter.

On the other hand, the narrowness of the range of types of primary relationships that we ordinarily study carries with it potentially severe bias, as noted earlier. It is important to expand that range, and to do so in a sufficiently systematic function as to allow an assessment of the theoretical understandings we have developed so far. Expanding the range can be facilitated by improving the procedures by which types of primary relationships can be identified, thereby enhancing our ability to recognise a type as one that has not generally been studied and as being different from what has been studied. The expansion can be across stages, contexts, cultures, and even species, as will be discussed shortly. However, even as the range of types is expanded, attention will have to be given to central themes—essences of relationships, perhaps—that will allow the types to be linked or contrasted. Each of these points requires some elaboration, starting with the identification of types.

Empirical attempts at systematic identification of types of personal relationships are not uncommon. Rubin's (1973) distinction between love and friendship and La Gaipa's (1977) factor analytically based conceptualisation of friendship are two obvious examples. Clark and Mills (1979) made the distinction (also Mills & Clark, 1983) between communal and exchange types of relationships that should also prove useful, largely because it is likely to spur research into the conditions under which exchange considerations become pertinent to the interactions between the members of a relationship. However, an approach taken recently by Keith Davis and Michael Todd (1983) is especially worthy of attention here because of its conceptual foundation and its objective.

Davis and Todd wished to identify the subrelations that exist in genuine, archetypal, and readily recognisable instances of love relationships and friendship relationships. They call such instances "paradigm cases," following the theoretical work of Peter Ossorio (1978); and the final sets of subrelations that Davis and Todd generated through careful conceptual and empirical work are called "paradigm case formulations," or PCFs. For example, the romantic love PCF has such subrelations as Enjoyment, Respect, Exclusiveness, Passion, Giving One's Utmost, and Fascination; and the friendship PCF includes Enjoyment, Trust, Mutual Assistance, but not Fascination or Exclusiveness. A given relationship can be altered by augmenting or deleting one or more subrelations and still continue to exist. For example, a love relationship without Trust *can* exist, and especially if it has an augmented Fascination subrelation—but it would be very destructive.

The paradigm case formulation of romantic love and friendship also conveys information about what kinds of action would violate the relationship and what kinds would be expressive of it. That is an important advantage, although along with the other approaches mentioned, the PCF battery of scales does not distinguish between stages in the career of relationship or ages of the participants, nor does it deal with types of relationships other than romantic love and general friendship. And, as Davis and Todd noted, it was developed primarily on the basis of the narrow population of subjects typically used for relationship studies. Furthermore, the PCF approach reflects cultural categories or conceptions of relationships, so the descriptions produced in one culture may not be applicable or informative to people from other cultures.

Once a PCF is completed, it will indicate the types of actions that would violate the relationship under study and the types that would affirm it. So, for example, when Morton (1978) found that spouses more frequently revealed intimate information to each other while being videotaped in a laboratory than did strangers, the difference may have reflected a cultural concept of the marital relationship as one that contains subrelations of trust, openness, support, and so on. Behaviors that manifest those features, given appropriate circumstances, are virtually prescribed by the cultural concept, or PCF, if the members of the relationship wish to demonstrate that such a relationship exists and is in good shape.

A PCF will also indicate the types of situations that a pair would select or create to affirm a relationship, or avoid to hide it. Similarly, the PCF will imply the types of situations a couple would avoid to protect it, or enter to threaten or violate it. A newly engaged couple might choose to enter situations in which they can display their new status, or where they would be afforded the opportunity to experience it. And an attached woman—or an attached man—might avoid situations in which certain subrelations of the attachment might be threatened, such as exclusiveness. An interesting example of acting to affirm a relationship is the "baby talk" that nursing home attendants direct toward their elderly or disabled charges (Caporael, 1981a, 1981b), who are in a dependent relationship to the attendant. And it is doubly interesting that the elderly people, many of whom were fully capable of refusing to accept the baby talk, never did—and thereby collaborated in the affirmation of the relationship.

As a final observation on the PCF approach, it is worth noting an important methodological point: The subrelations of a relationship are not construed as component parts or building blocks of the relationship. For example, a romantic love relationship is not constructed of some combination of respect, intimacy, fascination, and so on. Instead, the subrelations are construed as linguistic devices available in a culture for distinguishing between relationships and even within a relationship at various points in time. Nor can Davis and Todd's sets of subrelations be considered exhaustive, because other subrelations may make important distinctions in the quality of two or more relationships of the same type, such as romantic love, in a particular unusual situation that had not been taken into account in the original specification of subrelations. Thus, the subrelations are not tied to their relationship either on a statistically multidimensional basis or in a generative ("causal") sense; instead, they reflect the ordinary language that is available to members of the culture for making distinctions among various instances of a particular type of relationship. Methodologically, the PCF procedure is compatible with the stricture of Harré and Secord (1972) to pay more serious attention to what persons actually say about their actions and relationships.

Other investigators of relationships also have relied at one stage or another on the ordinary language of the community as applied to the relationships of interest. La Gaipa, for example (1977), extracted the themes of friendship that he ultimately factor analysed from open-ended interviews with 150 respondents. Interestingly, the major factors he obtained were quite similar to Davis and Todd's Friendship subrelations, as the latter authors note. The interviewing and content analysis procedure used by Peevers and Secord (1973) to assess developmental changes in children's concepts of persons also could be adapted to the study of relationships, with the objective of revealing the ordinary language available in the culture for distinguishing among relationships of a given type, such as "best friends." And in a work not yet published, Rosalie Burnett at Oxford is tapping people's construals of their relationship with a sibling or a friend by having them write a letter about the specified relationship to a hypothetical confidant. Burnett's procedure is discussed in a later section, but it is relevant here as a technique that takes advantage of the ordinary language distinctions made by respondents in their construals of their own close relationships. In general, the ordinary language construals can reveal to us culturally intelligible grounds for distinction within and between relationships, including grounds that we may not have anticipated or derived from our models.

One such ground is moral. Attention to the accounts people offer about changes in their relationships and about their judgments of the relations (see Harvey et al., this volume) is likely to disclose moral considerations as an essential and ubiquitous feature. It is important, however, to note that the issue of morality is not being suggested here as a feature of individual development or judgment, which it obviously is, but rather as a ubiquitous feature of personal relationships. It is inherent in the relational notion of commitment, which itself has received relatively little empirical attention (Backman, 1981). The issue of morality can be seen as arising from social interdependence (Haan, 1982); and it is part and parcel of everyday life (Sabini & Silver, 1982). In fact, a personal relationship is analogous to a protracted situation that contains moral matters among its affordances—that is, it inherently affords the pursuit and accomplishment of moral purposes. Empirical study of moral features of personal relationships should reveal covariations of the frequency and type of moral claims with the type and stage of the relationship, its "health," the social network in which it exists, and the embedding culture. Furthermore, the expression of moral claims will probably be found to become part of the active negotiation process (Backman, 1985; Duck, 1982) which includes evaluation of the legitimacy of those claims, thereby reflecting indirectly changes in the moral content of the relationship over time and type. Elucidation of the moral themes in primary relationships will facilitate expansion of the range and discrimination among the types of relationships that we study and therefore should be built into the procedures used to identify types.

It is also worth noting that the range could be expanded considerably by examining other species. Primary relationships within other species can provide information about both biological continuities and biological discontinuities. The value of the former is especially interesting: if we find similar phenomena characterising human and infrahuman relationships, will we be willing to explain them in the same terms? That is, if we rely on interpretative and attributional processes to explain the growth and regulation of human relationships, and if we find similar relationship patterns among infrahuman primates, are the latter to be explained in terms of the inferences drawn, judgments made, and intentions attributed to each other by monkeys, baboons, or chimpanzees? Hinde (1982) certainly would not rule that out a priori, since he conceptualises relationships—whether among humans or infrahuman organisms—as having cognitive as well as affective and behavioural concomitants. For example, interactions within some monkey groups may involve "the assessment by one animal of the relationship between two others" (Hinde, 1982, p. 220). That sort of descriptive construal is compatible with a large set of ethological data; and it certainly is consistent with the descriptions and photographs provided by de Waal (1982) in *Chimpanzee Politics*.

On the other hand, we may be unwilling to explain infrahuman relationships in the same terms by which we explain human relationships. In that case, we either are forced to reexamine the explanatory terms and assumptions currently in use for our species, or openly apply two different sets of conceptualisation criteria to what appear to be very similar patterns of relationship. The latter strategy, unfortunately, is not unlikely. It clearly is the case in the comparative study of communicative behaviour, especially that involving comparisons between language acquisition of children and sign language acquisition of various apes. As a review of the frequently contentious and occasionally vituperative literature of the "animal language" field reveals, different and sometimes shifting criteria are applied to children and chimpanzees or gorillas; the single and two-word utterances of a child may be interpreted on "rich" grounds based on assumptions about comprehension and ultimate achievement, while the single and two-sign gestures of a chimpanzee are held to much more strict criteria. The problem of dual criteria has not yet arisen in the comparative study of relationships, but it may well do so as more ethological material is published in the psychological and social psychological media. Facing the issue would eventually sharpen our understanding of relationships, and comparative material should be sought, not ignored (Cairns, 1979; Hinde, 1979, 1982).

So, clearly, it is incumbent on us to extend our attention to a wider variety of types of primary relationships and to do so in a way that will allow specification of the features that characterise them and of the kinds of actions that will affirm or violate them. But the understandings we gain will be seriously incomplete unless we collect three additional categories of information: information about the contexts within which particular types of relationships are ordinarily manifested, the courses or careers of those relationships, and what people actually do and say in the expression and experience of the relationships. These all entail further shifts in emphasis, each of which is considered in the following paragraphs.

MANIFESTATION CF RELATIONSHIPS IN WHAT
PEOPLE ACTUALLY SAY AND DO

The literature on relationships and their management is replete with illustrations of what people might say and do to accomplish some end, or of what they report having said and done. But analyses of what people actually *did* say and do, and of how those actions either manifested or regulated a specific relationship, are provided only rarely. Carl Backman, for example (1985), suggests that there is a dialectic process by which a couple in their ordinary daily conversation actually create new elements of identity. They recount events of the day, reconstruct the past, and extend themselves into the future by planning subsequent encounters. This creates new apparent elements of identity that each partner incorporates into the view he has of the other and thereby into the world he creates for the other. The partner, then, faces a world that promotes the new identity elements, and by acting in accord with the opportunities of that world he assimilates those new elements into his actual identity. This is claimed to be a constant and routine feature of enduring close relationships. But does it really occur? And if so, how? What does the process look like?

The identity dialectic in all likelihood really does occur, and the answer to questions about its appearance lies in a technology that is increasingly available to us, a technology that some of us feel will become as important for our field as is microscopy for the biological laboratory sciences (Bakeman & Ginsburg, unpublished manuscript). That technology is video, and we should use it to record what people actually say and do in the accomplishment of their relationships.

Using video technology to produce relatively permanent records that can be reviewed repeatedly and collected longitudinally is not difficult; but converting those video records into usable, analysable data *is* difficult. Nevertheless, methodological guides are available (see Bakeman & Ginsburg, unpublished manuscript) and the benefits are worth the effort. Applying recording techniques to conversations of couples would give us the opportunity to discover, in a methodologically reliable manner, how identity elements are conveyed in the coordinated utterances and other actions of the partners, and how the proposed altercasting process actually works to get the recipient to act in accord with new, imputed elements of identity. The previously cited studies by Linda Caporael of baby talk in a nursing home, in which conversations between caregivers and patients were audiotaped, clearly illustrate the use of altercasting, through which the caregiver casts the patient into a helpless and relatively docile role.

The greatest research use of video in the human behavioural sciences is in the child development area, and anyone who is interested in the study of relationships would do well to review some of that literature, since there is not much overlap, although a few users of video, like John Gottman, have made important contributions in both arenas (see Gottman, 1979a, 1981). Through the use of video, especially in combination with moderately longitudinal designs, an investigator can *observe* the emergence of intersubjectivity or mutually shared fields, the establishment of coordination and reciprocity in both timing and substance, short-term fluctuations in the state of the relationship, including fluctuations between communal and exchange states—and even the procedures of self-presentation and altercasting. In other words, the proper use of video allows us to create long-lasting records of interactions that can be analysed and reanalysed to discover the ways a relationship is manifested and regulated in what people actually do and say. But a special problem is raised when we focus on what people actually say: How do we identify and reliably code the meanings of their utterances?

It is an unfortunate fact that mainstream social psychology in North America, which deals almost exclusively with communicational phenomena, has had no systematic theory of language, discourse, and meaning. Fortunately, times are changing, and the new (third) edition of *The Handbook of Social Psychology* contains an excellent chapter on speech acts and discourse by Herbert Clark (1985). That chapter is likely to become the first contact with reasonably sophisticated analysis of discourse-in-context for most social psychologists, and it provides a set of tools to facilitate the shift in investigative emphasis to what people actually say to each other. This shift in emphasis is likely to have far-reaching ramifications, in part because speech act theory and discourse analysis allow for the construal of direct and indirect meanings, implications, and possibly even intentions as features of the situated speech act—that is, of the speech act as an interchange embedded in a context. This point requires some elaboration, especially since it is not necessarily recognised by the speech act theorists themselves (e.g., Clark, 1985).

Independently of whether speakers have intentions—they sometimes do— and independently of whether listeners actively interpret what they hear—they sometimes do—the contextualised utterances themselves embody intentionality and implications. Although a listener's description to a third party of what a speaker had just said to the listener might be couched in terms of the speaker's intentions, the information itself ordinarily is contained in the contextualised utterance of the speaker, provided the utterance is part of a communicative act. That is, in the performance of discourse, the speaker and hearer are engaged in coordinated activity (Clark, 1985) in which a mutually shared context is established, at least temporarily (Rommetveit, 1980). Moreover, within that context, the coordinated activities performed include acts that we call speech acts, which by their very nature *are* meaningful; the meaning of the speech act is in part its implications about the larger act(s) in which the speaker is engaged. For example, when a telephone caller asks the restaurant employee who answered the telephone, "Do you take credit cards?" the employee is likely to answer, "Yes, we do. We take American Express, Visa and MasterCard" (Clark, 1985). The employee offered more than was explicitly requested but not more than was implied as relevant, given the conventions of the restaurant trade in the Western United States: people ask such questions over the telephone as part of the preparation for going out to dinner, and they may not have the specific credit cards accepted by the restaurant. Furthermore, the employee also might say, ". . .but we're not open this evening," reflecting again the implication that the query is part of the larger act of preparation for going out to dinner that evening. If he or she were to reflect on that brief conversation, or describe it to someone else, the restaurant employee might well draw inferences about the caller's intentions, about what the caller had "in mind." That is, the way in which we talk about such matters. But the employee is unlikely to have done that during the telephone conversation; instead, he or she engaged in a coordinated, conventionalised, contextualised activity in which he or she most likely responded directly to the implications contained in the caller's utterance itself.

The caller, too, was engaged in the coordinated activity of a communicative act, and his or her utterance was designed to convey rather than disguise meaning. Given the culture, the topic, the caller's interaction partner and the conventions of service and payment, the caller's query not only asked a direct question but implied the larger act of which that query was an early component—preparation for going out for dinner that evening. Furthermore, the situated query also implied the sort of answer that would be appropriate as a response—including a warning not to come that evening because the restaurant would be closed.

The caller's query had both direct and indirect meanings; the answer to the direct propositional meaning was "Yes," and the response to the indirect meanings was to specify the accepted credit cards and to inform the caller that the restaurant would be closed that evening. The speech act conveys an indirect meaning that the listener is to take as having been intended by the speaker to be taken as intentional. Notice that the listener does not have to draw inferences or enter the mind of the speaker; the indirect meaning is contained in the conventionalised structure and context of the act. The act also has a perlocutionary force—the implication it carries as to the type of act that would be appropriate as a response. If the perlocutionary force is not matched by coordinated actions of the other party, then the system of coordination—the conversation—breaks down and the episode is restructured. (See Austin, 1980, for further discussion of speech acts as illocutionary and perlocutionary acts.)

Applying these concepts to the study of personal relationships is straightforward. For example, if we videotape episodes of interaction between relationship partners and analyse the episodes in terms of coordinated speech acts, we should be able to discover—in the situated acts themselves—the expectations of the actors. Furthermore, if the acts are expressions of liking or loving, which we can construe as different cultural modes for the expression of positive sentiment, then the acts also will have a discriminable perlocutionary force, and if the other partner does not match the perlocutionary force with sentiment-relevant coordinated acts, the episode will break down or change direction. Moreover, if such breakdown occurs frequently, the relationship itself may be in need of remediation. This sort of analysis of what interacting partners actually say and do, using video records, focuses attention on discovering the complex structure of the coordinated acts of the interactors. Thus, rather than looking for expectations about outcomes in states of mind, we would look for them in the implications of the coordinated, situated speech acts of interacting partners. Furthermore, the degree of coordination and synchrony (Cairns, 1979) in the relationship, the amount of reciprocity, imbalances in dominance, even the groundwork for intersubjectivity (Rommetveit, 1980) can be extracted from the properly coded video record in terms of the substance, occurrence, timing, and duration of actions (see Allison & Liker, 1982; Bakeman & Ginsburg, unpublished manuscript). The results of these shifts in emphasis will be increased information about what actually occurs in the expression of primary relationships. Light will be shed on the ''identity dialectic'' mentioned earlier in this section and on some of the social mechanisms by which the relationship is modulated. These are not necessarily processes that are under the control of either partner (see the discussions of joint processes by Shotter, 1980, and Ginsburg, 1980a) or of which either partner is aware, but they can be revealed by a careful analysis of the taped episodes (see Kreckel, 1982). However, that information will not be converted into systematic knowledge unless we also understand the contexts within which the information was generated and the ordinary contexts of occurrence of the relationships of interest.

THE CONTEXTS OF RELATIONSHIPS

The important point here is the view that for any and all human action, the meaning of an action depends in part on the context in which it is known or believed to occur (Bakeman & Ginsburg, unpublished manuscript; Ginsburg, 1980a), and that context includes not only the culture and situation and the antecedent events in the action sequence (cf. Clark, 1985) but the larger act that is in the process of being accomplished. For example, a handshake can be a part of a greeting, a farewell, or a contract ceremony, and its shared meaning depends in part on which of those acts it is helping to accomplish. The same holds true for speech acts—for example, a verbal reference by a person to a social error by his or her partner can be part of a tease, a denigration, a constructive criticism, or simple instruction. Thus, the concept of context as it pertains to the study of relationships is a multifaceted, complex one, and that complexity has to be acknowledged.

Furthermore, many of the contexts within which a particular type of relationship can be manifested are provided or authorized by the culture. However, they still must be chosen or created by the members of the relationship through coordinated activity, such as deciding whether to go to a party, or turning the lights down and having a romantic evening, and so on. The mutually protective nature of some types of primary relationships also may allow for the choice or creation, through joint action, of "unauthorized" contexts for the expression of the relationship (McCall & Simmons, 1978). In either case, active choice or creation on the parts of the two persons is involved—that is, active agency; in addition, the actions of choosing or creating the context are not individual actions, but *joint* actions. A final point is that the sorts of contexts that are appropriate—or even intelligible—for the manifestation of any particular type of relationship are likely to vary with the statuses of the persons and the history and career stage of the relationship. This point leads directly to the general issue of the career of a relationship.

THE CAREERS OF RELATIONSHIPS

Once again, the importance of longitudinal information about relationships and the deficiencies in most of our contemporary research have been recognised by others (Backman, 1985; Berscheid, 1985; Hinde, 1979). It is obvious that research is needed on the courses or careers of relationships, and our attention would be drawn more automatically and readily to the careers of relationships if we were to treat relationships routinely as developmental systems (see Duck & Sants, 1983), for a systematic statement of a similar position, and the volumes edited by Duck and Gilmour, 1981a, 1981b, several chapters of which urge increased attention to developmental processes). Developmental changes of the system can occur rapidly or slowly, depending on changes in its external world and in its component parts (Backman, 1985; Cairns, 1979; McCall & Simmons, 1982). For example, the addition of a new baby to a family with a $2\frac{1}{2}$-year-old child can drastically alter the relationship between that child and its mother. Other routine examples of changes to the immediate social network and potentially to the personal relationships within it include a child leaving home and the death of an aged parent. Changes in the world external to the immediate network also have to be considered, such as job, location, and friendship changes.

The impact of changes in the component parts on the relationship itself also is clearly demonstrated in longitudinal mother–infant studies. For example, in our present research, we videotape mother–infant interactions in the home every two or three weeks, starting at infant age of about one week; and over the past 17 months, as the infants have developed and matured, their relationships with their mothers have altered accordingly. By now, the babies are all mobile, and they all can indicate simple negation, either by gesture or by word. Those two routine developmental accomplishments—one largely biological and the other largely social—on the parts of the babies have had dramatic impact on the relationship: The mothers now have to chase the babies and persuade or entice them; it is clear that the relationships have entered a new phase of their career. Relationships often change in the face of increased knowledge or skill on the part of one or both parties. And as the other side of the same coin, relationships often change in the face of failed health of one of the members. The adult child with an elderly and progressively more infirm parent is a case in point, and one that although frequent has received relatively little systematic analysis.

The examples I have mentioned so far have been routine or ordinary for various types of primary relationships within our culture, and resultant changes in the relationships are likely to be seen as part of the relationship's career. The relationship would continue to mesh with its surrounding society and would not be treated as unusual by virtue of its developmental changes. However, some changes are not developmental, but a response to an unusual, extraordinary event or process. One of the members might win a million dollars or might lose a job (although this is becoming progressively less unusual); or a spouse could die suddenly at a young age; or an infant's development could become abnormal. It is important to recognise that developmental changes in a relationship are relatively easily accommodated by the surrounding social environment and are seen as part of the ordinary career of the relationship. Nondevelopmental changes are less readily accommodated by the ordinary social environment and should be distinguished.

A second point about the careers of primary relationships is that we should pay special attention to transition points or transition intervals and to the time periods that immediately precede and follow them. For example, the time periods before and after weddings will reveal important and relatively intense developmental processes of the relationship, at least for couples who had not been living together before the wedding. Peter Collett has a study of this sort in progress at Oxford. Similarly, Karl Kosloski, Carl Backman, and I, at Nevada, are using retirement as a transition point and examining the periods before and after that point to determine changes in the set of personal relationships and their linkage to the retiree's strategies for maintaining support for his or her self-view (Kosloski, Ginsburg, & Backman, 1982). A recent study by Johnson and Leslie (1982) also illustrates a focus on transition periods, although they looked at several transition stages rather than one. They found a pattern of withdrawal from social networks as young couples moved from occasional dating through various stages to engaged and married states. This has been replicated more recently by Milardo, Johnson, and Huston (1983).

One value of a focus on transitions is that it is likely to reveal features or subrelations of the relationship and its contexts by virtue of the responses of the relationship to their disruption. A relationship that was intimate but not exclusive could show considerable adaptive responding subsequent to a culturally supported transition to exclusiveness. Moreover, studies of this sort would extend our knowledge about what it is for a relationship to continue and yet be different—an issue that Hinde raised as troublesome (1979).

A concern with the career of relationships also raises several methodological issues, two of which can be discussed at this point. One is a design issue. A longitudinal prospective design clearly has important advantages for tracing changes in a relationship, but the transitions involved may be too long to be practicably studied longitudinally. An alternative that we have found useful in our retirement study (Kosloski, Ginsburg, & Backman, 1982) is the overlapping cohort design, which is a version of one of Cook and Campbell's (1979) quasi-experimental designs. In it, one sets up several cohorts of people, each cohort being at a different point in the career of the relationship under study. The members of each cohort are observed or interviewed on several occasions, at time intervals sufficiently separated to allow the cohorts to overlap. For example, we set up four cohorts, one of which had not yet retired and would not for a couple of months, another which had just retired, a third which had retired 2 months ago, and a fourth which had retired 4 months ago. The cohort members were interviewed four times, at 2-month intervals. We also used an age-equivalent, nonretirement contrast group, so the study generated data from a preretirement point to 1 year postretirement, but in a 6-month data collection period. The combination of repeated measures and partial overlap of cohorts allows us to identify developmental processes and other changes relatively free of confounding threats. The design is a reasonably efficient prospective way to study the course of a relationship. Comparable problems obtain in some biological and ethological research, and a similar design has been used (R. A. Hinde, personal communication, 1982).

The other issue is more complicated and pertains to something touched on earlier. We often cannot conduct prospective studies of relationships; and even when we do, we often wish to include retrospective items. But the recollective data produced by such items, whether in the form of narratives or ratings or sortings, are accounts of the past, and one of their functions is to make actions intelligible and perhaps warranted. The procedures for generating intelligible accounts are largely cultural products, shared by all of us, but they depend in part on the setting in which the account is being constructed and in part on its purpose. For example, an account concerning an action performed in the past may well differ when constructed as part of a plan for future action, or as part of an explanation of one's past to a loved one, or to a social scientist. Two accounts by the same person about the same event may differ but still both be authentic; the account is a *contemporary* action and its content will reflect what is present and important in the contemporary situation. For example, the account given to an investigator by a 70-year-old widower about his relationship at age 25 with his late wife will be very different from the account he would have given about it *then*. Fifty years ago, his wife would have been alive to support the account or disagree with it; the relationship would not yet have been faced with the enduring consequences of their actions; he would not yet have had the benefit of hindsight or of so many subsequent events from which to choose to connect to that earlier time. There is no escape from the fact that recollective data are *accounts* of the past given in the present, and both the respondents and we share the same cultural rules for intelligibility of actions and decisions.

On the other hand, the accounts are not necessarily inauthentic; they simply may be very different from accounts given at other times and places. Multiple interviews at more than one stage in the career of the relationship would help, but this is not always feasible. De Waele and Harré (1979) also addressed this problem; but although their analysis of the problem is trenchant, their solution is to use a team of psychiatrists, psychologists, physicians, social workers, and economists, totalling about six or eight professionals, to work in conjunction with each respondent to create an "assisted autobiography." The process takes about a year, which is feasible only because the respondents are a captive audience—they are all convicted murderers, housed in a Belgian prison.

Recognising that many of the self-report data about personal relationships are situated accounts that generally are produced in accord with cultural guidelines of intelligibility and acceptability forces us to face a variety of issues regarding the validity of those data. A number of the issues are discussed succinctly in the chapter by Harvey et al. (in this volume) and will not be repeated here; but it is clear that in treating our data as accounts, we find ourselves addressing such issues as the roles played and functions served by accounts, procedures for assessing the authenticity of accounts, and specification of context within which accounts are offered. That is, we become explicitly and self-consciously concerned with the uses to which we can put those accounts in our attempts to construct theories of personal relationships. Several years ago, Harré (1977) suggested that friendship and other interpersonal statuses be investigated as social relations that are actively maintained—as managed social relations. He proposed that gossip about friends or explanations about one's actions toward a friend serve as sources of relationship-relevant accounts, and that analyses of those accounts would provide information about the conceptual structure that people must have in order to be socially competent members of friendship relations. Thus, Harré recommends that accounts be used to reveal the conceptual resources of the individual that are necessary for competent maintenance of a type of relationship; he neither presumes nor recommends a reliance on their historical accuracy. The project at Oxford by Burnett, mentioned earlier, in which participants write a letter to a hypothetical confidant about an actual close relationship, also makes no necessary accuracy demands but is designed to reveal the ways in which people construe relationships of particular types. Authenticity of the accounts, rather than their historical accuracy, becomes the crucial issue— that is, the extent to which the accounts embody and reveal the conceptual resources demanded by the culture of the individual.

Unfortunately, there is no easy or simple test of ''authenticity'' of an account as a reflection of the cognitive or conceptual resources of a person. On the other hand accounts can also be used by the investigator to construct the cultural grounds on which actions can be made intelligible, warrantable, and relevant to the relationship. Those grounds would include the meanings, rules, roles, and values that underlie the intelligibility and warrantability of an action (see Ginsburg, 1979, 1980b) and should prove more directly accessible and more susceptible to empirical validation. Thus, I recommend that accounts indeed be gathered and analysed but that they be used to shed light on the temporally variable structure and processes of a relationship–a managed social entity— rather than on the psyches (including the memories) of its members.

In closing this section on the careers of personal relationships, it is worth noting that the issues of relationship development and those of context are closely interwined. Dickens and Perlman (1981) emphasised the importance of life cycle stages for our understanding of relationships, especially with respect to changes in both the nature and functions of close relationships over the life cycle. But the various stages of the life cycle, within any given culture, imply different opportunities and different sorts of challenges and problems. That is, the various stages establish different contexts, and personal relationships should be expected to vary accordingly.

PERSONS AS ACTIVE AGENTS

A final shift in emphasis that already is well under way is conceptual recognition of persons as active agents, as being capable of doing things for reasons as well as being impelled to do them by causes. Active agency has been very much a part of microsociological and ethogenic thought (Harré & Secord, 1972), speech and discourse theory (Rommetveit, 1980), and various theories of human action (von Cranach, Kalbermatten, Intermuhle, & Gugler, 1982; Ginsburg, 1980a, 1980b; Shotter, 1980); but it also is emerging in recent work in U.S. experimental social psychology. Kelley and Thibaut (1978), for example, explicitly consider the matrix transformation procedures to reflect ''the person as a causal agent'' (p. 324); and Snyder (1982) argues that people have the capacity to choose and to create situations that will best match their self-monitoring inclinations. The rapidly enlarging literature in self-presentation (Baumeister, 1982; Schlenker, 1980) and self-verification (Swann, 1985) also emphasise the active agency of the person.

The essence of the active agency conception is that people can choose, create, negotiate, and modulate the situations into which they enter; and the members of a relationship can negotiate with each other and also can negotiate, *as a unit*, with other people, about the situations which they enter and the character of the relationship which they display. As active agents, the members of a relationship are able to display to others a relationship of a particular character, such as young lovers, or middle-aged child with aging parent, and others will treat them accordingly. That is, others will provide for them a world that more or less allows them to behave in accord with the type of culturally recognizable relationship they have displayed to those others. In the study of relationships, Argyle and his colleagues (see Argyle, this volume) demonstrated that people choose situations in accord with the relationship being manifested, and both Erving Goffman (1971) and Desmond Morris (1977) have discussed the "tie-signs," such as hand holding, by which people indicate—wittingly or not—that a relationship of a particular sort binds them. More information is needed about how people in different cultures and different types of relationships do actively create a temporary world to express their relationship; but there is no question that they actively do so—and it is becoming increasingly difficult to conceptualise such actions as being causally determined.

There is one additional aspect of active agency that is especially pertinent to relationships. Most of the actions that express and regulate a relationship are not actions of a single individual but of two individuals acting in a coordinated fashion (Clark, 1985). The actions are *joint* actions (Shotter, 1980), and neither individual could explain his or her own action—a joint action—adequately in terms of his or her intentions, thoughts, or desires; and neither could we. Thus, although people are active agents, their actions in relationships are joint actions and always at least somewhat beyond explanation in terms of either person alone, thereby contributing to what Hinde (1979) noted as the emergent quality of personal relationships. The research implication of this is that the relationships, and the actions that express them, must be construed as objects of analysis in their own right and analysed accordingly—not as aggregates of more basic units, such as individual persons (see also Kelley, this volume). That would be as appropriate as conceptualising water as an aggregate of hydrogen molecules and oxygen molecules.

CONCLUSION: THE STRUCTURAL ANALYSIS
OF PRIMARY RELATIONSHIPS

I started this chapter by saying I was going to suggest some shifts in emphasis in the study of primary relationships. I have suggested, as have some others in this volume, that more attention be paid to context, to course, and to a wider variety of types of relationships. But in addition, I have argued that many of our data and several of our models reflect cultural rules for making actions intelligible, and that research for the most part has revealed social practices in the guise of psychological causation. To correct what I see as an error—the high priority given to notions of psychological causation—I have urged that much more effort be expended on recording and analysing what people actually say and do in expressing and regulating their relationships, using video technology and the conceptual tools of speech act and discourse theory. However, these recommendations are not meant to replace but rather to complement current work in the field and in some cases to stimulate a change in interpretation of the data. But the recommendations also reflect a particular methodological and metatheoretical view that I have called the structural analysis of situated action (Bakeman & Ginsburg, unpublished manuscript; Ginsburg, 1980a, 1980b). In closing, I would like to tie that view together with the study of personal relationships.

The situated action perspective is not a theory but a statement of what I think are true features of people and their actions, features with which any theory of human behaviour has to be compatible. The perspective also implies a methodology that differs from the conventional one on several points, two of which can be noted here. However, it should be emphasised that the two methodological perspectives are complementary rather than mutually exclusive.

First, an adequate analysis of action requires both reductive and holistic theorising. This is because all actions are composed of constituent parts that must be identified by decomposition of the action, *and* all actions occur in situations and as parts of larger acts and can be understood only in conjunction with an understanding of those larger units. Second, the analysis of action relies more heavily on part–whole descriptions than on linear, cause–effect descriptions. This places a greater reliance on descriptive research in the analysis of action and relatively less on the controlled experiment—but only *relatively* less. And, procedurally, an effort should be made to record whole episodes that then can be subjected to repeated, detailed analyses to reveal the various structural features and interdependencies. This can be contrasted with the controlled experiment, which ordinarily includes an input/output orientation from which the experimenter does not record the actual process by which the output was produced.

The shifts in emphasis recommended in this chapter are consistent with these methodological implications of the situated action perspective and can be summarised as emphasising structural analysis—that is, on identifying constituent parts and processes *and* the larger units within which the action of interest is embedded. To pursue this sort of shift in the study of enduring primary relationships will reveal more to us about the control processes of relationships as they are located in the patterned doings and sayings of the partners and in the social and cultural contexts of the occurrences of the relationships. This will provide a healthy complement to the present, dominant approach, which is heavily weighted toward the minds of individuals as the location of the controlling processes (see Backman, 1985, for a related view). The shift suggested in this chapter will facilitate the treatment of relationships as entities in their own right, complete with emergent qualities and deserving of analysis as such.

ACKNOWLEDGMENTS

Revision of a paper presented at the International Conference on Personal Relations, Madison, Wisconsin, 18–23 July 1982. Revision of the original paper was aided greatly by the facilities provided by the Department of Experimental Psychology, University of Oxford, the stimulating discussions with colleagues in that department and the sabbatical leave granted for 1982–83 by the University of Nevada, Reno. A detailed critique by Robert Hinde of the original paper was also very helpful and led to several changes, although certain points of disagreement remain.

4

Relationships, Personality, and the Social Situation

Robert A. Hinde
Joan Stevenson-Hinde
*Medical Research Council Unit on the
Development and Integration of Behaviour,
Madingley, Cambridge, England*

INTRODUCTION

The last decade has seen a rapid expansion in studies of interpersonal relationships. We now have the beginnings of a science, in the sense of an ordered body of knowledge. This is likely to have a profound influence on the development of psychology, since dyadic relationships have hitherto constituted a little-studied area between our knowledge of personality, individual behaviour, and mental functioning on one hand and the work of social psychologists, sociologists, and anthropologists on the other. Studies of the individual, of dyadic relationships, and of social groups can, in fact, be seen as levels of increasing complexity, each depending in some measure on the others, yet having emergent properties simply not relevant to lower levels of complexity (Hinde, 1976).

However, as any science develops it tends not only to become fragmented but also increasingly divorced from neighbouring areas of knowledge. If the study of relationships is to retain its vitality, it is crucially important that it be integrated with knowledge of both individual and group phenomena. This chapter first emphasises the importance of the mutual influences between relationships and the social situation on one hand and between relationships and individual characteristics on the other. This discussion is then illustrated by material taken from a study of the behaviour of preschoolers in home and nursery school.

CONVERGENCE BETWEEN STUDIES
OF RELATIONSHIPS, DEVELOPMENT, AND
PERSONALITY

The Dialectic Between Relationships and the Social Situation

Every relationship is set within and is affected by a network of other relationships: A's relationship with B is affected by B's relationship with C, and so on. Conversely, the properties of the social group are, in fact, determined by the properties of the dyadic and higher-order relationships within it. Such issues are commonplace to students of family and marital relationships (e.g., Parke, Power, & Gottman, 1979; Dunn & Kendrick, 1980). In addition, exchange and interdependence theorists partially incorporate aspects of the social situation in such concepts as "the alternatives comparison level" (Thibaut & Kelley, 1959) and in notions of what is considered as "fair" (e.g., Lerner, Miller, & Holmes, 1976), although here the concern is more with the individual's perceptions or beliefs about how the social situation affects *them* rather than with its total dynamics.

The social situation affects relationships also through norms that influence the conventions and expectations of the participants. The dynamics of a marriage, of a mother–child relationship, or of the friendship between two children are affected both by the expectations of the participants and by the relations between those expectations and perceived reality. Newlyweds bring to marriage expectations derived from their own parents, from their peers, and from others, which affect the future course of the relationship. Again, the influences are two way, for the norms of the group are transmitted and transmuted through the agency of dyadic relationships (see, for example, Andreyeva & Gozman, 1981, for a recent discussion).

The Dialectic Between Relationships and Individual Characteristics

The nature of every relationship is affected by the characteristics of the participants. Conversely, the social behaviour of individuals is affected by the relationships in which they participate. In the short term, an individual selects from all the behaviour that he or she might show that which seems appropriate to the relationship(s) in which he or she is involved. In the longer term, the individual's repertoire of possible behaviour, and thus his or her personality, is affected by relationships experienced: Whilst the effects of relationships (or their absence) on the individual may diminish with age, they continue throughout life.

Except for clinical psychologists and those concerned with marriage, this question of the dialectic between personality and relationships has been curiously neglected by social psychologists. Of course, there have been studies of the effects of the characteristics of the participants on the nature of relationships— such as Newcomb's (1961) analysis of the influence of authoritarianism on the way balance is achieved and, as a more recent example, Peplau's (Peplau, Cochran, Rook, & Padesky, 1978) study of the close relationships of lesbian couples. And the influence of relationships on the individual is central for many problems in psychopathology—for instance, recovery from depression (Vaughn & Leff, 1976), susceptibility to depression (Brown, 1982; Brown, Bhrolchain, & Harris, 1975), and a variety of other disorders (contributions to Parkes & Stevenson-Hinde, 1982). But in the main, social psychologists have pursued studies of the workings of relationships with little reference to the personalities of the individuals involved.

Developmental psychologists have inevitably had a much greater interest in the dialectic between personality and relationships. The individual characteristics of the infant (Dunn & Richards, 1977; Osofsky & Danzger, 1974) and those of the caregiver (Yarrow, 1963) affect the infant or child–caregiver relationship, and the nature of that relationship affects the characteristics of the child and perhaps also the mother. Thus both for understanding the dynamics of relationships, and for understanding social development, we must come to terms with the dialectic between relationships and the social situation and also with that between relationships and personality.

The Consistency of Individual Characteristics

In research on the influence of a child's relationships on the development of his or her personality, the propensities of the individuals concerned are properly assessed in the context of the relationship in question. Mothers are said to be "sensitively responsive," for instance, on the basis of their interactions with the child in question (e.g., Ainsworth, Blehar, Waters, & Wall, 1978). However, it must not be forgotten that individuals behave differently according to whom they are with. A parent does not necessarily show a precisely similar face in every relationship, or indeed to every child—he or she may be predominantly controlling to one and indulgent to another. Spencer-Booth (1968) documented a dramatic example in a rhesus monkey mother of twins. Apparently because of its greater activity, she controlled one of the twins much more rigidly than the other, restricting its access to the nipple. As a result, that twin behaved in a demanding fashion, and the mother's relationship with the two twins came to differ markedly (see also Hinde, 1969). Similarly human mothers may behave quite differently to twins (J. W. B. Douglas, personal communication, 1980; Minde, 1983). Reciprocally, children's behaviour when with one parent may differ from their behaviour with the other. An infant labelled as "securely attached" on the basis of behaviour in the Ainsworth "strange situation" with the mother present may behave quite differently with the father (Main & Weston, 1981). Measures of the behaviour of two individuals in interaction with each other must be seen as measures of their relationship and not necessarily as reflecting characteristics of the individuals concerned (Hinde, 1969, 1979).

That individuals behave differently according to whom they are with is, of course, familiar enough to the student of interpersonal relationships. Even 4-year-olds adjust the language they use according to whom they are with (Gelman & Shatz, 1977; Shatz & Gelman, 1973; Snow, 1972). The same issue is implicit in the symbolic interactionists' description of individuals as having a number of "role identities" which, though emerging as a consequence of interaction with a particular other, also provide both plans for action and the criteria by which action is evaluated (e.g., Goffman, 1959; McCall, 1970, 1974). Or, to take a different theoretical perspective, the interdependence theorist's insistence that the course of a relationship depends on rewards and costs, and the expectations of rewards and costs, acruing in the course of each interaction (e.g., Kelley, 1979) implies that every relationship is, in part, a product of its own history and anticipated future and is thereby differentiated from other relationships.

Such a view is also entirely in harmony with current trends in the study of personality. During the last decade, discussion has revolved around the reality of the consistencies that we believe we perceive in the behaviour of ourselves and others. The earlier view that individual differences in behaviour could be ascribed to individual differences along a number of trait dimensions came under fire because of the relatively low cross-situational consistency of the traits (Mischel, 1968). This led to an emphasis on situational determinants and an excessive neglect of person variables (Block, 1977). However, debate about the relative importance of person and situation variables is inevitably sterile (Mischel, 1973); and studies evaluating the contributions of Persons, Situations, and Person × Situation interaction to the variance in behaviour indicate the importance of the latter (e.g., Bowers, 1973; Endler & Hunt, 1968, 1969; Endler & Magnusson, 1976a, 1976b; Rausch, 1965; Schuster, O'Donnell, Murray, & Cook, 1980). One approach has been to search for "moderator variables" which affect the relations between the variables under study—or, more specifically, which allow for the way in which supposed basic dispositions might be affected by age, sex, or by other individual characteristics and by aspects of the situation (Alker, 1972), although this approach has encountered methodological, statistical, and conceptual difficulties (e.g., Wallack & Leggett, 1972; Zedeck, 1971). But if all people are not consistent some of the time about some things, at least some of the people are consistent some of the time about some things (Bem & Allen 1974; Bem & Funder, 1978; Kenrick & Stringfield, 1980; Rushton, Jackson, & Paunonen, 1981). The extent to which individuals choose, affect, and are affected by the situations they encounter is a crucial issue not only for students of personality but also for those of relationships and for developmental psychologists—although the involvement of two or more individuals more than doubles the complexity. Thus developmental psychologists (emphasizing that the behaviours of child and parent depend on whom they are with), students of relationships (emphasizing that the properties of a relationship depend on both participants), and personality theorists (concluding that individuals show limited consistency across situations) have reached a common point.

However, whilst the importance for integrating studies of relationships with that of personality has been emphasized by a number of writers (e.g., Carson, 1979; Duck, 1977b), the way forward is by no means clear—not least because of differences in opinion about the more relevant aspects of personality (Duck, 1977b) and the fact that these differ according to the nature or stage of a relationship (Duck, 1977a). But perhaps awareness of the dialectics between relationships and the social situation on one hand, and between relationships and personality on the other, should stimulate developmental psychologists to study how the effects of a relationship with particular characteristics on an individual may vary with that individual's nature or social situation—an issue already documented in the differing correlates to a given parental style shown by girls and boys, for instance (e.g., Baumrind, 1967, 1971).

In large measure the foregoing, of course, is looking to the future. The rest of this chapter demonstrates not progress along that road but evidence that the road is worth treading. It is concerned with a study in which we have obtained data on the same individual's behaviour in two or more relationships. The subjects were preschool-age children, chosen in part because the influence of relationships on personality should be susceptible to analysis at this age, and in part because, in the culture in which we have been working, children of this age are establishing in preschool some of their first relationships that are independent of the family. A major aim of the study was thus to assess how far the children's behaviour and relationships in preschool were related to their situation and relationships at home. To that end, in most of our work we have followed the usual practice in studies of the behaviour of the same individual in two situations and focused on the correlations between the two. Here, to emphasize the mutual influences between individual characteristics, personality and relationships, we follow a different course, examining some of the factors that limit the strengths of those correlations in the view that such an approach may throw light on the dynamic interaction between relationships and personality.

THE HOME SITUATION AND BEHAVIOUR
IN PRESCHOOL

Nature of the Study

The children, who all attended the same preschool and came from 2-child families, consisted of 11 firstborn girls, 6 firstborn boys, 10 secondborn girls, and 18 secondborn boys. (The uneven distribution of subjects between the sex and sibling status groups complicated the interpretation of inter-group differences). During a 2- to 3-week period at 42 months, when most children were in their second term, and again for 38 children at 50 months, each child was observed in preschool (indoors classroom, and outdoors playground) and home; and data on home background, family relationships, and the child's temperamental characteristics were obtained from maternal interviews. The observations were recorded as spoken commentary on tape and coded by a modification of Lytton's (1973) modification of Caldwell's (1969) coding scheme. Temperamental characteristics were assessed by a maternal interview based on one developed by Garside, Birch, Scott, Chamber, Kolvin, Tweddle, & Barber (1975). At 50 months, the mother also completed a mood scale assessing Irritability, Depression, and Anxiety (Snaith, Constantopolous, Jardine, & McGuffin, 1978).

Comparing particular types of behaviour (e.g., friendly behaviour, hostile behaviour) between home and school provided little evidence that the children's behaviour in school was similar to that at home or similar to that which their mothers showed to them at home (Hinde & Tamplin, 1983). Nevertheless, aspects of mother-child interaction showed meaningful patterns of correlations with other aspects of the child at home, such as mild behaviour problems and some temperamental characteristics (Stevenson-Hinde & Simpson, 1982; Hinde, Easton, Meller, & Tamplin, 1982; Simpson & Stevenson-Hinde, 1985). In addition, aspects of mother–child interactions as observed or reported in the home showed a meaningful set of correlations with observed behaviour to peers and adults in preschool (Hinde & Tamplin, 1983; Stevenson-Hinde, Hinde, & Simpson, in press). As so often happens in such studies, many of the significant correlations tended to lie in the .30 to .40 range. Here we focus on some instances where correlations were, on a priori grounds or from other evidence in the study, lower than might have been expected. We offer speculations on the shortfalls in the hope that they provide bases for further study.

Extent of Consistency Within the School

Differences in Behaviour to Different Others Within the School.   Children's behaviour in school could have been assessed from the frequencies with which they exhibited particular kinds of behaviour with all others. In practice, however, the behaviour they showed depended on whom they were with. Comparing first the total number of interactions with peers and with adults (teachers and helpers) when in the classroom and in the playground, there was no evidence that children who interacted frequently with adults also did so with their peers, the four correlations (two ages and two situations) being near zero. At 50 months, but not at 42 months, children who often initiated interactions with other children also tended to initiate interactions with adults. But when the frequencies of eight types of interaction directed to adults and to peers were compared, four (Friendly, Control, Semicontrol, and Dependent) each gave four near-zero correlation coefficients, two (Neutral conversation and Reactive hostile) gave one significant correlation, one (Active hostile) gave two, and only one (Informs) gave four.

Furthermore, the properties of interactions with adults and peers differed. Interactions with peers involved much more reciprocity than interactions with adults, and contained more Friendly responses, Neutral conversation, Active and Reactive hostility, but less Control and Dependency responses, than did interactions with adults. There were also differences in the extents to which different types of behaviour were associated in interactions with children and with adults. Thus, children who made many Initiations to peers also often made Play noises and played Excitedly, but this was much less true of children who made many Initiations to adults. Again, Active hostility to peers was much more common than Reactive hostility, but the reverse was true with adults (Hinde, Easton, Meller, & Tamplin, 1983). The extent of these overall differences in the behaviour shown to adults and to peers was assessed in an analysis of variance concerned with eight behavioural items. Whereas individual differences contributed only 0 to 3.9% of the variance on these items (none significant), context (i.e., interaction with peer versus adult) contributed 5.7 to 76.6% of the variance ($p < .001$ in all cases) (Hinde, Titmus, Easton, & Tamplin, 1985).

This, of course, merely documents the commonplace that preschoolers behave differently towards peers from the way in which they behave towards adults, but it raises the possibility that home experience may affect behaviour to peers and behaviour to adults differently. In passing, we note that, although there were few simple correlations between behaviour to adults and to peers, the two were related in other ways. For instance, adults tended to initiate interactions with children who did not receive initiations from peers, and children who showed much Active hostility to peers showed no tendency to score highly on hostility to adults but did tend to receive Reactive hostility from them.

Pursuing this to a slightly finer level, the children also behaved differently to different peers. Not only did individuals behave differently to boys and girls, but the behaviour they showed to children they knew well differed from that to children with whom they were less familiar: Children who were often together were more likely to talk to each other in each unit of time spent together than were children who were together less often (Hinde & Roper, 1982). A discriminant function analysis indicated that both boys and girls tended to show different behaviour to "friends" (defined in terms of time spent together) versus nonfriends, although the variance accounted for was much less than that contributed by individual differences (Hinde et al., 1985).

In case it should seem that we have laboured the point that children behave differently to different others, we note that studies of the influence of aspects of the home environment often use as dependent variables data on interaction with diverse undifferentiated others or data from a particular test situation (e.g., for prosocial behaviour). Such studies neglect the fact that relationships depend on both participants.

Cross-Situational Consistency Within the School.   Not only did children's behaviour differ according to whom they were with, but behaviour with the same other could vary with the physical situation. Data were collected both within the classroom and in the large playground, which was occupied by the children from three classrooms simultaneously. On the whole, those items that showed good split-halves reliability within the classroom also showed good cross-situational consistency. However, there were some exceptions. For example Friendly to peers gave Spearman rank-order reliabilities of .46[c] and .56[c] at the two ages, but cross-situational consistencies of .15 and .24 (the contrast would be even greater if the reliabilities could be converted by the Spearman-Brown formula to give reliabilities over the whole period on which the cross-situational consistency was based (see tables for explanation of correlations). Peers were freely available in both classroom and playground, and the absolute frequencies of interactions did not differ significantly between the two situations, so that floor or ceiling effects were unlikely to have been involved. Intuitively, of course, it seems reasonable that individuals' propensities to show a particular type of behaviour should be differentially affected by the situation.

There were also some items whose reliability in the classroom appeared low but nevertheless showed cross-situational consistency (e.g., Time spent with girls as a proportion of time spent with all children: reliability inside .10 versus consistency .60[c]; Large muscle play: .15 versus .44[b]). Perhaps the freedom of the playground allowed the free expression of propensities that in the classroom, in spite of its permissive atmosphere, could be expressed only unreliably.

Choice of Home Variables

Choice of variables was, of course, subject to the usual criteria of interobserver and split-halves reliability (e.g., Hinde et al., 1983). Beyond that we should expect measures of mother–child interaction to be more closely related to characteristics of mother and child that had some degree of permanence than to more temporary conditions of either partner. At 50 months, two relevant sources of data were available to us: the nine temperamental characteristics of the child and four characteristics of mother's mood—Depression, Anxiety, Inward Irritability, and Outward Irritability. These last three were intercorrelated (.38[a] to .60[c], Spearman rank-order correlations) and were also associated with two of the child temperamental characteristics, themselves also relevant to mood (Intense and Moody) and also intercorrelated. (.53[b]).

One might expect that measures of the mother's mood, which must be regarded as nearer the state end of the state–trait continuum (Allen & Potkay, 1981), would be less closely associated with measures of mother–child interaction than the child's temperamental characteristics, which had considerable durability (Stevenson-Hinde & Simpson, 1982). The data supported this view. While the three maternal items were related to only three items from the observational data on mother–child interaction, the two child items were related to many more. (As we shall see later, both maternal mood items and child temperamental characteristics relate to more aspects of mother–child interaction if the sexes are considered separately).

Age Changes

Two types of age change may be mentioned. First, in a number of cases, the school correlates of a given temperamental characteristic (assessed from mother's descriptions of behaviour in the home) sometimes differed markedly between 42 months and 50 months. For example, the temperamental characteristics Active (restless or "on the move") and Assertive (bossiness and fighting with peers at home) showed significant correlations with a number of school items involving control and hostility at 50 months, but few at 42 months (Table 4.1). Again, children assessed as Shy tended not to Initiate interactions with other children at 42 months ($-.33^a$) and to be often Passive ($.27^a$). At 50 months, by contrast, although tending not to Interact with other children inside ($-.42^a$) they were often With other children outside ($.34^a$), showed much Large-muscle play ($.33^a$), but tended to be Compliant ($.34^a$), seldom Initiating interactions with ($-.41^b$) or giving Strong controls to ($-.37^a$) adults, and seldom behaving Boastfully ($-.35^a$). They also seldom Cried indoors ($-.49^b$). Such changes are compatible with the expression of characteristics changing as the child settles in to school. At the later age the Active and Assertive children may feel more free to express "negative" behaviour, whilst the shy children may have overcome their initial tendency to withdraw—the latter being compatible with Thomas and Chess's (1977) view of the "slow-to-warm-up" child.

A second type of age change concerned the age-appropriate expectations of the parents. Ratings on three of the temperamental characteristics assessed—Moody, Unmalleable, and Intense—were summed to give an overall score on "Difficult." Difficult ratings did not increase significantly from 42 to 50 months and at both ages were correlated with mother's reports of tantrums and refusals (42 months, $.36^b$, 50 months, $.41^b$), seeking attention ($.50^c$, $.50^c$), and failing to comply with a repeated request made after an initial refusal ($.42^b$, $.36^a$). At 50 months, but not at 42 months, mothers reported that children with relatively high Difficult scores remained cross for longer after a tantrum (42 months, $-.34^a$ versus 50 months, $.45^a$), and their mothers were relatively harsh after repeated noncompliance ($.24$ versus $.35^a$). Relatively Difficult children had fathers reported as being even more harsh ($.09$ versus $.31^a$) than mothers, less aware of mother's daily life ($-.11$ versus $.43^b$), doing less with the child ($-.14$ versus $.33^a$), and annoyed by the child more often ($.19$ versus $.35^a$) than fathers of less Difficult children (Stevenson-Hinde & Simpson, 1982). The question thus arises, were the children actually behaving in a more difficult fashion at 50 months than at 42 months, even though the ratings showed no significant change, or were parents less tolerant of Difficult children at the older age? Since the ratings were based on descriptions of behaviour, the former seems unlikely. A

TABLE 4.1
Significant Spearman Rank-Order Correlations
Between the Characteristics Active and Assertive
and Interactions with Adults in School

	Child's Characteristics							
	Active				Assertive			
	42 Months		50 Months		42 Months		50 Months	
Interactions at School	In	Out	In	Out	In	Out	In	Out
Interacts adult				.36^a				.51^c
Adult Initiates				.38^a				
Adult Friendly				.36^a				
Neutral speech adult								.41^b
Dependent adult							.33^a	
Adult Disconfirms								.36^a
Gentle control adult					−.36^a			−.34^a
Strong control adult				.44^b			.39^a	
Adult Noncomply								.39^a
Adult Strong controls			.47^b					.49^b
Noncomplies adult			.35^a			.30^a		
Reactive hostile adult	.33^a							
Adult Reactive hostile			.37^b				.35^a	.33^a
Active hostile adult							.34^a	
Adult Active hostile	.34^a						.37^a	.36^a

$^a p < .05.$
$^b p < .01.$
$^c p < .001$, two-tailed.
Coefficients were calculated using both the absolute frequencies of the interactions (underlined) and the frequencies as proportions of total interactions (not underlined). In practice, the two usually followed each other closely: Only the higher coefficient is given here.

reasonable hypothesis is that the change in parent–child interaction with age resulted from a change in parental expectations.

Sex Differences

When data obtained in the home, either by the assessment of temperamental characteristics or from observation of mother–child interaction, were compared with the observational data obtained in preschool, differences in the patterns of correlations between boys and girls were often apparent. We can categorize these as follows according to the probable bases of the differences:

1. Differences arising from correlations that depend on extreme cases more prevalent in one sex than the other. If a correlation between home and school items depended primarily on individuals extreme on the items in question, and such individuals were more frequent in one sex than the other, a sex difference in

the correlation could appear. For example, items indicative of warm involvement with the mother gave stronger negative correlations with Active hostility to peers in boys than in girls (e.g., mother Positive to boys $-.53^b$ versus girls $-.18$; mother Neutral conversation $-.56^b$ versus $-.24$), and with Control of adults in girls than in boys (mother Neutral conversation, boys .10 versus girls $-.67^a$). In each case, the behaviour in question was more frequent in the sex in which the correlation was stronger (Hinde & Tamplin, 1983).

Similarly, in a number of other cases, differences between the sexes in patterns of correlations seemed to be related to sex differences in the frequencies of the behaviours concerned. For example, high Active ratings tended to be associated with low frequencies of a number of types of mother–child interaction. At both ages, correlations involving maternal physical friendliness, solicitude, and hostility were due primarily to boys (e.g., 42 months: mother Physically friendly, boys $-.59^b$ versus girls .09; mother Solicitous $-.44^a$ versus $-.26$; mother Active hostile $-.52^b$ versus .07), whilst those concerned with verbal interactions were stronger for daughters (e.g., mother Intellectual speech boys $-.12$ versus girls $-.47^a$).

2. Differential prominence of symptoms of similar basic relationships. In some instances, a particular school item related to one set of items in boys and another in girls, but in both cases this implied a mother–child relationship similar in quality. For instance, boys who showed Reactive hostility to adults in school had relationships with their mothers involving little Physical friendliness ($-.44^a$) or Neutral conversation ($-.51^a$), whilst with girls there was little maternal Solicitude ($-.47$) or warm Friendly interactions ($-.52^a$). In both cases the mother–child relationships seemed to lack warmth. Similarly, being Alone in school was associated with control and hostility between mothers and sons (sons, mother Controls .41^a; child Hostile .58^b versus daughters $-.15$ and .11) but in girls being Alone was associated with Compliance (.42^a versus boys $-.39$) with Disconfirming mothers (.37 versus .15).

3. Differences in maternal responsiveness. In a number of cases, sex differences in mother-child interaction seemed to be a consequence of a difference in maternal responsiveness to boys and to girls.

One example concerns the correlates of mother's mood. Although, as we have seen, there were few overall correlations between the mother's mood and measures of mother–child interaction, there were strong indications that this was partly due to marked sex differences (Table 4.2). Mothers' scores on all four scales were significantly positively correlated with Physical friendliness to girls, but the coefficients for boys were all negative or low except in the case of Inward Irritability. Mothers scoring high on Depression tended to be Solicitous to girls but not to be Solicitous to boys. The latter tendency was present also for Outward Irritability. Depressed mothers tended not to give Intellectual speech (and a number of related speech items not shown on the table) to sons, but the corresponding coefficients for daughters were near zero. Mothers who were Anxious or Outwardly Irritable were likely to have sons (but not daughters) who showed

TABLE 4.2
Sex Differences in Spearman Rank-Order Correlations
Between Maternal Mood and Interactions at Home
for 17 Girls and 21 Boys, Ages 50 Months

Interactions at Home	Depression		Anxiety		Outward Irritability		Inward Irritability	
	Girls	Boys	Girls	Boys	Girls	Boys	Girls	Boys
Mother Physically friendly	.56[a]	−.34	.72[b]	−.06	.51[a]	.06	.68[b]	.47[a]
Mother Solicitous	.46	−.42						
Child Dependence seeking		−.50[a]			−.48[a]	.54[a]		−.43[a]
Mother Active hostile				−.48[a]	.75[c]	.03		
Child Active hostile					.71[b]	−.04		
Mother Total verbal					.48[a]	−.45[a]		
Child Total verbal					.51[a]	−.42		

If a large sex difference (i.e., > .70 correlation points) occurred for any interaction, then other significant correlations involving that interaction were tabled as well ([a]$p < .05$; [b]$p < .01$; [c]$p < .001$, two-tailed). Coefficients were calculated using both the absolute frequencies of the interactions (underlined) and the frequencies as proportions of total interactions (not underlined). In practice, the two usually followed each other closely: Only the higher coefficient is given here.

Dependence responses to them. Finally, Outwardly Irritable mothers gave Active hostility to daughters, and received it from them, but there was no such tendency for sons.

In general, Physically friendly was not associated with other positive mother–child interactions (e.g., mother Verbal friendly −.08; mother Solicitous .01; mother Express pleasure −.04) and often appeared to the observers as expressive of maternal tension. On such a view, the data in Table 4.2 suggest that mothers high on all four dimensions used daughters, but (except in the case of Inward Irritability) not sons, for comfort. While Depressed mothers tended to reject sons, Outwardly Irritable mothers showed physical friendliness to daughters but also had many hostile interactions with them. The sons of Depressed mothers were likely to show Dependence even though the mothers showed little solicitude.

As a second kind of example, there was some evidence of differences in maternal responsiveness to the child's characteristics, depending on sex. This was most marked for the characteristic Shy [negative initial Approach responses to new stimuli (three items) plus poor Settling in (three items)]. Thus the home observations indicated that mother–child interactions were somewhat more tense with Shy boys than with Shy girls. The number of items concerned with positive or neutral interactions with the mother that showed a stronger *negative* correlation with the Shy scores, plus the number of negative home items (i.e., hostility, strong or inhibitory control) that showed stronger *positive* correlations, was greater for boys than for girls at 50 months (9 versus 1). Similarly, observer ratings and maternal reports of interactions indicated large sex differences in correlations involving Shy, especially at 50 months. For example, the higher the Shy score, the more sensitive were mothers to 50-month old girls (.35) but not boys (−.51[b]), the more mothers enjoyed girls (.50[a]) but not boys (−.52[b]), and the more reported joint activities with girls (.62[b]) but not boys (−.23).

However for seven other characteristics (Active, Irregular, Attention span, Unmalleable, Intense, Moody, and Assertive) the reverse was the case. The number of significant correlations indicated a more tensionful mother–child relationship in girls high on the characteristic in question than in boys (42 versus 17 at 42 months; 34 versus 18 at 50 months).

As a third type of example explicable in terms of differential maternal responsiveness, some types of behaviour in school showed different home correlates in boys and girls. Thus, at 50 months Active hostility to peers in school was also associated with maternal Control (.81[c]) and Hostility (.45[+]) in girls, but not in boys (.15 and −.27, respectively).

4. Scoring problems. There is a real possibility that any method for categorising interactions, by observers or by the mother, may overlook subtle differences in quality or meaning. For example, although a boy and a girl might receive equal scores on the characteristic Shy, the girl might be expressing the characteristic in a more appealing way than the boy: Thus there may be differences in the expression of a particular variable as well as in the mother's responsiveness.

Again, boys who were often hostile to their mothers tended to Interact infrequently with peers in school at 42 months (−.34[+]), while the opposite was true for girls (.41[+]). One possibility is that home hostility includes an element of "uncooperativeness" in boys but of "assertiveness" in girls.

Of course, we do not suggest that these are the only causes of such differences in patterns of correlations between the sexes. For example, a given temperamental characteristic could have different correlates amongst the other temperamental characteristics or amongst other dimensions of personality in boys and girls, and this could result in a different pattern of correlations. Innumerable such possibilities await exploration.

Multiple Determinants Versus Simple Correlations

This is perhaps the most important issue of all. The preceding discussion has been concerned with the relations between simple temperamental characteristics or items of behaviour at home and simple aspects of behaviour in preschool. In practice, we must expect that each school item would be related to numerous aspects of the child's personality. And if what goes on between mother and child is related to the child's behaviour in preschool, we should expect numerous aspects of the mother–child relationship to be related to each school item in numerous ways. For example, both friendly and hostile behaviour to peers in school was associated with lack of some aspects of warm involvement with the mother at home, but friendly behaviour was associated also with an absence of strong maternal control and hostility, whereas hostile behaviour to peers was associated also with maternal hostility. In an earlier study, Baumrind (1967, 1971) found that more self-reliant, explorative, and contented children were those whose parents were both nurturant and gently controlling, and some comparable findings emerged from the present study.

Such effects are likely to be complex, for there are certain to be interactions between the several "independent" variables. This must lead eventually to a multivariate approach to explore the variety of interaction (e.g., Plomin, 1982) as well as a longitudinal design to attempt to tease apart cause and effect.

CONCLUSION

Relationships between individuals involve properties not relevant to the behaviour of individuals in isolation, and social groups have properties not relevant to dyadic relationships. Relationships affect, and are affected by, the characteristics of the participants. Dyadic relationships affect, and are affected by, the social situation in which they are embedded. Thus not only does the study of relationships occupy an important middle ground within the social sciences, but its strength depends in part on the maintenance of links with studies of the behaviour of individuals and of groups. The present situation is favourable for this endeavour, for developmental psychologists, students of relationships, and personality theorists have come to have common ground in the view that whilst there are consistent threads in the behaviour of individuals, individuals may behave differently according to the situation.

Whilst an understanding of the dialectics between personality, relationships, and the social situation faces many difficulties, one course must surely involve attempts to tease apart the ways in which person and situation variables interact to affect behaviour. To this end, we have summarized some data from a study of preschoolers attempting to make some progress in that direction. We have sketched evidence that individuals show different behaviour according to whom they are with; behavioural measures reliable in one context may yet show poor cross-situational consistency and vice versa; and correlations between measures in different interactional contexts may change with age and be affected by the sex (and presumably other characteristics) of the child. Some of these issues may result from changes or differences in parental expectations of how children should behave. Furthermore, it is often necessary to take a more global view of relationships: For example, each aspect of behaviour at school may be better predicted by a combination of home variables than by any one alone, and the combination of relevant home variables may be different in each case. For instance, the combination of home variables related to frequent friendly responses to peers in school is not also related to infrequent hostile ones. The conclusion that behaviour is complicated is, of course, trite, but the type of data discussed here indicates an area in which complexity might become comprehensible if students of development, personality, and relationships would unite in an attack on process.

5

Dyads, Cliques, and
Conspiracies: Friendship
Behaviours and Perceptions
Within Long-Established
Social Groups

Barry McCarthy
Lancashire Polytechnic, England

INTRODUCTION

Over the past decade, research and theory in personal relationships have developed considerably both in breadth and in sophistication. The field of adult friendships, however, has received a relatively meagre share of this increased interest, as two recent reviews of the area indicate (Dickens & Perlman, 1981; Reisman, 1981).

There may be a number of reasons for this comparative neglect. In the first place, most young and middle-aged adults are engaged in one or a number of intimate heterosexual relationships, and it may be argued that such commitments, especially marriage and family, take precedence over mere friendships in the apportioning of scarce temporal and psychological resources. Second, friendships are seen as subordinate to the demands of occupational achievement. Toffler's (1970) provocative portrait of the late twentieth-century person with his or her modular, utilitarian, disposable relationships has not yet been borne out. In fact, it appears to be widely assumed that whichever side may win out in the conflict of choice between love and work, plain old friendship just isn't in the contest. From the standpoints just outlined, adult friendship's modest status in personal relationships research is entirely appropriate.

To some extent, the available evidence supports the notion of decline in relative importance of friendships in adulthood, with some suggestion of a recovery of status in old age, when familial ties may have weakened, when one's career has ended, and when death, illness, or disinterest has terminated or curtailed heterosexual involvements (for a review, see Huston & Levinger, 1978). Fischer and Phillips (1982), in a study of over 1000 adults in California, reported lowest frequencies of contacts with friends among married respondents with children. Stueve and Gerson (1977), however, found in a study of adult males in Michigan that having children tended to increase friendly links with neighbours. The issue is complicated still further by a general tendency for intimacy and frequency of contact *not* to be highly correlated in adult samples (Dickens & Perlman, 1981). In Stueve and Gerson's study (1977), for example, Michigan males rated relationships with neighbours with whom they associated regularly as less intimate than childhood friendships where contact in general was less frequent.

The number of intensive investigations of adult friendships remains small, however, and there are a number of intuitive and theoretical bases for the belief that friendships may be, or may be becoming, rather more important in the lives of adults than is often assumed. First, a small but probably increasing proportion of young adults, at least in the industrialised world, are declining for a variety of reasons to follow traditional routes into heterosexual/familial commitments. Second, divorced persons appear to be less precipitate in their return to the marital arena than heretofore, and single life-styles, including single parenthood, seem to be increasingly attractive options to many people. In coping with this challenging but also unnerving array of alternatives, friendship may become an increasingly important psychological resource. Third, even where marriage and family retain their preeminence in the list of relationship priorities, the vast majority of marital units operate within a network of kin, neighbours, work mates, and other friends; in order to understand the functioning of even the most blissful of conjugal dyads, researchers need to understand the network that constitutes its ecosystem (La Gaipa, 1981). Finally, alas, not all long-term heterosexual dyadic relationships are so very blissful. Whilst the accumulating literature on marital satisfaction/dissatisfaction does not now present as bleak a picture as once it did (Levinger, 1983), it is clear that participants in many marriages and cohabiting dyads are either positively wretched or at best unsatisfied, often for long periods of time. In such a context, individuals may rely on friendships outside the dyad to a considerable extent (e.g., Duck, 1982, on the role of the confidante at early stages of relationship dissolution).

What are the main characteristics that distinguish friendships in adulthood from other personal relationships? Clearly, most if not all distinctions will be quantitative rather than qualitative in nature. Recent reviews by Dickens and Perlman (1981) and by Reisman (1981) examine the area in detail; however, some broad patterns have been evident for a considerable time, and as these informed the design of the present investigation, I will summarise them here.

First come gender differences. Whilst sheer number of friends does not seem to vary reliably with gender, several studies have reported greater interpersonal intimacy and higher levels of self-disclosure among women than in male friendships (Booth, 1972; Crawford, 1977; Fischer & Phillips, 1982). Lewis (1978) suggested that the socalisation of boys in Western society makes intimate adult friendships relatively unlikely by virtue of males' high levels of competitiveness and homophobia (but see Peplau, 1983). A second possible factor in adult friendships concerns social class differences in friendship activities, with a more restricted range of behaviours and behaviour settings reported for working-class than for middle-class friendships (Allan, 1977), and with kin featuring more prominently in the friendship networks of working-class respondents than in those of the middle class (Hendrix, 1979). A few recent investigations also report age and social class homogeneity in adult friendships (Lowenthal, Thurnher, & Chiriboga, 1975; Verbrugge, 1977) and differences in the activities and apparent importance of friendships for married and unmarried persons (Booth & Hess, 1974).

McCall (1970) and Reisman (1981), among others, distinguish between casual, superficial friendly relationships (termed "associative" friendships by Reisman) and close or "reciprocal" friendships characterised by commitment, personal loyalty, and intimacy of interpersonal knowledge. In carrying out the preparatory work for my study, it became apparent that a third broad category of friendship might be required, neither deeply committed and exclusive, nor merely casual and role based. In the event, many of the relationships examined in the present investigation appear to fall into the third category, captured well by the connotations of the English term "mate": loyal but not exclusive, supportive but not intense, and above all, clique based rather than dyadic in activity patterns. Although the friendship gang or clique has long been seen as central to adolescent social relationships (Dunphy, 1963; Kon, 1981; Sullivan, 1953), it does not seem to have received much attention in the realm of adults' friendships; it is possible that the design of the present study, in the context of participants' membership of long-standing recreational groups, made clique membership a particularly salient feature.

My investigation examined behavioural and cognitive aspects of, and to a lesser extent changes over time in, friendships between adults. The objective was to accumulate descriptive data rather than to test hypotheses derived from theory; my persistent impression is that the ongoing relationships under study here were worlds away from the domain of existing relationship theories. This may be due to the fact that most theories of relationships are essentially theories of relationship initiation and development, and the majority of friendships in the present study were of long standing. In any event, several writers have recently identified the lack of a descriptive data base as a major obstacle to advance in social psychology generally (Elms, 1975) and especially in the area of personal relationships, our present concern (Hinde, 1979).

METHOD

I carried out my investigation in a coastal community in North West England between the early summer of 1979 and autumn of 1981. The area is primarily residential with little industry, and most adults are employed in servicing the seaside vacation trade or else commute to nearby industrial centres. Residing within the area, I utilised my own friendship network to gain access to three long-established social/recreational groups (a fourth group was also approached but declined to cooperate in the study): a fishing club, active on both sea and inland waters; the local branch of a national wildlife conservation organisation, interested mainly in bird study but with sidelines in other conservation areas; and a local amateur theatrical society. There were about 420 active members in these three groups. All three groups held evening gatherings on a regular basis, and in each case I initiated the study while attending one of these meetings and explaining the aims of the study to assembled members. With the cooperation of each group's elected officers, copies of all questionnaires and measures to be employed were distributed for examination, and enquiries were solicited from potential participants.

The expected duration and requirements of participation were outlined, and total confidentiality was promised. I explained that although volunteers were sought as individuals, pair relationships would be the main focus of interest, and interviews would be conducted on a dyadic basis.

Each volunteer received a package of materials, again outlining the main goals of the investigation and including a form to be completed by the participant and returned to me as quickly as possible. The form asked the participant to give his or her full name, age, gender, marital status, number in household including children, occupation, full address, and telephone number. On the same form, the participant was asked to name his or her friends within the group, "friend" being explicitly defined as:

1. Someone in the group who you like and choose to associate with in preference to others.
2. Someone who you believe would also name you as "friend."
3. Someone with whom you have been friends for at least 6 months.

In the case of each friendship nomination, participants were asked to estimate how long the relationship had been in existence. No restrictions of age or gender were placed on choices; kin and spouse choices were explicitly permitted, provided the group membership criterion was met. Although a few spouse choices were made, these dyads were not utilised in the main study.

The signing-up questionnaire was completed and returned by a total of 153 persons out of an initial distribution of 176, a remarkably encouraging response, presaging a high degree of interest and hospitality from the participants that persisted throughout, in spite of the periodic demands of the investigation. Officials of one group requested that data from the Group-Specific Attitudes Questionnaire be made available to them anonymously, so that group procedures might be improved; this was done, with participants' consent.

The 153 volunteers ranged in age from 18 to 53 years, although unfortunately only a handful were over 45, even though all three groups contained a substantial proportion of middle-aged members; the median age was 27.5 years.

Mutual choice pairs were identified within the volunteer pool from the initial friendship nominations. Excluding marital dyads and the very few kin choices left a total of 52 friendship dyads for further study, each participant being included in one dyad only.

Each of the 52 pairs was interviewed over a period of 6 weeks, either at one member's home or mine. In a session about $1\frac{1}{2}$ hours long each participant, working independently, rated the relationship for closeness on a seven-point scale and completed the following four questionnaires: 40-item Survey of General Attitudes, 7-item Group-Specific Attitudes Questionnaire, 9-item Self-Disclosure measure, and Schedule of Dyadic Activities for each of the 10 days immediately preceding the interview.

In a tape-recorded interaction following each session, the participants and I together discussed the questionnaires and other aspects of dyadic and group functioning in an unstructured and informal atmosphere.

After a period of 9 to 11 months had elapsed, in the late spring of 1980, the three groups were revisited; assembled members were reminded of the study and all original volunteers were asked for their renewed support. Of the original 153 participants, 140 came forward again for Phase 2; in addition, 27 new group members volunteered for the study. All participants again completed the Friendship Nomination Questionnaire, and 46 of the original 52 participant dyads, as well as 10 new mutual-choice pairings, were interviewed during the following weeks using the same instruments and measures as in Phase 1.

Finally, in the late summer and autumn of 1981 the procedure was carried out for the third time. On this occasion 123 of the original 153 volunteers again signed up, along with 22 of the 27 who joined at Phase 2 and 18 entirely new participants. These 163 respondents yielded 38 dyads from the original cohort of 52, with all 10 of the Phase 2 dyads participating again, plus 8 dyads newly recruited at the present phase. Interview sessions with these 56 pairs were carried out as they had been at earlier phases of the study.

Preliminary analyses of the dyadic activities data obtained at Phase 1, in conjunction with the taped discussion material, strongly suggested that the activity patterns of many friendship pairs typically occurred within a coterie of fellow group members, some of whom were also identified as "friends" by one or both members of the dyad. As this emerging impression strengthened, it seemed desirable to obtain more direct data on the nature and functioning of these cliques. Accordingly, at the commencement of Phase 2, assembled group members were informed that the study was being broadened to include groups of friends/acquaintances larger than the dyad. An item was added to the Friendship Nomination questionnaire at Phases 2 and 3, asking each respondent to name all other group members with whom they frequently interacted, whether or not these individuals met the criteria for "friend" specified earlier, and to indicate further which group members they frequently associated with in units of three, four, five, or upward. From these data, a total of 16 subgroups of from three to seven persons were identified with a very high degree of agreement between respondents; of the total of 86 persons named, 72 were already included in the pool of volunteers. Accordingly, one person from each of these 16 cliques was approached and asked to keep a record of all clique activities at which he/she was present, with at least two other clique members, during the next 4 weeks.

The observer, selected on the basis of a high level of sustained interest in the project, was instructed to show the Clique Activities Record Form to his or her comrades and asked not to proceed if any objected to the records being kept; this was done, and all cliques apparently cooperated willingly. A total of 96 Record Forms were returned from Phase 2 along with 80 from 18 cliques (the original 16, plus two newly established) from at Phase 3.

MEASURES

Before reviewing the main findings of the study, it seems appropriate now to outline very briefly the contents of the measures employed.

Survey of General Attitudes

This was a 40-item Likert-type instrument, dealing with issues chosen from a survey of the popular media. Items were selected to represent issues of a relatively enduring nature (e.g., nuclear disarmament, censorship of pornography, abortion, and the women's movement). The final questionnaire contained items covering a wide range of religious and ethical standpoints, political affiliations, and attitudes toward aspects of life-style such as work, relaxation, and entertainment preferences. Participants responded to each item at a seven-point scale, agree/disagree.

Group-Specific Attitudes Questionnaire

This was a 7-item instrument, also employing seven-point Likert-type scales, measuring attitudes toward aspects of the particular recreational group to which the respondent belonged. These aspects included satisfaction or otherwise with group size, general activities, and the conduct of the group's elected officers; ratings of the group's importance in the respondent's life and perceptions of the group's relative status compared with other groups engaged in similar activities.

Self-Disclosure

This measure contained nine questions relating to disclosure within the dyad: frequency, range, and degree of intimacy; rated importance of this aspect of the friendship; the extent to which attitudes toward other group members and group activities were disclosed.

Dyadic Activities Record

This was a day-by-day record of dyadic events covering the 10 days immediately preceding the interview: for each day, the nature, number, location, duration of activities; other persons present and whether group members or not; and number and nature of all telephone contacts. The format for this is similar to that developed by Wheeler and Nezlek (1977).

Clique Activities Record

This contained the day and date of each interaction: location and duration; names of those present, clique members and outsiders; brief description of activities engaged in and topics discussed; and any other items believed relevant by the observer.

RESULTS

First, I describe the broad pattern of interpersonal choices across the total of 70 dyads studied and relate these to residential propinquity, age, gender, and marital status.

Participants resided in a widely dispersed pattern across a number of townships, in a coastal strip some 12 miles long and 5 miles deep; residential propinquity did not, overall, have much bearing on friendship choice or activities. Comparison of dyads living more than 6 miles apart with those living within 1 mile of each other revealed no difference in rated closeness of the relationship and only trivial differences in patterns of social contact, with slightly greater use of the telephone by more distant friends. Sixteen pairs experienced change of residence by one member during the study period; although moving had no effect on perceived closeness of the relationship, moving nearer to the friend related to increased face-to-face contact. Moving farther away, however, did not lead to any reduction in contact rates. It seems to be the case in a district such as this, with good communications and relatively small distances, and with almost all participants comparatively young and mobile, that residential propinquity is unlikely to feature as strongly among the determinants of friendship as in some other settings (e.g., Nahemow & Lawton, 1975). In addition, membership of an active recreational group, as in the case of the present participants, is likely to further weaken the effects of distance by providing attractive, centralised facilities at which friends can meet.

Age homogeneity was a strong feature of dyadic choices in all three groups. Dividing the age range of dyadic participants into three equal segments 18 to 27, 28 to 37, and 38 to 47 years, and locating each dyad in a 3×3 matrix according to each participant's age category, demonstrated a highly significant homogeneity effect ($\chi^2 = 20.27$, df 4, $p < .001$). Median age difference across all dyads was 3.8 years. Gender homogeneity was less marked than the age effect but was still quite a strong factor in dyadic selection ($\chi^2 = 9.24$, df 1, $p < .005$). Interpretation of these data is rendered problematical by the fact that one of the three groups was overwhelmingly male in membership (there were 7 females out of an active membership of about 90). When the 18 dyads from this group are excluded from analysis, gender homogeneity appears somewhat attenuated ($\chi^2 = 5.56$, df 1, $p < .02$).

When participants were categorised as single, married, or divorced, only a nonsignificant tendency toward pairing of like with like was found with regard to marital status. A very clear finding, however, was for married participants to have friends of the same gender as themselves ($\chi^2 = 7.86$, df 1, $p < .01$). In discussion with dyads, there was general consensus among married respondents, both male and female, that close opposite sex friendship would be a source of strain within the marital unit.

Whilst it was envisaged that social class might emerge as an important factor in dyadic choice and activities, isolation of this variable did not prove successful in the present study. Discussion with group members indicated a high level of intragroup agreement that the fishing group was predominantly working class in membership, the theatrical group mainly middle class, and the nature conservation group more or less evenly balanced for social class. However, such a pattern did not emerge from the occupations cited by those who volunteered for the study. It proved impossible to establish satisfactory criteria for identifying social class in the present context, especially in the case of female respondents. Participants themselves were uneasy about being categorised in terms of social class, and the exercise was not proceeded with.

Attitudes

Contrary to a long-established trend in studies of personal relationships, general attitude similarity did not distinguish friendship dyads from nonfriend comparison pairs within the same group matched for gender and approximately for age. Similarity on each attitude item was considered to exist if (1) both participants responded at the same side of the midpoint on the seven-point scale and not more than one scale interval apart or (2) if each participant checked the scale at the midpoint. Comparison of overall similarity scores using Fisher's t for independent samples was carried out at each of the three phases of measurement, and no significant tendency toward greater similarity in friends was found on any occasion ($t < 1.00$). When the attitude measure was broken down into three conceptually distinct components (political/economic, moral/ethical, life-style) it was only in the life-style category that any significant differences emerged, with friends more similar than comparison dyads at all three phases of measurement (Fisher's t for independent samples, $p < .05$, one-tailed tests). In general, most participants responded readily and often extremely to attitude items; strong and consistent feelings and beliefs were evident on a wide range of important issues. Clearly, however, these convictions did not exercise a major influence on friendship choices or on dyadic persistence. When the 10 dyads that formed between Phase 1 and 2 of the study were compared with the 46 dyads already in existence at Phase 1, only one significant difference in degree of similarity was found, once again or the life-style preferences subscale of the questionnaire (Fisher's t for independent samples: $t = 1.88$, df 54, $p < .05$, one-tailed test) with newly formed dyads less similar than established ones. By Phase 3 this difference has disappeared: After the passage of a year the "new" dyads are manifesting as much agreement on life-style attitudes as the long-term pairs. The dyads have not, however, become significantly more similar in General attitudes than they had been a year before.

When one turns to the seven-item, Group-Specific Attitudes Questionnaire, however, some marked effects are evident. At all three phases of measurement, friendship dyads are significantly more similar than comparison dyads (Fisher's t for independent samples, $p < .01$, one-tailed tests). Recently formed dyads at Phase 2 became significantly more similar a year later (Fisher's t for correlated samples, df 9, $p < .02$, one-tailed test). This general pattern of attitude similarity data (across both General and Group-Specific questionnaires) is, to some extent, consistent with results of earlier investigations: Both Newcomb (1961) and Levinger and Breedlove (1966) found a similarity of attitudes toward relationship-relevant issues more predictive of friendship choice and marital satisfaction, respectively, than general attitude/value agreement. In my study, attitudes toward pragmatic issues such as ways of spending one's leisure and views of the group's activities and the adequacy or otherwise of its leadership may have had instrumental significance for the friendship that broad sociopolitical attitudes did not possess. The data on self-disclosure tend to support this conjecture.

Self-Disclosure

Overall, self-disclosure does not appear to be a major feature of the relationships investigated in my study. Data from directly comparable samples and measures in other investigations are not available but it would seem that in the present sample disclosure and verbal intimacy are low by any standard, with 44 out of the total 70 dyads in agreement that they "very rarely," "rarely," or "not often" discussed topics that either participant would not talk about with a casual acquaintance. Mean number of such conversations during the previous 10 days was a modest 1.84. On only 24 occasions over all three phases of the study did a participant claim to have raised some matter with their friend that he/she had never before mentioned to anyone else. When the 10 dyads newly formed at Phase 2 were followed up at Phase 3, no significant increase was evident in frequency, intimacy, or importance of self-disclosure.

Gender differences in self-disclosure are rather clear cut in line with the findings of much previous research: Female participants rated self-disclosure as more important in their relationships than males (Fisher's t for independent samples, $t = 2.71$, df 138, $p < .005$, one-tailed test). Of the 26 dyads who discussed personal matters "fairly often" to "very often," only two were male, although 28 of the total 70 dyads were male. The overall relationship between gender and self-disclosure is high: $\chi^2 = 10.32$, df 2, $p < .01$. In the 18 male/female dyads, however, females did not rate self-disclosure as significantly more important than their male friends, and these dyads resembled all-male pairings rather than female dyads in their rate and intimacy of reported disclosures—an interesting variant on the operation of a reciprocity norm in disclosure (the so-called "dyadic effect"; see Morton & Douglas, 1981).

Although discussion of private or intimate matters, as defined by participants, was a comparatively rare phenomenon, almost all dyads (65 out of 70) discussed other group members and group activities "often" to "very often." Not a single participant claimed "never" to engage in such gossip. In informal discussions with participants, it was clear from a very early stage of data collection that exchanging opinions of their fellow group members and of the group in general was a very salient aspect of the dyadic relationship. This is, of course, consistent with the pattern of attitude similarity already described. Interestingly, when participants' normally low rates of disclosure of personal matters were explicitly contrasted with their relative readiness to reveal often negative and disparaging views of other group members, many participants declared that this material was not really private and that their views were known to others apart from the dyadic partner. As we will see in examining clique activities, this claim appears to be substantially accurate: Gossip was rarely confined to the privacy of the dyad.

It may be noteworthy that it is in this area of self-disclosure that the only difference of any interest between the three groups emerged: Dyads in the theatre group manifested significantly more intimate dyadic self disclosure than in either of the other two groups ($F = 4.26$; df 2,69; $p < .05$), and participants from this group also rated self-disclosure as more important in their relationships than did other participants ($F = 3.18$; df 2,139; $p < .05$).

Activities

Patterns of dyadic activity were broadly similar across the three groups. A total of 18% of all interactions took place at the home of one or other partner, with, in general, an equal number of visits in either direction, but there were some exceptions. For example, married individuals tended to visit unmarried friends' homes more frequently and for longer periods than visits in the reverse direction; these differences did not reach significance. In addition, special circumstances such as acquisition of a video recorder by one dyad member led to (usually temporary) deviations from parity of home visiting. In newly established dyads, home visits accounted for a smaller percentage of interactions (12% compared with 21% in long-established dyads).

Of the total of 82% of interactions occurring outside dyad members' homes, 21% took place in other persons' homes (usually other group members), 18% were on group/club premises (theatre, meeting room, etc.) and the remaining 43% "elsewhere": mainly in outdoor activities or travel to group activities away from the area (the latter popular in all three groups), visits to the cinema or live entertainment (a mere 5% overall), or engagement in convivial interaction in a tavern or (rarely) a restaurant. The central role of alcohol consumption in the dyadic activities of friends across all three groups is striking; many visits to homes of third parties involved such activity and 71% of all interactions that commenced either at one dyad member's home or at the club/group meeting hall led to a visit to the local pub.

As reported earlier, preliminary analysis of the first batch of Activities data from Phase 1 suggested that, across groups, relatively few friendship activities (overall, 27%) were entirely and exclusively dyadic; hence the identification and study of clique activities at Phases 2 and 3 of the investigation.

Cliques

The cliques study, being something of an ad hoc arrangement, was much more crude than the dyadic friendships aspect of the investigation. Data consisted of unchecked written reports of 18 single observers completing a standardized form (see the foregoing discussion) at some time following each clique interaction in which the observer had participated. Observers were recruited primarily on the basis of their greater-than-average interest in the whole project and also on the basis of their central rather than peripheral status in the clique in question. In this way, I hoped to achieve consent for the observations from other clique members and to ensure that the observers would be included in a high proportion of the clique's activities during the measurement period.

A total of 176 clique interaction sheets were received from Phases 2 and 3. Among a great number of rather trivial facts (e.g., the great majority of clique activities took place in the evenings or at weekends) a number of interesting data emerged. Most clique activities lasted longer than dyadic interactions (mean 3.7 hours versus 1.8 hours), which may simply reflect the fact that a clique, unlike a dyad, does not normally have its interaction terminated by the departure of one individual.

As in the dyad, group-related discussion constituted a main activity, and a high proportion (47%) of clique activities occurred in the context of alcohol consumption. Many of the clique discussions were hostile and derogatory towards external targets; this crops up spontaneously in the "Comments" appended to 67 of the 176 clique interaction records. The target, where this is clearly mentioned, is most commonly another individual within the group (very often a group leader) or another clique within the group whose influence is described as excessive or as otherwise harmful to the interests of the clique doing the derogating.

Like dyads, cliques were predominantly either male or female, with 13 of the 18 entities studied almost or entirely homogenous with regard to gender. Age homogeneity was not quite so marked as in dyads, with 7 of the 18 units representing among their regular members an age span of over 10 years. It would seem from the absence of reports that personal disclosure is rare or absent in clique interactions, but it must be accepted that the relative crudity of the study procedure for cliques may have failed to catch much of the fine grain of clique interactions.

What is incontrovertible is that the great majority of dyads identified and studied during my study (57 out of 70) operated to a greater or lesser extent in the context of one of the larger cliques that existed within the group. Not one dyad could be found in which each of the two participants belonged to a different clique, although in the case of 8 dyads one member was active within a clique whilst the other was not.

CONCLUSIONS

Several aspects of these results appear to stand out as offering some food for thought about the nature of friendships in adulthood.

First, these friendships are markedly limited in scope and, in spite of that, are highly successful relationships. Of the 52 dyads recruited at the original measurement phase, 18 had been in existence for over 10 years, and another 20 had been functioning as friends for at least 5. The participants interacted frequently, often in what seemed to be well-worn verbal and behavioural routines, and yet the amount of mutual affection and positive regard within most of these dyads was readily and consistently evident to the observer. Nevertheless, these participants in established friendships appeared to refrain from discussing intimate topics and also avoided dealing with those broad sociopolitical and moral/ethical issues, agreement on which has been seen by many researchers as the vital bonding agent of friendship.

It is, of course, possible that in these friendships of long standing all necessary self-disclosure and attitude exchange had taken place long before the commencement of the study. That is now unknowable, but what is demonstrable, from data not reported here, is that friends frequently perceived each other's attitudinal positions accurately even in the apparent absence of relevant self-disclosure. There is some evidence that much of this interpersonal knowledge may be acquired indirectly via other clique members who provide a perspective on the partner not directly available to the friend him/herself.

It is possible, although merely speculative at this point, to suggest that the secret of these relationships' relative success lies in the participants' avoidance of irremediable and unresolvable issues of the world at large and of their own lives, in favour of concentrating on those smaller but also important issues and situations where agreement can be secured and relevant action taken.

Finally, the friendships I investigated clearly support and are in turn sustained by those larger subgroups that I have labelled cliques, after Dunphy's use of the term in his pioneering study of adolescent relationships (1963). Although I did not conduct a formal network analysis of these aggregations, my data clearly support those who have recently claimed that in order to understand adequately dyadic relationships we need to come to terms with the system of interpersonal linkages of which the dyad is usually a part. This may be particularly true, as my study, when friendships are based largely on activities, routines, and rituals; and when, within a large group or organisation, subgroups representing different interests and policy preferences evolve and contend for influence.

6

Gender Effects in Social Participation: Intimacy, Loneliness, and the Conduct of Social Interaction

Harry T. Reis
University of Rochester

INTRODUCTION

Gender exerts a strong influence over the conduct of social interaction. Females and males, it is said, differ in the styles of social behavior that they characteristically exhibit. Although most research focuses on the sex-of-subject variable, the impact of gender derives from other gender-related factors as well. One such factor is the gender constellation of the dyad or group. Consistent differences exist between interactions involving partners of the same sex and those involving opposite sex partners, so that analyses of sex differences in interaction style must specify the gender of the other group participants as well as that of the subject. A third aspect of gender relevant to social behavior is sex role. Individuals varying in the traits of masculinity and femininity generally show coherent, predictable differences in numerous features of their relations with others. When these three factors are considered simultaneously, it is apparent that gender, broadly conceived, is a fundamental factor in the complex organization and determination of everyday social interaction.

The popularity of these factors as research topics is in part due to their pervasive influence in daily life. By far the greatest attention has been paid to sex of subject differences. Although it is difficult to generalize from the vast literature, especially because of the diverse variations in conceptual background and nomenclature that characterize the research, many studies can nonetheless be reduced to a single finding: Men's socializing tends to be activity centered, whereas women's socializing tends to focus on the attitudes and feelings of the participants. I draw this conclusion from a great many studies conducted around the world in a great many empirical contexts: observations of behavior in work and social groups, questionnaires about friendship, interviews about participation in social networks, laboratory studies of interaction phenomena such as self-disclosure, and so forth. Although debates exist about the specific phenomena to which this generalized trend applies, as well as to its proper theoretical explanation and developmental origin, the point itself seems well rooted in the literature, not to mention common folklore.

Inquiry into the effects of a group's gender composition has been less extensive. Some specialized areas of research, such as conformity, leadership, reward allocation, simulation games, and helping behavior, have examined this factor. Very generally, these studies seem to indicate that, relative to same-sex groups, mixed-sex groups are more likely to elicit behavior consistent with sex-role norms, probably because impression management concerns are more salient in mixed-sex company, and sex-role conformity is a more viable strategy among strangers. Reasearch that deals directly with mixed-sex friendship is far less common, excluding, of course, the more narrow domain of dating, courtship, and marriage. Booth (1972), for example, found that fewer than one-fifth of his subject's friends were of the opposite sex. Similarly, Wheeler and Nezlek (1977) found that same-sex interactions predominated over interaction with the opposite sex by a ratio of slightly more than two to one. From all of this evidence, as well as from casual observation of everyday life, it is apparent that gender composition affects the pattern of social interaction substantially.

The third gender variable is sex role, or femininity and masculinity. There have been two major developments in our understanding of sex roles during the past 25 years. The first is that femininity and masculinity are not mutually exclusive opposites; instead, individuals may possess varying degrees of each trait, irrespective of their status on the other. The second advance occurred as psychologists began to conceptualize sex role not in terms of biological sex (or sexual orientation) but as stable predispositions to approach a variety of situations in a given manner. Spence and Helmreich (1978) described these traits as *communion,* a tendency to be concerned about closeness with others, and *agency,* a tendency to be self-interested and assertive. Empirical studies have supported both of these propositions, as well as the basic datum that, across a population, agency is more likely to be characteristic of males, whereas communion is more common among females. Despite the utility of this trait perspective, and despite its apparent relevance to the sex of subject variable discussed earlier, there are few existing studies examining the impact of femininity and masculinity on everyday social participation. Some research has dealt with social process variables, such as conformity, but there is little research concerning the descriptive elements of everyday social life.

AN EMPIRICAL STUDY OF SOCIAL PARTICIPATION

Although these conclusions are heavily (and necessarily) oversimplified, I hope it is clear that these three facets of gender are highly germane to the study of everyday socializing. In the research described in this chapter, my collaborators and I were concerned with two general questions related to these factors. First, we wanted to know how sex of subject, sex composition of the dyad, and sex role affect social participation. Second, we sought to clarify the relative role played by each of these factors in the experience of loneliness, an affectively unpleasant state in which social participation falls short of expectations.

As might be expected from my earlier comments, neither of these questions is entirely new. What is novel in our approach is an interest in the entirety of ordinary, day-to-day socializing. If social interaction is a core aspect of satisfactory *leben und arbeiten,* it is because of what transpires in everyday encounters with friends, family, and co-workers. This interest has dictated a naturalistic method of collecting data. It is exceedingly difficult to capture the numerous details that characterize social life over an extended period of time. Consequently, most researchers have adopted one or more of the following strategies: asking subjects to recall many details about their social activity during some preceding time period, such as the past 6 months; having subjects evaluate a few important summary dimensions, either over an extended period or in repeated instances; or observing subjects' interaction in a laboratory setting, so that finely detailed descriptions of behavior may be obtained.

All of these strategies have been, and will continue to be, valuable research tools. However, their usefulness is limited, if the goal is to provide objective accounts of ongoing social participation, as it naturally occurs in everyday life. For one, it is well known that memory and aggregation are subject to many sources of error, some of which can be traced to cognitive processing (Bernard, Killworth, & Sailor, 1982) and others of which are due to motivational biases in social and self-perception (Schneider, Hastorf, & Ellsworth, 1979). Observing single encounters may also be problematic in that such events may be less than representative of typical social behavior for a variety of reasons (Ickes, 1983). To avoid these problems, we decided to use a journal-like procedure, in which subjects describe each interaction that occurs during a specified time interval along a series of specific dimensions. To minimize memorial distortion, the records are completed daily. Because they ask for specific parameters about each event, aggregation problems are few. Finally, because the diaries are kept for virtually every interaction that takes place during a two-week period, the only systematic threat to representativeness stems from the selection of the time period itself. Elsewhere, we have discussed the limitations and advantages of this technique, known as the Rochester Interaction Record (RIR) (Nezlek, Wheeler, & Reis, 1983).

A sample of the RIR is shown in Figure 6.1. In the study following, we asked subjects to complete one of these forms for each interaction of 10 minutes or longer that occurred during a 2-week period. The forms were filled out as soon as possible after the interaction, but no less often than once a day. This regularity was encouraged by having subjects turn in their completed forms every second or third day. At the end of the record-keeping period, the subject was interviewed in

Date _____ Time _____ am __ Length: _____ hrs. _____ mins.
                                        pm __

Initials ____ ____ ____   If more than 3 others:
Sex   ____ ____ ____   # of females _____   # of males _____

Intimacy:	superficial	1	2	3	4	5	6	7	meaningful
I disclosed:	very little	1	2	3	4	5	6	7	a great deal
Other disclosed:	very little	1	2	3	4	5	6	7	a great deal
Quality:	unpleasant	1	2	3	4	5	6	7	pleasant
Satisfaction:	less than expected	1	2	3	4	5	6	7	more than expected
Initiation:	I initiated	1	2	3	4	5	6	7	other initiated
Influence:	I influenced more	1	2	3	4	5	6	7	other influenced more

Nature: Work   Task   Pastime   Conversation   Date

FIG. 6.1.   The Rochester Interaction Record.

depth to identify possible sources of inaccuracy. The records were then compiled by computer across all interactions and grouped into the various categories to be described shortly. In the study reported here, there were 43 males and 53 females, all of whom were seniors residing in campus dormitories. They kept the RIR for approximately two weeks in November 1980. After their interaction records were finished, the seniors completed a number of questionnaires, including the revised UCLA Loneliness scale (Russell, Peplau, & Cutrona, 1980) and the Personal Attributes Questionnaire (Spence & Helmreich, 1978), a measure of femininity and masculinity.

Sex and Sex Composition Differences in Social Participation

Five of the scales on the RIR pertain to interaction quality: intimacy, self-disclosure, other-disclosure, pleasantness, and satisfaction. These were summed into a composite labeled meaningfulness, separately for interactions involving up to three same-sex partners or opposite-sex partners. (Interactions including partners of both sexes, or more than three partners, were placed into mixed-sex and group categories and are not discussed here. However, their results are entirely consistent with those to be presented.) Table 6.1 shows the mean values for these composites. Same-sex interactions among males were significantly less meaningful than same-sex interactions among females, and all opposite-sex interactions. In other words, interactions that included at least one woman were perceived to be more meaningful than those that did not. Analysis of the individual scales revealed that this was true for all five components, although the pattern

TABLE 6.1
Sex Differences
in Interaction Meaningfulness

	Type of Relationship	
Sex of Subjects	Same Sex	Opposite Sex
Males	18.82	22.07
Females	21.38	22.07

Note. Meaningful refers to the composite of intimacy, self-disclosure, other disclosure, pleasantness, and satisfaction. The male same-sex relationship cell is significantly different ($p < .01$) from the remaining cells.

was more pronounced for intimacy and both disclosure items than for pleasantness and satisfaction.

This result supports our notion that both sex and sex composition affect the basic nature of a social encounter, at least insofar as its meaningfulness is concerned. Having at least one female in a dyad or group seems to enhance the intimacy of the interaction that occurs. Interestingly, having more than one female does not seem to produce an additive effect: females' same-sex interaction is no more meaningful than opposite-sex interaction.

One might propose that these results are due to the inclusion of interactions with all kinds of partners in these categories. Males, the argument goes, are selective in that they socialize intimately only with very close friends. Females, on the other hand, are more generally intimate. Accordingly, we sorted interactions into four categories, based on the subject's relationship with his or her partner: same-sex best friend, opposite-sex best friend (romatic or platonic), other same-sex friends, and other opposite-sex friends. The mean values for this breakdown are shown in Table 6.2. The same pattern of results is attained: Males' same-sex interactions, even with their best friend, is less meaningful than that of females and that involving opposite-sex partners. Once again, although this difference emerged for all five dimensions of the meaningfulness composite, it is stronger for the intimacy and disclosure items. Not surprisingly, interactions with other friends are perceived to be less meaningful than those with close friends. However, the same pattern of sex difference obtains, regardless of the level of friendship. Thus, the tendency of males to engage in relatively less meaningful same-sex interactions is pervasive, extending across close and superficial relationships. I comment on potential interpretations of this tendency later in the chapter.

Interaction quantity also appears to be influenced by the gender of the participants. Overall, females participated in significantly more interactions per day

TABLE 6.2
Sex Differences in Interaction Meaningfulness,
by Type of Relationship

	Best Friends			Other Friends	
		Opposite Sex			
Sex of Subjects	Same Sex	Romantic	Platonic	Same Sex	Opposite Sex
Males	19.77	22.67	21.67	18.50	20.60
Females	22.70	24.06	23.40	21.28	20.41

than males (male mean = 6.33, female mean = 7.45), which also tended to take more time per day (male mean = 325.98 minutes, female mean = 350.64 minutes). More interesting are the effects of sex composition. For both sexes, same-sex interaction is more prevalent than opposite-sex interaction. Fifty-three percent of males' interactions were classified as same-sex, compared to 25% that involved opposite sex partners. (Mixed-sex and group comprise the remaining interactions, which revealed no sex effects). This is a ratio of 2 to 1. Among females, 48% of their interactions were classified as same sex, whereas 31% included the opposite sex. This ratio is a bit more than 1.5 to 1. In other words, on average, every opposite-sex interaction was complemented by almost two same-sex interactions. These ratios are similar to other studies, such as Wheeler and Nezlek (1977).

Regarding the frequency of best-friend interactions, the picture is somewhat different. There is no sex difference in the number of same-sex, best-friend interactions, which occur an average of 1.26 times per day. Interactions with opposite-sex best friends tend to be more frequent, if and only if the partner is a romantic interest (on average 1.53 times per day). Note that this is true only for the selected subsample of subjects who had a romantic partner (58% of the females, 37% of the males). Interactions with a platonic opposite-sex best friend happen less often (0.60 times per day), as do interactions with other friends. Thus, one may infer that the relative prevalence of same-sex to opposite-sex interaction is even greater when primary romantic relationships are excluded.

Social Participation and Loneliness

Loneliness is an affectively unpleasant state in which actual social participation falls short of desired levels (see Peplau & Perlman, 1982, for a synthesis of various definitions that have been used). This discrepancy is typically thought of as occurring along either of two dimensions: The sheer amount of social contact is less than wanted or desired levels of emotional closeness with others are not achieved. In that the RIR is capable of distinguishing interaction quality from quantity, we sought to examine the relative role of these factors in the social experience of lonely and nonlonely persons. We also expected that gender would affect the social correlates of loneliness, for two reasons. First, if emotional closeness is an important aspect of avoiding loneliness, males would seem to be at a disadvantage, because the greater proportion of their interactions stems from the category that revealed the least meaningfulness, namely same-sex interactions. Second, despite the greater frequency of same-sex contact, much of college students' social goal-seeking behavior—not to mention most of the social anxiety they experience—concerns relations with the opposite sex. As a result the relative distribution of social contacts across same and opposite-sex partners could be expected to influence satisfaction with one's social life.

Table 6.3 presents the correlations between loneliness and two interaction summary variables: meaningfulness and time per day spent socializing. Meaningfulness was strongly correlated with loneliness for both sexes, in both same-sex and opposite-sex interaction. That is, subjects who rated their interactions as more meaningful were less lonely. Note that this pattern was true for all five scales composing the meaningfulness composite, but once again, the effect was stronger for intimacy, self-disclosure, and other disclosure than it was for pleasantness and satisfaction. Note also that the correlations are consistently larger among males, although the differences do not reach conventional levels of significance.

The results for interaction quantity depend on gender pairing. Among males, loneliness correlated significantly only with opposite-sex interaction: Males who spent more time with females were less lonely. Among females, the direction of this effect was identical, but the target was switched: Loneliness correlated significantly with same-sex interaction in that the more time a woman spent with other females, the less lonely she was likely to be. In other words, for both sexes, more interaction time with female partners was associated with less loneliness. Time spent socializing with males did not relate significantly to loneliness.

Other interaction-quantity variables produced compatible results. For example, the more frequently subjects interacted with women, independent of the

TABLE 6.3
Interaction Variables
Correlated with Loneliness

	Males	Females
Meaningfulness		
Same sex	$-.58^b$	$-.31^a$
Opposite sex	$-.52^b$	$-.46^b$
Time per day		
Same sex	$-.06$	$-.38^a$
Opposite sex	$-.46^b$	$.15$

$^a p < .05.$
$^b p < .01.$

duration of these interactions, the less lonely they were. The relative proportion of same-sex to opposite-sex interactions yielded a perhaps clearer result: The greater the percentage of one's interactions that included females, the lower the loneliness score. Correspondingly, the greater the percentage of interactions with males, the greater the loneliness. Thus, insofar as interaction quantity is concerned, socializing with females was a helpful manner of avoiding loneliness.

These results merge conceptually if one recalls that males' same-sex socializing was generally less intimate than those interactions that involved females. Less-lonely people had more meaningful interactions in general. However, since interaction with females tends to be more meaningful, any time spent with them raises the overall level of meaningfulness experienced. Interaction with males, whose mean level of meaningfulness is lower, is less likely to be beneficial, and, consequently, time spent with them is unrelated (or even negatively related) to loneliness. More simply, only those interactions possessing relatively high doses of meaningfulness are likely to help one avoid feeling lonely. Thus, the effect of interaction time as a buffer against loneliness depends on its meaningfulness.

Parenthetically, one can see the gender-conditional value of opposite-sex contact another way. Subjects were classified as to whether they reported an opposite-sex romantic partner or not. For females, having such a partner does not affect loneliness significantly: The mean loneliness scores are 20.16 and 24.27 for those with and without partners, respectively. On the other hand, among males there is a potent difference. The mean loneliness score among males with a romantic female partner is 16.88, whereas it is 31.15 for males not having a romantic partner. Thus, even though the mean levels of intimacy in opposite-sex interaction did not reveal a sex difference, it appears that a romantic partner provides a considerable emotional benefit for males that does not have a counterpart for females.

The gender asymmetry of these results forms the core of some interesting speculation. Just why should any interaction with a woman be helpful, whereas with a man the impact varies as a function of affective content? Three factors seem to be relevant. First, it may be that the affective value of interpersonal intimacy has an asymptote, beyond which additional increments are of slight consequence. If, as these data imply, females tend to surpass this asymptote, most interactions with them are likely to be rewarding. Interaction among males may not generally reach this asymptote, and consequently the experienced level of intimacy matters. Second, intimate interaction with a male partner is simply rarer, as we have seen, and hence may be more valuable when it occurs. This value derives from the loneliness-reducing effects of meaningfulness, but it is enhanced by the scarcity of this commodity. Among females, intimacy is more common and therefore less remarkable. A third, closely related possibility concerns adaptation levels. Given that males usually provide less emotional closeness in social interaction, people may come to expect less. High levels of intimacy from a male may therefore seem noteworthy and be experienced as more rewarding.

The preceding arguments all suggest that some males, and most females, engage in interactions that are characteristically and consistently meaningful. Across categories referring to different partners, meaningfulness ratings tended to correlate substantially, in the range of .4 to .7. More interestingly, it is notable that those men who interacted meaningfully were the same men who spent more time socializing with women. That is, among men, opposite-sex time per day correlated strongly with same-sex meaningfulness ($r = .49$) and opposite-sex meaningfulness ($r = .45$). Since interaction with the opposite-sex is a prize held in great esteem by this age group, it is apparent that high meaningfulness males possess a valuable attribute. For females, meaningfulness holds no such value. Opposite-sex time per day correlated nonsignificantly with opposite-sex meanfulness ($r = -.10$) and even negatively with same-sex meaningfulness ($r = -.33$). So the question is this: Are high-meaningfulness males taught to socialize meaningfully by female partners, or are they sought by women because they already possess this trait? These alternatives bring us to consider the third gender variable: sex-role orientation.

The Role of Femininity and Masculinity

In recent theories, femininity is typically conceptualized as a trait implying a communal or expressive orientation to situations. Persons possessing high levels of femininity are thought to be more concerned about others' feelings, more emotionally open, and more interested in establishing close relationships with others. Although there are numerous studies examining behavioral manifestations of this trait, there are none dealing with its consequences for everyday social participation. Based on the arguments and results presented to this point, it is reasonable to predict that persons high in femininity will report more meaningful interactions and will have spent more time socializing with female partners.

The first part of this prediction was confirmed only for male subjects. For them, femininity correlated significantly with the average level of meaningfulness in same-sex ($r = .34$) and opposite-sex interaction ($r = .35$). Among female subjects, the trend was in the same direction but not significant ($rs = .17$ and .11, respectively). Perhaps the decreased magnitude of these correlations for females is due to the asymptotic effect discussed earlier. Regarding interaction time, the results were as expected. Femininity was associated with more interaction time spent with women by both male ($r = .25$) and female ($r = .30$) subjects. Thus, persons high in femininity were more likely to socialize in an intimate manner (at least the males) and were more likely to socialize with more intimate partners. In passing, we should note that masculinity did not relate significantly to these variables.

The final empirical question to be addressed presently is the only one that deals explicitly with process. Earlier, I reported that the tendency to interact meaningfully was strongly associated with the absence of loneliness. If femininity, as a trait, refers to a general tendency to engage in more meaningful types of social interaction, then it may account for the link between meaningfulness and the absence of loneliness. That this is a viable possibility is suggested by the correlation between loneliness and femininity. For both sexes, more feminine persons reported less loneliness ($r = -.39$ for males, $r = -.36$ for females). In contrast, masculinity did not correlate significantly with loneliness. To explore this mechanism, femininity was entered into a series of hierarchical regression equations along with the two most salient predictor variables from our earlier analyses: (1) meaningfulness in interaction with males and (2) time spent socializing with females. The criterion variable was loneliness. The order of entry of the three predictors was varied systematically so that unique and shared variance components could be identified.

Among male subjects, 41% of the variance in loneliness could be ascribed to the optimal combination of the three predictors; of this, the component shared between femininity and either or both of the two interaction variables was 12%. The figures obtained from the female data were similar. Together, the three predictors accounted for 38% of the variance in loneliness scores; only 7% stemmed from variance shared by femininity and the interaction variables. Thus, it seems that although there is some overlap, femininity and social interaction contribute independently to the reduction in loneliness.

This relationship can be seen in Figure 6.2, which is a path diagram taken from the final regression step. Nonsignificant coefficients have been reduced to

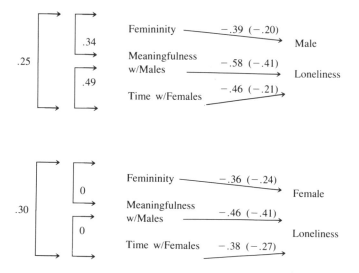

FIG. 6.2.   Path diagrams for predicting loneliness. (The numbers in parentheses are standardized regression coefficients. The remaining numbers are simple correlations, and correlations not significant at $p < .10$ have been replaced by zeros.)

zero for simplicity. Three features of this diagram are noteworthy. First, as just discussed, the three predictors all have substantial independent effects on loneliness. Femininity is clearly related to loneliness, but it is not responsible for the contribution of either interaction variable. Second, the path diagrams for females and males are remarkably similar, particularly the regression (standardized) coefficients. This indicates the relatively similar process by which the sexes become, or avoid, being lonely. Note, however, that this similarity requires a reversal of the gender-pairing factor: The best predictor for both sexes is meaningfulness with male partners. For males, this is encompassed in same-sex interaction, whereas for females, it is an opposite-sex interaction.

The third noteworthy aspect of Figure 6.2 concerns the interrelatedness of the predictors as indicated by the arrows between them. In males, the three predictors were substantially correlated among themselves, particularly same-sex meaningfulness and time spent with females. This tells us that there is a group of males who have close relationships with other males, who also spend more time with females, and who aren't lonely. Among females, in contrast, these variables tend to be relatively more independent. Some women avoid loneliness by spending time with women, whereas others do so by interacting meaningfully with men. (Chi-square analyses bear out these interpretations but are too laborious to report here.) We suspect that the relative ratio of same-sex to opposite-sex interaction, which was nearly 2 to 1, may be responsible for this asymmetry. That is, in their same-sex socializing, females have access to sufficient doses of meaningfulness and need not rely on their interaction with males to preclude feeling lonely. The relatively lesser time males generally spend with females necessitates also interacting meaningfully with other males, if they are to avoid loneliness. It would be interesting to examine the interrelation of these variables in a sample whose distribution of same- and opposite-sex interactions is less skewed.

SOME THEORETICALLY INTEGRATIVE REMARKS

Sex Differences in Social Participation

The clearest effect to emerge from this research concerns the meaningfulness of same-sex socializing. Compared to females, males' same-sex interactions were less intimate, involved less disclosure by either partner, and were less pleasant and satisfying. This difference was characteristic of both superficial and close friendships and so should be taken as evidence of a general style of interaction, rather than of a tendency to be more selective about the target of intimacy. Because a number of other studies have demonstrated similar results with very different methods, such as observation of single encounters and broad questionnaires (e.g., Caldwell & Peplau, 1982), the phenomenon appears to be quite robust and general.

How should this finding be interpreted? The classic explanation is, of course, that males are less willing to be intimate with each other by virtue of nature, nurture, or some combination of the two. Before accepting this conception, there is a viable alternative that should be considered. That possibility concerns the definition of an intimate interaction. It might be argued that males perceive intimacy differently than females. For one thing, there may be differences in how the same behavior is labeled. Males and females may use the scale of intimacy differently, such that the endpoint anchors have different psychological meaning for them, or perhaps the intervals between points vary. Even more problematic is the possibility that the sexes use different criteria to arrive at a rating of intimacy. For example, males may limit intimacy to the context of a heterosexual relationship whereas females may focus on emotional content along a broader set of dimensions. If either of these alternatives were the case (and there are of course other, more complex, possibilities as well), same-sex friendships would differ not so much in content but rather in how they were labeled. Although space does not permit fuller discussion of this issue, we have recently completed a set of experiments ruling out this alternative (Reis, Senchak, & Solomon, 1985). Thus, we may have greater confidence that the content of males' interactions with each other actually differs from those of females.

Returning to the present study, we also found that when males interacted with females, the level of meaningfulness rose to a point where it no longer diverged from females' same-sex interaction. This seems to suggest that men are capable of interacting meaningfully but prefer to do so in the company of women. It may be that women, by virtue of a more communal orientation, elicit intimacy from male partners. Alternatively, women may themselves provide whatever intimate content there is so that the interaction is seen as more meaningful largely because of the woman's contribution. This distinction requires future research in that it deals with the question of whether lesser intimacy among males is due to inability or unwillingness. Regardless of which possibility is eventually supported, it is important to note that a given male's social life is likely to contain appreciably less meaningful interaction than that of a female, if, as in our sample, men socialize with other men twice as much as they do with women. Thus, there is a paucity of intimate interaction and a predominance of task-oriented socializing. This pattern, which probably becomes more deeply ingrained over time, may be responsible for what I referred to earlier as the classic explanation of sex differences in social orientation: that males tend to take an instrumental/agentic approach, whereas females rely on a more expressive/communal style. The distinction is most apparent in our subjects' same-sex relationships.

Although sex-role orientation is thought to provide the psychological substrates of gender differences in some conceptualizations, this was only partly the case in our data. In males, femininity was associated with the tendency to interact meaningfully with either sex and to spend relatively more time in the company of females. These males seemed to possess the appropriate intimacy skills that would allow them to interact more frequently with partners who desire meaningfulness. Femininity appears to be one aspect of these skills, although our mediation analyses indicate that it only accounts for part of the variance. In females, femininity was related to time spent with females, but the association between these variables and meaningfulness was nonsignificant. Perhaps this is due to the asymptote effect proposed earlier: Beyond some level, extra dosages of intimacy may not matter. The relative prevalence of meaningful same-sex interactions for females may make femininity less of a discriminating factor. The firmest conclusion that can be drawn regarding femininity is that it accounts for a substantial chunk of the variance in sex differences in interaction style but that other factors are operative as well.

Loneliness and Femininity

One of the purposes of this research was to identify the specific aspects of social participation that, when deficient, lead to loneliness. Although both quantitative and qualitative correlates were obtained, our analysis indicates that the absence of meaningful interaction seems to be the primary factor. In other words, a person is likely to be lonely when he or she does not engage in intimate contacts with others. The frequency and distribution of socializing are relevant only insofar as they delimit the possibility that interaction will become intimate.

Elsewhere (Reis, 1984), I have argued that the expanding literature on health and social relations suffers from a lack of specificity. That is, existing measures of social support and social participation often fail to distinguish various aspects of social behavior from each other. Because these factors may be substantially correlated, they may be responsible for a misspecified conclusion when they are not separated empirically. For example, individuals who have a close intimate relationship with a confidant are also likely to have similarly intimate relations with others. From a theoretical standpoint, it is important to know which of these alternatives is a better predictor of well-being. In the present study, specificity was afforded in two ways: by the numerous different variables the RIR specifies and by sorting these variables on the basis of the other participant. Given the criterion of avoiding loneliness, a general pattern of interacting meaningfully with others was most important. The best individual predictors were meaningfulness in interaction with males and time spent socializing with females.

That interacting with females has benefits for mental and physical health is a finding that has emerged in other areas as well. For example, Jessie Bernard (1973) has proposed that marriage offers more advantages for husbands than wives. She believes this is due in large part to the communal functions that wives fulfill: emotional closeness and support, feelings of connectedness, and intimate interaction. Although husbands may supply these qualities for their wives as well, the contrast with preexisting same-sex friendships is smaller and thus the net benefit is less. Furthermore, only some husbands are likely to do so, similar to our finding that time spent interacting with males was not helpful; only those who interacted with males high in meaningfulness were less lonely. Another instance of this effect may be seen in Stroebe and Stroebe's (1983) review of widowhood research (see also Stroebe and Stroebe, Chapter 13). They confirm the common wisdom that mental and physical health problems are more prevalent among the recently widowed of both sexes. However, they also note that where there are sex differences, it is the widowers who are worse off. Our results imply that this is because males are more reliant on females for meaningful social contact than vice versa and because the relative prevalence of same-sex interaction provides widows with a higher base rate of meaningfulness than widowers.

Of course, not all marriages are good. In the health and social relations literature, it is currently debated whether marital status itself should be used as a predictor variable, given the diversity of relations that can be encompassed under its umbrella. A recent paper by Gove, Hughes, and Style (1983) moves toward resolving this issue and is consistent with what we have found among unmarried college students. Gove et al. demonstrate that although marital status is the best predictor of mental health among numerous typical predictor variables, the mental health enhancing benefits of marriage depend on it being a satisfying, intimate relationship.

Naturally, not every female furnishes or elicits greater meaningfulness in social interaction. They are simply more likely to do so than males. Recall that loneliness could also be abated by interaction with males who socialized meaningfully. Some of our results suggested that intimacy was displayed consistently and could be considered as a dispositional characteristic. Although intimacy skills may have many facets, one major component is femininity. High levels of femininity, together with high levels of masculinity, are commonly referred to as androgyny, a combination of traits hypothesized to promote optimal functioning across a variety of situations. Recent investigations have attempted to assess the relative contribution of masculinity and femininity to health and well-being. By and large, this evidence suggests that masculinity predicts mental and physical health—and psychological well-being—with femininity playing either a much smaller role or none at all (e.g., Jones, Chernovetz, & Hansson, 1978; Lubinski, Tellegen, & Butcher, 1981). However, we concur with Ford (1982) that these studies have tended to use criterion measures subtly biased in the direction of agency and self-assertion. Femininity ought to predict better functioning only with criteria concerned with emotional closeness and intimacy. It therefore bears emphasizing that this is exactly what we found: Femininity was associated with a meaningful interaction pattern and the absence of loneliness, whereas masculinity, in turn, was unrelated to these criteria. Thus, these data add empirical clout to the hypothesis that femininity is an important element of human well-being. Other studies have also supported the contention that femininity will appear beneficial when criteria relevant to social bonds are used. For example, Antill (1983) demonstrated that each spouse's satisfaction with their marriage was a function of the other spouse's femininity. We suspect this is because the spouse's communal orientation engenders more intimate interaction.

Before concluding, there is an interesting addendum that arises from Sears' (1977) analysis of sources of life satisfaction among the men in Terman's gifted children sample. These subjects were surveyed regularly about various aspects of affect and activity from adolescence into their early sixties. One set of questions concerned the relative importance of numerous sources of life satisfaction: occupation, family life, etc. As the men in Terman's sample retrospectively viewed their lives, family life satisfaction was seen as most important, more so than work. The greater priority of family satisfaction is even more remarkable considering that these children were selected for the study by virtue of high intellectual potential, and in fact did achieve substantial successes in their work lives. Moreover, femininity positively predicted family life satisfaction scores. From this and other longitudinal studies, we know that most men become more feminine over the life span, a trend that is probably related to ongoing, satisfying relationships. What better signpost is there for the value of meaningful social participation and femininity?

CONCLUSION

This research was primarily concerned with two questions: How do sex of subject, sex composition of the group, and sex role influence social participation? How do these factors affect the experience of loneliness? We focused on the specifics of everyday socializing, largely because it is the raw material from which broader social feelings are cast. Same-sex interaction was found to be more common than opposite-sex interaction, and these former interactions were found to be less intimate among males than females, regardless of whether the partners were best friends or not. Femininity was higher among subjects who reported more meaningful interactions and who spent more time with women. A similar pattern was shown by subjects who felt less lonely. These data should do nothing to lessen the conviction that gender, in its various manifestations, is a fundamental factor that differentiates numerous aspects of social life. But equally importantly, they demonstrate that the outcome is much the same for women and men. Both sexes are better off when they socialize in a more meaningful manner.

ACKNOWLEDGMENTS

I gratefully acknowledge the role of my collaborators in the research reported herein: Ladd Wheeler, Michael Kernis, Nancy Spiegel, and John Nezlek. Ellen Nakhnikian made valuable comments on the manuscript. Full explication of the methods and data from this research may be found in the *Journal of Personality and Social Psychology*, 1983, *45*, 943–953. Partial support for the research described herein was provided by the National Science Foundation.

DEVELOPMENT AND GROWTH OF RELATIONSHIPS

7

When the Honeymoon's Over: Changes in the Marriage Relationship Over the First Year

Ted L. Huston
University of Texas at Austin

Susan M. McHale
Ann C. Crouter
The Pennsylvania State University

INTRODUCTION

This chapter is based on a longitudinal study of the marital relationships of newlyweds. Data gathered from couples shortly after their weddings and then again about a year later were used to examine issues related to the hypothesis that husbands and wives become less romantic and less satisfied with the quality of their relationship over the first 15 months of marriage. The rationale for anticipating such changes was set forth more than 30 years ago by the noted sociologist, Willard Waller (1938), who wrote: "It has been said that marriage is the remedy for the disease of love, a remedy which operates by destroying the love." According to Waller (1938): "often such a process does take place, and it begins when the honeymoon's over" [p. 309]. He was writing about romantic love, a kind of love that he and others (e.g., Berscheid & Walster, 1974) believe is sustained by fantasy and illusion.

Waller's view is that marriage relationships change, in part, because new elements of each partner's personality enter into the couples' experience: "[First] gently, [then] with startling brutality, the real person and the reality of marriage pound at the portals of thought and at length enter" [p. 312]. Idealized images are replaced by more realistic ones and the partners act more like their ordinary selves. Sometimes couples discover areas of disagreement they had not known about before or find that their leisure interests are not as similar as they once had thought. Change in marriage is not wholly a function of new discoveries or emerging areas of disagreement, however. As Waller (1938) notes: "in the normal course of events, [marriage] soon loses its original intensity. Habits of adjustment to the other person become perfected and require less participation of consciousness. The wide area of the taken for granted is a basis of mutual faith and understanding'' [p. 311].

Our data about marriage relationships bear on most of the ideas set forth by Waller (1938), and thus we are able to test his ideas against the realities of contemporary marital life. Major changes in married life have taken place since Waller (1938) wrote his treatise on the family. Women have entered the labor force in ever increasing numbers (Waite, 1981); sex-role attitudes have moved away from strongly traditional views (which stress the differences in the rights and responsibilities of men and women) (Thornton & Freedman, 1979); a greater emphasis is being placed in popular writings on the importance of companionship in marriage; and the divorce rate has risen considerably (Cherlin, 1981). In addition, it is increasingly common for couples to live together before marriage (Clayton & Voss, 1977; Spanier, 1983), a phenomenon that may affect how the transition to married life is perceived and experienced.

In this chapter, we are concerned with changes that take place during the first year of marriage. As we explore this issue, we examine whether these changes differ under two conditions that are increasingly frequent in today's society. The first condition has to do with premarital cohabitation. Since many couples live together before marriage, it is necessary to consider the possible effect of cohabitation on the ways husbands and wives adapt to one another as newlyweds. The second has to do with whether or not couples become parents during their first year, usually because the bride was pregnant at marriage.

We first focus our attention on two levels of analysis: (1) the feelings that marriage partners develop about each other and about their relationship and (2) the behavioral organization of the marital relationship. Thus, we begin by exploring whether Waller's depiction of the demise of romance holds up in our sample of newlyweds. Then we examine what couples actually do together in terms of behavior in the context of married life, searching for behavioral changes that parallel (or deviate from) changes in the feelings and attitudes that spouses report. Waller's analysis (1938) suggests that, as the euphoria associated with the early months of marriage wears off, the spouses' attitudes about each other and their relationship will become more firmly anchored in their treatment of each other. Thus, in the concluding section, we examine how husbands' and wives' feelings (or attitudes) toward each other are related to features of the behavioral organization of their marriage.

THE STUDY

The data to be discussed in this chapter were gathered in the context of the "PAIR Project," a longitudinal study of the early years of marriage. The acronym "PAIR" stands for "Processes of Adaptation in Intimate Relationships," and it reflects our focus on the ways in which partners involved in marriage adapt to one another over time. The PAIR Project was designed to follow a sample of newlyweds through the first $2\frac{1}{2}$ years of marriage, tracing the development of such patterns of marital interaction as the division of labor, leisure, conflict, and the expression of positive and negative affect. An important feature of the original purpose of the project was to gather detailed information on courtship so that the early years of marriage could be studied in the context of the history of each couple's relationship.

Data for the study were collected in three phases, with the first phase taking place in the spring and summer of 1981. Couples were initially identified through marriage license records, available in the courthouse of each of four predominantly rural counties in central Pennsylvania. All of the 168 couples who participated in the first phase were interviewed within 3 months of their weddings and all were in their first marriage. The participants in the study were representative of those married during the sampling period in terms of their age at marriage (husbands and wives averaged 23.5 years of age and 21 years, respectively) and in regard to the type of work their parents did (predominantly skilled and semi-skilled labor).

The second and third phases of data collection were timed to take place at yearly intervals. The data presented in this chapter pertain to changes in marriage relationships over the first year: Thus, we limit ourselves to material gathered during the first two phases of the project. Two primary data collection procedures were used each year. First, each couple was interviewed, usually in the couple's home, by a male and female interviewer from the PAIR Project. After a brief period in which questions were addressed to the couple as a unit, the male interviewer accompanied the husband and the female interviewer accompanied the wife into different rooms for separate, but virtually identical, interviews covering an extensive range of information.

At the end of the face-to-face interviews, arrangements were made with each couple to telephone them on nine different evenings during the 2- to 3-week period after the interview. These phone interviews were designed to gather data about the activities that husbands and wives carry out at home and during their leisure time. These activity data were used to develop behavioral descriptions of marriage relationships. The phone call procedure gave us a detailed picture of what couples in our sample were actually doing, both together and apart. Moreover, acquiring these data on nine different days gave us a satisfactory sampling of most types of behavioral events (Huston & Robins, 1982); we can be fairly confident that the overall picture for the 9 days is representative of the couple's life-style, at least during that particular period in their marriage.

Measures of Partners' Feelings About the Relationship

In developing our measures of couples' subjective evaluations of the marriage, we looked for instruments that focused specifically on respondents' feelings about their relationship rather than have them describe typical behavioral patterns. As Norton (1983) points out in a recent critique of measures of marital quality, instruments that combine items that require the individual to *evaluate* the marriage with items that ask the respondent to *describe* the relationship (in terms of such dimensions as communication, showing affection, and companionship) run the risk of making invalid assumptions about how multiple dimensions of married life go together. Measures that combine description with evaluation run the risk of leading scholars to conclude that behavioral patterns that correlate with positive evaluations are part of those evaluations, rather than antecedents and consequences of them. In addition, Norton argues that it is a questionable practice to examine, for instance, the extent to which communication patterns or demonstrations of affection are related to marital quality if these very constructs are part of the marital quality instrument itself. We decided to utilize measures of partners' subjective evaluations—their feelings or attitudes about the relationship—because we had other methods with which to gather indicators of couples' behavior and interaction patterns.

At both phases of data collection, spouses were asked to evaluate their marriage in four ways during the face-to-face interview, using the previous 2 months as a frame of reference. First, spouses reported on the extent to which they had been satisfied or dissatisfied with the frequency with which particular positive or affectional and specific negative interpersonal events have been occurring in their relationship. Thus, for example, they read a statement such as "My partner expressing approval of me or complimenting me about something I did," and then indicated whether they would like the behavior to have been happening about as often as it had been, more often, or less often. If they would like to have seen the behavior occurring either more or less often, they further indicated whether they wanted it to happen "somewhat more (or less)," "much more (or less)," or "very much more (or less)." The items were scored by counting "about the same" as "0" and "very much more (or less)" as "3"; the other two responses were scored "1" and "2," respectively. The total extent of dissatisfaction with the quality of interaction was derived by summing the scores across the 17 items (10 of which were positive and 7 negative).

It is important to note that the 17 specific behaviors asked about in relation to spouses' satisfaction with marital interactions were the same interaction events (with one exception) they reported on during the nine telephone interviews. Thus, at least with regard to the socioemotional aspects of marital behavior, we know both how often specific affectively toned events actually occurred and how satisfied husbands and wifes were with that level of frequency.

Husbands and wives also rated their feelings of *love* for one another and their *ambivalence* about their relationship, using scales developed by Braiker and Kelley (1979). These scales have been found to be increasingly negatively correlated as couples evaluate their relationships at varying stages of involvement, ranging from casually dating to marriage and into the third year of marriage (Kelly, Huston, & Cate, 1985).

The fourth measure, the Marital Opinion Questionnaire, was designed to measure marital satisfaction. We anticipated Norton's (1983) criticisms of the standard scales, and chose to follow the logic used by researchers interested in identifying correlates of life satisfaction (see Campbell, Converse, & Rodgers, 1976). These researchers, in their search for life-style and life context correlates of well-being, recognized the importance of developing a measure of "well-being" that did not include in the measure reference to the life circumstances that might be associated with it. The index of *marital satisfaction* we used was adapted from the measure developed by Campbell, Converse, and Rodgers (1976) to measure life satisfaction. This instrument is a 10-item semantic differential scale on which respondents characterize their marital relationship in terms of a series of bipolar adjectives such as miserable-enjoyable, rewarding-disappointing, and full-empty. Seven points separate the two adjectives, and scores can range from 10 to 70. The marital satisfaction scores correlated strongly with the extent to which the marriage partners were satisfied with their relationship in general, as measured by a single question put to them after they had completed the marital satisfaction questionnaire ($r = .72$, $p < .01$, for Phase 2).

Data on Partners' Activities

As we described previously, information about activities that partners are actually performing—alone, together, and with various other individuals—was collected during nine telephone interviews at each phase. During each interview, husband and wife reported separately about specific activities and interactions that occurred in the preceding 24-hour period. Thus, we were able to obtain accurate information about a broad spectrum of behavior patterns of each spouse while avoiding many of the problems associated with alternative approaches such as direct observation or global reports of participants.

Identifying Activity Patterns.   The activities selected for investigation were derived through two separate processes. In the first, we requested a group of newlyweds, drawn from the same population as our sample, to keep detailed diaries of their daily activities for a 2- or 3-day period. At the same time, we reviewed previous research employing diary records (e.g., Berk & Berk, 1979; Russell, 1978; Walker & Woods, 1976; Wills, Weiss, & Patterson, 1974) to identify activities participants were asked to record. We used the material from these two sources to derive a list of activities. The list was subsequently modified and refined through pilot research. The activity spheres selected for study were (1) household tasks, including general chores and child care tasks (for those couples with children), (2) leisure/recreational activities, (3) husband–wife interaction, including both affectional and negative exchanges, (4) conflict, and (5) conversations. Details are given in Table 7.1.

TABLE 7.1
Information Gathered About Marriage from Phone Interviews

Region	Examples	Nature of Data Gathered About Activities
A. Household Tasks		
General tasks	Grocery shopping; make beds; make dinner; do the dishes; run errands; do laundry; mow lawn; rake leaves	Number of times the activity was carried out, if at all. For each occurrence, whether the activity was performed with or without the spouse
Child care tasks	Feed child; bathe child; change or dress child; put child to sleep	Number of times the activity was carried out, if at all. For each occurrence, whether the activity was performed with or without spouse
B. Leisure Activities	Watch TV during daytime; read a book, magazine, or newspaper; go to a bar, tavern, or nightclub; go to a movie; go to a park or on a picnic; play a table game; go to a sporting event; exercise or play a sport	Number of times the activity was engaged in, if at all. For each occurrence, information was also gathered regarding (1) who else, if anyone, was involved—these "others" were coded according to the nature of their relationship to the respondent and his or her spouse—and (2) the length of time involved
C. Interaction	Was there a time when your husband/wife: Did something nice for you that you didn't expect. Showed anger or impatience by yelling, snapping, or raising his/her voice at you	Number of times the event occurred, if at all
D. Conflict	Disagreements, arguments, or differences of opinion	Number of occurrences, if at all. For each occurrence, topic of conflict
E. Conversations	Includes all conversations in person or on the phone, that lasted 5 minutes or longer; excludes conversations that occurred at work/school that were related to tasks respondent was doing	For each conversation, information was gathered regarding (1) who else was involved (coded according to the nature of the "other(s)" relationship to the respondent and his or her spouse and (2) the length of the conversation

The nature of the data obtained regarding each activity sphere is summarized in the right side of the table. In reference to the first three spheres (i.e., household and child care tasks, leisure activities, and interaction), each spouse was asked to provide information about the occurrence of every activity contained on a previously compiled list of activities. The lists of household, child care, and leisure activities were extensive, incorporating the majority of activities in which spouses engage relevant to these domains. The list of interaction activities included a sampling of pleasant and unpleasant interpersonal events. Table 7.2 shows the household tasks and child care (Section A), leisure activities (Section B), and interaction events (Section C) we inquired about.

The final two sections of the phone interview focused on conflict and conversations. Spouses were asked to indicate the number of times they had disagreements, arguments, or differences of opinion and to describe the subject of each conflict. With regard to conversations, the spouses were asked to enumerate every occasion when they conversed with one or more individuals for a period of 5 minutes or longer, excluding those converations that took place at work and pertained to their work role. For each conversation, spouses were requested to indicate with whom the conversation was held as well as its duration.

One noteworthy feature of this method is that respondents report on each individual occurrence of each event. Aggregation is carried out by the researcher with the aid of the computer when the series of calls is completed—and not by the respondent, thus avoiding any demand for mental arithmetic and its associated risks. In addition, this method ought to increase accuracy of recall due to the relatively short period involved. Finally, the events sampled are clearly delineated, and the respondents are asked about the occurrence of each event. Thus, events are less likely to be misassigned or forgotten altogether. By gathering data on repeated occasions, it is possible to amass the kind of descriptive information necessary to characterize the husband–wife relationship in terms of the spouses' joint and independent activities. The approach also allows certain methodological checks to be carried out. The extent of day-to-day fluctuations in tasks reported can be examined; this information can be used to assess the adequacy of the length of time during which sampling is done. Reactive effects of the method can be explored by seeing whether there is any systematic change in the frequency of events reported over the time period sampled.

The approach we used was chosen over other forms of self-report, such as diary keeping and methods in which recording is done concurrently with the occurrence of events (e.g., using counters or beepers), for several reasons. We were concerned about the likelihood of obtaining the necessary cooperation that these approaches require of respondents. Many of our respondents, we felt, would be unwilling to carry through with such procedures. Concurrent recording is more intrusive than retrospective reporting and thus might lead to greater reactive effects. Also, in practice, there is rarely any control over whether recording actually is done concurrently, even when records are collected often

TABLE 7.2
List of Household Tasks, Leisure Activities, and Interpersonal Events
Used with Phone Interviews

A. Household Tasks

---

1. *Shopping/Errands*
   Go grocery shopping
   Run errands
   Buy household supplies
   Buy wife's clothes
   Buy husband's clothes
   Make an expensive purchase
2. *Indoor Maintenance*
   Make the bed(s)
   Straighten up the house, put things away
   Clean the house (mop, wax, dust, vacuum)
   Take out the garbage
   Do laundry
   Do ironing
   Decorate the house, arrange furnishings
   Do repairs around the house
3. *Finances*
   Pay bills
   Budget, plan, or review expenses

4. *Food Preparation/Clean-up*
   Make breakfast
   Make or pack lunch
   Make dinner
   Do the dishes
   Do baking or canning
5. *Outdoor Maintenance*
   Gardening (pulling weeds, planting vegeta-
      bles, etc.)
   Repair car or other vehicle
   Make home improvements (carpentry, roof-
      ing, etc.)
   Wash or wax car or other vehicle
   Mow lawn, rake leaves, shovel snow
6. *Child Care*
   Data were not used in the analyses reported
      in this chapter

B. Leisure Activities

---

1. *Home Activities*
   Watch TV during daytime
   Watch TV during evening
   Listen to records, tapes, or radio (not just
      background music)
   Read a book, newspaper, or magazine
   Work on a hobby (carpentry, collecting,
      embroidery, etc.)
   Play a musical instrument
2. *Going Out for Entertainment* (I)
   Go to a party
   Go dancing
   Go to a restaurant or other eating place
   Go to a movie
   Go to a concert
   Go to a play
   Go to a sporting event (football, or basket-
      ball game, race, etc.)[a]
3. *Socializing*
   Entertain friends or relatives in your own
      home
   Visit friends or relatives in their homes

4. *Sports and Games*
   Go for a walk
   Play a table game (cards, Monopoly, check-
      ers, puzzles, etc.)
   Play pool, pinball, or an electronic game
   Go hiking, camping, or backpacking
   Exercise or play a sport (such as jogging,
      softball, bowling, etc.)[a]
5. *Going Out for Entertainment* (II)
   Go to the park or on a picnic
   Go to a fair, outdoor show, exhibit
   Go shopping or browsing
   Go to a garage sale, auction, or flea market
   Go for a drive or motorcycle ride (just to
      drive around)
6. *Miscellaneous Activities*
   Go to a meeting of a hobby club or interest
      group
   Go to a meeting of a service club, commu-
      nity organizaton, or political group
   Go to the library
   Go to church, or other religious activity
   Go to a class or lesson

C. Interaction Events (Socioemotional Behavior)

1. *Positive/Pleasing Behaviors*

   Spouse expressed approval of you or complimented you about something you did

   Spouse did or said something to make you laugh

   Spouse said "I love you"

   You talked together about things that happened to each of you during the day while you were apart[b]

   You had sexual intercourse[b]

   You expressed physical affection with your spouse, such as kissing, hugging, or cuddling (outside of sexual intercourse)[b]

   You shared your emotions, feelings, or problems with each other[b]

   Spouse initiated sex with you

   Spouse did something nice for you that you didn't expect

2. *Negative/Displeasing Behaviors*

   Spouse seemed bored or uninterested while you were talking

   Spouse dominated a conversation with you, such as by interrupting you or not giving you a chance to talk

   Spouse showed anger or impatience by yelling, snapping, or raising his/her voice at you

   Spouse criticized you or complained about something you did or didn't do

   Spouse turned down or avoided your sexual advance

   Spouse failed to do something you asked him/her to do, or that you asked to get done (such as not running an errand, coming home late, or something like that)

   Spouse did something, knowing it annoyed you (some habit like leaving on a light, not picking up his/her clothes, or something like that)

[a]Respondents indicated the sport they observed or participated in and the responses were coded.
[b]These are joint, or mutual, behaviors rather than individual behaviors exhibited by the spouse.

from participants (e.g., Wheeler & Nezlek, 1977). For all of these reasons, we believed that short-term retrospective reporting posed fewer problems than concurrent recording.

We did deviate from our pattern of using the telephone records to map behavioral patterns in two cases. During face-to-face interviews, we asked respondents to complete Braiker and Kelley's (1979) scales for *conflict* and *maintenance*. The conflict scale is a five-item instrument that asks the respondent to generalize about the extent to which the couple has disagreements, arguments, expressions of anger, and the like. The maintenance scale, also comprised of five items, asks respondents to generalize about the extent to which the couple engages in behavior designed to enhance their relationship, as in talking through differences of opinion or making efforts to change behavior to make it more satisfying to the spouse. We included these two scales because they measured behavior that is fairly infrequent, behavior that might not be picked up reliably by our telephone procedure.

Summarizing Acitivity Patterns.   It should be clear from our description of the way in which behavioral activity data were collected that the raw data can be aggregated into a number of variables, depending on the purposes of the investigator. For the analyses reported in this chapter, we were interested in four general areas of behavior, as summarized in Table 7.3.

The first area of interest is *companionship*. Couples whose relationship is cohesive, or whose lives are intertwined, perform many activities together. They may share in carrying out work around the house, go to movies or on outings together, socialize with others as a couple, and spend time in conversation. We were interested in ascertaining how couples change over the first year of marriage in terms of the extent to which they engage in leisure activities with each other and take the time to talk together. To begin to explore these phenomena, we developed four measures of different aspects of companionship, as Table 7.3 describes.

Our second focus is *instrumental role performance*. One way in which a marriage evolves over the first year can be seen in the patterns of household labor developed by the couple. As Table 7.3 shows, we were particularly interested in the issue of specialization, both as measured by differences in the relative extent to which the husband and wife are involved and the degree to which household task activity in a marriage is sex typed. It is possible to identify, for instance, how frequently the husband and wife cross over and carry out household tasks traditionally considered the work of persons of the opposite sex (Atkinson & Huston, 1984). To what extent does the wife mow the lawn, do household repairs, or work on the car? How often does the husband make dinner, clean up the house, or do the laundry?

Socioemotional behavior is another important domain in the marital relationship that might evolve and change during the first year of marriage. As Waller (1938) explains, during the courtship and honeymoon period, spouses generally attempt to put their best foot forward. This means anticipating the partner's needs, refraining from criticizing or complaining, and behaving in an affectionate and approving manner toward the partner. If Waller is right, we can expect to see activities designed to enhance the relationship and other positive behaviors to decrease over the first year and to observe negative interactions and conflict to be on the rise. Again, four operationalizations of these constructs are summarized in Table 7.3 under the heading of socioemotional behavior.

Finally, we were interested in young couples' patterns of *involvement with others*. Does participation in leisure activities with friends or kin change over the first year of marriage? Ryder, Kafka, and Olson (1971) suggest that early in marriage, after the honeymoon, couples begin to reintegrate themselves with friends and kin. Do such patterns of involvement differ for husbands and wives (Bott, 1957)? These questions are answered below in our analyses of the PAIR Project data set.

TABLE 7.3
Measures of the Behavioral Properties of Marriage

I.	*Companionship*	
	A. Overall amount of companionship (D)	Average number of household and leisure activities done together per day
	B. Extent to which companionship takes place in recreational contexts (D)	Proportion of joint activity that is leisure in nature
	C. Amount sharing of leisure time (D)	Average number of minutes per day spent together in leisure activities
	D. Amount of time spent conversing with each other (D)	Average number of minutes per day spent in conversation
II.	*Marital Role Performance*	
	A. Extent of participation in household tasks (I)	Average number of household tasks completed per day by husband/wife
	B. Relative extent of husband's and wife's involvement in household tasks (D)	Proportion of the household tasks carried out by the wife
	C. Sex typing of the participation of husband and wife in household tasks (D)	Proportion of the household tasks done by the person traditionally assigned
III.	*Socioemotional Behavior*	
	A. Expression of affection (I)	Average number of times per day husband/wife says or does something that is positive or pleasing
	B. Expression of negative feelings or displeasure (I)	Average number of times per day husband/wife says or does something that is negative or displeasing
	C. Maintenance (I)	Extent to which husband/wife indicates he/she carries out activities that enhance or maintain relationship
	D. Conflict (I)	Extent to which husband/wife indicates that they argue, fight, or feel resentful toward each other
IV.	*Involvement with Others*	
	A. Amount of involvement with kin (I)	Number of times husband or wife is involved in leisure activities with kin
	B. Amount of involvement with friends (I)	Number of times husband or wife is involved in leisure activities with friends

D = Dyadic measure; I = Individual measure.

RESULTS

Relationship Change Over the First Year of Marriage

We base these analyses on the 100 couples for whom we have complete data for both the face-to-face interview and the nine telephone call interviews at both Phase 1 and Phase 2. In planning these analyses, we considered the fact that some of the couples either had cohabited before marriage and some had become parents during their first year of marriage. Specifically, 35 couples had lived together for at least one month ($\bar{X} = 10.3$ months) prior to marriage, and 37 had a child during the first year of married life. Cohabiting couples might be less romantic at the time of marriage, and their experiences in early marriage may not fit as clearly as the others the pattern described by Waller (1938). In addition, previous research indicates that, for many couples, the transition to parenthood may require readjustments in other role commitments and activities (Cowan, Cowan, Coie & Coie, 1978; Rossi, 1968). Consequently, we elected to use a data analysis strategy that would allow us to compare and contrast cohabitors and noncohabitors and parents versus nonparents across the two points of measurement.

As a first step, two multivariate analyses of variance (MANOVA) with repeated measures were performed. The first used as the dependent variables the dyadic measures shown in Table 3; the second employed the individual measures as dependent variables. The MANOVA for the dyadic variables had three independent variables, each with two levels: phase, cohabitation before marriage, and parental status (at Phase 2). Phase was treated as a repeated measure variable. The MANOVA for the individual measures included the same three classifying variables but, in addition, used spouse as a repeated measure.

Significant effects were found in both of the MANOVA tests for phase, parental status, and phase × parental status. The MANOVA involving the dyadic variables also showed a significant main effect for cohabitation, whereas the MANOVA for the individual level variables revealed significant effects for the spouse variable and the spouse × parent interaction. The other two-way interactions were not significant for either MANOVA; nor were any of the higher-order interactions significant. We will report all significant univariate statistics for main effects and interactions for the variables that were significant using the MANOVA tests. Our main objective is to trace changes that occurred in the marriage regardless of whether couples lived together before marriage or whether they became parents.

Since our MANOVA tests did not show an interaction between cohabitation and phase, we do not discuss cohabitation other than to note the differences here in the relationships of couples who cohabited compared to those who lived together for the first time after marriage. The cohabiting couples, compared to those who did not live together until marriage, were less traditional in terms of the relative involvement of the husband and wife in carrying out household tasks, $F (1, 96) = 8.83$, $p < .01$. With regard to the couples who became parents, all of the interactions between phase and parent group are such that the direction of the changes over time hold up for both groups. Some of the changes are greater, however, among the couples who became parents, and when such is the case we discuss the differences. In general, though, we focus on the phase effects that reflect changes that occur between shortly after marriage and the time just after the first anniversary.

Changes in Couples' Feelings During the First Year.   Our data confirm Waller's scenario about changes in how spouses feel about marriage when the honeymoon is over. All four of our indicators of husbands' and wives' subjective evaluations of marriage show a decrease in their sense of satisfaction over time. Beginning with the measure that is perhaps the most specific and concrete, we see that couples became increasingly dissatisfied with the quantity of their interactions with one another over the year, F $(1, 95) = 23.4$, $p < .01$. Further analysis of the questionnaire revealed that husbands and wives became dissatisfied with the extent to which their spouses initiated pleasurable activity, showed negativity, and the frequency with which the two of them shared physical intimacy.

Changes in respondents' reports of feelings of love and ambivalence reinforce the notion of a decrease in the extent to which individuals felt positive about their marriage during the first year. In terms of love, analysis of variance revealed a significant main effect for phase, F $(1, 95) = 21.4$, $p < .01$, showing that husbands and wives, regardless of parental status or whether they cohabited before marriage, felt less in love after a year of married life. Paralleling the decrease in love over the first year of marriage was an increase in ambivalence, F $(1, 95) = 12.8$, $p < .01$.

Our global measure of marital satisfaction confirmed the picture developed by the foregoing analyses. The couples in our sample decreased significantly in their reports of marital satisfaction between the time shortly after marriage and their first anniversary, F $(1, 95) = 21.1$, $p < .01$.

Wives reported more dissatisfaction with interaction than did their husbands, both early in marriage and a year later, F $(1, 95) = 8.0$, $p < .02$. The same pattern was found with regard to husbands' and wives' feelings of love. Husbands were more in love with their wives than vice versa, both during the "honeymoon" period and a year later, F $(1, 95) = 6.05$, $p < .02$.

The four measures we have used to chart changes in the feelings spouses have about their relationship and their partner require somewhat different kinds of evaluations. These include ratings about the satisfactoriness of husband–wife interaction, attitudes partners have about each other (love), their sense of ambivalence about maintaining their relationship, and their general satisfaction with married life. These constructs are moderately intercorrelated early in marriage and the intercorrelations increase from the honeymoon period to a year later. The changes in subjective evaluation over the first year of marriage reveal a consistent pattern. Husbands and wives were less satisfied with their patterns of interaction, less in love, more ambivalent, and less satisfied with the married life in general. These findings confirm Waller's ideas about changes in cognition that occur when the honeymoon is over. These results do not mean, however, that these couples were unhappy, disillusioned, and dissatisfied with their lot. After a year of marriage, they were less euphoric than they were shortly after marriage, but their responses still fall on the positive side of the continuum for each variable. Let us now shift away from reports of feelings and subjective evaluations of marriage to examine changes in actual behavior. Do couples' behavior patterns change in ways that are consistent with their decreased satisfaction with the relationship?

Changes in Behavior and Activities During the First Year.   The discussion of behavioral changes in marriage parallels Table 3. The four measures having to do with companionship shown in the table, when considered together, provide complementary information about how married life changes over time. Even though some social scientists have suggested that marital companionship is highest shortly after marriage and that it declines thereafter, our data did not reveal such a pattern. The total number of joint activities reported by the spouses early in marriage averaged 30.6 activities over the 9 days (or 3.4 activities per day); the average dropped somewhat, but not significantly, a year later to 25.8 (or 2.9 per day).

The type of companionate activity changed somewhat over the year, however, in that there was an increase in the proportion of activity centering around instrumental tasks rather than leisure, $F (1, 96) = 10.45, p < .01$. Moreover, couples who became parents had a higher proportion of joint instrumental to leisure companionship, overall, $F (1, 96) = 8.60, p < .01$, and their companionate activity evolved away from the recreational sphere and toward the instrumental area more so over the year when compared to nonparents, phase × parent interaction, $F (1, 96) = 38.7, p < .01$. The amount of time husbands and wives reported spending together in leisure activity declined about 20% over the first year of mariage, $F (1,96) = 16.94, p < .01$, with newlyweds reporting that they spent 4.1 hours per day doing leisure activities together compared to an average of 3.2 a year later. A similar, though somewhat less strong, drop occurred in the extent to which the husband and wife reported spending time talking with one another, $F (1, 96) = 8.96, p < .01$. The average couple 2 months into marriage reported talking together about 1 hour and 20 minutes per day; a year later the average had dropped to a few minutes over an hour per day.

Sex role patterns were somewhat traditional, and they changed very little over the year. Wives did significantly more of the housework, $F (1, 95) = 116.3, p < .01$, and, although the overall amount of housework changed over the year, depending on whether couples become parents, $F (1, 95) = 38.7, p < .01$, there was no change in the proportion of housework done by the wives. Wives were involved in about 64% and 65% of the household tasks during the newlywed period and a year later, respectively. The stability of the traditionalism in sex-role patterns is also evident in the sex typing of the spouses' participation in household tasks. We measured the extent to which husbands and wives ''cross over'' and become involved in tasks traditionally assigned to the opposite sex. The extent of crossover was about the same at both time periods (Phase 1: 35%; Phase 2: 36%). Although we have yet to break the data down according to whether spouses carried out the tasks alone or together, it is our impression that much of the crossing over that does occur takes the form of helping the spouse traditionally assigned a task to complete it rather than performing the task alone.

Perhaps the most striking change that occurred over the first year had to do with *socioemotional behavior*. Changes in the affective tone of interaction were most evident in the reduced rate at which partners did and said things that brought each other pleasure, F (1, 95) = 55.3, p < .01. The change in the amount of pleasurable activity, as measured by our phone procedures, was dramatic and general. The number of pleasurable activities that spouses reported declined by about 40% overall and, as we can see in Table 7.4, the decrease was generally consistent across the activities about which we inquired. Husbands and wives a year into marriage were considerably less affectionate, less approving, and less disclosing than they had been as newlyweds. This general decline in emotional responsivity is also reflected in the decreased extent to which spouses reported that they spent time talking about the quality of their relationship, made efforts to change their behavior to resolve problems, or disclosed their wants and concerns to one another, as measured by the maintenance subscale of the Braiker and Kelley (1979) instrument, F (1, 95) = 11.58, p < .01.

The picture that emerges from the data regarding conflict and negativity are more complicated. When we consider the frequency with which negative, or displeasing, events were reported by the husbands and wives during the phone interviews, we find that the rates of such behavior were very low, and they did not change from the newlywed period to a year later (see Table 7.4). If we assume that the negative behaviors are generally representative, and moreover that they are as representative of the kinds of negative things spouses do to one another as the pleasurable behaviors are of the positive things that happen, then the data would suggest that the affective tone of marriage becomes increasingly neutral. On the other hand, it is possible that the sampling period was too short to pick up changes in negative patterns, given that they apparently occur much less frequently. We suspect that day-to-day fluctuations in the extent of negativity and conflict is much greater than is the case for affectional behaviors, particularly for couples who are generally happy and who have not been married long. When husbands and wives were asked to generalize about the extent of negativity and conflict in their marriage, using the Braiker and Kelley (1979) measure, they reported an increase in such behaviors and patterns over the year, F (1, 95) = 6.80, p < .01.

In turning to the bottom part of Table 7.3, we move away from the marital dyad to examine the extent to which husbands and wives are involved with others. There was no change over the year in the frequency with which husbands

TABLE 7.4
Specific Behavioral Changes in Affective Interaction
in the First Year of Marriage

Behavior	Phase I[a]	Phase II[a]	F Ratio	p Value
Pleasing Behaviors				
Spouse approved or complimented partner	1.40	.98	28.1	< .01
Spouse did or said something to make partner laugh	3.55	2.35	24.5	< .01
Spouse said "I love you"	8.37	4.71	46.2	< .01
Spouse initiated sex	.49	.30	22.3	< .01
Spouse did something nice for partner	.68	.49	31.2	< .01
Couple had sexual intercourse	.64	.40	33.3	< .01
Shared physical affection (outside of sexual intercourse)	6.55	3.98	43.0	< .01
Shared emotions, feelings, or problems	1.54	1.01	15.2	< .01
Talked about day's events	1.24	1.16	1.9	n.s.[b]
Displeasing Behaviors				
Spouse seemed bored or uninterested	.25	.24	.0	n.s.
Spouse dominated conversation	.18	.18	.0	n.s.
Spouse showed anger or impatience	.42	.42	.0	n.s.
Spouse criticized or complained	.37	.35	.3	n.s.
Spouse turned down or avoided sexual advance	.06	.05	.1	n.s.
Spouse failed to do something partner asked, knowing it would annoy partner	.43	.25	4.6	< .05

[a]Average frequency per day.
[b]n.s. = non-significant.

or wives were involved in leisure activities with either kin relations or friends. Husbands and wives did differ, however, in their patterns of involvement with others at both phases. Traditional sex roles specify wives as "kinkeepers," with the husbands being more involved with friends. Such a differentiation of activity with others was found for couples in our study. The wives were involved in leisure activities with kin about 50% more often than husbands; wives averaged about 1.6 leisure activities per day with kin compared to 1.1 for husbands, F (1, 95) = 46.9, p < .01. The difference in involvement of husbands and wives with friends was less great but nonetheless statistically reliable, F (1, 95) = 4.84, p < .03. Husbands averaged 1.7 activities per day with friends; wives averaged 1.4 activities.

We can now elaborate our summary of how marriages are structured and how that structure changes. The most notable stable feature of marriages is their traditionalism. Wives do most of the housework, and couples assign household tasks primarily on the basis of gender, with husbands generally carrying out tasks such as household repairs, car repairs, and outdoor maintenance and with wives usually doing the cooking, cleaning, and the like. When we consider the spouses' involvement with friends and relatives, we find further evidence of the sex role traditionalism of the couples in that wives engage in more leisure activities with kin and husbands with friends.

In contrast to the stability in the role structure of marriages, notable changes occur in their emotional tone. Not only do spouses evaluate their marriage less favorably after a year, but it appears that they are already beginning to take each other and the relationship for granted. The overall amount of companionship does not change, but by the beginning of the second year it has started to become more incidental to activity rather than the focus of activity. Since instrumental activity is apt to be less pleasant than leisure time, the partners may begin to associate one another with neutral, even negative, subjective states, the result of which might contribute to the erosion of their attraction toward each other (cf. Lott & Lott, 1974). Another notable change is the dramatic reduction in the extent to which the marriage partners say and do things that bring pleasure to their spouses; similar drops occur in the extent to which spouses show their affection by hugging, kissing, or having sexual intercourse.

Our data also bear on Waller's (1938) suggestion that spouses are more likely to get on each other's nerves once they settle into marriage. The new tension, according to Waller, is the result of both an increase in the extent to which previously hidden and problematic elements of each spouse's personality enter into the relationship and the rise in the likelihood that spouses will express their disappointments. Whatever the reasons, the data gathered using the Braiker and Kelley (1979) measure show an increase in negativity from the honeymoon period to a year later. It remains to be seen, however, whether these changes are temporary or indicative of more permanent changes in the affective tone of marriage. Moreover, until we examine the interconnections between the behavioral patterns and measures of satisfaction, it is difficult to determine whether these changes foretell the beginnings of a process of disaffection and disaffiliation.

The Interplay Between the Subjective Evaluations of Marriage and Behavioral Patterns

Waller's (1938) analysis of the early period of marriage draws attention to two key issues that bear upon our effort to find connections between husbands' and wives' feelings about one another (and about their marriage) and their behavior in the marriage. Newlyweds are apt to be very much in love, blind to each other's faults, and careful to behave in ways they hope will reinforce each other's positive image. Although the data we presented previously do not bear on all of these ideas, we know that the spouses are generally very much in love and satisfied with their marriages, and that even though they change in both of these regards over the year, the changes are subtle. The typical husband and wife feel far from neutral about each other, with the differences among the couples being more a matter of degree of satisfaction (or love) than a matter of some couples being satisfied (or in love) and others being distressed (or hostile). In addition, even though the affective tone of marital interaction changes over the year, it is still highly positive. This does not mean, of course, that some newlyweds do not become disillusioned or unhappy early in marriage; indeed 12 couples who participated in the first phase were separated by the time we sought them out for Phase 2.

The interconnections between the attitudes (i.e., marital satisfaction) that spouses have about one another and marital behavioral patterns have been the focus of several investigations. These earlier studies, however, have used samples that differ considerably from ours in that they have studied either (1) couples who have been married for a much longer period of time (couples who are more differentiated in regard to both their current level of satisfaction and the length of time they have had to work out a style of relating to one another) (Cousins & Vincent, 1983; Wills, Weiss, & Patterson, 1974) or (2) couples who have been selected to be extremely different in marital satisfaction, with one group of couples regarding themselves as highly satisfied and the other group seeing themselves as distressed, generally to the point of seeking counseling (e.g., Billings, 1979; Gottman, 1979a; Margolin & Wampold, 1981).

Our group of couples, in contrast, is in the early stages of trying to find out about themselves and their spouses as marriage partners. Attitudes and behavioral patterns are in the process of being put into place, as the husbands and wives find out what each wants out of the relationship and what each is willing to contribute to make it work. Waller's analysis, the data we have on the extent and the variability in the marital satisfaction and behavior of our couples, and the results of earlier research (with couples who are more varied in attitudes and behavior) provide a context for putting our data together with the earlier research in order to work toward an understanding of the ways in which marital relationships might change as partners become disaffected.

Table 7.5 shows a striking pattern of correlations in that husbands' and wives' evaluations of their marriage are consistently related to the socioemotional character of their interaction and minimally (if at all) related to the extent and nature of their companionship, their marital role patterns, or to the amount of involvement of either spouse with friends or kin. Sixty-three of the 64 correlations having to do with the socioemotional character of interaction are in the direction consistent with the idea that the affective quality of husband-wife behavior reflects the spouses' extent of positivity about their relationship and vice versa. Although this generalization holds for both the honeymoon period and a year later, a more careful look at the breakdown of socioemotional activity into affectional (positive) and negative behaviors suggests that spouses' attitudes toward one another (and the marriage) are related to affectional behaviors during the honeymoon but not after a year of marriage. During the newlywed period the more husbands and wives feel positively about each other and the relationship—that is, the more in love they are (and for husbands the more satisfied and less ambivalent they are)—the more affectionally responsive they behave toward one another. A year later affectional behavior does not have much to do with the marital attitudes of either husbands or wives.

The attitudinal correlates of negativity show more consistency in association across time, and this is particularly true with regard to the correlations between negativity of interaction and the extent to which husbands and wives report dissatisfaction with the quality of their interaction. There are some striking differences between the two phases in the correlations between negativity and attitudes, however. In every case, the correlations are as strong or stronger a year into marriage as compared to when the couples were newlyweds. Consistent with Waller's (1938) idea that husbands' and wives' are reluctant to express their dissatisfactions early in marriage, we find little association during the newlywed phase between the evaluations spouses make of their marriage and their propensity to behave negatively toward their marriage partner. A year later, however, the connections between attitudes and behavior become stronger, with seven of the eight relevant correlations being statistically significant at Phase 2 compared to only two of eight at Phase 1. The contrast in the correlational patterns across the phases is most dramatic with regard to negativity and marital satisfaction. Shortly after marriage, no relationship is evident between husbands' and wives' marital satisfaction and their propensity to behave negatively (husbands: $-.15$, $-.09$; a year later, however, both husbands' and wives' satisfaction is reflected in the extent of their negativity (husbands: $-.44$, $p < .01$; wives: $-.33$, $p < .01$). Moreover, the correlations between one spouses' negativity and the others' marital satisfaction are somewhat stronger a year into marriage as compared to when the couples were newlyweds. The correlation between wives' negativity and husbands' marital satisfaction showed a moderate increase from $-.08$ to $-.23$ ($p < .05$); the comparable figures for wives were $-.36$ ($p < .01$), and $-.49$, ($p < .01$), respectively.

The general conclusion that attitudes about the marriage partner and the marriage relationship are more firmly anchored in the extent of negativity rather than in the extent of affection is consistent with previous research that has used samples of couples who have been married much longer (e.g., Wills et al., 1974). One possible reason for the stronger linkage between negativity of behavior and spouses' attitudes is that husbands and wives may be more likely to reciprocate negative behaviors than positive behaviors. To explore this possibility, we examined whether husband–wife pairs were more similar in the extent to which they treated each other negatively as compared to positively. The results of this effort did not lend support to the idea that husbands and wives are more likely to be similar in negativity than positivity. Indeed, for both phases, the intracouple similarity was greater for positive behaviors than for negative behaviors. Another explanation lies in the possibility that negativity between partners in marriage is more stable than affection, and thus the patterns measured during one period may

TABLE 7.5
Correlations Between Marital Attitudes and Behavioral Properties

	Wives								Husbands							
	Dissatisfaction with Interaction		Love		Ambivalence		Marital Satisfaction		Dissatisfaction with Interaction		Love		Ambivalence		Marital Satisfaction	
	Phase I	Phase II	Phase I	Phase II	Phase I	Phase II	Phase I	Phase II	Phase I	Phase II	Phase I	Phase II	Phase I	Phase II	Phase I	Phase II
I. Companionship																
A. Overall amount of companionship	-.03	.15	.03	.11	-.22ᵃ	.04	.18	-.05	.08	.10	.25ᵇ	-.04	-.03	.05	.19	-.08
B. Extent to which companionship takes place in recreational contexts	.10	-.09	-.03	.00	.13	-.12	-.07	.06	.09	-.07	.17	-.11	.03	.04	-.13	-.11
C. Amount of sharing of leisure time	.03	-.12	.14	.06	-.12	-.10	.11	.12	.01	.05	.21ᵃ	.19	-.10	-.10	.15	.15
D. Amount of time spent conversing with each other	.01	-.14	.05	.03	-.10	-.05	-.04	.08	-.07	-.05	.09	.05	-.14	-.11	.20ᵃ	.05
II. Marital Role Performance																
A. Extent of participation in household tasks by husband	-.01	.15	-.12	-.21ᵃ	-.07	.12	-.02	-.13	.06	.26ᵇ	.09	.06	.07	.14	.02	-.07
B. Extent of participation in household tasks by wife	-.01	.14	-.14	-.09	.03	.12	-.04	-.10	-.03	.09	-.02	-.15	-.07	.20ᵃ	.00	-.15
C. Relative extent of husband's and wife's involvement in household tasks	-.02	-.04	.01	.08	.09	-.04	-.03	-.01	-.02	-.06	-.08	-.07	.00	.05	-.02	-.07

D. Sex typing of the participation of husband and wife in household tasks	$-.07$	$.10$	$-.05$	$-.21^a$	$.02$	$.05$	$.00$	$-.12$	$-.05$	$.22^a$	$.00$	$-.09$	$-.02$	$.13$	$-.06$	$-.09$
III. Socioemotional Behavior																
A. Expression of affection by husband	$-.16$	$-.09$	$.30^b$	$.13$	$-.23^a$	$-.03$	$.21^a$	$.02$	$-.18$	$-.15$	$.30^b$	$.17$	$-.15$	$-.08$	$.26^b$	$.07$
B. Expression of affection by wife	$-.09$	$-.07$	$.31^b$	$.10$	$-.22^a$	$.00$	$.17$	$.02$	$-.13$	$-.17$	$.24^a$	$.23^a$	$-.11$	$-.13$	$.23^a$	$.11$
C. Expression of negative feelings or displeasure by husband to wife	$.37^b$	$.40^b$	$-.12$	$-.26^b$	$.27^b$	$.27^b$	$-.36^b$	$-.49^b$	$.30^b$	$.35^b$	$-.12$	$-.26^b$	$.15$	$.32^b$	$-.15$	$-.44^b$
D. Expression of negative feelings or displeasure by wife to husband	$.11$	$.28^b$	$.03$	$-.14$	$.20^a$	$.18$	$-.09$	$-.33^b$	$.33^b$	$.40^b$	$-.10$	$-.17$	$.10$	$.24^a$	$-.08$	$-.23^a$
IV. Involvement with Others																
A. Amount of husband's involvement with kin	$.04$	$.02$	$-.09$	$.01$	$-.05$	$-.04$	$.19$	$.06$	$-.06$	$-.11$	$.04$	$.09$	$.01$	$-.13$	$.07$	$.23^a$
B. Amount of wife's involvement with kin	$-.01$	$-.10$	$-.04$	$.03$	$-.04$	$.09$	$.10$	$.19$	$-.02$	$-.10$	$-.13$	$.02$	$.07$	$.04$	$.05$	$.11$
C. Amount of husband's involvement with friends	$.12$	$.10$	$-.13$	$-.07$	$.16$	$.07$	$.10$	$.19$	$.13$	$.02$	$-.19$	$-.16$	$.10$	$.12$	$-.23^a$	$-.11$
D. Amount of wife's involvement with friends	$.14$	$.04$	$-.03$	$.09$	$.05$	$-.10$	$-.11$	$-.08$	$.14$	$-.02$	$-.21^a$	$-.02$	$.12$	$.00$	$-.11$	$-.12$

[a] $p < .05$.
[b] $p < .01$.

be more representative of marital patterns over a longer run. We found, however, that the extent to which husbands and wives behaved affectionately or positively toward one another during the newlywed period was just as predictive of later positivity as early negative behavior was of later negativity.

As noted earlier, the pattern of correlations regarding marital attitudes and socioemotional behavior contrasts sharply with the results pertaining to companionship, marital role performance, and involvement with others. These findings would seem, at first glance, to be inconsistent with previous research, but again it is important to keep in mind that our sample consists of generally happy newlyweds, whereas the earlier research was conducted with couples married for many years, some of whom were very dissatisfied and had been unhappy for years (cf. Orthner, 1975; Wills et al., 1974). Husbands and wives may adjust their leisure time activities to include or exclude one another only if they are *dissatisfied* and have been for some time. The same thing can be said, in general, about the relationship between dissatisfaction and the extent to which husbands and wives seek the company of others. The general failure to uncover connections between role performance and measures of satisfaction seems a bit more puzzling. Most of the couples are neither strongly traditional nor nontraditional in sex role attitudes. It may be that patterns of role behavior are generally aligned with the preferences of the husbands and wives, and that were we to control for role preferences, we would find that it is only when the actual pattern is inconsistent with preferences that dissatisfaction sets in (Peplau, 1983). It is also possible that role performance takes longer to have an impact on marriage when compared to the affective quality of interaction. Role expectations are varied and couples may be more inclined to assume that role understandings need to be worked out. Thus, when a newly married husband fails to do the dishes or clean up the house, his wife may be patient in her attempts to change his behavior, recognizing that deciding about who should be responsible for what needs to be worked out. In contrast, negative events, when they occur, have more of a sting to them.

CONCLUSIONS

The pattern of findings reported in this chapter suggest that Waller's (1938) ideas about the transition to married life hold true more than 45 years after the publication of his classic treatise on the family. Moreover, the pattern is consistent across couples, regardless of whether they cohabited before marriage or became parents before their first anniversary. Waller (1938) described the process well when he wrote:

> As the area of privacy diminishes, the opportunity for idealization diminishes at an equal pace. As intimacies increase, the opportunities for disgust are multi-

plied. . . . It is of the nature of early marriage interaction to tend toward an unusual intimacy. . . . It is not surprising, therefore, that the honeymoon so often ends in conflict [p. 313].

It is somewhat surprising that the couples in our study who had lived together before marriage experienced the same decline in romantic feelings and positive interaction as those dyads who set up housekeeping after marriage. We had suspected that cohabitors would have gone through this process much earlier and would not show the same pattern as the other couples. There are several possible reasons why the expected results were not obtained. First, it should be remembered that only 35 of the couples in the sample had lived together before marriage, and although they cohabited an average of more than 10 months, there was considerable variability around this average. Perhaps most of them did not live together a sufficient time for the processes Waller describes to be set in motion. If so, we would expect a different set of findings to emerge in a study of couples who had lived together for longer periods of time. Another explanation is that the act of marriage itself is such a significant event in our culture, an event so imbued with romance, that it is perceived similarly by those who cohabit and those who do not. Thus, regardless of how well they may have known each other prior to marriage, couples may find themselves putting their best foot forward until they have settled into marriage.

It is clear that we have found Waller's ideas to be particularly useful in understanding how couple's adjust their feelings and behavior during the first year of married life, but our findings deviate from Waller's scenario in an important way. Waller's depiction of these changes implies that they are inevitable and that they apply to virtually everyone. We found that couples' negativity at the end of the first year of marriage could be predicted by their negativity shortly after marriage, and that negativity in marriage appears to have a corrosive effect on the spouses' feelings toward one another. The implication of these feelings is that couples experiencing conflict, negativity, and tension during courtship and early marriage are ''at risk'' for having problems later on in their relationship. It is interesting that the same continuity does not hold true for love. These results suggest that professsionals who are involved with couples at early stages in their relationships, that is, premarital counselors and family life educators, would be well advised to be attentive to early signs of negativity and to be less concerned about outward manifestations of love and affection. With this in mind, we conclude by echoing Waller's prescient commonsense advice that: ''educative programs with regard to family life are probably at their best when they liberate the young from conventional patterns that are not workable at the present time, and equip them with attitudes of tolerance and flexibility and techniques of meeting the crises that are certain to arise'' [p. 307].

ACKNOWLEDGMENTS

We wish to thank Jean Atkinson, Elliot Robins, and Anisa Zvonkovic, all of whom participated in the planning and execution of the research described in this chapter. We also express our gratitude to Shelley MacDermid for her help in carrying out the data analysis.

Work on this chapter was supported by National Institute of Health Grant MH 33938, Ted L. Huston, Principal Investigator.

8

Charting the Development of Personal Relationships

Steve Duck
Dorothy Miell
University of Lancaster,
Lancaster, England

INTRODUCTION

If we are just asked what characterises the interactions of acquaintances and friends in real life, we might declare that they are essentially private encounters shared between intimates; that they would be significantly longer than other interactions and more concerned with close sharing; that over time, as partners grow closer together, the interactions would be more intimate, more satisfying, and more "stable."

If, on the other hand, we consulted the research literature on friendship and interpersonal attraction we would probably be inspired to predict that friends would be characterised, by and large, by similarity; or that the intimacy of a relationship increases as a function of increasing discovery of similarity between the partners; or that satisfaction, intimacy, and similarity would be correlated; or that future expectations about the state of the relationship would predict satisfaction, and so on.

Whatever we believed, either before or after conducting this thought experiment, one thing is certain: Useful standard research literature on the actual conduct of real friendships over an extended period could not be consulted to settle any disputes between opposing views—because there is hardly any. This is surprising for three reasons: First, there has been an increasing emphasis in social and clinical psychology recently on the discovery of how people actually conduct their lives, so that normal and abnormal patterns can be more clearly delineated; second, inventive new methods of recording social participation and courtship growth have been reported recently by Wheeler and Nezlek (1977) and Huston, Surra, Fitzgerald, and Cate (1981); third, the breakdown or unsatisfactory development of friendship is being increasingly recognised as a major source of clinical problems (e.g., Feldman & Orford, 1980). There is both an urgency of need and a ripeness of time, therefore, for long-term studies of friendship growth.

This chapter reports a study conducted over 18 weeks in which participants kept daily records of up to two of their most significant interactions of the day and described their intimacy, duration, location and satisfaction; reported on their nature; and indicated the sex of partner, type of surrounding group (if any), and initiator of the interactions. As we indicate, the data suggest that several intuitions about friendship are deeply suspect as well as showing that some of the assumptions of psychological theories are questionable in fact. Most striking, however, is the observation that individuals express considerable uncertainty about their partners, feeling vague, ambiguous, and unsure about the constancy of their friends. Although we report here a study of students, our other ongoing studies on clinical patients and on "real people" suggest the same thing (Miell & Duck, 1985). People have generally little confidence about the relationship's future form, are constantly storm tossed by the vicissitudes of daily life, and are full of mild "existential terror" about their friends and their friendships. The likely future form of the relationship is a particular source of doubts and anxieties in both normal and clinically disturbed individuals.

It is also clear that many people are less confident about their own activity than psychologists have tended to assume. Discussions about past encounters, clarification of their own and partners' meanings, and reinterpretation of previous interactions are all major forces for social intercourse in this area. Perhaps psychologists are wrong to have assumed so centrally that people know what they are doing at the time when they do it. Often our subjects got together with precisely the intention of analysing and raking over what they had done earlier: In many cases, their business was to decide just what *had* happened rather than to dispute over causes for it or interpretations of it.

The reason for the unreliability of many of psychologists' assumptions about relationships is a simple one. Despite the vigorous researching of interpersonal attraction in recent years, it remains true that we have not properly studied (and hence do not really know) what people actually *do* in real-life voluntary acquainting. The emphasis of the research has fallen on experimental manipulation of variables presumed to be relevant, rather than on the discovery of their actual relevance in real life. Emler (1981) has recently identified several paradoxes in such an imbalance, most important of which is that investigators have the wrong model of social behaviour and so choose the wrong things to study. Hence particular selected variables are overrepresented, and their influence is unduly emphasised. Consequently their true-life significance is distorted in theoretical explanations of the phenomena. Worst of all, we never find out that (when given the choice) people behave in ways different from those that we assume. For instance, large assumptions have been made that liking, commitment, and estimated futurity of an acquaintance are essentially correlated—but no measures of these variables have been taken longitudinally.

Also, laboratory studies necessarily foreshorten and isolate interactions which, in real life, are not only extended but embedded in a context of other interactions. Emler also notes that attraction researchers assume that friends discuss their attitudes, personalities, and chronic states or characteristics when, in fact, they talk about personally relevant events—and just gossip. Such criticisms of the research into attraction amount to the claim that laboratory findings have unknown explanatory relevance until one knows more about how they reflect the actual conduct of the human enterprise. This can be achieved only through the study of spontaneous real-life acquainting, but the familiar call for more longitudinal studies is as frequent as it is unheeded. Social psychology has *not* yet told us how people start, conduct, maintain, and develop their centrally important voluntary interpersonal relationships. Until it does, clinicians will have to rely on intuition and guesswork about the way relationship turmoil bears on psychological turmoil.

From the perspective of a different research tradition, Hinde (1979; 1981) adds direction to the above familiar criticisms of laboratory work in attraction. He argues that a science of relationships will have to be founded on a fuller descriptive base and that we cannot begin to differentiate and taxonomise relationships until we have records of relevant dimensions of their actual conduct, such as their intensity, the range of behaviours that is manifested, and the changing patterns of liking and commitment that characterise their growth. By such means, we explore more than the unrepresentatively outstanding contours of relationships (the present risk of relying on laboratory studies), and we delineate the base rate against which those contours arise and are experienced. Clearly their relative importance can then be more easily understood and given its true theoretical status.

In the context of the study of courtship, Huston et al. (1981) have made a start in providing records of actual courtships over an extended period. These authors had married couples report on the progress of their courtship toward marriage. Using confidence of eventual marriage as the indicator, Huston et al. (1981) recorded the relationship between courtship growth and significant events. By this means the authors were able to distinguish 4 types of courtship that had previously lain unsuspected beneath the research data on courtship and its causes. However, the study has the drawback, fully discussed by the authors (Huston et al., 1981, pp. 61–63), that it was retrospective in character and dealt only with the reminiscences of couples who, at the time they completed the study, had succeeded in reaching the goal point—marriage. Clearly, for all sorts of reasons, the couples' recollections are likely to have been affected by many kinds of processes such as rationalisation, selective forgetting, reconceptualisation, and idealisation. Thus, although the study represents a major conceptual and methodological advance from which useful information can be extracted, it does not offer a complete solution to the problems of investigating spontaneous relationship growth in vivo—and, in fairness, it must be reiterated that the authors do not claim that it does.

In another area of social psychology a method for contemporary study of social participation has been developed by Wheeler and Nezlek (1977) and Reis, Nezlek, and Wheeler (1980). These authors have devised a record sheet by means of which participant subjects were able to record all their day's interactions of more than 10 minutes, to record their impressions of the nature of the interaction, and to rate the interaction and their partner(s) on various dimensions of assessment. Records were completed for only short period, however, but by such methods the authors were able to determine sex differences in, and the effects of physical attractiveness on, social participation. Because of their different intentions and purposes, these authors did not take (as Huston et al., took) measures of commitment to the relationship or its likely future and so on. Nevertheless, the basic method seems to be potentially as useful in measuring the natural growth of friendships as it has been in assessing social participation.

Our study employs a method founded on the Wheeler and Nezlek method but modified to suit the study of friendship growth. We also followed Wheeler and Nezlek in the choice of a population for study (i.e., students in a dormitory residence block) but we did this particularly because we needed a population that commenced the study unacquainted yet had a high probability of encountering and becoming acquainted with others in the sample. We departed from the Wheeler and Nezlek method in the length of our study, because we believed that the study of friendship initiation and growth requires longer than does the acquisition of a representative sample of human social participation. Our study lasted 18 weeks.

THE PRESENT STUDY

Method

The method of our study is briefly summarised as follows: Both male and female participants recorded each day the two most significant interactions of the day, using standard report sheets and their own criteria for "most significant." There were two 10-week periods for the data collection (each representing one university term), but in the first period, data collection began in the third week of term and covered the remaining eight weeks of Term 1. Subjects were all undergraduate students at a small campus university located 3 miles outside a major English city and were between 18 and 27 years old, with a mean age of 18.4 years. All were volunteers who received payment for their participation in the study. Of the 94 who originally agreed to take part, 74 completed the study (43 females, 31 males).

Subjects completed a daily record sheet. The form of the sheet follows closely on that reported by Wheeler and Nezlek (1977) but includes measures of intimacy and estimated future of relationship as appropriate to the purposes of the study. Subjects were instructed to record up to two of their most significant interactions with friends or acquaintances on campus each day. They reported on the location, duration, nature and initiator of the interaction, making choices between classes. Subjects recorded their satisfaction with it, the intimacy of it, its likely impact on the future of the relationship, and their current views of the similarity between themselves and their partner. Other data were also recorded concerning the sex of partner, whether the interaction was in a dyad or in a group, and the topics of conversation. Record sheets were collected every week and participants were thus unable to refer to their previous comments about their partners once this had been done.

Analyses and Results

Two major types of analysis were carried out: first, the duration, initiator, location, and nature of the interaction were examined, providing evidence about the changes in social participation occurring over 18 weeks. This analysis compared the pattern of results obtained from male and female subjects over the two terms in conversations with same-, opposite- and mixed-sex groups of others in a series of three- and four-way ANOVAs (analyses of variance).

Second, data on the intimacy satisfaction, and estimated future of relationship along with similarity perceived by the participants were analysed. Again, ANOVA comparisons were the main analyses employed.

We report each comparison briefly and summarise main findings: first the data on social participation and then the data on interaction quality.

Social Participation Data.   The two main questions here are: (1) What characterises social interactions between acquaintances and friends? (2) How does such participation change over time, presumably as the relationships develop?

The subjects in this study were asked to record the two most important interactions they had taken part in each day, regardless of the sex of their partner(s) or the size of the group involved. However, the subjects chose as most important significantly more of their same sex interactions (Term 1: $F = 21.89$, df $= 2,64$, $p < .001$ Term 2: $F = 57.71$, df $= 2,52$, $p < .0001$), and 60% of the time reported dyadic rather than large-group interactions throughout both terms. Thus, perhaps unsurprisingly, subjects placed most importance on their interactions with one same-sex other throughout the 18 weeks of the study. However, the result of the analysis of the length of time spent in these interactions is counterintuitive. In both terms, the subjects reported short interactions, generally less than an hour long, significantly more than longer ones (Term 1: $F = 200.29$, df = 2,64, $p < .0001$ Term 2: $F = 171.25$, df = 2,52, $p < .0001$). This pattern is especially marked in the most commonly reported same-sex interactions, with male subjects in particular reporting as many long (1 to 2 hours) as short conversations when in a mixed-sex group ($F = 3.01$, df = 4,128, $p < .05$).

It surprises us that whereas intuition supposes that friendship is quantitatively as well as qualitatively different from casual acquaintance, these results indicate no support for the belief. Short interactions are the order of the day, their significance coming from the person with whom they are conducted. We also note in passing that Wheeler and Nezlek (1977) took a period of greater than 10 minutes as the criterion for recording an interaction. Turning to the location of the recorded interactions, the results were again contrary to expectations. In the first term subjects do not choose to meet in their own private rooms as often as in more public places, such as coffee bars, pubs, kitchens, and sports centre with off-campus meetings being recorded least ($F = 62.5$, df = 2,64, $p < .001$).

This pattern is especially true of the female subjects, but for males there is no significant difference between the number of opposite sex interactions in public and in private. By Term 2, however, both sexes are reporting more interactions in their private rooms, $F = 26.2$, df = 2,52, $p < .001$). For males these are predominantly opposite-sex interactions, but the female subjects chose to record more same-sex private interactions ($F = 7.05$, df = 4,104, $p < .01$). Thus, although all subjects choose their same-sex interactions as their most important ones, it is only the females who report meeting these friends most in private, especially once the relationship has become established (in Term 2) as we would have expected. The male subjects, however, meet their same-sex friends mainly in public places, even after having known them for two terms, yet report interactions with opposite-sex partners in their own rooms. Off-campus interactions remained significantly fewer throughout both terms, presumably because these students lived on campus and spent the majority of their time there, with their trips off campus mainly associated with visits to their homes, which were not recorded on the diary sheets.

A third finding relates to the initiator of the interaction. Surprisingly, the subjects relatively infrequently reported initiating the encounters themselves. During the early days of the friendship, in Term 1, subjects generally see the encounters as mutually initiated ($F = 11.57$, df = 3,96, $p < .01$), and in Term 2, the partner is often seen as the initiator ($F = 11.2$, df = 3,78, $p < .01$). Again, there are sex differences in this pattern, however, with females making no consistent distinction between the possible initiators of interactions in Term 1 but by Term 2 recording their partner as the initiator most often ($F = 6.74$, df = 6,120, $p < .01$). The males, however, tend to record their interactions as mutually initiated in both terms (Term 1: $F = 3.97$, df = 6,96, $p < .01$, Term 2: $F = 2.58$, df = 6,78, $p < .05$). The very few records of interactions where the subjects see themselves as the initiator of the interaction suggests to us that participants perceive other people as their friends, rather than themselves as other people's friends.

Finally, the data on the nature of the recorded interactions produced further suprises for intuition. One might expect friends to report that much of their time is taken up with personal conversations, in which they share their secrets, problems, and personal opinions. However, throughout our 18-week period, for both male and female subjects, "chat" is the most often-used category for recording their important interactions with "share," "pastime," and "task" being referred to much less frequently (Term 1: $F = 27.29$, df $= 3,96$, $p < .001$, Term 2: $F = 72.01$, df $= 3,78$, $p < .0001$). This finding—that superficial conversation is the main form of interaction between friends—supports Emler's (1981) contention that gossip has a central role in conversations between friends. When the subjects do report the sharing of personal information, it is more in Term 2, after the relationships have had a chance to develop and a level of trust has been established between the partners. For males, these "sharing" conversations are reported more in their opposite-sex interactions, whereas the female subjects report more disclosures overall, and in particular in their same-sex encounters ($F = 2.84$, df $= 6,192$, $p < .05$). "Task" interactions are reported most in same-sex interactions in both terms, and "Pastime" interactions are most often recorded for mixed-sex interactions, as would have been expected.

In short, then, when one looks only at the social participation data rather than at the data on quality of interaction, there are a few surprises in store for intuition; new friends interact for short periods of time, in public rather than private places, and view themselves as essentially passive or receptive rather than as initiative in encounters that are predominantly chatty rather than significantly "sharing" or based on joint activity. This surprising pattern has been found predominantly in the interactions of male subjects suggesting perhaps that our intuitions about social participation rates have been based primarily on the interactions of females and do not as accurately reflect the interactions of males.

Interaction Quality. When one considers interaction quality, the surprises are less for intuition than for the research and theoretical literature on the subject. The assumption that intimacy and satisfaction are related, or that present intimacy relates to future expectations, cannot be upheld by our data. Ratings of intimacy, satisfaction, assumed similarity to partner, and estimated future for the relationship are in fact significantly different from one another throughout the 18-week measurement periods (Term 1: $F = 27.29$, df $= 3,114$, $p < .001$, Term 2: $F = 32.17$, df $= 3,66$, $p < .001$), although satisfaction with, and estimated future for, the relationship are nonsignificantly different from each other yet are both significantly different from the other scales. Evidently, subjects do not base their relationship judgments entirely on those that research psychologists have come to use. Intimacy does not promote confidence in the relationship's future; similarity does not create satisfaction; the probability of a successful future for the relationship is not determined by the partner's level of similarity.

Intriguingly, males report greater intimacy in their interactions than do females, right across the 18-week period (Term 1: $F = 5.7$, df $= 3,114$, p

$< .005$, Term 2: $F = 2.82$, df $= 3,66$, $p < .05$) and in defiance of all known social psychological laws! It is true that the females' overall ratings across the scales are significantly higher than the males' ($F = 6.07$, df $= 1,22$, $p < .05$), but this is because females see more future and greater similarity in their relationships and are generally more satisfied with them, not because their interactions are more intimate. However, caution is necessary in interpreting ratings of intimacy levels in interactions. Absolute levels of intimacy are likely to be less salient to the partners in a relationship than the interpersonally negotiated relevance of what is being said (whether objectively intimate or nonintimate), as Miell (1985) notes. Thus the women in this study may not actually be discussing items that would in themselves be judged by observers as more intimate than the men but they may believe their interactions to be intimate as topics that are important in their relationship are discussed. Friendships during the first two terms of a student's life at the university are likely to be subject to many fluctuations and full of uncertainty, and this study is unique in providing data over the whole of this period. From these data emerge many interesting points about how friendships develop during these terms and especially about the marked changes that are evident in the students' ratings of their friends before and after the Christmas break. In the last week of the Michaelmas term, the students' ratings of intimacy in their interactions, satisfaction with, and future for their relationships all drop markedly, suggesting that the subjects are becoming generally less satisfied with their newly formed relationships at the university possibly because they are looking forward to their return home, where they have friends of longer standing. The first week of the Lent term, however, is characterised by higher ratings on all four scales relating to the quality of interactions with their friends (indeed, perceived levels of intimacy and similarity were higher than at any time during the first term). Obviously, the students return after Christmas with a much stronger commitment to their friends at the university than they had before the vacation, and an examination of the comments made by the subjects on the diary sheets suggests that this is mainly due to their experiences with their friends at home over Christmas. It seems that many of the students expect to find the relationships with their friends at home unchanged after their 10-week absence, yet actually discover that they have altered; with both partners in the friendship having made new friends, and in many cases having lost the common ground (of school, joint activities, etc.) on which the friendship was based. The students return to the university realising that in fact they have more in common with their relatively "new" friends there, and that it is worth them investing more effort into developing these relationships (evidenced by the increasing amount of time spent meeting friends in private in the second term).

At the end of the second term, ratings of the interaction quality—especially intimacy—increase, rather than decreasing sharply as at the end of the first term. From their comments, the subjects report having more intense interactions during that last week before Easter while the prospect of returning to friends at home is seen almost as an interruption to the development of university friendships; this is an obvious change from their feelings before Christmas.

Finally, there is an intriguing oddity about the reports. There is a marked uncertainty recorded by the subjects about their friendships. In the free comments section, people were reporting things such as: "We are very close but I'm not sure if he wants the relationship to last," "I can't tell if she thinks she will still like me as the term continues" (and incidentally we, as researchers, knew that the partner was recording a future relational probability of 7 out of 7 at this point!). This astonishing and general feature of the diaries, found in all participants in the study, strongly suggests a kind of uncertainty given no weight at all in present theoretical formulations of relationships and relationship growth. Particularly it suggests that each person tends to see the other as the person who controls and is responsible for the existence of the relationship. It implies that, in a curious way, people see others as their friends but are reluctant to call themselves other people's friends.

In sum, then, the qualitative data suggest that long-term development of naturally occurring relationship contains elements that have so far eluded researchers and theorists alike. Precisely those measures of relationship growth that are most frequently used interchangeably (i.e., intimacy, similarity, expectation, and satisfaction) are, in fact, statistically different in behavior—and the general tenor of uncertainty that actually characterises relationships has hitherto been given no theoretical weight at all.

CONCLUSIONS

What do we conclude from this long-term study of naturally occurring personal relationships? The clearest conclusion is that both intuition and present theoretical models are unsatisfactory. Friends conduct themselves and their relationships in public, for short encounters, with superficial chat as the main ingredient. There are no long, intense, private intimacies here that we might have expected.

A second conclusion is that the development of friendships is rather an uncertain, nonlinear (fluctuating), speculative business rather than the automatic, linear, and straightforward process supposed by the literature. For this reason, subjects appear to give considerable thought to the strategic control of relationships and strive to correct the feelings that they do not know where they are going. If present cognitive models of social relationships overemphasise the linearity of development in relationships, they (surprisingly) underestimate this element of strategic control.

Third, we conclude from the foregoing that there exists a virgin and important area of research in this field: namely, the comparison of contemporary accounts of relationship growth with retrospections about the same relationship (but see Duck & Sants, 1983). Too often we are told that biases inhere in retrospective accounts without *anyone* having the data to support such a view. We suspect that retrospection about relationships is a major force in their shaping. Far from being pernicious or biased, such activity is essential to the creation of a relationship. Ginsburg (1981), for instance, has argued that retrospective analyses suffer from the flaw that they represent only a *perspective* on what has occurred in a relationship. We agree. However, psychologists deal with perspectives: That is our stock in trade and we must not fall into the mistaken assumption that the present is not also a perspective. Reports and accounts of the present or very close past do not represent some indisputable truth, nor are all other reports of it to be dismissed as past or future perspectives. The present is a perspective just like the past and the future. It may be that the dynamics of the three differ, however, and psychologists must in future explore the details of this possibility with vigour.

What is required in this context, then, is systematic investigation of the dynamics of retrospections. These dynamics constitute not an artifact of psychological research but a significant set of psychological processes without which relationships probably do not develop. At present, however, psychologists do not know how such retrospections work nor how their dynamics persist and influence relationships. Yet the processes by which individuals come to perceive themselves as members of a relationship and the influence exerted by these crystallisations are, we believe, enterprises of great moment (Duck, 1980; Duck & Sants, 1983). They have a major psychological interest that needs exploration and we are currently exploring it by retrospective interview techniques (Miell & Duck, 1985).

Finally, we observe that our method already embodies both simultaneous recording and short-term retrospection: The facts of the interaction (location, duration, etc.) are unlikely to be influenced by the fact that diaries were recorded at the end of the day. Other, qualitative, aspects of the encounters may have been recorded, however. As with most studies of interpersonal attraction and acquaintance, this one focuses on individuals' activities in the relationship (albeit, from a new perspective). However, in everyday life, people are able to report experiences of regret, disappointment, and satisfaction that illustrate the discrepancy or correspondence of some actual event with their prior expectations about it. Equally, people report retrospections about events, attempting to interpret them and "replaying" them—indeed, such replays are a major source of pleasure and pain with reference to social interaction. Both expectations and retrospections are likely to influence performance in subsequent encounters. It is clear that we all *know* that many things important to the conduct and future of a relationship can occur in the absence of the relationship partner. Yet despite knowing this, researchers persist in focusing on the here-and-now of the present encounter without investigating persons' plans, beliefs, and schemes that guide them in those present encounters. We urge future researchers to pay more attention to the nature of such out-of-relationship activities and their influence on voluntary real-life acquainting. This proposal seems to us to offer many avenues for advancing beyond previous research styles and to indicate several other directions for future exploration. We also feel that it will produce some interesting surprises. For if our present study can be summarised at all in a pithy phrase, that phrase is: The people out there living their lives and having their friendships don't know much about psychological theories—although the converse statement also seems defensible!

ACKNOWLEDGMENTS

The study reported here was first described in a paper presented to the One-day International Conference on Long Term Relationships, Oxford, November 21, 1981. We are grateful to Michael Argyle, Peter Collett, Jerry Ginsburg, and Elaine Hatfield for their advice and encouragement, and we gratefully acknowledge the financial support of Programme Grant No. HR 5382 from the Social Science Research Council.

9 Interaction Characteristics of Disengaging, Stable, and Growing Relationships

Leslie A. Baxter
Communications Department
Lewis and Clark College

William W. Wilmot
Department of Interpersonal Communication
University of Montana

INTRODUCTION

Many investigators have examined the basic dimensions or attributes of social behavior. While some consistency has emerged from a vast body of data (see Triandis, 1977, for a review), the findings are limited by the relative paucity of work that examines social behavior embedded in ongoing relationships. Important features of relationships are necessarily excluded from consideration when research questions focus on how *individuals* typically behave or on how interaction *encounters* are organized, regardless of the relationship in which these phenomena are enmeshed. A number of recent critics have underscored the need to study *relationships* as a basic unit of social organization (Duck, 1980; Duck & Gilmour, 1981a; Hinde, 1979). The study reported in this chapter expands our understanding of personal relationships by examining perceived changes in the ongoing constituent encounters of which relationships are made.

METHODOLOGICAL ISSUES

A Relationship-Level Approach

Knapp (1978) has advanced a framework for assessing interpersonal communication. Extending social penetration theory (reported by Altman & Taylor, 1973), he suggested eight dimensions on which relationship communication could vary:

1. Uniqueness: the extent to which relationship partners develop an idiosyncratic communication system.
2. Depth: the extent to which a relationship's communication system is characterized by self-disclosure.
3. Breadth: the extent to which a relationship's communication system is extended over a broad range of topics and activities.
4. Efficiency: the extent to which relationship partners accurately communicate with one another, free of misunderstandings.
5. Flexibility: the extent to which relationship partners have multiple ways of expressing a given thought or feeling to one another.
6. Spontaneity: the extent to which relationship partners are free of hesitation and caution in communicating with one another.
7. Smoothness: the extent to which relationship partners synchronize their communication styles.
8. Evaluativeness: the extent to which relationship partners give positive and negative feedback to one another.

In an initial empirical test of the dimensions, Knapp, Ellis, and Williams (1980) found that the eight-dimensional structure collapsed into three basic dimensions: (1) Personalized Communication—closely aligned with the Depth dimension and secondarily with Uniqueness and Flexibility; (2) Synchronized Communication—primarily drawn from the Smoothness dimension and secondarily from the Spontaneity and Efficiency dimensions; and (3) Difficult Communication—primarily drawn from the Efficiency dimension and secondarily from the Smoothness dimension. Baxter (1983), using an expanded item pool from that employed by Knapp et al., produced a five-dimensional structure, basically replicating the second and third factors that Knapp et al. found while unpacking their Personalized Communication factor into its three component factors of Personalness, Flexibility, and Uniqueness.

Relationship-as-Process

The evidence on Knapp's thesis is somewhat mixed (see Baxter, 1983). However, it is a move in the proper direction toward a relationship-based unit of analysis. Furthermore, his approach stresses that communication relationships vary across time. Conceptually, his stance is process oriented, examining the processes of relationships as they change over time from initiation to deterioration. Unfortunately, the overwhelming majority of studies reported in the literature utilize methodology that precludes charting relationships in process. In a recent study, Wilmot and Baxter (1983) distinguished between relationship-as-state and relationship-as-process conceptualizations of interpersonal relationships. Much of the existing research and theory in interpersonal relationships exhibits the relationship-as-state conceptualization (i.e., closeness as a stable state). Thus, research has contrasted such relationships-as-state as "acquaintances" and "romantic partners." A relationship-as-process conceptualization of interpersonal relationships recognizes that, although some relationships may be stable at a given level of closeness, many relationships are "in process" either in growing more distant or in growing closer. A relationship-as-process conceptualization recognizes that importance of distinguishing stable relationships from more fluid relationships. The relationship-as-state conceptualization is thus meaningful only among relatively stable relationships. For relationships that are in flux, a stable state view may be inadequate and misleading.

Research designs that are cross sectional assume a "relationship-as-state" conceptualization that does not extrapolate to process notions of communication. As Arundale (1980) said: "If one desires interpretations in terms of change over time, one must have data containing information on change over time; yet only some research designs include the operations needed to generate such data [p. 230]." More specifically, if one amasses data from a cross-sectional design (such as studying some individuals in the initial states of a relationship and others in the ending phases), the relationships between the variables have to be assumed to hold throughout.

There have been continuing calls for process models of communication in interpersonal communication, but as Kline (1978) noted: ". . . hearing the calls and acknowledging them are no excuses for inaction [p. 202]." If we are going to conceptualize relationships as "in process," then data from static cross-sectional views will not be sufficient. What is needed is data from "change over time" designs, which parallel a motion picture with successive "frames" of information spaced so they include the necessary information on relationships in process (Arundale, 1980, p. 231). In an ongoing relationship, where the participants have multiple interactions with one another, each interaction encounter could serve as a "frame" of the overall relationship. The recurring communication experiences are what build the relationship; they are the "building blocks" that construct a relationship (Forgas, 1979, p. 9). Thus, data should be gathered from successive encounters if one wishes to draw conclusions about relationship movement over time.

Examination of the everyday functioning of relationship encounters is limited. In a pioneering study, Wheeler and Nezlek (1977) asked first-year university students to keep diaries of their interaction encounters for a 2-week period of time. The researchers were primarily interested in comparing male and female social participation profiles—the average number of encounters experienced daily, whether the encounters were dyadic or larger in size, the proportion of encounters initiated by the subject, the locations in which the encounters occurred, the average duration of an encounter, the activities enacted during one's encounters, and the reported intimacy of and satisfaction with the encounters. In a second study, Reis, Nezlek, and Wheeler (1980) examined the effects of physical attractiveness on social participation; university students who differed in perceived attractiveness were asked to keep diary records comparable to those of the first study on the social encounters with others. Most recently, Duck and Miell (Chapter 8) asked first-year university students to keep diary records on their two most significant interactions of the day for a period of 20 weeks, focusing on perceptions of similarity to, and liking for, one's interaction partners, in addition to the descriptive features noted in Wheeler and Nezlek (1977).

Collectively, these three studies probe people's actual interaction encounters. Unfortunately, from a relationship-level perspective, two of the three studies focus on individual-level issues (e.g., attractiveness and social participation) or on encounter-level issues (e.g., location and duration), rather than studying the ongoing progression of relationships per se. Like the Duck and Miell study, we use the diary method to inform us of relationships through time.

The Diary Method

Wheeler and Nezlek (1977), Reis et al. (1980), and Duck and Miell (this volume) share in common the diary method of self-report, soliciting the cooperation of the research subject as a "coinvestigator" because she/he both engages in relationship encounters and records them. Fortunately for others interested in using the diary method, these researchers report that the recording is reasonably accurate and does not disrupt the normal functioning of people in their social encounters. Furthermore, the diary method allows for process conceptualizations to be tested by process data.

This conceptualization-data isomorphism, however, is not the only methodological concern. Since close relationships are, by their very nature, not amenable to ongoing unobtrusive data collection, some other method must be used to glean information from the participants in the relationship. Interactions not available for public access can be tapped by (1) recall of relationship experiences or (2) responses to hypothetical scenarios. Both of these data bases, however, have been criticized. Recall is subject to the usual problems of memory. With hypothetical scenarios it can be argued that forecasting behavioral choices is a problematic way to assess real choices. The diary method, although not immune from criticism, does offer two distinct benefits over retrospective reports and role-playing data: *immediacy* and *concreteness of stimuli*.

The typical interpersonal relationship study that relies on self-report data asks respondents to recall a relationship of theirs that can be described by a given relationship term or phrase (e.g., "your best same-sex friendship"), which in turn is evaluated by the respondent on the particular variables of interest in the study. The respondent is asked to report on a highly abstract construct—the relationship overall—rather than a more concrete phenomenon such as a specific relationship encounter, as in the diary method. Furthermore, the respondent of the typical investigation may be recalling a particular relationship that is rather remote temporally from the data collection occasion. One's "best friend" may be someone removed from day-to-day interaction by months or decades, as in the case of Rands and Levinger's (1979) study. In contrast, the diary method has more immediacy with the actual relationship experience, typically being reported on the same day as the encounter itself.

Role-playing studies indirectly access people's recalled relationship experiences. In the prototypical study, the subject is asked to imagine a specified hypothetical relationship and project what the relationship's interaction would be like (Knapp et al., 1980) or to act out how people in such a relationship would behave (Keiser & Altman, 1976). In imagining a particular relationship type, subjects naturally draw on their recollections of their experiences with the given relationship type, and thus, by contrast, the diary method still has comparative advantages of immediacy and concreteness of stimulus.

The reliance on recalled relationship experiences and relationship role playing maximizes the likelihood of data that are biased by people's implicit theories of relationships (Hinde, 1981). Thus, closer relationships may, for example, be characterized by greater self-disclosure than less close relationships in the research literature, not because closer partners always disclose more but because the respondents have an implicit expectation that disclosure should happen in close relationships (Bochner, 1982). Parks (1982), drawing on Sennett's *The Fall of Public Man* (1977), argues that our culture has a pervasive "ideology of intimacy," which in fact manifests itself in individuals' implicit expectation that our close relationships will be characterized by maximum openness, honesty, and understanding. Of course, people's implicit theories of relationship are not abandoned simply because of the process of diary recording; respondents will have implicit theories of the way things should be in their relationships that they will bring to the encounters. However, the immediacy and concreteness of the particular interaction encounter may limit the impact of biasing implicit theories. If a respondent is asked to recall the nature of the communication that transpired in his or her relationship with the same-sex best friend, for example, the respondent may recall it as open and effective ("We're best friends and have been since high school, so of course we're honest, open, and free of communication breakdowns."). The recalled data from an individual encounter gets filtered through the expectations for the relationship. In contrast, the concrete particulars of interaction may still be salient when the respondent assesses the encounter rather immediately after its conclusion ("We just talked about trivialities today, but that doesn't happen too often between us."). In fact, Nisbett and Ross (1980) summarize a substantial body of perception research that supports this rather anecdotal advocacy of diary-based data. Summarized in their vividness principle, Nisbett and Ross suggest that persons remember more as opposed to less vivid stimuli, and stimulus features that enhance vividness include concreteness and sensory, temporal, or spatial proximity. A just-concluded interaction encounter is both concrete and temporally proximate and thus is likely to remain salient in the perceiver's memory.

THE PRESENT STUDY

Research Questions

In monitoring day-to-day encounters in ongoing relationships, we complement extant research that is overly reliant on individual-level analyses, static-state conceptualizations of relationship, and persons' implicit theories of relationships. In contrast to the composite profile of interpersonal relationships that emerges in existing work, encounter-by-encounter monitoring of relationships may provide us with a different view of what happens in relationships. Recalled and hypothetical one-shot descriptions may bypass potentially valuable information. For example, there may be substantial instability in interaction behavior across a relationship's encounters. Indeed, interaction instability has long been posited as characteristic of interpersonal relationships. Almost a century ago, Georg Simmel argued that instability was inherent to social relationships between people. And more recently, Knapp and his colleagues (1980) have echoed the same point:

> Most relationships are composed of co-existing forces which seem in opposition to one another. Warmth behaviors are mixed with cold. Intimacy is not conceptualized as a continually increasing amount of any type of behavior. We will likely see some public behaviors, some awkwardness, some rigidity, some stylizedness, some difficulty and some hesitancy in intimate relations. For most relationships a degree of instability is part of the definition of stability [p. 264].

Yet attention to this facet of relationships has been notably absent in the research literature. In addition to interaction instability, interaction characteristics from both the Knapp model (Baxter, 1983; Knapp, 1978; Knapp et al., 1980) and the encounter monitoring research tradition (Duck & Miell, this volume; Reis et al., 1980; Wheeler & Nezlek, 1977) were included for study.

Consistent with Knapp's process-oriented theory of relationship change, we were interested in the interaction features of relationships that were disengaging as opposed to relationships that were growing closer. Simultaneously, however, we were interested in comparing relationships that had stabilized in closeness to those that were in flux (disengaging or escalating). In sum, this study addressed the following questions:

1. To what extent do disengaging relationships and escalating relationships differ in their reported interaction characteristics?
2. To what extent do stable relationships differ from relationships in flux in their reported interaction characteristics?

Subjects

The sample consisted of 58 university-level students, 27 females and 31 males, ranging in age from 18 to 45 with the vast majority in the 18 to 22 age bracket. Subjects were drawn from the respective institutions of the authors, one a moderately sized public university and the other a small, private, liberal-arts institution. Data were collected from October 1981 to January 1982. Subjects received a copy of the results of the study as compensation for their participation.

Diary Records

Subjects were asked to identify two of their interpersonal relationships for diary monitoring: one same-sex relationship and one opposite-sex relationship. Thus, the data set was comprised of diary reports on two relationships from each of the 58 subjects, producing a total data set of 907 encounters embedded in 116 relationships. For each relationship, subjects filled out a Background sheet that indicated the sex of the subject, his/her age, the age and sex of the target relationship partner, the judged closeness of the relationship at the beginning of the diary monitoring period, and the duration of the relationship to date.

At the conclusion of each face-to-face or telephone encounter of at least 5 minutes' duration, subjects were asked to fill out a Diary Entry sheet. Diaries were maintained on both relationships for the same 2-week period of time. The Diary Entry sheet solicited much of the same information obtained by Wheeler and Nezlek (1977). However, it contained additional communication elements as well: the topics that were discussed, the overall importance of the encounter, the perceived effect of the encounter on the overall relationship definition, and nine semantic differential scales designed to measure the three relationship communication dimensions—Personalness, Smoothness, and Efficiency—which are common to the two empirical tests of Knapp's eight-dimensional model (Baxter, 1983; Knapp et al., 1980).

Analysis Variables

Analysis variables were formed for each relationship for which the one-sided diary data were obtained. The variables were as follows:

1. *Relationship process*—whether the relationship was growing apart, growing closer, or stable in closeness for the period of diary collection. This was a constructed variable based on subject perceptions of relationship change per encounter. Subjects were asked to respond on a seven-point scale to this item: "How do you think this specific encounter affected the overall relationship between you?" (-3 = much more distant, 0 = no change, $+3$ = much more close). A net change score was computed for each relationship based on the mean of the episode entries. The relationships with a minus net change score were defined as disengaging ($N = 10$). Relationships with a net change score of zero were defined as stable ($N = 16$). And relationships with a net change score greater than zero were regarded as growing closer ($N = 90$).

2. *Talk embeddedness of encounters*—the proportion of a relationship's encounters that enacted talk for talk's sake, as opposed to the enactment of a recognized social activity (e.g., playing a game, writing a joint report, etc.).

3. *Number of encounters*—the total number of encounters for a relationship during the 14-day diary monitoring period.

4. *Encounter breadth*—the mean number of different topics discussed per encounter.

5. *Encounter satisfaction*—the mean of the encounter satisfaction scores computed across a relationship's total encounters.

6. *Encounter importance*—the mean of the encounter importance scores computed across a relationship's total encounters.

7 & 8. *Interaction Effectiveness and Personalness*—the mean Effectiveness and Personalness scores computed across a relationship's total encounters. The three dimensions of communication common to the Knapp et al. (1980) and Baxter (1983) studies were selected. Specifically, three semantic differential pairs comprised the Personal Communication dimension on a priori grounds: impersonal–personal, in-depth–superficial, and guarded–open. Three adjective pairs formed the Smoothness dimension: strained–relaxed, informal–formal, and difficult–smooth flowing. Three adjective pairs comprised the Efficiency dimension: attentive–poor listening, great deal of (mis)understanding, and laden with (free of) communication breakdowns. To test the validity of these a priori designations, a principal components factor analysis with varimax rotation was applied to the nine adjective pairs across all 907 encounters. An eigenvalue at least equal to 1.00 was necessary for factor acceptance. An item loaded on a factor if it had a primary factor loading $\geq .50$ with no secondary factor loading $\geq .30$. The factor analysis produced a two-factor solution that accounted for 68.4% of the variance. Table 9.1 reproduces the factor loadings.

It is apparent that factor 1 is a hybrid factor of Smoothness and Efficiency; we labeled the factor Effectiveness. The second factor is a rather straightforward Depth dimension, one we labeled Personalness. An Effectiveness score and a Personalness score were computed for each encounter by averaging the values of those items that loaded on the respective factor. Finally, relationship interaction

TABLE 9.1
Factor Loading of Communication Quality Items

Item	Factor 1	Factor 2
Personal/impersonal	.23	.55[a]
Relaxed/strained	.84[a]	.22
Attentive/poor listening	.36	.68
Informal/formal	.49	.17
In-depth/superficial	.12	.87[a]
Smooth flowing/difficult	.87[a]	.15
Open/guarded	.79[a]	.30
Great deal of (mis)understanding	.63	.43
Free of/laden with communication breakdowns	.73[a]	.21

[a]Item loaded on this factor.

Effectiveness and Personalness scores were computed as the means of their respective encounter scores.

9. *Effectiveness stability*—the standard deviation of the encounter Effectiveness scores for a given relationship.

10. *Personalness stability*—the standard deviation of the encounter Personalness scores for a given relationship.

Results

The nine dependent variables were: talk-embeddedness of encounters, total number of encounters, encounter breadth, encounter satisfaction, encounter importance, interaction effectiveness, interaction personalness, effectiveness stability, and personalness stability. Correlations were computed among these variables in order to determine whether a multivariate statistical analysis was warranted. Results are dispayed in Table 9.2. Because substantial inter-correlation was apparent in the dependent variable set, a multivariate statistical test was employed initially. Furthermore, because of substantial research literature that reports sex differences in interpersonal relationships (e.g., Eakins & Eakins, 1978; Knapp et al., 1980; Wheeler & Nezlek, 1977), respondent sex was included in the statistical analysis for control purposes. A nonorthogonal, two-factor MANOVA (multivariate analysis of variance) was selected, with the Relationship Process factor entered into the analysis after the Respondent Sex factor.

The two-way MANOVA produced significance at beyond the .05 level for all possible effects. Significant multivariate main effects were found for Respondent Sex (Wilks' lambda = .71; $F = 4.71$; df = 9,102; $p < .001$) and for Relationship Process (Wilks' lambda = .67; $F = 2.52$; df = 18,204, $p < .001$). In addition, a significant interaction was found for Respondent Sex × Relationship

TABLE 9.2
Correlation Matrix of Dependent Variable Set

	Variable Item Number[a]								
	2	3	4	5	6	7	8	9	10
2	—	−.11	.05	.09	.07	.05	.12	.04	.07
3		—	−.01	.13	.18[b]	.19[b]	.20[b]	.16[b]	−.01
4			—	.19[b]	.12	.14	.14	−.06	.07
5				—	.64[b]	.57[b]	.56[b]	−.12	−.07
6					—	.21[b]	.49[b]	.16	−.08
7						—	.49[b]	−.36[b]	−.01
8							—	−.09	−.18[b]
9								—	.39[b]
10									—

[a]Numbers correspond to those in text under "Analysis Variables" section.
[b]Significant at beyond .05 level for 116 relationships.

Process (Wilks' lambda = .72; F = 2.01; df = 18,204; p = .01). Mean scores are reported in Table 9.3.

Table 9.4 summarizes the information relevant to the single significant discriminant function that emerged for the interaction effect. Consistent with Wilkinson's (1975) reasoning, multiple statistical perspectives were employed in order to interpret the interaction effect. Based on both the magnitude of the canonical component loadings and the magnitude of the univariate F ratios, the interaction effect is primarily attributable to the encounter importance variable. Based on follow-up *Least Significant Difference* (LSD) tests, females reported their stable relationship encounters as significantly more important than those in growing relationships, which were significantly more important than encounters in disengaging relationships. Among males, however, growing relationship encounters were more important than those in either disengaging or stable relationships, with encounters in the latter two process types failing to differ significantly.

Table 9.5 presents follow-up information relevant to the Relationship Process main effect. The canonical loadings and univariate F ratios suggest that the effect is largely a function of encounter satisfaction, interaction effectiveness, and interaction personalness. For all three dependent variables, follow-up LSD tests indicated that disengaging and stable relationsips failed to differ significantly from one another; in all three instances, however, both disengaging and stable relationships had significantly lower scores than growing relationships.

Only number of encounters, effectiveness stability, and personalness stability failed to contribute to the multivariate main effect for Respondent Sex. Canonical loadings and univariate F ratios are summarized in Table 9.6.

TABLE 9.3
Mean Scores for Dependent Variable Set

| | Relationship Process × Sex | | | | | | Relationship Process | | | Respondent Sex | |
| | Disengaging | | Stable | | Growing | | | | | | |
Dependent Variable	M	F	M	F	M	F	Disengaging	Stable	Growing	Male	Female
Talk embeddedness	.67	.77	.61	.66	.64	.76	.71	.63	.66	.64	.75
Number encounters	10.17	5.25	5.60	7.50	7.96	8.14	8.20	6.31	8.05	7.79	7.82
	(N = 6)	(N = 4)	(N = 10)	(N = 6)	(N = 46)	(N = 44)					
Topic breadth	3.36	5.20	3.76	4.62	3.93	4.67	4.10	4.38	4.29	3.85	4.70
Encounter satisfaction	4.04	4.45	4.29	4.44	4.99	5.39	4.20	4.35	5.19	4.79	5.21
Encounter importance	3.93	4.55	3.23	5.48	4.53	4.98	4.18	4.08	4.76	4.26	5.01
Interaction effectiveness	4.54	3.78	4.78	4.84	5.24	5.79	4.24	4.81	5.51	5.10	5.54
Interaction personalness	3.94	4.10	3.84	4.45	4.46	5.19	4.01	4.07	4.83	4.31	5.03
Effectiveness stability	.98	1.04	.69	1.06	.86	.81	1.01	.83	.84	.84	.85
Personalness stability	1.25	1.16	.90	1.13	1.08	1.14	1.21	.98	1.11	1.07	1.14

155

TABLE 9.4
Canonical Component Loadings and Univariate F Ratios
for Sex $\times$ Process Interaction

Dependent Variable	Canonical Loading	Univariate F Ratio
Talk embeddedness	.10	.14 (2,110)
Number encounters	−.24	2.83
Encounter breadth	.01	.56
Encounter satisfaction	.13	.23
Encounter importance	−.65	5.88[a]
Interaction effectiveness	.12	3.07[a]
Interaction personalness	.02	.49
Effectiveness stability	−.30	1.31
Personalness stability	−.11	.23

[a] $p < .05$.

Discussion

Relationships were typed as disengaging, stable, or growing based on net change in reported relationship closeness over a 2-week diary monitoring period. Nine interaction features were monitored from encounter to encounter in these relationship process types. Overall, the interaction features varied by both relationship process type and respondent sex.

Results indicated that the relationship types differed primarily on the interaction attributes of encounter satisfaction, interaction effectiveness, and interaction personalness. Fully compatible with Knapp's theory of relationship growth and decay, disengaging relationships were characterized by less reported effectiveness and personalness of communication than were relationships undergoing

TABLE 9.5
Canonical Component Loadings and Univariate F Ratios
for Relationship Process

Dependent Variable	Canonical Loading	Univariate F Ratio
Talk embeddedness	−.05	.41
Number encounters	−.15	1.65
Encounter breadth	−.05	.05
Encounter satisfaction	−.68	16.81[a]
Encounter importance	−.39	3.62
Interaction effectiveness	−.76	13.34[a]
Interaction personalness	−.54	6.58[a]
Effectiveness stability	.15	.61
Personalness stability	−.01	.53

[a] $p < .005$.

TABLE 9.6
Canonical Component Loadings and Univariate F Ratios
for Respondent Sex

Dependent Variable	Canonical Loading	Univariate F Ratio
Talk embeddedness	−.35	5.47[a]
Number encounters	−.01	.01
Encounter breadth	−.43	8.64[a]
Encounter satisfaction	−.51	11.94[a]
Encounter importance	−.62	17.94[a]
Interaction effectiveness	−.42	8.15[a]
Interaction personalness	−.66	20.09[a]
Effectiveness stability	−.01	.01
Personalness stability	−.11	.56

[a]$p < .05$.

growth. The parallel finding on satisfaction suggests the centrality of effectiveness and personalness in interpersonal relationships. However, contrary to Knapp's theory, disengaging relationships were not characterized by less frequent encounters or by reduced topic breadth. The disengaging relationships in this sample may have continued their encounters because of circumstances (e.g., joint classes or activity commitments that continued despite the relationship disengagement). Alternatively, these disengaging relationships may have been in the earliest stage of disengagement, a period whose primary attributes may be increased superficiality and ineffectiveness of communication; avoidance and total withdrawal from contact may occur much later in the disengagement process. Similarly, topic breadth was not reduced in the disengaging as opposed to the growing relationships. Again, substantial reduction in topic breadth may characterize the disengaging relationship only in more advanced stages of dissolution; in early stages, the relationship parties may be employing a diversity of topics in order to prevent the conversation from personalizing in depth on a given topic.

Interestingly, stability of effectiveness and personalness qualities across encounters did not contribute to the relationship process main effect. Several theorists have argued that disengaging relationships should be characterized by reduced "vibration" or instability as they deteriorate (Baxter, 1982; Frentz & Rushing, 1979; Lerner, 1979). Instead, these findings indicate substantial variation regardless of relationship process.

Relationships that stabilized in closeness displayed less satisfaction, effectiveness, and personalness than relationships undergoing growth; furthermore, stable relationships did not differ significantly from disengaging relationships on these three attributes. These findings may point to a danger in relationship stability. As Lerner (1979) argued, a relationship can withstand only so much stability before the parties experience boredom and stagnation in the relationship. Subsequent research needs to investigate the tolerance boundaries of relational stability, determining the circumstances under which "sameness" becomes stagnating rather than comforting to relationship parties. Our data suggest that "sameness" is less satisfying when the relationships have stabilized at moderate levels of closeness. Our respondents were reporting on relationships at intermediate levels whereas more intimate or less intimate stable relationships might not lead to lower satisfaction than did the growing relationships. The precise factors leading to these effects of stability are, however, still in need of investigation.

The pattern that emerges on these three attributes was evident as well on encounter importance, but for males only. Males perceived the encounters of growing relationships as more important than those of disengaging and stable relationships, with no significant distinction in encounter importance for the latter two relationship process types. In contrast, females reported greater encounter importance for stable relationships, with growing relationships ranked second in encounter importance and disengaging relationships ranked third. The gender differences in this case are in contrast to the systematic differences in the above areas and are not readily interpretable.

An overall difference was found between males and females, with females reporting higher scores on most of the interaction measures. The presence of a sex difference is not surprising, and the pattern evident in the results is quite consistent with sex role socialization research and theory. The greater personalness associated with females confirms their socialized expressiveness. And, consistent with the findings of Wheeler and Nezlek (1977), females engage in more talk for talk's sake than males do. These two characteristics may relate causally to one another; the enactment of social activities may constrain the level of personalness which can occur in interaction, unlike talk for its own sake.

Although males and females differed on what relationship type was accorded more encounter importance, females reported greater encounter importance in general than males did. The greater importance which females attached to their relationship encounters is also quite compatible with sex role socialization patterns. Females are traditionally socialized more than males to value interpersonal relationships for their inherent worth, whereas males are socialized more than females to value instrumentality (Gilligan, 1982). The fact that so few of these encounters were embedded in instrumental activities perhaps provided sufficient warrant for traditionally socialized males to devalue their perceived importance and perhaps their effectiveness and potential for satisfaction, as well. Conversational talk, however, is a valued commodity for the relationship-oriented female.

Females reported more topics of discussion per encounter than did males. Given the greater importance that females typically attach to their relationships, they may simply have monitored the relationship encounters more carefully than males, recalling more of the conversation than males at the point of diary entry. Alternatively, females may not have better recollection of conversations but may simply engage in talk of greater breadth. Fishman (1978) has observed that females more than males assume responsibility for keeping a conversation running smoothly (what Fishman graphically described as "interaction shitwork"). Raising many possible topics of discussion is one conversational device to maintain a smooth-flowing conversation; in establishing a broad range of possible topics, one enhances the likelihood of finding something of mutual interest to both interactants. The increased topic breadth finding, then, may support Fishman's hypothesized "interaction shitwork" as a female attribute.

SUMMARY

This examination of close relationships has reflected three specific foci: (1) the analysis focused primarily on relationships and only secondarily on the individual attribute of sex; (2) the relationships were conceptualized and operationalized in process terms; and (3) the data were collected over time on an encounter-by-encounter basis with the use of respondent diaries. By necessity, the diary method is cumbersome to monitor with large numbers of participants, and our sample size was not large. Furthermore, we accessed perceptions of relationship encounters from only one party in the relationship; dual-perspective diaries from both relationship parties would clearly constitute a preferable way to monitor relationships. Finally, we focused on friendship relations, whereas other close relationships might manifest distinctly different patterns. On the positive side, these data flow from an isomorphic set of assumptions between conceptualization and measurement. Studying relationships from a process perspective is a relatively unexplored approach, and it holds promise for a richer description of the role of communication in ongoing relational dynamics.

10

The Relation Between Patterns of Friendship, Self-Concept, and Conceptions of Friendship in Six-Year-Olds

Harriet K. A. Sants
Medical Research Council Unit on the
Development and Integration of Behaviour,
Madingley, Cambridge, England

INTRODUCTION

With a few exceptions (e.g., Piaget, 1932; Sullivan, 1953) theories of social development have made one or both of two assumptions: first, the child becomes a competent adult through his relationship with his parents (e.g., Bowlby, 1969; Guntrip, 1961; Sears, Maccoby, & Levin, 1957); second, the child mainly learns about the social world by learning about the characteristics of other people rather than by developing capacities to conduct relationships (e.g., Flavell, 1974; Livesley & Bromley, 1973). Where interest has been focused on relationships, research has concentrated on children's beliefs or conceptions about relationships without relating them to the children's actual relationships or interactions with others (e.g., Bigelow, 1977; Selman, 1981). Until recently, these assumptions have led to a relative neglect of the role of peers in social development and of the possibility that different types of relationships may have different effects on the process of social development. Previously, only a few theorists such as Piaget and Sullivan recognised peers as having a significant influence on development.

Theorists who have concentrated on the parent–child, particularly the mother–child relationship, have tended to assume that all subsequent relationships derive from it. They see the child as developing personality and social style as a result of experiences with the mother. Although children may later be influenced by relationships outside the family—and obviously the nature of relationships changes—this is seen as gradual and it is assumed that there is a continual link between earlier and later experiences (e.g., Bowlby, 1969). Little account is taken of the possibility that children may have qualitatively different experiences and learn different things in the context of relationships with people other than

161

their mothers. This does not imply that a child's relationship with his/her parents is not important to social development but rather that relationships with others, particularly peers, may be equally so, contributing a different dimension to this development.

It has often been argued that there is a contrast between peer relationships and child–adult relationships (Piaget, 1932; Sullivan, 1953). The child's relationship with adults is usually unequal, with the adult being in a position of authority. Because of this, the adult is more likely to be instructing the child, directly or indirectly, in the rules for social life, such as customs and others' expectations of the child, than negotiating or inventing new social worlds, as a child could do with a peer with whom he/she is on an equal footing. Children come to understand the social world either *through* adults or *with* peers (Youniss, 1980). If children do get a rather different kind of social experience with peers compared to adults, then it is quite likely that the role of peers in social development may indeed be important and possibly different from that of adults. This is particularly true of school-age children who, obviously, spend more time with peers than younger ones. At school, too, children are encouraged to play with, do things with, and compare themselves with other children. For the first time they are confronted with a wide variety of possible relationships and interactions. This they have to learn to cope with, with the help of their peers.

As children construct their social world, an individual child needs to evaluate his/her competence in dealing with it. Because an individual's beliefs, styles of behaviour, and concept of himself or herself are often shared by others, they can be validated by the consensus of those other people (Festinger, 1954). If the people who are chosen as judges do not agree, then either the belief may be changed or different judges chosen, that is, the individual finds new friends or acquaintances. Thus, Duck, Miell, and Gaebler (1980) argue that there is an important functional relationship between friendship and personality in that friendship can be an important process in the development and validation of an individual's personality. However, other types of relationships apart from friendship may also be part of this process and may be more significant in validating different aspects of personality. Research that has looked at aspects of personality and behaviour with peers has concentrated on the correlates of peer acceptance and popularity and the children's behaviour toward peers in general rather than differentiating relationships (e.g., Barnett & Zucker, 1980; Moore & Updegraff, 1964; Smith, Tedeschi, Brown, & Linskold, 1973). Behaviour toward selected others may be rather different from the impression given by the sum of social behaviour to all peers. Similarly, the out-of-context "sum" of personality and social knowledge may give rather a different impression of an individual compared with the picture presented in the context of particular relationships.

Despite the recent upsurge of natural observation of preschool children, there has been almost no observation of this kind of school-age children. Studies that have included observational data have only used limited behavioural categories, usually concentrating on one type of interaction, for example aggressive ones. None of the studies have taken into account the relationship of the participants of the interaction, interactions with all peers being added together. If it is the case that particular relationships are more significant for the development of some aspects of social knowledge and personality than others, then this kind of grouped data could give a very misleading picture. Studies of the links between specific aspects of social interaction and personality or social knowledge carried out in a laboratory or other contrived setting may also give incomplete or misleading information. It is unlikely that personality or social knowledge develop only through experience of relationships in restricted contexts. Particular relationships will have their impact on social development in all the contexts where they occur. Thus a study in a controlled situation may only give information on links between personality, social knowledge, and relationships that specifically emerge in that new context as a result of previous social experience. In order to get a more direct and wider perspective on these links it is, therefore, essential to collect observations of a range of behaviour in its natural context.

This chapter describes some of the results from a study that tried to do just this. As far as is known, this is the first study that has tried to relate personality and social knowledge to social behaviour using extensive observations of children's behaviour as it occurs naturally. The study looks at one particular aspect of personality—self-concept. The self-concept is one of the aspects of personality most likely to be clearly linked to relationships with or treatment by others, because it can be directly validated by others, for example, rejection clearly indicates dislike. Thus if peers do have an important influence on the development of personality, then a child's treatment by them should be associated with his or her self-concept. The study also takes one aspect of social knowledge— conception of friendship. This aspect was picked because it relates to the two types of relationship chosen, within which to look at social behaviour. Children were observed interacting with friends and peers who were not friends. The study will, therefore, help to indicate the importance of peers in social development and of the possible differential significance of two types of relationships.

THE STUDY

Method

The sample consisted of 30 subjects—15 girls and 15 boys—aged between 6 years, $3\frac{1}{2}$ months and 6 years, $4\frac{1}{2}$ months. The distribution of the children's IQs represented that of the general population (girls: mean = 104, sd = 15.3; boys: mean = 100.9, sd = 12.7) and no child was known to have a serious physical or emotional problem. The children were drawn from two schools, coming from five different classes, spread over two academic years. Both schools had a mixed catchment area but most families were upper working class or lower middle class.

Each child was observed continuously for 12 15-minute periods, 6 in the playground and 6 in the classroom, giving a total of 3 hours per child. Observational data from the playground and the classroom were always analyzed separately and this chapter examines the playground data almost exclusively. The situations in the playground and in the classroom were rather different in that in the playground the children could always choose whom they associated with, whereas in the classroom they were often directed to their places by the teacher. Group tasks in the classroom also meant that children often had to interact there with peers regardless of their relationship with them. In the classroom, the main objective is to get work done so many children chose to get on with their work rather than talk to a neighbour and thus had fewer interactions in the classroom than in the playground.

The observations were taken in the form of continuous, verbal description recorded on a small tape recorder, which was then transcribed into a written form. The children's activities were recorded at four levels:

1. *Settings* that described the general types of activity the child was involved in, for example, vigorous play, art.
2. *Social participation* that described the kind of interaction the child was having with his companions or if he was alone.
3. *Instantaneous categories* that described particular activities or verbal exchanges within the settings.
4. *Qualifiers* that are adverbs and described how any behaviour at level 3 was done, for example, with affection, with hostility.

Most of the behaviour categories were similar to those used by Hinde, Easton, Mellor, and Tamplin, (1983).

Although a large number of items of behaviour were recorded, several items were combined into categories for many analyses. The categories relevant to this chapter are described as follows:

Ignoring. A child does not respond to another's overtures, verbal or nonverbal, when there is no doubt that he must have seen or heard them.

Hostile. A child shows verbal or nonverbal aggression.

Control. A child makes any suggestion or request.

Inhibiting/rejecting. A child stops another from doing something, snatches a toy, or refuses to let another child play.

Showing affection. A child shows any physical sign of affection, a verbal indication of it or says something in an affectionate tone.

Helping. A child does something for another or shows them how to do it.
Disagreeing. A child says anything in disagreement, contradiction, or
criticism.

For all instantaneous categories, the name of the child who was the object of the
behaviour was recorded and the subject if the child being observed was the
object. In the case of Control, whether or not the attempt at control was complied
with was also recorded.

In addition to the observations, each child was given three interview or test
sessions. The first session consisted of three tests: verbal IQ, reading and number
tests. The second session was for a self-concept test. This was a 20-item, five-
point rating scale, Q sort as used by Block and Block (1969) and Block (1961).
The test was administered twice — once asking the children what they thought of
themselves and once what they thought their best friend thought of them. Scores
for three of these items—Good at schoolwork, Good at sports, Is attractive in the
way he/she looks—were summed to give a combined score. This score was
assumed to give some indication of the child's self-esteem as physical appearance, ability at sports, and schoolwork are three of the most obvious areas
where a child can compare himself or herself with others. These three items, the
indicator of self-esteem, and the following items—Likes to talk, Likes to try new
things, Helpful, Has lots of ideas, and Happy—are the only ones discussed in
this chapter.

The final session consisted of an informal interview on the child's views and
experiences of friendship. Answers to three questions (Why is X your best
friend? What would the best friend in the world be like? Why do you think
someone wouldn't have any friends?) were categorised into three levels of
friendship conception, similar to those used by Bigelow (1977) and Selman
(1976):

Level 1. Friendship is seen as a momentary, physicalistic affair. A close
friend is someone whom the child likes the look of, who lives next door, or with
whom they are playing at the time.

Level 2. Friendship is seen as a relationship but it is one way only. A child is
a friend if he or she does what is wanted. A close friend may be known better but
this only means knowing likes and dislikes.

Level 3. Friendship is seen as a two-way relationship requiring cooperation
and give and take. However, it may be that there is a lack of conception of
continuity and argument may end the relationship.

For each question, children scored 1 to 3 depending on whether their answers
fell into level 1, 2, or 3. The scores were then summed to give a combined score
representing the overall level of their friendship conception. There were significant correlations between the scores on all three of the questions (r_s 1, 2 = .36, p
< .05; r_s 2,3 = .46, p <.01; r_s 1,3 = .38, p < .05).

Results

Differences in Behaviour Between Friends and Children Who Are Not Friends.   Rates of behaviour with friends and children who were not friends, for all children who had friends available and interacted with them, ($N = 25$ in the playground) were calculated by the following ratios:

$$\frac{\text{Frequency of behaviour with friends}}{\text{Total number of interactions with friends}} \times 10$$

and

$$\frac{\text{Frequency of behaviour with nonfriends}}{\text{Total number of interactions with nonfriends}} \times 10$$

Ignoring was measured as the percentage of approaches by others that were ignored by the child being observed, *being ignored* as the percentage of approaches by the child that were ignored by others. Friends were taken as those children who were named as friends in the interview.

In the playground the children gave to and received less hostility from friends and ignored them less (Fig. 10.1). Although children successfully controlled nonfriends more often than friends, the percentage success rate of all control statements to nonfriends was not significantly different. On the other hand, children both had control attempts made more frequently towards them by friends than nonfriends and were more likely to be controlled successfully by their friends ($p < .05$). There were no significant differences in rates of positive behaviour between friends and children who were not friends (Fig. 10.1).

Self-Concept and Treatment of Peers.   The results indicated an association between self-concept and treatment by peers. Children with a poor view of themselves and low self-esteem suffered the most hostility from others (Table 10.1). This link held both for the children's own assessment of themselves and what they considered their best friend thought of them (social self).

A further indication of a link between the children's view of themselves and their relationship with peers was given by the association between claiming to be happy and several behaviour categories (Table 10.2).

However, it seemed to be the case that self-concept was linked to treatment by peers in general rather than those with whom the children had a particular relationship. The patterns of associations between self-concept measures and behaviour with friends compared with nonfriends in the playground were very similar. Also, there was no relation between number of friends chosen and any of the self-concept measures.

Nevertheless, links between types of social participation and some of the measures did suggest the possibility that friendship may provide a different

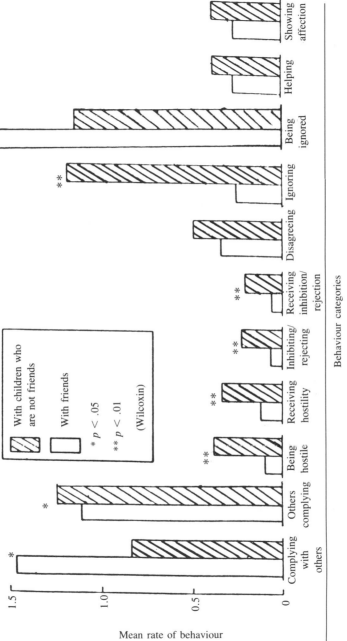

FIG. 10.1 Differences in behaviour between friends and children who are not friends in the playground.

TABLE 10.1
Spearman Rank Correlation Coefficients
Between Self-Concept Measures and Receiving Hostility
($N = 30$)

Measure	Social Self		Own Assessment	
	Classroom	Playground	Classroom	Playground
Self-esteem	$-.40^a$	$-.53^b$	$-.12$	$-.40^a$
Looks attractive	$-.32^a$	$-.39^a$	$-.03$	$-.39^a$
Good at school	$-.26$	$-.62^b$	$-.21$	$-.17$

$^a p < .05.$
$^b p < .01$ (one-tailed test).

context for the development of associations between activities with peers and views of oneself compared with others kinds of relationships. In the playground, interactive play and parallel play showed opposite significant correlations with four measures, depending on whether the play was with friends or nonfriends. Children who said that they liked to talk ($r_s = .38, p < .1$), liked to try new things ($r_s = .52, p < .05$), and thought that they were helpful ($r_s = .41, p < .1$) were more likely to engage in parallel play with their friends. Children who said that they did not like to talk ($r_s = -.40, p < .1$), did not like to try new things ($r_s = -.61, p < .01$), and were not helpful ($r_s = -.43, p < .05$) spent the most time in interactive play with their friends. Children who spent the most time in parallel play with nonfriends said that they had lots of ideas ($r_s = -.55, p < .05$), whereas those who spent the most time in interactive play with nonfriends said that they did not have many ideas ($r_s = -.44, p < .05$).

Friendship Conception and Social Behaviour.   As might have been expected, level of friendship conception was linked to some behaviour categories. Children with a high combined score for friendship conception were more likely

TABLE 10.2
Spearman Rank Correlation Coefficients
Between Claiming to Be Happy
and Treatment by Peers ($N = 30$)

Treatment	Coefficient
Receiving hostility	$-.25$
Receiving inhibition/rejection	$-.55^b$
Being ignored	$-.35^a$
Time spent with others	$-.39^a$

$^a p < .05.$
$^b p < .01$ (one-tailed test).

to organise and tell other children what to do and to ignore them but less likely to be the victims of hostility and to be ignored (Table 10.3).

A more detailed examination of whom the children were interacting with revealed that all of these associations were more marked with nonfriends than with friends. In the playground, rate of successful control and ignoring others were significantly positively correlated ($r_s = .44$, $p < .01$ and $r_s = .36$, $p < .05$) with friendship conception when the others were not friends but not when they were (all $r_s < .2$). Similarly, receiving hostility and inhibition/rejection and being ignored by those who were not friends ($r_s = -.31$, $r_s = -.27$, and $r_s = -.39$; $p < .05$) were negatively correlated but not to the same extent if the children were victims of this kind of behaviour from friends (all $r_s < .2$).

Discussion: Context, Relationships, and Self-Concept

The results from this study suggest that there are links between peer interaction, self-concept, and friendship conception, thus confirming the view that peers, are an important influence on social development. As indicated in the Introduction, much research on social development has assumed that "peer interaction" or "peer relationships" are unitary concepts and as such can be related to other aspects of the child's personality or social style as a whole. The results from this study also suggest that this assumption may not necessarily be justified, since they showed that children's behaviour with friends was different from that with nonfriends and that behaviour with friends was not linked to aspects of self-concept and friendship conception in the same way as behaviour with nonfriends.

The children were found to distinguish between friends and nonfriends by reducing "negative" behaviour toward friends. The children were more likely to be hostile or aggressive and to inhibit, reject, or ignore children who were not friends than friends. Most studies of children's friendships have shown that joint activities of friends are characterised by more positive behaviour, such as sharing, cooperation, or affection (e.g., Aiello & Jones, 1971; Charlesworth & Hartup, 1967; Galejs, 1974). However, the evidence for this is equivocal. For example, Berndt (1981) found no increase in sharing with or helping a friend in a task compared with a nonfriend. On the contrary, boys actually shared less with friends compared with nonfriends. Confusion also arises because most of the relevant studies have been done on preschool children rather than children over 5 years old, and it is not necessarily the case that the friendships of children under 5 are characterised in the same way as those of school-age children. Where older children have been studied (e.g., Berndt, 1981; Chapman, Smith, & Foot, 1980; Foot, Chapman, & Smith, 1977), the results are usually based on the children's behaviour during set tasks rather than free play. These two situations may bring out different aspects of the children's friendships.

A general point emerges from these confusions: Behaviour that characterises a particular relationship may vary from age to age and between different contexts

TABLE 10.3
Spearman Rank Correlation Coefficients Between
Level of Friendship Conception and Behaviour in the
Playground ($N = 30$)

Behaviour Category	Coefficient
Receiving hostility	−.33[a]
Being ignored	−.36[a]
Organising others	.55[a]
Success in controlling others	.41[a]
Ignoring others	.44[b]
Receiving inhibition/rejection	.27

[a] $p < .05$.
[b] $p < .01$ (one-tailed test).

at the same age. It may, therefore, be important to take age and context into account when looking for links between relationships and personality or social knowledge, because the salience of a behaviour within the context of a particular relationship may not remain the same at all times.

The results of this study provide evidence for the interplay between children's developing personality, in this case self-concept, and their interactions with peers. Children with a poor view of themselves tended to suffer from the most rejection and hostility and to claim to be least happy. Since the data were only collected from one age group and at one time, it is not possible to draw any firm conclusion about the development of the self-concept from the results. However, the implication of the findings is that being treated badly by peers is likely to confirm or create a poor self-concept in a child. Rejection by peers acts as a continual validation of the child's poor view of himself or herself. It could be that the self-concept is formed entirely by the experiences that a child has with his or her parents and that both poor self-concept and the characteristic patterns of interaction with peers may derive from a particular kind of parent–child relationship. Nevertheless, if it is the case that children have a relationship with parents different in kind from that with peers, then it is quite likely that the aspects of the self-concept related to peer interaction may also be different. The view of oneself from a dependent role, which is usually the one played by the child to the adult, will not necessarily be appropriate to cope with a more equal relationship, as is usual with peers. It would be very surprising if the increase in interactions and close relationships with peers experienced by children entering school did not have some effect on their developing self-concepts. The results from this study are consistent with this view.

These results did not show different associations between behaviour in one relationship and self-concept as compared with behaviour in a different kind of relationship and self-concept. Children with a poor view of themselves suffered rejection and hostility from friends and nonfriends. However, friendship did seem to provide a special context for links between other aspects of self-concept and types of play. There is an interaction between types of play and relationship with companions resulting in different kinds of associations with the self-concept. Children who said that they liked to talk, try new things, and were helpful tended to engage in parallel play with their friends; whereas those who said that they did not like to do these things and were not helpful tended to play interactively with their friends. In the case of nonfriends, children who played most in parallel with nonfriends said that they had lots of ideas whereas those who spent most time in interactive play said that they did not have many ideas. Although an interpretation of why these particular self-concept items should be related to behaviour in this way is difficult, the picture does emphasise the importance of bearing in mind that not only is the context of the relationship important for its impact on the developing self-concept, but also what the participants regularly do together.

Social knowledge, as exemplified in this study by friendship conception, was also found to be related to peer interaction, but in this case the importance of the context of the relationship was illustrated more clearly. The results show that the children who had the best developed concepts of friendship were the most likely to control or organise others and to ignore them but the least likely to be ignored or be the victims of hostility. However, all these associations were more marked when the children were interacting with others who were not friends rather than with friends. One interpretation of this is that a high level of friendship conception may be more related to general acceptance or success than to behaviour within the specific context of friendship. For example, a child with a low or average level of friendship conception may be as successful as one with a high level in controlling friends because they and their friends see compliance as part of being friends. On the other hand, children with a high level of friendship conception may have more confidence about their social acceptance (they were less likely to be victims of unpleasant behaviour and more likely to ignore others) and may have more knowledge in general about people and so be better able to manipulate everybody, even without the advantage of being friends. Children with a high level of friendship conception may not differ from their peers in terms of having more satisfactory friendships or in the way in which their social development proceeds within the context of those friendships, but they may differ in terms of their competence with the wider peer group.

The findings of this study are consistent with the view that peers have an influence on the development of personality and social knowledge and that this influence may vary depending on the nature of the peer relationship. It is more likely that such interactions between different relationships and aspects of social development will be picked up as a result of observations of children in their natural environment rather than in a setting provided by a researcher. Once it is clearer which relationships and which context (e.g., home or school) have what kind of effect on which aspects of social development and personality, it might be more useful to look at a restricted setting. In the meantime, it is important to bear in mind that not only are peers very likely to play an important role in social development but that the role may vary depending on which peers are focused on and when.

11 The Development of Preferred Relationships in Preschool Children: Child–Child and Child–Adult Relationships

Grazia Attili
Institute of Psychology,
National Research Council,
CNR, Rome, Italy

INTRODUCTION

The study of social relationships of children implies a systematic analysis of the social *objects* the child may come in contact with as well as of the social *functions* these objects may have. In fact, even if similar social objects can be characterized by similar functions, there need not be a direct relation between object and function. For instance, in spite of the fact that "the mother" (an object) and "behaving like a mother" (a function) have often been considered highly correlated terms, some recent studies seem to indicate that other figures such as fathers or grandparents are just as adequate in carrying out this function.

Until the beginning of the 1970s, the influences of the psychoanalytic model, with its emphasis on relationships with adults, and of Piagetian theory, with its emphasis on the egocentric nature of the child's intelligence, discouraged research in social development aimed at studying the formation of relationships other than the mother–child relationship. This more-or-less exclusive focus of research on the mother as a preferred social object has resulted in an impoverished view of social functions and in a lack of systematic analyses. If functions like "feeding," "protecting," or "taking care" are the only ones taken into consideration it may seem meaningful to study the mother (or the father) as the most important (and, perhaps, the only) social object. In the life of a small child, however, other social functions can be traced, such as "play" and "exploration," with respect to which social objects other than his/her mother might turn out to be more appropriate. This very awareness has stimulated a renewed interest in peer relations (e.g., Asher & Gottman, 1981; Foot, Chapman, & Smith, 1980; Hinde, Easton, Meller, & Tamplin, 1983).

173

What is being stressed, particularly by developmental psychologists, is the importance for a child of having relationships with people who are at an equal level of maturity (cf. Bronson, 1975b). To relate with other children on a similar level permits the growth of differentiated behaviours and social responses appropriate to and effective in different situations through direct experimentation with inappropriate behaviours. Behaviours like rough play or aggression, for instance, can have the function of training the young child in self-defence or attack (where appropriate) but are immediately inhibited in interaction with adults.

In interactions, particularly in friendship relations among peers based on reciprocity and a two-way rapport, there is, however, ample room for those behaviours that are functional in the development of social competence (Hartup, 1975, 1978a, 1978b), or such capacities as interpersonal perception, self-understanding and sensitivity to others' behaviours (Hinde et al., 1983; Youniss, 1980).

Few studies have analyzed the nature and determinants of positive social relations among preschool children, especially how preferred relationships are formed and develop over time (Attili, Hold, & Schleidt, 1982). Nor have studies examined the extent to which peer relations differ from relations children establish with adults (Hinde et al., 1983), in order to individuate the social functions that these different social objects carry out in children's lives.

Even if adult–child and child–child systems appear to influence each other (Vandell & Mueller, 1980), the differences already found between them, even in younger children, (e.g., Bronson, 1975a; Vandell, 1980), would argue for a functional independence between them (Attili, 1983; Attili & Camaioni, 1983). This does not rule out the possibility that individual differences in social behaviour directed at a strange adult and at a peer might be affected to a certain extent by prior relations the child experienced at home (Hinde et al., 1983) and vice versa, but it does imply that children need to engage in accurate social reality testing in their interactions (Foot et al., 1980) as well as to acquire security from an adult.

THE PRESENT STUDY

The research reported here is a longitudinal study based on direct observation of children's social behaviour and designed to achieve various objectives. The first objective was to verify if and to what extent children between ages 3 and 4, attending a preschool, are able to establish specific relationships among themselves, whose intensity and nature would qualify them as preferred relationships. Children attending a preschool were used because a preschool is one of the places where children are confronted simultaneously with strange adults and strange peers.

In sociometric studies (where friendship among children has been most studied), each child has to identify a number of his/her best friends (Miller & Maruyama, 1976), but the differing degrees of acquaintanceship or the positive affect that characterize the child's relationships are not examined, ignoring what is a continuous dimension of friendly affect (Foot et al., 1980). Furthermore, this approach tends to polarize all the remaining children into a homogeneous group of nonfriends. A second objective, therefore, has been to analyze the development of these friends' relationships, or preferred relationships, to verify if this differentiation is stable over time and if this stability is correlated with the degree of acquired familiarity so that it provides a dimension of continuity in the transition from not being friends to being friends, and vice versa. The present study also attempts to analyze the differences between the preferred relationships established with peers and those established with the adult (teacher) in order to relate them to the different functions these relationships carry out. Other questions concern the extent to which the ability to establish preferred relationships with both adults and peers might be correlated to a broader degree of sociability. Finally, the study examines the nature of social behaviour directed toward the adult and toward the peer, when preferred partners and the influence of familiarity on it.

Method

Setting and Subjects.   Although the present study is an exploratory one with a small sample, the results are based on a considerable amount of observation for each subject and show some significant differences as well as trends in line with the literature on childrens' social behaviour and sex difference. The study was conducted in a preschool located in a central part of Rome inside a large public park. It involved 23 children (9 girls and 14 boys) ranging in age from 3 to 5 years, attending the same preschool class but partly newcomers and partly already familiar with one another. The analysis of the preferred relationships formed inside the class was based on observing the behaviours shown by 8 children (4 boys and 4 girls) ranging in age from 3 to 4 years (mean age: 40 months) who were all newcomers to the class and had no previous experience of a day nursery. All the children belonged to upper-middle-class families, defined on the basis of the parents' level of education, income, and the part of town they lived in, according to the indexes used by Hollingshead and Redlich (1958).

Data Collection.   Each focal child was observed for 8 months, that is, from the first day of school to the end of the school year. There were two 5-minute videotape observation sessions per week for each child. Owing to normal absences from school during the year, there were between 36 and 41 (with an average of 38) observational sessions with an average of 190 minutes of observation for each child. The observations were always performed at the same time (from 10 to 11 A.M.) when children were inside their classroom with the same teacher and, for the most part, were allowed to play freely.

Coding Procedure and Data Analysis.   Tape recordings were usually transcribed on the same day using a coding scheme including 83 behavioural units grouped into 43 broader comprehensive categories. For each observed social exchange, the initiator, his/her action, the target, and the target's response as well as the identities of the two nearest neighbours were always noted. The reliability of the use of the complete coding inventory was high: Comparisons between two trained observers who coded social interactions from the same videotape recording of preschool free play gave agreement scores exceeding $X = 80\%$.

The number of behavioural categories was subsequently reduced both by eliminating some rarely used or unreliable items and by intuitively grouping other ones in broader categories. The final list had 17 categories, including positive social contact (A), negative social contacts (B), and neutral contacts (AB) (see Table 11.1). Total interactions of focal children with adult and peers were assessed.

The data analysis was based on the relative frequency of behaviour shown by each child to others in each of the three terms of the school year (each term being roughly the same length). Relations between items were assessed by Spearman rank order correlations; differences were assessed by Student's two-tailed test, the X2 test, and Fisher's exact probability test.

Results

Two Determinants of Interaction Frequency.   Initially, two questions were asked: First, were the children who had a greater number of interactions with peers also the ones who had a greater number of interactions with adult, or were the two phenomena not related?

Second, was the frequency of adult-oriented and peer-oriented behaviours correlated not so much with the actual amount of time spent together (shared attendances) as with the degree of familiarity measured by the duration of time since first meeting? As far as is known, these two issues regarding familiarity— as measured by temporal duration of acquaintance and by frequency of shared attendances—have not previously been distinguished in studies of friendship.

Adults Versus Peers as Targets of Interaction.   I found that boys who interacted more with peers tended to interact less with the adult ($r_s = -0,80, p < .5$) while in contrast, the girls who interacted more with peers also interacted more with the adult ($r_s = 1.00, p < .001$).

TABLE 11.1
Categories of Preschoolers' Social Behavior.
A: Positive, B: Negative, AB: Neutral Social Contact

Behaviour	Description
A	
Proximity	Within arm's length of another child
Look	$\geq$ 3 sec
Parallel play	The same game with two objects; it is not clear who started the play
Social play	The same game, with same object, alternating roles: it is not clear who started the play. Interactive play
Imitative play	The same game (with an object or role game) and it is clear that is an imitation of somebody else who started it
Contact-seeking behaviour	Offering objects, smiling, laughing with eye contact, attention-seeking behaviour (showing, inviting to look, calling by name)
Approaching	Moving toward, following
Body contact	Showing affection, embracing, kissing, caressing, comforting with gestures, body touching
Distal behaviour	Supporting, comforting verbally, starting a verbal interaction (asking, telling), agreeing or allowing verbally, inviting to play verbally
B	
Object conflict	Taking on object or trying to take it or resisting taking it away
Dominant aggression	Ordering, forbidding, excluding, contradicting
Avoidance	Going away, because aggressed or ignored. Sometimes approaching again within 30-sec period.
Aggression	Aggressive behavior patterns with body contact or verbally (insulting, threatening)
AB	
Rough-and-tumble play	Wrestling match with a smiling face
Playful aggression	Teasing, irritating with a smiling face
Dominant acts	Initiating role or object games or activities, or proposing games (successfully), explaining something
Subordinate acts	Compliance, obeying

For most of the children (seven out of eight), there was a significant positive correlation between attendances shared with peers and amount of interactions during the first term, while by the third term for most of the children (six out of eight) there was no longer any significant correlation. For all the girls, the correlation ceased to be significant by the third term. With regard to interactions with the adult, however, there was no significant correlation with number of shared attendances for either term. The differences here may reflect the different nature of children's relationship with peers and with adults, the latter being dependent in character so that children to some extent *have* to interact with the teacher.

Preferred Partners.   Preferred partners were operationally defined as having at least 10% of the focal child's other-directed behaviour directed toward them.

This fitted in with observers' intuitive judgments, as well as a distribution of interaction, which meant that preferred partners were receiving more than the mean number of interactions from the focal child.

Adult Versus Peers as Preferred Partners.   With the above criterion as a basis, it was found that both boys and girls showed a tendency to have as preferred partners both the adult and their peers during the first term while during the third term all the boys had only peers ($p < .001$) and just some girls still had both as preferred partners.

Presented in this way, the data underrepresent the importance of the adult as a preferred partner because each child could have had up to 10 preferred partners in each term, but only one adult was available. When the preference criterion was reached by both the adult and one or more peers, it was the adult who was the more "chosen" of the two in every term except for boys in the third term who chose only peers.

As for the number of preferred partners, the number of children who were preferred partners tended to increase over time, while the adult was increasingly less a preferred partner.

Are Children Who Had Preferred Partners More Sociable in General? Results showed a positive although not a significant correlation between the occurrence of peer- (PP) and adult-oriented (PA) choices (boys $r_s = .10$, girls $r_s = .65$); an inverse correlation was instead found between the selection of preferred partners (peers or the adult) and a more generalized sociability (SB) (PP/SB boys $r_s = -.65$, girls $r_s = -.40$; PA/BS boys $r_s = -.85$, girls $r_s = -.85$).

The children who had the adult or peers more frequently as their preferred partner were those who had less interaction overall with their peers.

Consistency of Relationships with Preferred Partners.   There were 33 relationships between focal children and peers that reached the 10% criterion (see foregoing discussion) in at least one term, and 7 with the adult. These relationships could involve either close preferred partners (a three-term relationship), sporadic preferred partners (a single-term relationship), or maintained preferred partners (a two-term relationship).

For both peers and adults, close relationships (CR) were less frequent than maintained ones (MR) and sporadic relations (SR) were more frequent than either. For peers, increasing preferred relationships (IPR)—that is, relationships that increase in time, either starting from a condition of nonpreference ($< 10\%$) and reaching in the third term the criterion threshold for being considered preferred relations ($> 10\%$) or starting out with an existing preference condition and growing with time—were more frequent than decreasing preferred relationships (DPR)—that is, either those reaching a condition of nonfriendship in the third term, or those that might have considered friendship relationships but with time underwent a process of involution—($p < .02$); but adult–preferred relationships were all decreasing relationships. In one case, the adult was never selected as a preferred partner (NR).

Nature of Social Behaviour Directed to Preferred Partners of Different Types. Here are considered the relationships with the adult and the children when either were selected in any of the three school terms as preferred partners (children: 50 times, the adult: 11 times). The only behaviours considered were those shown to the preferred partners with a frequency of at least 10% of the frequency with which those behaviours were shown to all other possible partners.

Behaviours Shown to Peer-Preferred Partners: Sex Differences. Figure 11.1 shows the percentage number of child-child couples (based on 50 child–child dyads) sharing a preferred relationship and showing behaviours that comply with the criterion percentage. The behaviours are shown in the order of their total frequency in boys and correspond to the categories described in Table 11.1.

For both sexes, Proximity, Contact Seeking Behaviours, Looking, and Social Play were among the most frequent behaviours. There were negligible differences between boys and girls for most behaviours. However, there were indications of differences in behaviour style. For girls, Body Contact and Distal Behaviour were more common than Contact Seeking Behaviour, and Body Contact was more common than Distal Behaviour. For boys, Contact Seeking Behaviour was more common than the other two.

With regard to the three types of play, boys showed more Social Play than Parallel Play ($t = 3.06$, $p < .005$) or Imitative Play, but there were no differences for girls.

Behavior Shown to Adult When a Preferred Partner: Sex Differences. Many types of behaviour common in interactions with peers were absent or infrequent in interactions with the adult (Fig. 11.2).

The only behaviour frequent in both sexes were Approaching, Looking, Body Contact, Avoidance, and Actual Proximity. In girls, Contact Seeking Behaviour and Distal Behaviour were also common. The sex differences were significant only for Distal Behaviour ($t = 2.34$, $p < .005$).

Approaching and Following significantly characterized relations with adults ($t = 5.58$, $p < .001$), and Distal Behaviour tended to occur more often in girl–adult dyads than in girl–peer dyads, while it tended to occur more often in boy–peer interaction than in boy–adult interaction. Body Contact tended to occur more often in boy–adult dyads than in boy–peer dyads and more in girl–peer dyads than in girl–adult dyads.

Increasing and Decreasing Relationships: Influence of Familiarity. The next concern was with the transition from not being to being preferred partners

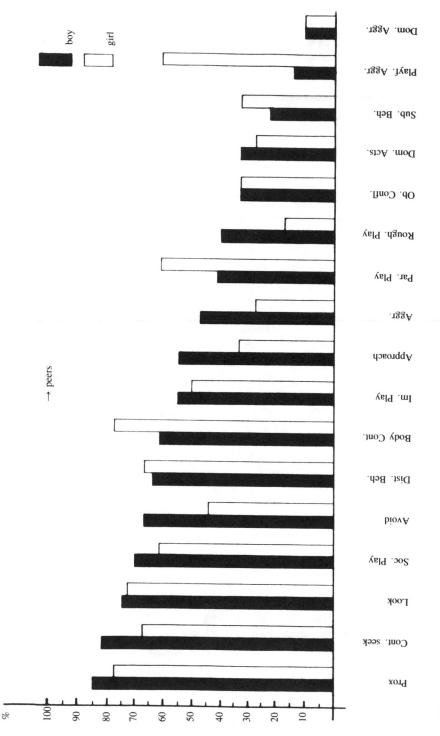

FIG. 11.1. Behaviors directed toward peers chosen as preferred partners (percentages calculated on 50 child–child dyads; for significance of T tests see text).

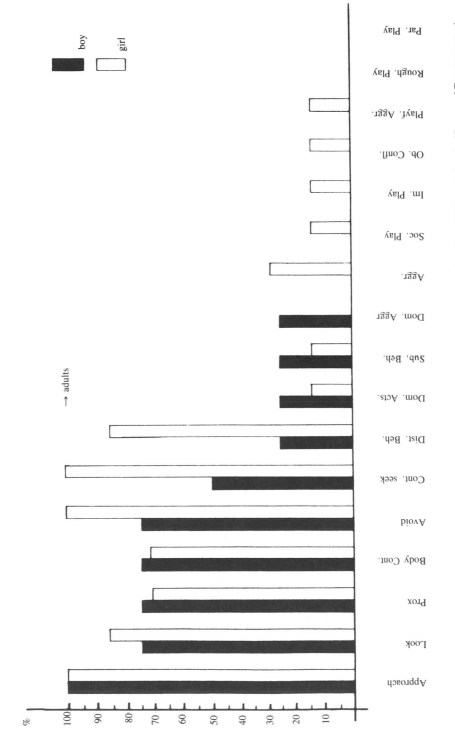

FIG. 11.2. Behaviors directed toward adults chosen as preferred partners (percentages calculated on 11 adult–child dyads; for significance of T tests see text).

(let's label them friends) and vice versa. This meant looking at relationships that became preferred relationships only in the third term (IR $N = 13$), and those that reached the criterion of 10% of interactions in the first term but ceased to be a preferred relationship by the third term (DR $N = 8$)

Are the two types of change accompanied by differences in the behaviour shown? Furthermore, we can ask whether familiarity affects the behaviour shown first by comparing friendships that appear in the first and in the third term and second by comparing the behaviour shown in the first term before the friendships appear, and the behaviour shown in the last term after the friendship ceased to exist. Let us compare first the behaviour in child–child dyads who reached the criterion of a preferred relationship in the first term (DR) with the behaviour shown in preferred relationships achieved only in the third term (IR). Imitative Play, Approaching and Following, Object Conflict, Body Contact, Playful Aggression, and Aggression were more common in first-term friendships than in third-term friendships. Conversely, Proximity, Looking, and Social Play were more common in third term preferred relationships.

Second, behaviours frequent in first term friendships need familiarity to appear outside a friendship, so that they were not always found if friendship was yet to come, in the first phase of an IR, but they were still present when there was no longer any friendship, in the last phase of a DR. The increased number of preferred partners in the third term necessarily resulted in a lower frequency of interaction in each case. Social play became much more common than parallel and imitative play in third-term friendships, whereas in the first-term friendships, these three types of play were equally frequent. Furthermore, whereas social play was the type of play more present (imitative play did not appear at all) in the first phase of a relationship that leads to a friendship, imitative play was more present and parallel play did not appear any more when the friendship ceased to exist.

In the relationships with the adult ($N = 8$, including *all* relationships), most behaviours follow the decreasing trend of the relation, so that many did not appear at all in the last term. Object Conflict and Dominant Aggression were present only in the second term; Dominant Acts, Subordinate Behaviours, Contact Seeking Behaviours, and Distal Behaviours increased in the second term and diminished in the third term. The second term seemed to be a critical time for allowing more complex patterns of interaction to emerge.

SUMMARY AND CONCLUSIONS

The present study set out to examine the differences between preferred relationships that preschool children establish with the adult (teacher) and/or with peers. Amongst other things, I found that an inverse correlation existed between peer-directed social behaviour and adult-directed social behaviour in the boys and a positive and significant correlation in the girls. Furthermore, girls had both adults and peers as preferred partners more than the boys. As for the development of relationships and occurrence of preference, however, both the boys and the girls moved from a greater preference for the adult in the first term to an almost exclusive preference for the peers in the third term. Only the girls continued to be oriented toward the adult even in the third term; while preference for peers, in terms of the number of choices made, increased over time, preference for the adult decreased.

The fact that the children did not select just peers until the third term, when they had become familiar with both the physical and social environment, may be interpreted as evidence of the independence of function that the two relations perform; the relation with the adult (even a stranger) seemed to satisfy those needs for security and protection elicited by a nonfamiliar situation and nonfamiliar interactants (as happened in the first part of the year). After this, relationships with peers were preferred, because they are more useful in the development of interpersonal perception and sensitivity to the other's signals.

This would also explain why all the relationships with the adult decreased over time in terms of frequency of interaction while the greater part of the relations with peers increased. In addition, it would explain why, at the level of content of interaction, in relationships with the adult, there were either very few or no behaviours that implied a reciprocity or symmetry in turn taking, like those used in play. More prevalent were the behaviours aimed at seeking contact, behaviours that also characterize mother–child attachments (Ainsworth & Bell, 1970; Ainsworth, Bell, & Stayton, 1974; Bowlby, 1969, 1973)) and relate fundamentally to the need for security.

The particular behaviours common to both relations were maintaining contact, showing affection, and starting or continuing social interactions like looking, starting verbal interaction, and telling a story—all of which seem to express a preferentiality in selection that is independent of the interactant.

The girls were more adult oriented than the boys, and they used a broader spectrum of behaviours with adult than with peers. Girls expressed their preference for the adult through verbal interaction and requests for attention more than the boys and more than they did with peers, and they expressed their preference for the adult also through negative types of behaviour—or both negative and positive—such as conflict for objects, playful and teasing provocation, and aggressive behaviour, both verbal and nonverbal. These male–female differences confirm on a qualitative level what we have found on a quantitative level.

This finding is confirmed by other observational types of research work (Blurton-Jones, 1972; Hinde et al., 1983; Lott, 1974). It should be made clear, however, as Hinde et al., (1983) point out, that the adult (the teacher) in these studies was always a woman, so we do not know what the results would be if there were a male adult in the preschool. Also, it might be the differentiating behaviour of the adult with the boys and the girls that produces this diversity of response in the two sexes. Most of the research to date has shown differences in the responsivity of the adults to boys and girls, whether the adults be the mothers or fathers or the preschool teachers (Alfgren, Aries, & Oliver, 1979; Clarke-Stewart, 1973; Smith & Green, 1975). This naturally does not exclude the possibility that the differing behavior of boys and girls could in turn provoke a differing response in the part of the adult (Attili & Camaioni, 1981). For example, many studies reviewed by Maccoby and Jacklin (1974) attribute the greater tendency on the part of the girls to interact more with the adult to a greater dependency present in girls.

In my view, an explanation might be found in a tendency on the part of the girls as well as of the boys to select the person more able to transmit information consistent with the social and biological role that they must assume (thus the older person of the same sex) and who can most readily enable them to perform acts aimed at fulfilling this role. This interpretation finds support in a tendency from both females and males to prefer among older children partners of same rather than opposite sex (Attili et al., 1982).

As for peers, the trend toward greater aggressiveness in boys (Abramovitch, Corter, & Land, 1979; Brodzinski, Messer, & Tew, 1979), the greater amount in girls of friendly behaviour expressed in body contact (Hinde et al., 1983; Whiting & Edwards, 1973) and of verbal interaction, and the greater presence in the boys of interactive type of play (Hinde et al., 1983), compared to the imitative or parallel play (in the girls all three were equally present), the greater presence in boys of approaching and following (Emmerich, 1971; McIntyre, 1972) and of contact-seeking behaviour were trends that did not reach statistical significance in this study. With regard to body contact and contact-seeking behaviour, Bronson (1975b) did not find any sex difference in a sample of younger children. What was instead significant was a greater frequency of rough-and-tumble play in the boys and more playful provocation of aggressive acts in the girls.

Finally, looking at the influence of familiarity on the content of a preferred relationship in the development from not being friends to being friends and vice versa, it seemed that familiarity had a great effect on behaviours like look, approach, following, conflict over objects, the expression of affection through body contact, and imitative play. These behaviours recurred very often even when a relation was *no longer* a preferred one but the familiarity was high, while they were very seldom in evidence *before* a relationship had become preferred and when the children were not yet familiar with the physical and social environment (first term). With the exception of proximity, look, and social play, all of which seemed to be present more often when there was more familiarity as well as greater friendship (third term), all other behaviours that characterize friendship were found more frequently in those pairs that formed a friendship "at first sight" (in the first term) than in those whose friendship had grown with time (in the third term).

It would seem that in the first term the social roles are still to be negotiated so that it is necessary for the children to engage in more complex interactions, while in a friendship which occurs in the third term, the roles are already established, and children are more free to be involved almost entirely in interactive social play.

ACKNOWLEDGMENTS

This work was carried out with the support of the National Research Council of Italy Grant. 104480/10/8205551.

The data discussed in this chapter are part of a more comprehensive project that is a transcultural study of social behavior in Italian and German children. The part of this project involving Germany is led by Barbara Hold and Margret Schleidt, of the Max-Planck Institut fuer Verhaltensphysiologie, Forschungsstelle fuer Humanethologie, Seewiesen, W. Germany.

I am very grateful to the principal, the teachers, and the children of the public preschool Scuola Materna Statale "Contardo Ferrini," experimental section, Forte Antenne, Roma, for their cooperation.

I am also very grateful to Raffaele Felaco and Norberto Pizzo, who helped in data collection and videotape transcription, to Rodolfo Nencini and Dario Salmaso for their suggestions for the statistical analysis, and to Wanda Bronson and Robert A. Hinde, for their helpful comments to the manuscript.

IV DISORDER AND REPAIR OF RELATIONSHIPS

12

Attribution in the Termination of Close Relationships: A Special Focus on the Account

John H. Harvey
Texas Tech University

Ann L. Weber
University of North Carolina at Asheville

Kathryn S. Galvin
Texas A & M University

Heather C. Huszti
Nettie N. Garnick
Texas Tech University

INTRODUCTION

Back in the mid-1970s, George Levinger (1977) concluded a perceptive essay on close relationships in our time by suggesting that a possible major reason for relationship dilemmas was people's inarticulateness in addressing issues in their relationships. No doubt that suggestion still is generally tenable today. However, we feel that people are increasingly becoming verbal, if not articulate, in trying to understand their relationship problems. The spoken and written records that they are providing form what we believe is a foundation for a useful literature concerned with an attributional approach to relationship breakdown.

At various points in a lifetime, an individual asks "why" questions about a significant other, the course of relationship events, or even about oneself vis-à-vis close relationships. Questions such as the following are common: "Why does he do those things that he knows will hurt me?" "Why is she so stubborn and selfish?" "Why can't I live without her?" "Why did we fight about such petty matters?" Not only do individuals ask "why" questions, but they also provide answers. They explain how events occurred; they depict others and themselves; and they tell stories often containing a rich array of plots, characters, and patterns of interaction. These stories have been referred to as accounts by Robert S. Weiss (1975) in his work on marital separation and by attribution investigators including Orvis, Kelley, and Butler (1976) and Harvey, Wells, and Alvarez (1978). To clarify a little what constitutes an account, we are emphasizing the storylike character of accounts often containing multiple interpretations and inferences. Thus, singular attributions about other (e.g., "he is a bastard") or self or singular cause–effect statements (e.g., "he made me cry") would not constitute accounts in our view. Surely these are lines in the script, but the script typically has many lines.

We argue here that as self-reports, accounts are a valuable means for understanding the actors and events of a close relationship. Accounts provide clues about the individual respondents, the groups with whom they are involved, and the historical contexts surrounding them. They also provide clues about the gamut of psychological processes attendant to the termination of close relationships—from penetrating rational analysis to unmitigated panic and fright.

Although of recent advent, attributional research using free response or archival techniques is beginning to appear in the literature (e.g., Felson & Ribner, 1981; Harvey, Yarkin, Lightner, & Town, 1980; Lau & Russell, 1980; Peterson, 1980; Wong & Weiner, 1981). Accounts given for relationship problems, however, have only begun to receive the attention they deserve. They are rich specimens of attribution and should be amenable to careful analysis and empirical scrutiny. We provide some of that analysis in this chapter.

EXAMPLES OF ACCOUNTS

Some of the best illustrative evidence of accounts are found in Weiss' (1975) reports from people in the process of marital separation and in Hunt's (1969) records of accounts given by persons reflecting on extramarital affairs in which they had been involved. The first example is from Weiss (1975) as he quotes a man in his late 30s:

> I've been on a yo-yo. My wife would come up for the weekend and wow, we'd have a hell of a time. And then Monday she'd go back to her school, leaving me with the children. And I know she has somebody there. And then I wouldn't hear anything, no phone call. So I would say, "Jesus, I must have been lousy." I must have been a terrible lover, or I just didn't do this right or that right or, you know, all kinds of thoughts go through your head. And you feel really lousy. And no phone calls, no nothing. And this went on until just recently. And she came up and she was in such a hurry to get back that I said, "Once you leave, just stay away" [p. 35].

Sometimes, as in Hunt's examples (1969), accounts are a means of articulating self-awareness as a result of relationship events:

My outlook on life was completely changed by what happened. The affair made me aware of my own need to think and to communicate with someone I am deeply in love with. Before, I was asleep; ever since, I have been awake—and living with a sense of incompleteness. Yet I do not regret what happened. I would rather *know*, and not have what I want, than live out my life without ever having known. But it's so difficult. For a whole year I haven't been able to tell my husband I love him, not even in bed. . . . There was a time when I looked forward to my future with him when the children would be older and on their own; now I try not to think of that future. We don't quarrel, and he loves me in his own way, but I don't know how to survive within this marriage [p. 93].

Another example from Hunt better illustrates the type of account that addresses "why things happened the way they did"—in this case, why an affair took place:

Who could ever imagine anything like that happening to my marriage? My husband was the squarest, straightest of men—a deacon in the church, a Little League Dad, a Cub Scoutmaster, a non-drinking, crew-cut junior executive. But I let it happen: Our marriage had become nothing but a kind of corporate enterprise without my ever taking time to wonder about it. How it got that way I don't know. It seemed as if we were so busy with children. the house, and local activities, that we never paid any attention to each other; we never said anything real to each other. As for sex, I was bored by it. I felt I could live nicely forever without it, and tried to avoid it as much as possible. I hardly ever thought about any of this, but when I did, I told myself that every marriage goes through phases of this sort and there was nothing to worry about. I was living in never-never land, refusing to see the truth or do anything about it [pp. 233–234].

Accounts are not exclusive to marital relationships. In her book on women and depression, Maggie Scarf (1980) documents many accounts of conflicted and ended relationships among the unmarried. In this example, a 28-year-old woman reflects on the possible causes of the demise of a long-term on-again, off-again relationship with a man who "would not make a commitment" to her:

I was more mature, in many ways, than Philip was. . . . It was as if I had, in some way, a stronger sense of who I was . . . and this was, I think, threatening to him. So he would push me away and be rejecting. And yet . . . I always understood. I understood this, and didn't drag him into long hassles about it; I was pretty tolerant. . . . With Philip, though, it was the first time . . . I ever became that involved. And yet it didn't work out. I *knew*, almost at once, that it wouldn't work [p. 221]

The authors related the foregoing stories to therapists and writers—somewhat impartial audiences—and not at all typical for most accountmaking. As we note later, the nature of the audience has a shaping influence on the style of the account. Consider the self-justification in the following account from Feirstein (1982), given to the subject's closest male friend by a 32-year-old man on the verge of divorce:

> Your goals change. The things you want out of life change. When Beth and I got married, I was 26 and she was everything I ever wanted. She was pretty. She cooked. She dressed beautifully. But then things changed. Some people get fat after they get married. Others let themselves go. Beth stopped growing. She was brought up to be pretty and get married—and now that I'm 32, being pretty and cooking well just isn't enough. . . . The problem is how can I work with bright, intelligent women all day long and then go home at night to the young bride? It just doesn't work. It's too hard to get ahead alone today. I don't want to keep dragging somebody through life [p. 46].

As a final example of the diversity of accounts, it is important to note that with media influence in our culture, certain "themes" recur in accounts, perhaps patterned after popular movies and songs. Plot structures may be borrowed from these media themes to give closure to one's personal experiences. Russianoff (1982) quotes one of her 20-year-old female patients in this regard:

> Two years ago, there was this disco hit, "Victim," and the words were about this woman whose boyfriend dumped her. And he had always been unfaithful to her, anyway. And she just hates being a victim, but she knows she'll be back in the same boat, anyway, because every time she turns around she's back in love again. I identified like crazy with this song, playing it over and over. It was kind of the story of my life. And at the same time, I had just broken up with this guy who was fooling around, just like in the song, and I was determined never to be the victim of a man again. That's what I thought. But at the same time, I was looking for another man, you know? [p. 41].

MAIN CHARACTERISTICS OF ACCOUNTS

Perhaps the most fundamental characteristic of an account is that it often has all of the components of dramatic presentation such as plot, characters, scenes, lines, on-stage happenings, behind-the-scenes happenings, and so on. As such, accounts are similar to what Abelson (1976) has called scripts and to the elements of self-presentation in everyday life according to Goffman (1959). In this story form, accounts serve as summaries of action, thought, and feelings that stretch across time and different people and that embody many levels of intensity and currents of direction. Somewhat similar versions of accounts are provided by the sociologists Scott and Lyman (1968) and by Harré (1981) in presenting the so-called ethogenic position in social psychology. Also, it is possible to construe

Bartlett's (1932) venerable research on the effect of social factors on forgetting as containing seeds of an accounts perspective.

We suggest that an individual develops an account much as if he or she is searching for hypotheses to fit the data: The best fitting story will "explain" it all, and will become the (current) True Story. An account that maintains that a relationship was "wrong from the start" will have different implications from one which plays on a theme of "wrong place, wrong time" or "just one of those things." As an individual experiences more than one close relationship, the accounts may add up and even influence each other. Given the time necessary for one to "rack up" such experience and to require review of it, we should also recognize that such emotion-laden thought packages probably develop around midlife for most people and then become wedged in memory, remaining with the individual to the grave.

The "When" of Accounts

While accounts are formulated at other times than breakdown—such as at the beginning of a commitment or of a period of conflict—it is during the dissolution period that accounts become a matter of personal history. Now that the story has a formal ending, the author may go back and "flesh out" the characters and events so that they *predict* the outcome. Hindsight should be 20-20 vision. Accounts are formed to make retrospective sense out of what may have been quite beyond understanding while it was happening.

Our argument about when accounts occur seems consistent with the reports of Weiss' (1975) respondents. These individuals indicated that their most pronounced period of trying to make sense out of their marital troubles was immediately prior to, and for months and even years after, actual separation. Also congenial to the argument are recent data collected by Schwarz and Clore (1982) suggesting that negative mood states—which are far more frequent than the euphoria sometimes accompanying separation—are more likely to stimulate active attributional processing than positive mood states.

The basic assumption behind the argument that accounts occur most frequently around the time of the end of relationships is that account making serves the human's drive for homeostasis in all physical and psychological systems. Accounts often represent the product of the psychological process of a search for a level of tranquilizing understandings. And this point takes us to the "Whys" of accounts.

The "Whys" of Accounts

Quest for Understanding and Control. Any adequate characterization of accounts will reveal a breadth of motivation involved in their use. At the most basic level, accounts involve quests for understanding. Weiss (1975) addresses this motivation as follows:

The account is of major psychological importance to the separated, not only because it settles the issue of who was responsible for what, but also because it imposes on the confused marital events that preceded the separation a plot structure with a beginning, middle, and end and so organizes the events into a conceptually manageable unity. Once understood in this way, the events can be dealt with: They can be seen as outcomes of identifiable causes and, eventually, can be seen as past, over, and external to the individual's present self. Those who cannot construct accounts sometimes feel that their perplexity keeps them from detaching themselves from the distressing experiences . . . [p. 15].

Accounts may be like rumors or "urban legends" in that they seek to satisfy a need for simple understanding even if they are in fact simplistic or outright inaccurate. The account sometimes leaves out ambiguity and confusion and retells a tale in black and white, for the purpose of tying together all the loose ends. Consider the following account in Weiss (1975), in which the narrator, a man in his 30s, reduces complicated event sequences into simplistic cause-effect statements:

One of the events that led to my divorce was my brother's death. No question about it. That's a very tough thing, the first time you lose somebody you are close to. I mean friends die, but I was never affected by it, not like that. But my brother was the closest person I had. I was very, very grief-stricken when he died. And my reaction was to bury myself in work. I took on a very heavy project which I should never have taken on. It took me two and a half years, during which I paid no attention to my wife's needs, all I did was work. . . . I'm sure of it. There is no question in my mind that is what happened in my relationship with my wife. And then she found a lover, because I wasn't home [p. 16].

Many of the suddenly separated describe the breakup in terms of "a shot out of the blue" or "the world crashing down around me." For such persons, accounts contribute to a sense of gaining some control over the emotional vicissitudes of separation and a sense of predictability about the future. They search their memories of past experiences for some missed clue or advance warning. The postbreakup account may be a report on such clues, finally unearthed, as in, "Now I know what it was! Now I understand why it ended—and it won't surprise me again!" Consider the following account from Weiss by the man in his 30s:

I didn't know anything was really wrong. It was like a bomb dropping. Oh, we had been married, a lot of years, and I knew we had a couple of problems, but I would say, "I feel sorry for all these people who are married and the marriage gets very dull. We still love each other." And we did, you know, in terms of sex. That is why it was such a bomb falling on me. Now I see it was there all the time, but our way of communicating was so poor that it just never got to me [p. 28].

The Presentational Motive.   While accounts may have as a principal function the clarifying effect that Weiss noted, we believe that they fulfill several other functions as well. Most important, accounts have a social–presentational function. To a variety of publics, people present the stories of their relationships. They present these constructions sometimes simply for purposes of information. Perhaps more often, people present their stories as a means of influencing others, and these influence attempts may take a variety of forms.

A recent analysis by Jones and Pittman (1982) cogently outlines various tactics people use across different types of situations, including: ingratiation, self-promotion, exemplification, and supplication. In ingratiation, the ingratiator is viewed as concerned with influencing others to like him or her. Behavioral tendencies toward conformity, favor doing, and other enhancement may serve the ingratiator's goal. In self-promotion, the actor presumably seeks the attribution of competence by the other. Jones and Pittman cite Ringer's 1973 book *Winning Through Intimidation* as highlighting many of the ploys and mannerisms people may use to convince others they are worthy or their time, attention, or business. In exemplification, the actor seeks to project integrity and moral worthiness. The exemplifier may present the self as honest, disciplined, charitable, self-abnegating, or as a martyr for a cause. Finally, in supplication, the actor may attempt to exploit personal weakness or dependence. Jones and Pittman suggest that by stressing personal inability and emphasizing dependence on others, the supplicant makes salient a norm of obligation or social responsibility. Thus, supplication is the strategy of advertising one's dependence in order to solicit help.

Each and all of these tactics may be found in account making. For example, Harvey et al. (1978) collected the following part of an account that a newly divorced woman reported giving to a male friend: "I'd say to myself, 'my husband is right, I'm sure a terrible person, I'm such a bastard . . . no one will ever want me again.'" In a sense, this woman is engaging in what Jones and Pittman call supplication. As much as believing herself, she probably is asking for help and to be wanted and loved again.

We would argue that, quite frequently, people select the particular accounts they present depending on who is listening. The audience's receptivity and reaction must be anticipated and the account tailored accordingly. A same-sex friend, for example, may elicit an account that blames other and exonerates self. Weiss (1975) notes that, after a separation, members of a parting couple may have to agree on who gets "custody" of which friends. A tale telling may be instigated to win such an audience in the first place: "Listen to my side of it; I've been wronged; you'll agree after you've heard it all." On the other hand, an opposite-sex potential lover may elicit mixtures of self-promotion and supplication because the account-giver is not sure either what is true or what account will present self in the best light or which strategy will be effective in making the potential lover see the self in just the right light to embark on a new relationship. Or the account giver may take another tack and relate a story to the potential lover that is designed to check the other's suitability as a partner. Thus, an account may be a way of saying, ''This is a test.'' Having a ''story'' may be a sign of having sufficient experience and wisdom to consider another relationship, now wiser and less error prone. On the other hand, too much self-promotion or vilification of one's ex-lover may make the other think that he or she could later suffer the same fate and hence become wary of going too far. Since account giving is such a pervasive activity, it probably is important for individuals to find friends who will listen and are likely to accept the account given. They may even reinforce the lines with ''I know just what you're saying—he's such a jerk. I just never had the heart to tell you.'' It may be the case that accounts with their repertoire of common lines and themes are therapeutic for audience and account giver as well—especially in their assurance of social comparison and camaraderie.

The account giver may indeed seek an audience to echo such other-critical sentiments. However, as noted by Harvey, Weber, Yarkin, and Stewart (1982), friends' concurrence with self's criticisms of the ex-partner may be discomfiting during the ''getting over'' phase. One may go overboard with such an obloquy, leading the account giver to become defensive of the departed other, as he or she wonders, ''Wait a second—how could I have been in love with such a loser?''

As self-presentations, accounts concerning relationship breakdown still are given for the fundamental purpose of restoring or reconstructing self-identity. As Katz (1981) implies in his book on stigma, divorcing individuals may perceive themselves as both faulted human beings and as disadvantaged (e.g., too physically unattractive to maintain a relationship). Indeed, among singles' groups, the divorced and separated sometimes distinguish themselves from the never married, by referring to themselves as the ''Walking Wounded.'' The dual perspective of presenting oneself as both ''wronged'' and ''inadequate'' may engender in others feelings of antipathy and compassion. Again, so often we probably search out others who come down on the side of compassion. Weiss (1975) notes that a major task for the separated individual is reconstruction of a sense of identity. Account making appears to be one way of summarizing one's experiences for others and thus seeking the community that will assuage the search for that new sense of self.

Another aspect of the self-presentational character of accounts is that sometimes they may be presentations whose sole audience is oneself. They are private ruminations. But this privacy in no way diminishes the possibility that the individual is promoting self to self or asking for self's sympathy: As Mead (1934) argued, the mind is the importation within the individual of the social process. The individual takes the role of other and reacts as other would respond, and in so doing, the individual imaginatively shares the conduct of other. For that matter, accounts, like cognitive maps, remain private and are not accessed, they are merely represented by individuals' self-reports. The account one relates to a therapist may not be the same one told to oneself. It may be that, to be effective, or to seem "true," accounts must be *told*; they must have an audience. Private, self-rehearsed accounts may only be schemas or formulas until they are "tried out" on listeners.

Finally, while we believe that self-presentational motivation is a prime influencer of accounts, in no way do we mean to suggest that individuals are not making an honest attempt to explain meaningful events in their lives. They may well be making such an attempt, and/or they may be unaware of the role of presentation processes in their account-making.

Emotional Release.   Another motive behind accounts is that of emotional release. In her forthcoming book on affect in close relationships, Berscheid (in press) suggests that the magnitude of affect experienced in a relationship on a daily basis may imperfectly telegraph the magnitude of affect the participants may experience upon dissolution of the relationship. Indeed, the accounts people tell in the end may contain a vast reservoir of thought bundled with feeling. Quite apart from searching for understanding or presenting to other or anything else, this role of accounts is the release of affective energy that has built up to an unbearable point. In effect, the account may serve as a catharsis to help purge such feelings as distress, anger, insecurity, confusion, loneliness, and depression.

ACCURACY AND DIVERGENCY IN ACCOUNTS

The question of accuracy in social perception, or about the criteria for assessing accuracy, is recurrent in the literature of social psychology. Most recently, however, this question has surfaced again in the attribution domain with regard to Ross' (1977) argument that the pronounced tendency to make dispositional attributions represents "the fundamental attribution error." There now is a mini-literature about the reasonableness of this concept (see Funder, 1982; Harvey, Town, & Yarkin, 1981; Reeder, 1982). Given the intricacy of most accounts, it seems unlikely that debates about the legitimacy of the concept of fundamental attribution error will be particularly instructive to unraveling the ratio of truth to distortion in people's accounts of relationship difficulty. In light of what we have said about the many functions accounts serve at this time in people's lives, perhaps it could be argued that the "most fundamental attribution error" would be any attempt to provide a simple story for a terribly complex event.

There is more than a modicum of evidence and speculation that couples often diverge greatly in their explanations for the causes of the demise of a relationship. Studies by Harvey, Wells, and Alvarez (1978) and more recently by Fletcher (1983) provide suggestive data about the extent of this divergence and the content dimensions on which it often occurs. Sex differences are a focal issue in these divergencies. Men and women come to different conclusions about why their relationships ended. This trend is suggested by a recent survey of reasons given for divorce. Men ranked "conflict of sex roles" very high as a problem area; it was low in women's rankings. Women focused on marital infidelity and emotional immaturity as high-ranking reasons—reasons not highly ranked by men.

SOME CONCLUDING CHARACTERISTICS OF ACCOUNTS

The example read earlier of the man who described his life as having been like a yo-yo suggests that accounts may invoke vivid imagery, and their scriptal character makes the events described quite amenable to vicarious experience. Contemporary music is replete with fragments of easily imagined accounts. These fragments tell of lovers or ex-lovers who are "always on my mind." They may indicate a hope that other entertains similar images as the following lyrics suggest:

Do I ever cross your mind?
Darlin' do you ever see
Some situation somewhere
That triggers your memory?
And do you ever wonder
What became of all the time?
Darlin' do I ever
Ever cross your mind?

A further example of a contemporary theme, this song by Stephen Sondheim, illustrates the "dailiness" of accounts and their vivid images:

Not a day goes by, not a single day,
But you're somewhere a part of my life
And it looks like you'll stay.
As the days go by
I keep thinking, When will it end?
Where's the day I'll have started forgetting?
But I just go on thinking and sweating and
cursing and crying
And turning and reaching and waking and dying.
And no, not a day goes by, not a blessed day,
But you're still somehow part of my life
And you won't go away,
So there's hell to pay. . . .

We could go on and on with song lyrics, sometimes with different genres of songs—"you picked a fine time to leave me, Lucille." But all would signify the vivid imagery of many accounts. As these examples suggest, many of the "universal themes" of accounts have found their way into popular songs. These prove to be convenient vehicles or primers for novice account makers. As Russianoff (1982) quotes from one of her patients:

> Every relationship I've had has had its soundtrack. There are, in each case, the songs we courted to, the songs we made love to, the songs we broke up to—all these songs reflected our feelings, or my mood, at each stage of the game. And always the lyrics say basically the same thing, that love is paramount in anyone's life. And losing love, or not finding it in the first place, is the greatest tragedy in the world [p. 41].

Accounts are scriptal and yet unique and personal at the same time. They are scriptal in the sense that they incorporate major elements that are common to most people. But also there are stylistic differences. One person may present a more "macho" type of account, while another presents the self-martyr image. It is probable that the precise image conveyed about oneself is tailored to the audience. A woman may tell her female friends, "The bastard just walked out on me!" and yet turn around and report to her mother, "We both felt we ought to stop seeing each other for a while." The narrator may, of course, accept different images of himself/herself at different times and may maintain a mental "master account" that ties together the various subaccounts into a cohesive, unified-theme story. The whole account, like an iceberg, remains mainly submerged and private, although aspects are revealed and related to selected audiences.

The relating of accounts, and their precise themes, may be strongly influenced by cultural values as cued by the media. In the last 5 years, with greater frequency and poignancy, such issues as divorce, child custody, and relationship breakdown have been the focus of several popular films: "Kramer vs. Kramer," "Shoot the Moon," "An Unmarried Woman," and "Starting Over," among others. These films reinforce the messages long available in popular literature, magazines, and television: Relationships and marriages break up, often for "a few simple, basic reasons," and people react and respond in "a few basic and simple ways." Do such images affect accounts, or is it increased account making that invites popular treatments of formerly touchy or taboo subjects or themes? There is little of both, we think. The images of films and popular literature, like those of popular music, are powerful in themselves. Account makers will feel freer to discuss their experiences and borrow themes and heroics from the media in creating their own stories.

In an effort toward developing accounts that embody the full flavor of the relational experience, the individual may rework the account during each presentation. Through this process of drafting and revising, each fragment of experience or stray memory that may have been triggered by the presentation can be integrated within the overall framework of the relationship account. Left untended, these fragmented thoughts and impressions may result in the discomfort associated with what some clinicians might describe as an "incomplete gestalt." Thus, through an almost obsessive need to organize and reorganize the numerous relationship components, a sense of completion, at least at the cognitive level, is achieved. It should be pointed out, however, that this Zeigarnik-like process of feeling a need to complete the story may not occur on occasion. It simply may be too painful to fill in all the details. Once agian, we may have been beaten to this point by another popular set of song lyrics: "Memories may be beautiful and yet, What's too painful to remember, We simply choose to forget. . . ."

CONCLUSION

Accounts like relationships themselves do not end, psychologically at least, but are ongoing and cognitively integrated. The individual seeks to explain the world primarily to himself/herself. The master account is maintained and modified, parts of it are publicized and tested, and all relationship experiences are added to, and interpreted in light of, this "continuing story."

We might ask whether accounts could be formalized, solicited, and used better to understand a complex of relationship issues. There is no question that people can generate accounts, but many seem merely to be reporting, with little sense of control or perspective over their creations. It may be possible to heighten people's awareness of the usefulness of accounts by encouraging them to relate or write them, perhaps interweaving fact and fantasy.

As people become mature and experienced in interpersonal relations, it may be possible for them to "capture" the account-making process, and to take control of its direction and usefulness, filling in the gaps with helpful insights, and reviewing the master account for central themes and self-revelation. In so doing, the individual may feel less a "pawn" of recurring themes, scripts, and/or relational habits and better able to respond to the uniqueness inherent in each close relationship.

In Kelley's (1979) acclaimed book on personal relationships, he suggests that personal relationships provide a means—although perhaps never fully realized—of establishing contact with others and thereby lessening the recognition that our experiences of the world are essentially private and subjective. We suggest, in conclusion, that the development of accounts based on the individual's perceptions and experiences with significant others serves both a need for assimilating these private aspects of experience and as a vehicle for sharing hopes and fears intrinsic to close relationships.

ACKNOWLEDGMENTS

Some of this work was completed with the assistance of funds from the Texas Tech Research Council. We are grateful to Ellen Berscheid, Gerald Ginsburg, and Harold Kelley for comments on an earlier version of this chapter.

13

Beyond Marriage: The Impact of Partner Loss on Health

Wolfgang Stroebe
Margaret S. Stroebe
University of Tübingen

INTRODUCTION

A message one gets clearly from scanning the contents of this book is that in adopting a new name, the area of personal relationships has considerably widened its scope. With a few notable exceptions (e.g., Duck, 1977c) most texts on interpersonal attraction published in the late 1960s or 1970s (e.g., Berscheid & Walster, 1969; Huston, 1974; Mikula & Stroebe, 1977; Rubin, 1973) fail to refer to many of the themes covered in this book. Topics such as ''loneliness,'' ''disordered relationships,'' or ''dissolution and repair of relationships'' were either not considered part of attraction research or not studied at all.

In this chapter we extend the limits of this field even further. Going beyond relationships, we ask what happens to individuals who lose their partners either through death or through divorce. There is a great deal of research that firmly links widowhood to steep increases in depression, mental illness, suicide, physical ill health, and even death from natural causes (Stroebe & Stroebe, 1983). There is also some evidence that the health consequences of losing a partner through divorce are comparable to those of losing him or her through death. In this chapter we focus mainly on bereavement for two reasons: First, the health consequences of bereavement have been studied more extensively than those of divorce. More importantly, however, since we typically have to draw on studies that do not employ pretests, the direction of causality is somewhat more clearcut in the case of bereavement than divorce.

Because many may be unfamiliar with the pitfalls of this type of research, we begin with some methodological comments. Then, the evidence linking conjugal bereavement to health deterioration is summarized. Following this, we present evidence on health consequences of divorce and discuss similarities and differences in the impact of divorce and widowhood. Finally, we outline a theoretical interpretation of these findings.

METHODOLOGICAL CONSIDERATIONS

The Need for a Control Group

Like cigarette smoking, grief is not directly linked to a specific and distinct cause of death. It is assumed to aggravate or accelerate existing health problems. The impact of grief on health can therefore never be demonstrated in a single case but only by comparing the health of large numbers of bereaved individuals to that of a nonbereaved control group. If the widowed group is found to be significantly less healthy than a nonwidowed group (both groups being comparable in terms of characteristics such as sex, age, or socioeconomic status), then we have support for the assumption that the experience of losing a partner is associated with health deterioration.

The comparability of control and treatment groups is the major problem in any research in which random assignment is precluded. However, in the case of bereavement research, the problem is complicated by the fact that, for obvious reasons, there are exceedingly few studies in which the health of the widowed is examined prior to the death of the partner. Thus, most investigations of health consequences of bereavement utilize posttest only designs with non-equivalent groups. The deplorable weaknesses of this type of design are discussed by Cook and Campbell (1979).

Fortunately, the equivalence of bereaved and nonbereaved groups is not equally threatened in all areas in which bereavement reactions have been studied. It poses the most serious threat to longitudinal studies of mental and physical health, since they examine only small samples of those widowed who are willing to be interviewed and who may be systematically different in health from those who refuse. For most longitudinal studies of mortality and suicide, on the other hand, nonequivalence is less of a problem because archival data (medical records, vital statistics, etc.) is used and typically segments of the widowed population are compared with age- and sex-matched segments of the married population.

Strategies of Design

Longitudinal Versus Cross-Sectional.   Both longitudinal and cross-sectional types of design typically involve some cross-sectional comparisons, that is, comparisons of the health of a bereaved sample with that of a nonbereaved control group. However, whereas cross-sectional studies tap the dependent measure (e.g., health, suicide) in both groups only at one point in time, and thus only allow a cross-sectional comparison, longitudinal studies examine the same subjects repeatedly. Thus, in addition to the cross-sectional analysis of differences between the control and bereaved sample at a given point in time, longitudinal designs allow us to examine health changes over time.

The Choice of Data Base.   An investigator may be able to use epidemiological data based on large-scale surveys conducted by national agencies (e.g., Office of Population Censuses and Survey) or he or she may have to collect his or her own data. Using national statistics has the advantage of providing information about large sections of the population. However, because national agencies are not in the habit of collecting information about psychological variables (e.g., personality traits, anxiety levels) any investigator interested in this type of information would have to collect his or her own data. Thus, in the area of bereavement, national statistics have been of most use in studies of the suicide and mortality risk of the bereaved. There are two major drawbacks, however, to using this type of epidemiological data. First, these statistics do not allow one to subdivide the widowed samples according to the duration of bereavement, because this information is typically not presented. Such information is important, however, because the impact of bereavement on health is greatest during the first year of bereavement. Second, these statistics do not allow one to keep track of individuals who remarry (i.e., who are selected out of the widowed into the married category). If we assume that the healthier widowed are more likely to remarry, the lower health of the widowed as compared to the married group could be due to such selection effects.

In studies based on in-depth interviews of bereaved and nonbereaved individuals, remarriage is less of a problem, because investigators can typically keep track of individuals who remarry. Unfortunately, these studies have their own set of shortcomings. First, there are problems with sample size. Studies based on in-depth interviews rarely achieve (or even approach) the sample size of the large-scale epidemiological surveys. Second, there are problems of representativeness. Most interview studies of recently bereaved individuals use samples of convenience. Furthermore, because refusal rates are typically quite high, sampling is practically based on self-selection.

Illness and Illness Behavior

In discussing research on the effects of bereavement on health, we need to keep in mind the fact that most health measures do not directly reflect bodily conditions but are based on either medical diagnosis or subjects' self-reports. This is an important difference for a number of reasons. First, self-perception of illness, like any self-perception, is likely to be affected by various aspects of the social context, particularly if the internal illness cues are weak and ambiguous. Thus, symptoms such as spells of dizziness, stomach pains, or mild attacks of influenza are so ambiguous that there will be great interpersonal as well as intersituational variability in whether they are interpreted as within the range of normal health or as signs of illness (e.g., Pennebaker, 1982). Second, quite apart from the self-perception of health, treatment-seeking behavior is affected by contextual factors (e.g., availability of medical help, health insurance) as well as bodily conditions (cf. Mechanic, 1978). Third, physicians' diagnoses and treatment recommendations are not based exclusively on bodily conditions but also take into account the past history and present circumstances of the patient. Thus, one might expect that the information that a patient has recently lost a spouse could affect the diagnosis. For example, physicians may tend to downgrade certain symptoms as due to grief and prescribe some form of mild psychotropic medicine.

In summary, then, our health measures cannot directly tap the bodily condition of the bereaved individual but are based on self-reports of symptoms or on a physician's diagnosis. Therefore, some of the differences observed between samples of bereaved and nonbereaved individuals may reflect the direct effect of bereavement on self-perceived health or on treatment-seeking behavior rather than a difference in bodily conditions. This possibility should always be kept in mind when interpreting research relating bereavement to mental or physical health data.

Conclusion

After this rather sobering discussion of shortcomings and weaknesses of research into the relationship between bereavement and health, one might feel tempted to side with those critics of bereavement research who argue that most of the studies in this area are flawed. And indeed, we could not deny that there is some truth to this opinion. However, our conviction that bereavement is linked to deteriorations in the mental and physical health of the widowed as well as to increased risks of suicide, accidents, and mortality from natural causes is not based on any single study but on the convergence of findings from numerous investigations across all major areas in which normal and pathological grief reactions have been manifested. These studies have used longitudinal as well as cross-sectional designs, prospective as well as retrospective strategies, and epidemiological data as well as in-depth interviews. We would argue that, since these different designs and data bases are associated with frequently opposing biases, it is the consistency of findings that justifies one's trust in their validity.[1]

---

[1]Because of the differences between whites and nonwhites in patterns and rates of illness and mortality, and because more information is available for whites (e.g., on marital and widowed roles and support systems), the data presented and discussed in the following paragraphs are predominantly for whites.

HEALTH CONSEQUENCES OF CONJUGAL BEREAVEMENT

Depression

Sadness and depression are such integral parts of grief that it would be very unusual in our culture if a person who had recently lost his or her spouse would not show signs of depression. In the normal course of bereavement, we expect the widowed for some period after the loss of their partner to be sad and depressed, to suffer sleep disturbances, to have frequent fits of crying, and to show little interest or pleasure in usual activities.

What then distinguishes such normal from abnormal or pathological depression? In his classic analysis of normal and pathological grief, Freud (1917) suggested a number of differences between the two states. Normal grief was characterized by painful dejection, a loss of interest, and an inhibition of activities. Pathological grief reactions, on the other hand, which Freud attributed to the existence of ambivalence toward the lost person, were, in addition, characterized by feelings of guilt, self-reproach, and a lowering of self-esteem. However, in recent studies of bereaved individuals (Parkes, 1972) feelings of self-reproach and guilt have been found to be very much part of the normal grief response as well. There is no clear-cut boundary that divides depression in normal grief from clinical depression. Grief becomes clinically relevant when the depressive reactions are excessively intense or when the process of grieving is unduly prolonged.

Several studies have shown that samples of widowed individuals are significantly more depressed than married controls (e.g., Carey, 1977; Clayton, Halikas, & Maurice, 1972; Radloff, 1975; van Rooijen, 1979). This marked increase in the incidence of depression has not only been demonstrated for recent bereavement but also in studies conducted more than a year after partner loss. Thus, van Rooijen (1979), who compared depressive mood scores of 194 women who had been widowed for over $1\frac{1}{2}$ years to a group of 73 nonwidowed women, found mood levels to be significantly more depressed among the bereaved than among the nonbereaved women. Defining severe depression in terms of distribution of scores and using a cutoff point at 2 standard deviations above the mean of his control sample, van Rooijen found that 36% of his widowed sample had scores above this point. However, since the questionnaires were only returned by 63% of the original sample of eligible widows, the representativeness of this estimate for the total widowed sample is somewhat unclear.

Lower depression percentages were reported in a study by Bornstein, Clayton, Halikas, Maurice, and Robins, (1973). These investigators used criteria suggested by Feighner, Robins, Guze, Woodruff, and Winokur (1972) for the diagnosis of depression. Bornstein et al. (1973) found that while 35% of their sample could be categorized as depressed when examined one month after the loss, this was true for only 17% one year later. Again, implications of these results for assessing the depression rate of the total widowed sample are unclear because the refusal rate for participation in the study was 42% (Clayton, Halikas, & Maurice, 1972).

Although the widowed who were categorized as depressed in the van Rooijen (1979) and the Bornstein et al. (1973) studies were definitely impaired in their functioning, their illness does not seem to have been sufficiently severe to have motivated them to seek psychiatric treatment. There is evidence, however, that widowed individuals are also overrepresented among psychiatric patients (e.g., Parkes, 1964a; Stein & Susser, 1969). Thus, in a study of 3,245 patients admitted to the Bethlehem Royal and Maudsley Hospitals in London from 1949 to 1951, Parkes (1964a) found that the number of patients whose illness followed the loss of a spouse was six times greater than expected. Furthermore, comparing the percentage of patients whose illness was diagnosed as "Reactive or Neurotic Depression," Parkes observed that 28% of the bereaved group but only 15% of the nonbereaved patients fell into that category. Thus, among these psychiatric patients, a significantly larger proportion of bereaved rather than nonbereaved individuals were diagnosed as clinically depressed.

It seems then, that even after more than one year of widowhood, approximately one in five bereaved persons suffer from extremely depressed mood states. Even though this depression does not seem severe enough to motivate individuals to seek psychiatric treatment, it is bound to seriously impair functioning in everyday life. The fact that few, if any, of these individuals feel in need of psychiatric care is probably due to their ability to attribute their mood state to the loss experience. Since it is normal in our culture to be depressed after the death of one's spouse, these individuals probably expect little improvement in their condition following psychiatric consultation.

Suicide

In view of the close relationship between depression and suicide (Dominian, 1976) and, as we have just noted, between depression and bereavement, it is not surprising that the suicide risk of the bereaved is considerably higher than that of comparable married controls. The pattern was first pointed out by Durkheim (1897/1951) and is still apparent in more recent suicide statistics (e.g., National Center for Health Statistics, 1970). Furthermore, MacMahon and Pugh's study (1965) confirmed that, at least in part, the high suicide rate among the widowed was due to the excess risk in the early years of bereavement. They found that the suicide risk among the widowed was highest during the first year of bereavement and subsequently decreased over the next few years. Their data further suggest that the clustering within the first four years was more marked for males than for females.

These results were supported in a recent longitudinal study of bereaved mortality conducted in Finland (Kaprio & Koskenvuo, 1983), in which death rates of a cohort of 95,647 widows and widowers were monitored for a 5-year period. In a comparison of widowed suicide rates with the sex and age adjusted suicide rates of the general population, the authors reported a peak in widowed suicide risk during the first week of widowhood. They also confirmed that this excess was much more marked for men than for women (66-fold versus 9.6-fold). After this period, the excess mortality was of the same order for both sexes (2 to 3 fold). Similar findings were reported in a much smaller study conducted in Germany (Bojanovsky & Bojanovsky, 1976).

Physical Health

The widowed are far more prone to suffer from physical illness than comparable married individuals. This was found in a large-scale examination, conducted by the National Center for Health Statistics (1976) in the United States, of the relation between marital status and physical health. There is also evidence that the increased risk of physical illness is closely connected with recent bereavement (e.g., Maddison & Viola, 1968; Parkes, 1964a).

There are some studies, however, that did not find any physical health deterioration following bereavement (Clayton, 1974; Heyman & Gianturco, 1973). As part of the longitudinal aging project at Duke University, Heyman and Gianturco (1973) examined the health of 41 elderly subjects (all over the age of 60) before and after bereavement. No health deterioration could be observed. To account for this unexpected finding, these authors suggest that the elderly might be psychologically prepared for bereavement and the role of widowhood. Thus, losing a partner is less of a shock for them than for the younger age groups. A further explanation could be that their sample had lived in small communities in a rural area for many years and thus could draw on a well-established network of friends and neighbours. As we show later, social support is one of the factors that alleviates the impact of bereavement.

No such special circumstances can be called on to account for the outcome of a study by Clayton (1974). She examined the physical health of 109 widowed individuals (average age 60), selected from the death certificates of St. Louis City and County, during the first year of bereavement. The study failed to find significant differences between the widowed and a nonwidowed control group on the number of physicians' visits, hospitalization, and use of tranquilizers. This failure to find an impact of bereavement on any of her health measures is rather puzzling but may be due to sample size.

Mortality

The most intriguing and most stable findings in this area are those linking bereavement to significant increases in mortality. When Farr first analyzed French mortality statistics in 1859, he noted that widowed mortality rates were higher than those of married individuals of the same sex and age. The same pattern still holds true today for a wide range of countries (e.g., Kraus & Lilienfeld, 1959; Stroebe, Stroebe, Gergen, & Gergen, 1980). Ratios derived from age- and sex-specific death rates for the widowed and the married clearly suggest that widowed rates exceed those of comparable married persons, with the excess being particularly marked for the younger age groups. There is also a sex difference, with widowed men having consistently higher ratios compared with married men than widowed women compared with married women.

One would be happy to accept these data as convincing evidence that bereavement is linked to high mortality. Unfortunately however, this type of cross-sectional data does not allow one to control a number of alternative variables that might account for, or at least contribute to, this pattern. The most important of these uncontrolled factors is remarriage. If we assume that the probability of marrying again is higher for healthy rather than unhealthy widowed, we would have to expect a permanent drain of the healthiest widowed into the married category, thus raising the average health rate of the married and lowering the average health rate of the widowed. Since remarriage rates are higher for widowers than for widows, and higher for the young rather than the old, this alternative explanation could account for most aspects of the pattern. Other variables that might increase the proximity of death rates for the married are "joint unfavorable environment" (e.g., low social class), "mutual infection," "joint accidents," not to mention a number of "statistical artifacts and biases" (Stroebe, Stroebe, Gergen, & Gergen, 1981).

Nevertheless, longitudinal studies that controlled for these factors still confirm the excess mortality rates of widowed over married. The classic study of this kind was conducted by Young, Benjamin, and Wallis (1963) with a follow-up by Parkes, Benjamin, and Fitzgerald (1969). In this study, death rates of a cohort of 4,486 widowers age 55 or over were monitored for a period of 9 years after bereavement. When death rates were compared to those of married men of comparable age, a significant increase in the mortality of the widowed was found for the first half year of bereavement. This excess is followed by a return to the normal mortality level for married men of comparable age.

These results were supported by the findings of a recent large-scale longitudinal study conducted by Kaprio and Koskenvuo (1983) in Finland. In this investigation, death rates of a cohort of 95,647 widowed persons of both sexes were examined for a 5-year period. Comparing their mortality to the age and sex adjusted rates for the total population, the authors found that a significant increase in widowed mortality for both sexes occurred mainly during the first 4 weeks of bereavement. After that, widowed mortality rates were not notably different from those of the total population. Comparable results have been reported in a number of other longitudinal studies (e.g., Ekblom, 1964; McNeill, 1973; Niemi, 1979) that typically observed the greatest excess during the first 6 months.

In view of the relative consistency of research findings in this area, the results of a study by Helsing and Szklo (1981) are puzzling. These authors, who followed a sample of 1,204 widowers and 2,828 widows for a 12-year period, found a significant excess in widowed compared to married mortality for men but not for women. Even more surprising, however, is the fact that the authors did not find any evidence for a greater excess in the mortality of their widowers during the first year of bereavement. They concluded that the mortality risk for widowed males persists for many years after the spouse's death, which is clearly different from the conclusions of Parkes et al. (1969), Kaprio and Koskenvuo (1983), Niemi (1979), and McNeill (1973).

While this discrepancy cannot be explained, it is much less difficult to account for the failure of small-scale studies such as that of Clayton (1974) to find a significant excess in widowed mortality. Even had the results paralleled those of Young et al. (1963), with a sample of 109 widowed only 5 deaths could have been expected in the widowed group as compared to 3 in the married control group.

The problem of sample size can be circumvented by using a retrospective case-control design (i.e., by starting at a cause of death expected to be excessive among the bereaved and working one's way backward). This procedure was adopted in a study by Cottington, Matthews, Talbott, and Kuller (1980) who examined the circumstances of 81 Caucasian women aged 25 to 64, who had died suddenly from arteriosclerotic heart disease. Results revealed that relative to matched controls, the women who had died from heart disease were six times as likely to have experienced the death of a significant other within the last 6 months.

Causes of Death Excessive in the Widowed.   Are bereaved individuals really most likely to die of a "broken heart" as folklore and Lynch's (1977) popular book would like us to believe? Conclusions will be somewhat different depending on whether they are based on evidence from longitudinal or cross-sectional studies. In one of the most thorough longitudinal analyses of causes of death among the widowed, Parkes et al. (1969) found that cardiovascular diseases were indeed most excessive: "Taken together diseases of the heart and circulatory systems account for two-thirds of the increase in mortality during the first six months of bereavement" [p. 741]. According to the cross-sectional evidence compiled by Stroebe, Stroebe, Gergen, and Gergen (1982) from data published by the National Center of Health Statistics in 1970, cardiovascular diseases rank behind violent causes of death (accidents, suicide, homicide), in women and in men behind tuberculosis and liver cirrhosis as well, in the order of causes of death in which the widowed show an excess over married individuals. They are closely followed by various forms of cancer, which are also excessive in the widowed.

Two differences between longitudinal and cross-sectional studies are likely to contribute to this discrepancy, that is, differences in duration of bereavement and in sample size. Although we assume that bereavement merely aggravates or accelerates existing disease processes, a myocardial infarction is a faster acting cause of death than tuberculosis, liver cirrhosis, or cancer. We would, therefore, expect coronary diseases to be a more excessive cause of death in a sample of individuals who have only been bereaved for a few months rather than for several years. Thus, in their longitudinal study, Kaprio and Koskenvuo (1983) found coronary disease to be mainly excessive during the first month of bereavement.

Differences in the length of bereavement of the widowed samples studied in longitudinal and cross-sectional studies cannot account, however, for the failure of the Parkes et al. (1969) study to find an excess for violent causes of death among the bereaved. This discrepancy is probably due to differences in sample size. Because violent deaths are much less frequent than deaths from natural causes, particularly in the older age groups studied by Parkes et al., the sample of the Parkes et al.'s study may have been too small to register increases in violent deaths among the bereaved.

In this context, the treatment of base rates has to be mentioned as a thorny problem. Because widowed to married excess is expressed as a ratio of widowed to married rates of mortality due to a given cause of death, rare causes of death, if they are affected by the emotional stress of bereavement, are more likely to become excessive than causes such as coronary disease or cancer, which already have a very high base rate in the population. However, even if we consider differences in rates rather than ratios, we find in the Kaprio and Koskenvuo study that 248 more widowed than expected die from violent death, compared to an increase of 273 in death from natural causes. Thus, even in absolute numbers the increase in violent deaths is nearly as sizable as the increase in death from natural causes.

Conclusions

A few years ago, in a critical review of empirical studies of the bereavement-mortality relationships (Stroebe et al., 1981), we concluded that: ''neither the loss effect nor its associated hypotheses concerning age and gender rest as yet on convincing evidence'' [p. 87]. In view of the findings of a number of studies that have been published since our manuscript went to press (e.g., Cottington et al.,

1980; Helsing & Szklo, 1981; Kaprio & Koskenvuo, 1983), we now feel greater confidence in assuming that the increased mortality of the widowed is due to a loss effect.

HEALTH CONSEQUENCES OF DIVORCE

The evidence on health consequences of divorce, although mainly based on cross-sectional data, consistently links divorce to health risks that are at least as serious as those of widowhood (Bloom, Asher, & White, 1978). The following paragraphs briefly summarize this evidence and evaluate the relative risk to health on becoming divorced and widowed.

Reviews of studies of the relationship between mental illness and marital status by Crago (1972) and by Gove (1972a) suggest that the mental illness rates of divorced and separated individuals are not only excessive when compared to the married but also when compared to the widowed.[2] Thus, in a review of 11 studies conducted during the previous 35 years, using rates of admission into psychiatric hospitals as an indicator of mental disorder, Crago (1972) consistently found that admission rates for adults were highest for the divorced/ separated groups and lowest for the married, with the widowed holding an intermediate position. The same pattern was reported in the review by Gove (1972a) who limited his analysis to studies conducted since World War II, but included information from household surveys and nonhospital health services in addition to hospital admissions.

A comparable pattern of marital status differences has been observed with regard to physical health. Based on data from an extensive survey of residents of 88,000 households in the United States in 1971–1972, the National Center of Health Statistics (1976) reported that divorced individuals have higher rates of illness and debility than the married on all health indicators employed. Rates for the divorced are comparable to those for the widowed on three out of four indicators (days of restricted activity, limitations of activity due to chronic conditions, and physicians visits per year). On the fourth indicator (acute conditions), divorced individuals have higher rates than the widowed. Carter and Glick (1976) suggested that this may be the result of tensions associated with the disruption of marriages that end in divorce.

---

[2]The concept of mental illness has come under strong attack recently, and we agree that there are severe shortcomings in looking at the prevalence or incidence of psychiatric disorders in general (particularly the reliance on inception rates alone) to draw conclusions about risk and outcome. As Gove (1979) argued, 'To treat all phenomena that receive a psychiatric label as the same disorder makes about as much sense as a doctor treating all persons admitted to a general hospital . . . as suffering from the same disease (p. 23)'. Nevertheless, to proceed beyond this stage of global analysis, we need information on diagnostic specific disorders. To our knowledge, no such information according to the duration of bereavement or divorce (compared with controls) is as yet available.

Marital status differences in mortality rates again follow the familiar pattern, with divorced individuals having higher rates than the married. (National Center for Health Statistics, 1970). Furthermore, divorced mortality rates even exceed those of the widowed, although this excess is much more marked for males than for females (Carter & Glick, 1976).

Divorce has also been linked to significant increases in suicide rates (Bloom et al., 1978). Thus, Shneidman and Farberow (1965), in an analysis of suicides committed in Los Angeles County during 1957, found that 13% of the suicide victims were divorced and 3% separated. These figures were more than twice what one would expect on the basis of the proportion of divorced and separated individuals in the general population of Los Angeles. Comparable findings were reported by Gove (1972b) using U.S. national statistics as well as suicide statistics for Canada, New Zealand, Sweden, and Switzerland.

There are a number of reasons for caution in interpreting the data on the divorced and in drawing comparisons with the widowed. Data are lacking on predivorce health characteristics. This is critical because, in the case of health deterioration of the divorced, the direction of causality is even more ambiguous than in widowhood. It seems quite possible that ill health could, in some instances, be the cause rather than the consequence of divorce. Particularly, the mental instability of one of the partners is likely to cause the breakdown of a marriage. In support of this hypothesis, Briscoe and Smith (1975), who compared samples of bereaved and divorced depressive probands, present some evidence that suggests that the divorced patients may have had psychiatric problems before undergoing the divorce. The divorced depressed probands reported significantly more previous episodes of depression than the bereaved and also had significantly more first-degree relatives who had suffered from depression. A second reason for caution is the fact that remarriage rates are higher for the divorced than for the widowed (Carter & Glick, 1976).

Despite this problem of establishing the direction of causality in investigations of the health of the divorced, there are good reasons to argue that the divorced are at least as vulnerable as the widowed to the detriments in mental and physical health. First, as was found for the widowed, there is great consistency across different areas of health: The divorced have excessive rates for suicide, depression, mental illness, physical ailments and illnesses, and mortality. One would not expect this consistency if the causal relationship were in the opposite direction, that is, if the health problem were the cause of divorce. Furthermore, while it is likely that depression or mental illness precipitates divorce, the case for physical ill health would be harder to make (for instance, one could equally well argue that this would prevent rather than facilitate divorce). Yet, as the data showed, rates for physical as well as mental illness are higher for the divorced than the married. Second, that divorce could have as devastating effects as loss of a partner through death seems intuitively convincing. There are some important similarities between being divorced and being widowed: Both are partnerless, are entering a devalued status (marriage is still socially desirable), go through a grief reaction, and experience many changes in social relationships.

There are obviously also numerous differences between divorce and widowhood. What might make things worse for the widowed is the lasting attachment and the fact that the marriage had worked. While attachment may linger for some divorced, particularly those reluctant to undertake the proceedings, in general one would expect the widowed to look back on and yearn for a happier marriage than one that had ended in divorce. After all, the termination of the former was not voluntary or desired. On the other hand, certain aspects of the situation that divorced persons find themselves in would lead one to predict devastating effects on health. They do not have the unconditional support that is offered to the bereaved, some relationships will cease as some other persons side with the ex-spouse, and there is a stigma attached to being divorced that there is not to being widowed. Perhaps one of the worst aspects for the divorced, at least for individuals who have been forced into a divorce by their partner, is the feeling of rejection, which again the widowed are spared. Furthermore, whereas cultural norms function for the widowed to indicate appropriate behavior and others help to transmit these, there are no such rules for the divorced (e.g., no mourning customs), and few people perceive the divorced as needing help and support. If we accept the data on the health of the divorced and the analysis of their situation indicated here, then we must conclude that the divorced are at as high, if not higher, risk to their health as the widowed and as much in need of support as the bereaved. Thus, the following theoretical analysis of the impact of partner loss is applicable not only to loss through death but to loss through divorce.

TOWARD A THEORETICAL EXPLANATION OF THE IMPACT OF PARTNER LOSS ON HEALTH

There is a large body of research that links psychosocial stress to various somatic and psychiatric disorders and that isolates the neurochemical and hormonal processes assumed to mediate these relationships. According to a definition suggested by Lazarus and Launier (1978), a situation is stressful when: ''environmental or internal demands (or both) tax or exceed the adaptive resources of the individual, . . .'' [p. 296]. Thus, conceptually, stress is neither a feature of the situation alone nor of the person, but depends on the relationship between individual resources and environmental demands. This does not imply that situations cannot be ordered along a continuum of stressfulness. For example, driving on a sunny day along an empty road is certainly less stressful than driving through heavy rain during rush hour. But the extent of the stress experienced by the driver will also depend on his or her resources—driving skills and the state of the car.

At this point, we first present a social psychological analysis of the sources of stress in bereavement and divorce. Our interpretation is based on the assumption that partner loss causes deficits in a number of areas that can broadly be characterized as loss of social support and of social identity. We then continue with a discussion of the role of individual resources in modifying stress. Although bereavement or divorce are considered highly stressful life events (Holmes & Rahe, 1967), which tax or exceed the coping resources of most individuals, the magnitude of individual stress will be moderated by the availability of coping resources. We conclude with a discussion of the physiological and behavioral mechanisms assumed to mediate the impact of stress on health.

Sources of Stress in Bereavement and Divorce

A marital couple is a small social organization with a differentiated system of roles regulating the division of labour as well as the distribution of rewards. Since marital partners perform a number of emotional and instrumental functions for each other, the loss of one partner implies the loss of these functions for the other. In the following the major deficits likely to result from the loss of a marital partner will be outlined.

Loss of Instrumental Support.   Like the productivity of any social group, success or failure of the marital group in solving problems involving goal achievement and adaptation to demands from the outside world depend largely on the adequacy of the group's resources vis à vis the task demands. Resources include all relevant knowledge, abilities, or skills possessed by the group members (Steiner, 1972). While loss of a marital partner reduces task demands only slightly, it usually results in a considerable reduction in the resources available to respond to task demands.

Marital couples typically share a number of task functions such as earning money, performing household chores, and bringing up children. Even today, marital division of labour usually follows traditional sex-role boundaries, with the wife acting as ''housekeeper'' while the husband occupies the more powerful role of provider. The loss of one partner forces the other one to take over most of his or her functions. Thus, the higher the specialization of these roles in a marriage, the more drastic are the effects of the loss of one of the partners. For example, if a husband has never been involved in performing household chores, the loss of his ''housekeeper'' may present a number of difficult problems. Similarly, if a wife has never been responsible for the financial affairs of the family, she may come under great strain.

Loss of Validational Support.   Success or failure in transactions with one's environment are not merely a function of ability. They also depend on the validity of an individual's evaluations of the level of his or her ability as well as the difficulty of the task. Since such evaluations often take place under ambiguous circumstances, they are highly dependent on social comparison processes. As Festinger (1954) argued, if there are no objective criteria to assess the validity of one's evaluations, such judgments will have to be based on social reality. Because of the closeness of the marital relationship and the similarity in important social characteristics (Lewis & Spanier, 1979), it seems only plausible to assume that spouses serve mutually as bases of social reality. Thus, loss of a partner may lead to drastic instability of such judgments.

Social comparison processes also play an important role in evaluating the appropriateness of one's own emotional responses (Schachter, 1959). Reference persons are needed to stabilize one's emotional reactions, particularly in novel, emotionally arousing situations. It seems likely that marital partners rely on each other for such evaluations. Since bereavement or divorce is novel and emotion arousing for most individuals, the loss of a central reference person is particularly devastating. As Glick et al. (1974) have shown, almost 40% of those bereaved are concerned that they may lose their sanity. Matters of mental health are typically very ambiguous and one needs somebody close to assure one that one's actions, thoughts, or emotions are the result of emotional stress rather than early symptoms of a mental breakdown.

Loss of Emotional Support.   Of all the deficits resulting from partner loss, the loss of emotional support that involved providing empathy, caring, love, and trust seems to be the most important (House, 1981). There is consensus among personality and clinical psychologists (e.g., Beck, 1967; Erikson, 1963; Rogers, 1968) about the importance of positive self-regard for mental health. The partner's expression of caring or love may therefore serve an important function in bolstering one's feeling of self-worth or esteem. Sociologists have been well aware of the importance of this "therapeutic" function partners perform for each other. Bernard (1968) referred to it as "stroking" and writes: "One of the major functions of positive, expressive talk is to raise the status of the other, to give help, to reward; in ordinary human relations it performs the stroking function. As infants need physical caressing or stroking in order to live and grow, even to survive, so also do adults need emotional or psychological stroking or caressing to remain normal" [p. 137].

Loss of Companionship Support.   In a good marriage, the partner is a companion with whom one shares many experiences from joint holidays to togetherness in a time of crisis. Although marriages vary in terms of reliance on each other for companionship, the loss of this function is frequently deplored by widowed and divorced alike. Feelings of loneliness are probably the result of the inability of the widowed or divorced individual to find comparable sources of companionship and emotional support.

Loss of Social Identity.   In addition to causing these deficits in social support, the loss of a marital partner is likely to affect one's self-concept. The social groups to which we belong are important determinants of the conceptualization of "self" and form the basis for "social identity." Tajfel (1978) defined social identity as: "that part of an individual's self-concept which derives from his knowledge of his membership to a social group (or groups) together with the value and emotional significance attached to that membership" [p. 83].

Since his or her membership of the marital group is likely to be central for an individual's social identity, leaving the status of "married persons" and entering that of "widowed" or "divorced" will necessitate a reconceptualization of self. The impact of that reconceptualization on self-esteem will depend on individual as well as societal evaluations of the different status categories. It is therefore difficult to predict whether the effect of this status change will be greater for the divorced or the widowed. If we focus on societal evaluations, the divorced should be worse off, since the status of "divorced" is likely to be evaluated less positively than that of "widowed". If, on the other hand, individual evaluations are considered, divorced individuals should typically be better off, since their voluntary exit from the marital group suggests a less positive evaluation of that status than can be assumed for the widowed.

Coping Resources and Social Support

Individual differences in coping resources are at least as important as situational variations in determining bereavement outcome. In analyzing these differences we distinguish four types of resources: *personality related resources, skills, financial resources,* and *social support.* In the following paragraphs, the function of these resources in coping with bereavement or divorce are discussed.

Personality-Related Resources.   It seems reasonable to assume that individuals with stable and well-adjusted personalities should be better able to withstand the onslaught of stressful life events such as bereavement than people who are unstable and poorly adjusted. While there is some support for this hypothesis in studies of the relationship between unspecific stressful life events and health (e.g., Henderson, Byrne, & Duncan-Jones, 1981; Johnson & Sarason, 1978; Smith, Johnson, & Sarason, 1978), there is little conclusive evidence from research on bereavement. An extensive study conducted by Vachon, Sheldon, Lancee, Lyall, Rogers and Freeman (1982) as part of a 2-year longitudinal study of bereavement reported a plausible relationship between personality measured with the 16 Personality Factor Questionnaire (PFQ) (Cattell, Eber, & Tatsuoka, 1970) and the level of distress reported after 2 years, using the General Health Questionnaire (GHQ) (Goldberg, 1972). Vachon et al. (1982) found that their "enduring high distress group" had lower scores on Ego Strength (Factor C) and higher scores on Guilt Proneness (Factor O) and Anxiety (Factor Q_{11}) than the widowed characterized as "enduring low distress group" on the basis of the GHQ. Unfortunately, however, an interpretation of these findings in terms of a stable correlation between the GHQ and the 16 PFQ is hard to rule out in the absence of a nonbereaved control group.

More convincing support for the role of personality in moderating bereavement outcome can be found in a study of suicide following bereavement (Bunch, 1972). When comparing bereaved individuals who had committed suicide to a bereaved control group that had not, Bunch found that significantly more suicide than nonsuicide controls had had psychiatric treatment before bereavement. Most of these had been suffering from depressed mood, sleep disturbance, and anxiety. This suggests that predisposition to psychiatric disturbances rather than situational stress factors connected with the loss itself is critical in a suicide outcome to bereavement.

Skills.   Since we argued that the stress of bereavement is partly due to the fact that the widowed has to take over some of the functions previously performed by the deceased, we predict that widowed individuals should experience the less stress, the greater their skill in performing these new duties. A wife who cannot drive a car and cannot balance a bank account or a husband who cannot cook or perform any other household chores will be initially worse off than individuals who have acquired the skills needed for these tasks. Unfortunately, we know of no studies that tested these hypotheses, either with the widowed or the divorced.

Financial Resources.   Even if individuals do not possess the skills needed to take over from their spouses, they may not experience much stress if they are able to find others to perform these tasks for them. One way to induce others to work for one is to pay for their help. For example, a widower who has been left with two small children can reduce some of the stress inherent in this situation, if he can afford to hire a housekeeper to perform some of the instrumental aspects of the spouse's role. At the other end of the scale, it certainly adds stress to the situation if the remaining spouse has to worry about how to make ends meet. Nevertheless, the relationship between socioeconomic status and bereavement outcome cannot be clearly predicted. The negative impact of insufficient financial resources may be counteracted by the more extended social support networks (Walker, MacBride, & Vachon, 1977), better provision of emotional and social support (Gorer, 1965), and lower involvement with marital partners (Lopata, 1973) of working-class persons.

Social Support.   Next to a stable personality, social support is probably the most valuable resource in facing potentially stressful demands. Even if individuals neither possess the skills needed to take over from their spouses nor the means to pay for help, they will receive all the help they need if they have neighbours, friends, and/or relatives who are willing to support them. In addition to fulfilling informational and material support functions, social support networks can also provide emotional support, companionship support, and validational support, which by its very nature cannot be elicited by financial inducements.

The importance of social support has been demonstrated in a number of studies on unspecific stressful life events that typically found that individuals who have close relationships to supportive others are better able to withstand stressful life events than individuals who do not have this kind of support. For example, Brown and Harris (1978) reported that the impact of stressful life events on the mental health of their sample of London women was moderated by the general level of intimacy with a spouse and the amount of social support typically received from that partner. Similar results have been reported by Eaton (1978) and Surtees (1980).

An early investigation of the impact of social support on bereavement outcome was conducted by Maddison and Walker (1967). In a questionnaire study of 132 widows, they found that widows assigned to a "bad outcome" category on the basis of self-reports of their physical and mental health 13 months after bereavement also perceived their interpersonal relationships as less supportive during the crisis than widows classified as the "good outcome" group. However, since the social support measure was taken retrospectively at the same time as the health measures, the causal direction is rather unclear.

Further evidence for the importance of social support in moderating bereavement outcome comes from a longitudinal study by Vachon et al. (1982) who related the level of perceived social support to mental health. Vachon et al. (1982) reported that low satisfaction with social support 1 month after bereavement was a good predictor of poor outcome 2 years later.

Mechanisms Mediating the Impact of Stress on Health

The final and probably most intriguing issue we discuss here is *how* stressful life events such as bereavement or divorce can lead to a health deterioration. After all, the death of one's spouse does not operate in the same manner on one's bodily system as the entry of some alien bacterium or lethal instrument. The health consequences of stressful life events such as bereavement are likely to be mediated by behavioral as well as physiological changes. In our discussion of mechanisms mediating health deterioration, we focus first on the impact of loss on behavior.

In a persuasive analysis of health behavior, the economist Becker (1976) suggested that every death is more or less a suicide. Most of us take care of our health by limiting our tobacco and alcohol consumption and by engaging in some physical exercise. Undoubtedly, however, we could do much more for our health (e.g., become vegetarians, stop smoking and drinking altogether, or give up our stressful jobs). Thus, we sacrifice a somewhat better health or longer life because it conflicts with other aims. Becker (1976) speculates: "that there is an 'optimal' expected length of life, where the value in utility of an additional year is less than the utility foregone by using time and other resources to obtain that year. Therefore, a person may be a heavy smoker or so committed to work as to omit all exercise, not necessarily because he is ignorant of the consequences . . . , but because the lifespan forefeited is not worth the cost to him of quitting smoking or working less intensively" [pp. 9–10].

In describing their feelings after the death of their partner, bereaved individuals typically report that, at least initially, life no longer seemed worth living. The significant increase in suicides in the period immediately following the loss (Kaprio & Koskenvuo, 1983; MacMahon & Pugh, 1965) attests to the seriousness of these claims. Even some of the "accidental" deaths are probably outright suicides, while others may be the result of a combination of stress and lack of care. In such an emotionally arousing and stressful situation, accidents are likely to happen and can only be avoided if additional attention is paid to one's safety. However, with the value of life so significantly reduced, the bereaved are unlikely to make great efforts to attend to their own safety.

Other causes of death in which widowed rates are excessive when compared to married rates could be considered as the result of a slow process of self-destruction. Thus, the commonest *known* causes of liver cirrhosis are heavy drinking over many years and malnutrition. Since even advanced cases of alcoholic cirrhosis can be improved or virtually cured by abstention from alcohol and a regulated diet, death from cirrhosis can be considered at least partially self-inflicted.

The increase in mortality due to tuberculosis is probably a joint result of lack of health care and the immunosuppressive effects of stress. Since tuberculosis can typically be arrested or even cured by drug treatment, the excess of tuberculosis deaths among the bereaved suggests that medical treatment may not have been sought in time. A poor diet is also a factor contributing to the illness, for tubercle bacilli thrive in the presence of malnutrition and tuberculosis patients require a good mixed diet with sufficient protein and vitamins.

Because tuberculosis infections are frequently counteracted by the healthy body's own natural defences, the increase in these infections may also reflect the impact of bereavement on the immune system. Since Selye's (1946) classic work on the effect of stress on the immune system, it has been known that stress increases individual susceptibility to infectious diseases. Consistent with this assumption, more recent research has found evidence for the immunosuppressive effects of bereavement (Bartrop, Lazarus, Luckhurst, Kiloh, & Penny, 1979; Goodwin, Bromberg, Taszak, Kazubowski, Messner, & Neal, 1981).

There is some speculation (e.g., Frederick, 1971; Solomon, 1969) that the immunosuppressive effect attributed to stress, which reduces the organism's chance to recognize and destroy foreign tumour cells, could also be responsible for the relationship between psychosocial stress and cancer. Sklar and Anisman (1981) advanced a similar but more general argument when they suggested that the mobilization of resources or the potential exhaustion of resources due to extended stress experiences may render the organism less capable of efficiently contending with malignant cells.

The impact of stress on the cardiovascular system has received much attention by the popular press as well as by researchers in medicine and psychology (e.g., Dembrowski, Weiss, Shields, Haynes, & Feinleib, 1978; Glass, 1977). Three different mechanisms have been identified by which stress can contribute to coronary heart disease. First, stress is likely to accelerate the development of atherosclerosis by increasing the secretion of catecholamines and corticosteroids. Catecholamines, jointly with the corticosteroid cortisol, mobilize fat stores. Thus, increased production of catecholamines and cortisol leads to increased levels of serum cholesterol. Serum cholesterol is a major factor in the formation of plaques (i.e., fatty deposits), which consist mainly of excess amounts of serum lipids. While some plaque formation is quite normal, substantial occlusion can impair the blood supply to the heart. There is now ample evidence from studies of animals as well as humans that links stress experiences to increases in serum cholesterol (e.g., Friedman, Byers, & Brown, 1967; Paré, Rothfeld, Isom, & Varardy, 1973; Rahe, Rubin, & Arthur, 1974). Second, catecholamine increases the tendency of blood to coagulate. This is a great advantage when an organism is wounded, but it may contribute to the formation of blood clots thereby blocking arteries, especially arteries already narrowed down due to the formation of atherosclerotic plaque. Third, increases in catecholamine output lead to increased blood pressure. The pressure produced in the arteries as the heart pumps blood through them will be elevated by any of three changes: (1) increased cardiac output (i.e., the amount of blood pumped out of the left ventricle per minute); (2) constriction of the blood vessels; and (3) increases in the fluid volume. The sympathetic nervous system regulates blood pressure by controlling cardiac output and vasoconstriction through the release of catecholamines.

Further strain on an already damaged heart and the risk of sudden death may result from processes described by Engel (1978). He argued that the inability to cope with a negative emotional situation may simultaneously activate two contradictory biological reactions to emergency situations, namely the "fight–flight" and the "conservation–withdrawal" systems. While the "fight–flight" system moblizes the bodies resources for massive motor action, activation of the "conservation–withdrawal" system leads to inactivity, that is, to internal withdrawal from the situation. Normally the two systems inhibit each other, but Engel (1978) proposed that situations of uncertainty and hopelessness may lead to a simultaneous activation of both systems. For healthy individuals, the result may be vasodepressor syncopes or benign arrhythmias, but for people who already suffer from heart trouble, this additional strain may lead to death.

Conclusions and Implications

Intense stress can lead to health deterioration either directly, by affecting various neurochemical and hormonal processes, or indirectly, by changes in individual health behavior. Such stress is neither a feature of the situation nor the person but results from situational demands that tax or exceed the resources of the individual. Although loss of a partner is a situation experienced as stressful by most people, the magnitude of stress is likely to be moderated by aspects of the situation as well as differences in individual coping resources.

In his classic treatment of bereavement, Parkes (1972) lists a number of situational variables that have been shown to affect the magnitude of distress. For example, bereavement is likely to be more stressful not only if the partners had been strongly attached to each other but also if some degree of ambivalence had existed in their relationship. Type of death of the spouse has also been shown to affect outcome. Health consequences tend to be more serious if the death of the partner is sudden and unexpected (e.g., due to an accident) rather than anticipated (e.g., the result of a chronic disease). Parkes reasoned that the loss was less stressful if individuals had had some time to prepare themselves for it. On the basis of our analysis of social deficits (Stroebe et al., 1980, 1982) we suggested that marital roles and interaction patterns are critical for bereavement outcome. For example, the level of division of labor practiced in marriage should affect the stress experienced by the surviving partner. With a strict division of labour rather than a sharing of marital tasks, the surviving spouse is likely to be less used to performing functions that were previously part of the duties of the deceased spouse.

Of the resources we considered important in moderating the stress of bereavement and divorce, the availability of a social support system has been investigated most extensively. And indeed, it seems reasonable to suppose that the impact of the deficits can be ameliorated by supportive others. Obviously, nobody can replace the lost person, but others can help to make the situation less stressful by offering not only information and material aid but also companionship and emotional support.

Neighbours, relatives, and friends can also help in what is probably the most daunting task facing widowed or divorced individuals—the task of adjusting to their new social identity. As we suggested earlier, membership of the marital group contributes to social identity. Therefore, once the status is no longer held (as in widowhood or divorce) a reconstruction of self is required. Lopata's work (e.g., 1973, 1975, 1979) provides an extensive consideration of this issue. Drawing on the theory of symbolic interactionism (Berger & Luckman, 1966; Mead, 1934) and from her own detailed analyses of role changes and identity reconstruction in Chicago widows, Lopata (e.g., 1973) reasoned that marital partners serve a major function for each other in the formulation of identity, which takes place through a complex social interaction process. Over time, this will have led to relatively stable definitions of the self, the other, and the situation. On death or divorce, reformulation of these prior identities is required. The more pervasive and important the marital relationship, the more reformulation will be needed on its dissolution. In line with this analysis, we argue that the deficits accompanying death or divorce, which we have already described, deliver a shattering blow to the self-concept. Loss of information or task functions leads to a reassessment of one's own competence. Loss of validation support leads to loss of confidence in one's own judgments. Loss of emotional and companionship support leads to loss of self-worth, esteem, and feelings of personal security. Most centrally, loss of social identity leads to loss of the stabilized and definite self-concept that had emerged through interaction with the spouse over the years. The resultant depressed and hopeless psychological state of the grieving spouse is one of high risk for psychological and physical ailments.

In this perspective, coping resources may be regarded as factors that bolster a positive self-concept. Personality variables such as self-esteem are clearly relevant. Perhaps most important, however, and empirical research supports this, is the presence of, and interaction with, substitute support figures who, by taking on some of the functions of the lost spouse, guide and help the bereaved or divorced person toward a new, positive self-concept that is in line with the changed circumstances in which the bereaved or divorced find themselves. Loss of a loved partner is, in many ways, loss of the self, or, to put the message in literary terms, ''one's not half two. It's two are halves of one'' (e. e. cummings).

14 Examining the Causes and Consequences of Jealousy: Some Recent Findings and Issues

Robert G. Bringle
Purdue University at Indianapolis

Bram Buunk
University of Nijmegen, The Netherlands

INTRODUCTION

Until the second half of the 1970s, most publications on jealousy were based on clinical studies of extreme manifestations of jealousy such as paranoia and delusions concerning infidelity of the spouse (e.g., Mooney, 1965; Vaukhonen, 1968), homicide as a consequence of real or imagined infidelity (Mowatt, 1966; Psarska, 1970), and the link between jealousy and alcoholism (Hahn, 1933). In apparent contrast with these writings, the prevalent attitude in society prior to the mid 1970s was that jealousy was not pathological at all; on the contrary, analyses of the writings in popular magazines in this period show that a certain amount of jealousy was viewed as the natural evidence of love and was good for marriage (Brinkgreve & Korzec, 1978; Clanton & Smith, 1977).

Since the beginning of the 1970s, we have witnessed remarkable changes in attitudes toward jealousy among scholars as well as in certain segments of society. With the increasing emphasis on personal growth and autonomy in marriage and other intimate relationships—manifested in popular writings such as *Open Marriage* by George and Nena O'Neill (1972)—more and more people came to see jealousy as a deficiency in their relationship and as something wrong with themselves that had to be overcome.

The view that reconceptualizes "normal" jealousy as being problematic has undoubtedly resulted in social psychologists being sensitive to the lack of knowledge concerning such an omnipresent and often overwhelming emotion. Most programs of research on jealousy of which we are aware started around 1974; this includes our own independent work as well as research by Greg White, Jeff Bryson, and Ralph Hupka. Yet after a decade, published studies are still few in number and limited in scope because many of the findings that are currently available are conceptually scattered and have not been cross-validated.

First, we intend to summarize some of the conceptual issues that have shaped recent research. Furthermore, we will present a general overview of our own research on jealousy: in doing so, we will examine personal, situational, and relationship factors influencing jealousy; the relative importance of these determinants; and how persons cope when jealous. Finally, we will provide some suggestions concerning future directions for research. For the purpose of this chapter, we define jealousy as the aversive emotional response to a partner's real, imagined, or potential attraction for a third person.

CONCEPTUAL AND METHODOLOGICAL ISSUES

Jealousy as Label Versus Situation

One issue in which approaches to jealousy can differ is the extent to which they focus on "jealousy" as a *label*. For example, one can ask people directly how jealous they are in a specific relationship, or one can look at the structure of feelings and behaviors that are, according to the respondents, characteristic of their jealousy (e.g., Bryson, 1976; White, 1981a). This strategy allows respondents to determine how the term applies to themselves and their relationships. In contrast, other approaches have focused on the way people react to certain specific *situations* or events that are generally considered as jealousy evoking (e.g., Bringle, 1981a; Buunk, 1980c, 1982a). Because of the many different connotations of the word "jealousy," these researchers have preferred to look at the reactions of respondents to well-defined situations where the meaning of the intensity or reaction type is more clearly defined and less equivocal than when one asks people to reflect on instances of "jealousy."

Jealous Versus Upset

When one follows the situational approach just mentioned, two different courses can be taken. One can proceed to ask people how "jealously" they would react in such a situation (e.g., Bringle, 1981a). However, because jealousy has a negative connotation in our culture, it is possible (although only anecdotal evidence is available to support the possibility) that people may resist labeling their reactions in this way, even when they do feel badly as a result of a specific event that is, to an observer, clearly a jealousy-evoking event (cf. Clanton, 1981). Therefore, in some research, the word "jealousy" is avoided as a response label and respondents are simply asked to indicate how "upset" they had been or how aversively they would react in a certain situation (e.g., Bringle, 1982; Buunk, 1982a).

Anticipated Versus Actual

Another issue in which situational approaches differ is whether they focus on *anticipated* jealousy (e.g., Bringle, Renner, Terry, Davis, 1983; Shettel-Neuber, Bryson, & Young, 1978) or on jealousy that *actually* occurs or has occurred (e.g., Bryson, 1977; Buunk, 1980b). This issue is important because the way people actually react can often be very different from their anticipated reactions, and this may be particularly true of strong emotions such as jealousy. Although there are examples of researchers creating experimental procedures designed to evoke jealousy (Bryson, 1977; Mathes, Phillips, Skowran, & Dick, 1982a) others have relied on reports of jealousy that had occurred in the recent past as a consequence of an extramarital sexual relationship of the spouse (Buunk's research on this is discussed later).

Qualitative Versus Quantitative

A last main issue in which research on jealousy can be distinguished is whether one focuses on the *qualitative* or *quantitative* aspects of jealousy (Bringle & Williams, 1979). A qualitative approach tries to distinguish several distinct ways in which jealousy is experienced or expressed and examines patterns of reactions (e.g., Bryson, 1976; Francis, 1977). In contrast, a quantitative approach assumes that there are individual differences in the intensity or frequency of global jealous reactions and examines correlates of these differences. There is no necessary contradiction between the two approaches, and the qualitative approach has typically also been quantitative. For example, it can be theoretically important to look for the different correlates of different jealousy reactions, such as anger or depression.

Sampling

In addition to these issues, there is the issue of subject populations from which samples have been drawn. Most research on jealousy has been conducted on relationships of college students that are either relatively uncommitted or, even when there is a clear commitment, have been of rather short duration. There is sufficient reason to suppose that in long-term, committed marriages jealousy plays quite a different role and has different causes and consequences than in relationships that are in their early phases of development. For instance, there are likely to be many important differences between the jealousy experienced by casually dating couples when one of the partners dates another person, and the jealousy that will arise in a marriage of 20 years when one spouse, after always having been faithful, becomes involved in an extramarital relationship.

PERSON DETERMINANTS OF JEALOUSY

Although there are numerous characteristics of persons that can influence how they respond to jealousy-evoking events, one approach that has been taken is to consider how personality characteristics are related to the intensity and/or frequency of jealous reactions. It is also possible to assume that there are reliable individual differences in reactions to jealousy-evoking events, an approach that has been termed "dispositional jealousy" (Bringle, 1981a).

Study 1

One of the personality characteristics most frequently referred to in discussions of jealousy has been self-esteem. Low self-esteem has been regarded both as a predisposing characteristic to jealous reactions and as a consequence of having been jealous. In a study using college students (Bringle, 1981a), persons who reported high dispositional jealousy tended to be those who had low self-esteem ($r = -.38$, $p = .01$). This relationship has been found in three studies by other researchers (e.g., Jaremko & Lindsey, 1979; Manges & Evenbeck, 1980; White, 1977), although there are exceptions (Buunk, 1982a; White, 1981a). The Bringle study also found that dispositionally jealous persons were more dissatisfied with their lives than those reporting less jealous reactions ($r = -.46$, $p < .01$), a finding that is conceptually consistent with the self-esteem relationship. Furthermore, White (1981b) has presented evidence that the effects of self-esteem on jealous reactions may be mediated through perceived inadequacy in a particular relationship.

The final variable investigated in this study was locus of control. It was anticipated that jealous persons would have an external locus of control because jealousy is viewed as a reaction to real or imagined threats. This was confirmed ($r = .30$, $p < .01$) and has been replicated by White (1981d), although Jaremko and Lindsey (1979) failed to replicate this relationship.

Study 2

A second study on personality correlates replicated these findings and extended them (Bringle, 1981a; Bringle, Evenbeck, & Schmedel, 1977). Using Steiner's (1974) benevolent–malevolent scale with a sample of 90 college students, jealous persons were again found to be more externally controlled ($r = .36$, p

< .01), and to a lesser degree, malevolent in their attitudes toward the world ($r = -.25, p < .05$).

Anxiety has been construed as resulting from individuals believing that the world is threatening and that they have little control over it (e.g., Lazarus, 1968). Because of the findings in the first study concerning self-esteem and locus of control, it was expected that jealous persons would also be quite anxious. Using Zuckerman's Anxiety Scale, the second study found this to be the case ($r = .36$, $p < .01$). Three subsequent studies have supported this finding (Buunk, 1982b; Jaremko & Lindsey, 1979; Mathes, Roter, & Joerger, 1982b).

Study 3

Given that jealous persons are anxious, it may be possible to find examples of ways in which they attempt to manage the anxiety that is associated with a threatening interpersonal environment. Rokeach's (1960) view of dogmatism was identified as one such defensive reaction. Dogmatic persons have been shown, in spite of attempts to control their anxiety, to be more anxious, rigid, and self-deprecating (Vacchiano, 1977). A third study (Bringle, 1981a; Bringle et al., 1977) found jealous persons to be more dogmatic ($r = .35, p < .01$).

Study 4

Because of the central role that arousability assumes in cognitive theories of emotion (Arnold, 1960), it seemed reasonable to investigate the relationship between arousability and jealous reactions. Bringle and Williams (1979) included two measures that each relate to arousability. The screening–nonscreening dimension (Mehrabian, 1976) characterizes nonscreeners as individuals whose response to an environmental stimulus is of greater amplitude and duration than screeners. The second dimension included in the study, Repression–Sensitization (Byrne, 1961; Byrne, Barry, & Nelson, 1963), identifies repressors as being highly defensive when faced with threatening stimuli. This defensiveness results in avoidance strategies, little anxiety, and a lack of awareness of sources of threat. Both of these dimensions were found to be independently related to jealousy responses, such that highly jealous persons were more likely to be both sensitizers and nonscreeners. White (1981d) has recently replicated this finding for Repression–Sensitization.

Although the correlations obtained in this type of research are moderate, ranging from .30 to .45, the pattern of correlations is consistent with theoretical speculations concerning jealousy. Thus, these findings offer some evidence that there is continuity between relatively stable personality characteristics in individuals and how they perceive and react to jealousy-evoking events.

SITUATIONAL AND RELATIONSHIP DETERMINANTS
OF JEALOUSY

Although numerous studies have examined situational and relationship factors as determinants of jealousy (Bryson, 1977; White, 1977, 1981a, 1981b), most of these have used college samples. The following research by Buunk presents findings based on more heterogeneous samples with regard to background.

Study 1

In a first, exploratory study, a questionnaire was administered to a heterogeneous sample consisting of 250 Dutch persons. The majority of persons in the sample (77%) were older than 35. Most respondents were married (79%), and some were cohabitating (21%). All educational levels were represented, as were several degrees of sexual permissiveness—ranging from people who were members of the sexually liberal Dutch Association for Sexual Reform (NVSH) to people belonging to a rather conservative ecumenical church denomination (for a description of the sample, see Buunk, 1980c). The first question explored in this study was which *situational* variables determined the degree of jealousy people would anticipate experiencing. However, because of considerations outlined before, the word "jealousy" was avoided; people were simply asked to what extent they would feel *upset* if their partner and someone of the opposite sex were to engage in certain behaviors, varying from having fun and dancing to being involved in a long-term affair.

The results showed that those behaviors that involved some erotic or sexual component, such as flirting, petting, and sexual intercourse, triggered much more jealousy than other behaviors, even when these other behaviors included a rather high degree of intimacy with the third person, such as talking about intimate matters (Buunk, 1978). Not only is intimacy with a third person that occurs outside a sexual relationship not as likely to arouse jealousy as when it occurs within such a relationship, but sexual relationships without emotional intimacy were found to evoke more jealousy than intimacy alone. Of course, there are individual differences in this respect. Although these effects were quite reliable, cross-cultural research (Buunk & Hupka, 1984) suggests remarkable differences between cultures in the types of behavior that are perceived as most or least threatening.

In addition to the jealousy-evoking behavior, this study also examined the importance of characteristics of the third person. When presented with several potential kinds of people with whom the spouse could have intercourse, more jealousy was evoked on the average by socially *undesirable* persons—such as people who were described as physically unattractive or disliked by the subject (Buunk, 1978). Apparently, it was a shock to respondents' self-concepts to learn that someone they loved was attracted to an undesirable other. Thus, these results suggest that such a blow to their self-value in their mate's eyes is, in general, a more important aspect of jealousy than the fear of losing the partner; indeed, if fear was the dominant factor in jealousy, respondents would have been more threatened by a sexually attractive and likable person who could possibly replace them.

Because of the apparent salience of sexual and erotic behavior in determining jealous reactions, Buunk constructed a scale to measure this variable by summing up responses to the following five behaviors: the spouse having a long established sexual relationship, falling in love, sexual contact, petting, and flirting. The scale has a high reliability (alpha = .94). In contrast with several American studies on jealousy, females scored significantly higher on this scale than males (Buunk, 1978, 1980a). Second, despite many propositions in the clinical and sociological literature about the link between jealousy and feelings of inferiority and a negative self-image (e.g., Hansen, 1980; Lobsenz, 1977; Mead, 1970), in this study jealousy among males was not significantly correlated with a low self-esteem, as measured by a Rosenberg-type of scale, while there was a significant correlation for females, $r = -.20, p < .05$.

As social exchange theory (Burgess & Huston, 1979; Thibaut & Kelley, 1959) would predict, two other variables turned out to be much more important: first, emotional dependency, defined as the relative importance of the relationship with the partner compared to other things in life; second, one's own extramarital inclinations, a variable neglected in most other jealousy research. Subjects who indicated that they would, if the opportunity presented itself, engage in each of the five erotic and sexual behaviors that were used in the scale for jealousy indicated far less upset than respondents who said they would refrain from such involvements. This finding was replicated in other studies, even when the influence of other factors was controlled for (Buunk, 1982b). Such findings suggest that the norm of *reciprocity* concerning extradyadic relationships is operating in jealousy in that people are inclined to allow their partners the same level and kind of involvement as they are claiming for themselves. It is also possible that a high degree of extramarital involvement makes one less dependent on or more detached from the marital relationship. In both cases, the lower degree of jealousy to easy to explain.

Study 2

Because the findings in the previous study were based on anticipated reactions, they have to be viewed with some caution. Therefore, a second study was conducted with 218 Dutch persons whose partner had, in fact, had at least one extradyadic sexual relationship during the past 2 years. Respondents were selected mainly via advertisements in several periodicals. Most respondents were married (87%), some (13%) were cohabiting. More than half of the sample

(52%) were between 27 and 36 years of age; more than a third (36%) were older than 36 (see Buunk, 1980b).

The first question in this study dealt with the experience of jealousy; specifically, what exactly is it that people *don't* like about the fact that their partner has a sexual relationship or contact with another person? What do they perceive as the painful or unpleasant aspects of such an involvement? Eleven possible perceptions were each presented two times: First, respondents were asked to respond with respect to the partner's most significant extramarital relationship in the past; second, with respect to their partner's extradyadic sexual involvement in general. The four perceptions mentioned most often on both of these measures were (1) affective deprivation, the idea of getting less attention than before; (2) the perception that the partner enjoyed certain things more with the other person; (3) feeling excluded from the activities of the partner; and (4) uncertainty. Together, these perceptions point to a perceived threat to the exclusivity and intimacy of the primary relationship. Another frequently mentioned perception—the unpleasant feeling of no longer being the only one for the partner— reflects a related source of upset. It is noteworthy that the fear of losing the partner turned out to be of relatively minor importance. Apparently, as was the case in the last study discussed, jealousy is not necessarily grounded in a fear of losing a loved one.

Thus, what is important, besides a blow to the perceived evaluation by the mate, is the violation of exclusivity and intimacy. This emphasizes the importance of having an exclusive area of feelings and behaviors with the partner that is not supposed to be shared with others and that are supposed to be superior to other relationships both partners may have (Buunk, 1978, 1980a). Note again that, although this exclusive area embraces more aspects than the sexual relationship with the partner, jealousy as a feeling of violated exclusivity was especially sensitive to any sexual involvement of the spouse. Thus, exclusivity appears to be of central importance to understanding jealousy. It seems that the exclusivity of some behaviors and activities is valued by most couples in Western culture. However, couples probably also differ widely in the *areas* they consider exclusive in their relationships and in the *degree* to which they view their relationships as exclusive.

A second question in this study concerned the way people *coped* with the fact that their partners had an extramarital relationship. Embracing probably only a few of the possible coping strategies, a factor analysis of a scale of 13 coping items clearly revealed three factors (see Buunk, 1982a). The first factor indicated mainly the strategy of *avoidance*. Several items loading high on this factor referred directly to retreating on one's own and avoiding the spouse. The other items loading high on this factor included negative feelings toward the spouse, the rival, or oneself, such as the wish that the spouse end the affair, reproach toward the rival, wishes for revenge, and feelings of self-doubt. The picture this factor evokes is that of a person escaping the situation and worrying. On the average, about 20% of the respondents reported reacting in this manner at least sometimes.

The second factor referred also to an individual strategy and can be called *reappraisal* because it refers to cognitive attempts to reduce one's jealousy. More than half of the sample had used this strategy at least sometimes. The strategy seems to include first, a critical attitude toward one's own jealousy and, second, direct attempts to get the jealousy under control, for example, by re-evaluating the whole situation.

The most frequently mentioned coping strategy appeared in the third factor, *communication*. Nearly all respondents indicated that they tried to have open and frank discussions with their spouse about the whole situation. No less than two-thirds tried to do the same with the third person. It must be emphasized, however, that the more people felt jealous, the more their communication style was characterized by behaviors such as blaming the other, nagging, complaining, and trying to get their own way by any means (Buunk, 1980a).

The last question in this reasearch examined correlates of jealousy. First, neuroticism or general anxiety was not only correlated with the felt intensity and frequency of jealousy but also with the coping styles of avoidance and reappraisal. Second, jealousy resulting from the most significant extramarital relationship of the spouse was less intense when the respondent had been involved in at least one extramarital relationship. So, again, reciprocity seems to be an important concern. However, emotional dependency was only slightly correlated with jealousy in this sample. Third, also in this study, women reported more intense upset than men. Fourth, low self-esteem again did not or only slightly correlated with jealousy (Buunk, 1980a, 1982b).

THE RELATIVE IMPORTANCE OF PERSON AND SITUATIONAL DETERMINANTS OF JEALOUS REACTIONS

Most studies to date have focused predominantly on either a person or situational determinant of jealousy to the exclusion of the other. Studies that have compared person and situational determinants (Buunk, 1982b; White, 1977) have found that a specific personality characteristic—self-esteem—was less important in predicting jealous reactions than situational factors (e.g., relative level of involvement in the relationship). However, the interaction effect of the two factors was not evaluated in these studies, so that the possibility of a Person × Situation interaction has not been directly considered in any study. While taking only one perspective is not necessarily a critical weakness in any particular study, decisions about the direction of future research will depend on a comparative evaluation of the different perspectives.

Taking the conceptual distinction inherent in the work of Endler and Magnusson (1976a) on the interaction of personal and situational determinants of behavior, four possible approaches emerge. The first approach attributes most of the variability in jealous reactions to individual differences—an approach often characterized as the trait approach. The second possibility, representing a behaviorist perspective, is that situational cues account for differences in reactions.

A third perspective, which is a combination of the trait and behaviorist approach, and one that is actually closest to what trait theorists have proposed in practice, is the dispositional view. According to this view (Bringle, 1981b; Bringle & Williams, 1979), it is not assumed that an individual will always display the same degree of emotionality to different events, nor is it assumed that the same event will elicit the same reaction in all persons. The dispositional view does state that there are meaningful person effects *and* situational effects. That is, it posits that there are meaningful and reliable differences among individuals in their propensity to become jealous and among jealousy-evoking events in their propensity to elicit jealous reactions. Thus, reactions across a variety of situations should be correlated for individuals, and vice versa. The dispositional perspective, then, can be viewed as subsuming the "trait" and "behaviorist" approaches to analyzing jealous reactions. The fourth perspective assumes that some interaction of the person and situational determinants accounts for the pattern of reactions, *and* it states that neither the person nor situation main effect will be important.

Study 1

Since the dispositional and interaction predictions are somewhat mutually exclusive, in that the dispositional view predicts significant person and situation main effects while the interaction view posits that these main effects will be unimportant, the methodology proposed by the interactionists can provide some guidance as to the relative importance of determinants of jealousy. In the first study on this issue, 20 jealousy-evoking events were presented to 302 respondents who were asked to rate the intensity with which they would expect to feel jealous, envious, angry, sad, fearful, and guilty for each of them (Bringle et al., 1983). Using a three-way analysis of variance (Endler, 1966), the variance components for Subjects, Events, Affective responses and their interactions could be estimated. A dispositional view of jealousy was supported by the fact that there was a sizable Person main effect (15% to 16%) and Situation main effect (11% to 12%). However, the largest single component was the Person × Situation interaction (16% to 19%). Thus, in addition to finding reliable person and situational differences, the data also showed that different individuals perceived different levels of threat in the various situations.

Study 2

Given that the Person × Situation interaction was sizable, a study was designed to analyze the nature of this interaction (Bringle et al., 1983). In this study, the situational factors were conceptually separated into two components, the jealousy-evoking event, and the specific partner who is associated with that event. Furthermore, the particular partner was viewed as being unique both as a person and also because of the nature of the relationship between the partner and the jealous person. These conceptual distinctions were then designed into a questionnaire that would allow an evaluation of the separate components. Seventy-one female respondents in the study were presented with three jealousy-evoking events like the following:

> Your partner has been playing tennis every Saturday for the past month with the same person. This Saturday you decide to meet him for a drink, at which time you discover his tennis partner is a stunning young woman with a terrific serve.

In each of the situations the actual threat was unclear; thus, the characteristics of the partner and the type of relationship one has with the partner can maximize or minimize the amount of perceived threat and upset. The three events were responded to for each of the following three actual partners: the respondent's current partner, the most recent partner with whom she had been romantically involved, and next-most-recent partner. Thus, respondents rated how "threatened" and "upset" they would feel if each event happened with each of these three actual partners.

Again, an ANOVA was used to estimate the relative importance of variability attributable to Subjects, Partners, Jealousy-evoking events, and the interactions. Because the three situations were purposely similar in nature they did not affect results greatly. The largest component was Subjects (34.6% to 37.4%). The Subject × Partner interaction (34.3% to 35.2%) accounted for the next greatest proportion of variance and indicates that, within respondents and across events, different partners evoked differing levels of threat and upset.

While the analysis of variance procedure allows the relative contributions of the person and situational components to be assessed, this type of analysis fails to explain how or why the variables interact. Thus, the question of *why* the partner is important in producing different reactions in the same person remained to be explored. In addition to responding to the situations, the respondents also rated the balance of power in each of the three relationships on the items "who's more in love" and "who's more involved" and the personality characteristics of the three partners. Analyses showed that individuals who reported being more in love and more involved, and presumably had less power in the relationship, reported more threat and upset. When considered together, the personality characteristics of the partners did not explain any additional variance.

These findings demonstrated again that there are reliable individual differences in jealous reactions, but that, within this rank order of persons, respondents reported that the intensity of their reaction was different for different partners. Furthermore, this study not only replicates the finding that interpersonal power is an important determinant of jealous reactions but goes beyond that finding by demonstrating that it is a predictor of intrasubject variability in jealous responses. Thus, we now know one reason that the same person will display different intensities of reactions is because of relationship differences with different partners and not differences in the partner's characteristics that were studied.

Since both the dispositional and interaction predictions were supported in the first study discussed in this section, these results do not provide overwhelming support for either point of view. However, the fact that a null finding on either the person factor, the situational factor, or their interaction was not obtained is important in guiding future research. Although any particular set of results is consistent with several interpretations (Olweus, 1976, 1977), the results are interpreted as supporting continued effort in attempting to theoretically understand and empirically investigate jealousy from the point of view of either the person, situation, or their interaction.

Clanton (1981) has commented that to construe jealousy in a dispositional fashion is counterproductive because it stereotypes and stigmatizes jealous persons and leads to the conclusion that they are "profoundly and irretrievably jealous" [p. 264]. However, to speak of dispositional jealousy is not to apply a clinical label of behavioral pathology, but, rather, to employ a conceptual perspective that this research endorses as a meaningful part of a larger picture. No one has ever assumed that traits would explain all of the variability in jealous responses. To interpret correlations between jealousy and personality traits of .3 and .4 as if they were 1.0, as Clanton has done, is as inaccurate as assuming them to be .00. The present findings do imply that future work on jealousy that ignores person-based determinants will be incomplete. Thus, no one of these different paradigms will be comprehensive and an approach to conceptualizing and investigating jealousy that balances intrapersonal, interpersonal, and societal influences will be most worthwhile.

FUTURE ISSUES FOR RESEARCH ON JEALOUSY

Person Issues

As a final topic, we will discuss several issues that may play a future role in the better understanding of jealousy. Concerning person-oriented issues, the area of social cognition may provide some valuable inputs into jealousy research. Whereas the traditional cognitive theories of emotion (e.g., Lazarus, 1968; Schachter, 1964) portray cognition as a necessary part of the emotional experience, Leventhal (1980) and Zajonc (1980) have recently argued that affect can arise in the absence of conscious cognitive activity. Their position is that all cognition is accompanied by affect, but that affect can occur as the result of only minimal processing of which the person is not aware.

One suggestion is that "interrupts," which are defined as unexpected events occurring or expected events not occurring (Berscheid, 1983; Fiske, 1980; Mandler, 1975), can release the partially independent affective response. Conscious cognitive activity, including attributional processes, can follow this affective response and influence subsequent reactions. Such ideas could have important implications for understanding responses to jealousy-evoking events and how people manage these responses (see Berscheid, 1983; Bringle, 1981a).

Since the mid 1970s, virtually all of the research on jealousy has been conducted on what is now referred to as "normal" jealousy, in contrast to "pathological" jealousy. However, the relationship between jealousy and personal and interpersonal adjustment has not been attacked directly. A number of possible relationships between jealousy and adjustment can legitimately be considered. For example, there could be no relationship between jealousy and adjustment. That is, the absence of jealousy can be associated with both healthy and unhealthy outcomes, as can the presence of jealousy. In contrast, some psychologists seem to assume a negative linear relationship that describes increases in jealousy as being increasingly maladaptive. Others have implied a positive relationship such that jealousy is good and its absence is not healthy because it indicates a lack of love and emotional responsiveness. Humanists could argue that both extremes of emotionality are not healthy, but that emotions, in general, are beneficial to persons and their relationships. Or again, any jealousy could be viewed as bad; or only extremely intense jealousy could be construed as unhealthy. In the future it will be necessary to obtain more definitive assessments of these issues.

Situational Issues

Concerning situational issues, the research results presented earlier suggest that it is mainly threats to the perceived evaluation by the spouse and the exclusivity of the relationship that are relevant, and that especially the *sexual* aspect of the partner's involvement seems to trigger these threats. However, it still is largely unclear *why* this sexual aspect is so important. This seems such a fundamental question that it should be given high priority in future research.

In addition to the results presented here, White (1981d) has also presented an analysis of threats. He used both judge's ratings and factor analysis to identify the following four motives: sexual attraction, nonsexual attraction to the rival, dissatisfaction with the relationship, and desire for greater commitment. Only "commitment" failed to produce significant correlations on measures of the subject's jealousy, the partner's jealousy, perceived threat in the relationship, and anger to hypothetical jealousy-evoking incidents. Thus, we now have several descriptions of categories of threats that are perceived in relationships. However, at a more general level, there is currently no theoretical basis that integrates the nature of perceived threats. Such a framework is needed and we anticipate that it will draw from attribution theory.

Person and Situation Issues

Concerning the interplay between person and situational determinants of jealousy, Bem and Allen (1974) and Snyder (1979) have demonstrated the importance of considering that some individuals may display more consistency across time than others. In addition, Snyder (1979) and Mischel (1977) suggest that situations may vary in their tendency to elicit behavior that is consistent with a person's underlying disposition. In the future, it will be necessary to consider moderator variables such as these in understanding jealous responses from both a personality and situational point of view.

Relationship Issues

Relationship variables, which have had the most success of any variables in predicting jealous reactions, clearly deserve subsequent attention. The most important variables here all seem in one way or another to be connected with *dependency* on the relationship. This has been supported by other studies (Berscheid & Fei, 1977; Bringle, Evenbeck, & Schmedel, 1977; Buunk, 1980c; Manges & Evenbeck, 1980; White, 1981a, 1981b) as well as by the data presented earlier that linked jealousy to emotional dependency and to a low degree of extramarital involvement. However, findings summarized earlier have shown that among people for whom the partner actually had been involved in an extramarital relationship, emotional dependency is hardly related to jealousy. Why this is the case is not completely clear. What *is* clear, however, is that dependency is not a unidimensional construct and that it probably has different meanings in different phases of a relationship. In the beginning of a relationship, the concepts of relative involvement and comparison level for alternatives may be relevant. However, as suggested earlier, it is questionable whether this is also true for long-lasting, committed relationships where dependency can, for example, be formulated in terms of the sources of satisfaction one has in addition to the intimate relationship (e.g., work, hobbies, or friends). In addition, other variables such as trust and communication style may be as important and should be examined more closely.

Using the Endler and Magnusson conceptual framework, it is not always clear if relationship variables such as relative involvement and dependency are more appropriately construed as situational or interaction variables. This problem may reflect the factors that Kelley (Chapter 1) has referred to that identify relationships as qualitatively distinct at a conceptual level from person and societal influences. However, future work can also focus on identifying those person and situational factors that result in some relationships showing balance and some inbalance; that is, determining why individuals end up in particular types of relationships. Greg White's (1981b) model represents an attempt to delineate these factors, and his research shows that discrepancies between own and partner's characteristics, such as physical attractiveness, produce differences in relative involvement.

Cultural Issues

There are also issues at the subcultural and cultural level that deserve attention. As Ralph Hupka (1981) has shown, cultural variables concerning property rights, the availability of sexual gratification, and the meaning of marriage and progeny account for cross-cultural variations in the incidence and severity of male jealousy reactions. Also, cultures prescribe which situations should be labeled jealousy evoking, what the appropriate reaction is, and which behaviors are most threatening. Similarly, within a culture, the norms and values one has toward extramarital relationships will influence the intensity and manifestation of jealousy. However, except for some studies among swingers (Gilmartin, 1977) and homosexuals (Ludwig, 1982), research has hardly paid any attention to the undoubtedly complex but nonetheless relevant interplay between norms and jealousy. It is evident that sexual jealousy is often a problem for people with permissive norms on extramarital sex. However, it is also clear that people who do get influenced by permissive norms, in general, develop a willingness to attempt to handle and reduce their jealousy—sometimes with success (Buunk, 1980a; Ramey, 1975). Nevertheless, sometimes such people fail in adapting their feelings to their norms (Denfield, 1974) and probably become less permissive, although how this interplay works is still not clear.

CONCLUSION

In conclusion, we think research on jealousy has made a promising start. Relevant questions are being attacked, even if few definite answers have yet been found. We hope that studies in this area will continue and will develop more closely in line with each other. More research is clearly needed, not only to provide more insight into jealousy itself, but also because such insight will give us more understanding of some of the fundamental aspects of intimate relationships such as intimacy, exclusivity, conflict, love, trust, and dependency.

ACKNOWLEDGMENTS

Portions of this chapter were prepared while the second author was an Honorary Fellow at the Family Study Center. I thank Professor Ira L. Reis of the center for his valuable comments. The research described here and the stay at the Family Study Center were supported by the Netherlands Organization for the Advancement of Pure Research (Z.W.O.)

15

Loneliness and the Degree of Intimacy in Interpersonal Relationships

Jenny de Jong-Gierveld
Vrije Universiteit
Amsterdam

INTRODUCTION

Feelings of well-being for most people appear to be related to the quantity and perceived quality of the person's network of social relationships. Ideally, this network should consist of social relationships with varying degrees of emotional contact, including a more personal, satisfying, mutually shared relationship (Derlega & Margulis, 1982; Levinger & Snoek, 1972; Litwak & Szelenyi, 1973). The realization of such a network of relationships is of crucial importance for alleviating loneliness. We define loneliness as the experiencing of a lag between realized and desired interpersonal relationships as disagreeable or unacceptable, particularly when the person perceives a personal inability to realize the desired interpersonal relationships within a reasonable period of time.

It is important to distinguish between loneliness and objective social isolation. By objective social isolation, we mean the absence of all those relationships between people exhibiting a certain degree of durability. Loneliness concerns a situation in which the number of meaningful, lasting, interpersonal relationships is *experienced* by the person as deficient, either qualitatively or quantitatively, and as less than satisfying in meeting the person's desires. Some researchers state that objective social isolation and feelings of loneliness may be two separate and perhaps independent conditions (Fischer & Phillips, 1982). This statement of nondependency might have to do with the scope of their investigations. Fischer and Phillips (1982) concentrated on quantitative aspects of the network—the *number* of available relationships—and consequently neglected the relevance of personal perception factors concerning the network of relationships. In our opinion, it is important for loneliness researchers to pay attention to specific aspects

241

of the person's social network as well as to the person's perception of the quality of the relationships-as-realized.

THEORETICAL BACKGROUND

The theoretical notions presented in this study are based on an analysis of relevant literature (Lazarus, Averill, & Opton, 1970; Perlman & Peplau, 1981) and our own empirical studies concerning loneliness (de Jong-Gierveld & Aalberts, 1980, 1982). These notions can be characterized as a cognitive approach with its emphasis on cognition as a mediating factor between characteristics of the social network and the experience of loneliness. Within this framework, attention is directed toward characteristics of the social network as well as toward evaluative aspects. We first focus on one of the more relevant characteristics of the social network: the presence or absence of a partner. In many Western countries, the number of people living without partners is rapidly increasing. In the United States, Canada, as well as in some European countries like Holland, Belgium, France, and the United Kingdom approximately 20% of the households consist of a single person. Another 5% of the (Dutch) households consist of a mother or father without a partner, living with offspring.

Several researchers evaluate this demographic development positively, emphasizing the benefits of being single (Adams, 1976; Libby, 1977). However, Adams and Libby are speaking of a rather specific group of singles—upper-middle-class college graduates. Perhaps this explains their positive position concerning singleness. Others have clearly shown the negative side of this development (Gove & Hughes, 1980; de Jong-Gierveld & Aalberts, 1980, 1982; Lynch, 1977; Starr & Carnes, 1972). "Living without a partner, either alone or as a family head, means that socially integrating possibilities with other adults exist only outside the household" (Kobrin & Hendershot, 1977). Weiss (1973) concentrating on a direct relationship between the presence or absence of a partner and feelings of loneliness, characterizes the situation of loneliness that pertains to all those people who have either lost or never had a close emotional attachment to a partner as "emotional loneliness." This should be distinguished from "social loneliness" which is related to the absence of satisfying relationships with friends, neighbours, etc. In these ideas, intermediating cognitive processes are ignored. In doing so, a series of important questions remains unanswered, such as for people living with a partner, what is the significance of less-satisfying and even nonsatisfying partner relationships with regards to loneliness? And for people living without a partner is it possible to remedy emotional loneliness through the integration of other adequate, substitute, emotional attachments? Is there a difference in the perceived degree of intimacy between partner relationships and these other (substitute) attachments? In summary: The *purpose* of this study is to examine in detail the relation between:

1. Aspects of the network of social relationships; especially the presence or absence of a partner.
2. Some characteristics of the subjective perception of the quantity and quality of the realized contacts (particularly the degree of intimacy).
3. The development and perpetuation of feelings of loneliness:

THE PRESENT STUDY

Method

Respondents.   Data were obtained from a sample of 556 adult men and women (ages 25 to 75). The sample was stratified on sex and marital status. Names and addresses of the subsamples of single, married, divorced, and widowed men and women were selected at random from the population registers of Haarlem, an older city (population about 175,000), Purmerend, a rapidly growing commuter city with many highrise apartments (population about 33,000), and Nieuwkoop (population about 9000), a village in the "green heart" of Holland. We managed to interview 248 people living with a partner (included in this category are unmarried couples living together), 150 people living alone (a one-person household), and 86 mothers or fathers living with the children ("parents without partners"). There were some other categories recognized in the sample, such as older unmarried and divorced men and women (still) living with their parents, and men and women living with brothers and sisters. The numbers of people in these categories were rather small and were therefore disregarded for this study. The interviews lasted from 2 to 3 hours, followed in most cases by an informal conversation about loneliness.

Questionnaire and Procedures.   Several loneliness measures were utilized in the survey, including a 34-item multidimensional measuring instrument incorporating three dimensions of loneliness:

1. *Emotional characteristics of loneliness* refer to the absence of positive emotions such as happiness and affection and the presence of negative emotions such as fear and uncertainty.
2. *Type of deprivation* refers to the nature of the missing relationships. In this regard, it is crucial to collect information concerning those relationships that the person considers to be essential. This component obviously varies greatly according to the category of individuals being studied. This dimension can be further differentiated into three subcategories: feelings of deprivation associated with the absence of an intimate attachment, feelings of emptiness, and feelings of abandonment.

3. *Time perspective* can also be further differentiated into three subcomponents: the extent to which loneliness is experienced as being unchangeable, the extent to which loneliness is experienced as temporary, and the extent to which a person resigns himself or herself to loneliness by attributing the cause of the loneliness to others. (see de Jong-Gierveld, 1978; de Jong-Gierveld & Raadschelders, 1982).

While multidimensional scales have the potential for identifying variations in the experience of loneliness (de Jong-Gierveld & Raadschelders, 1982; Russell, 1982) the focus of this study is not directed toward types of loneliness. In analyzing the relationship between loneliness and some other variables, we used the answers on the self-report loneliness question: the numbers of people stating they are "one of the moderately, very or extremely lonely people in society." In regards to the validity of this measure, a correlation of .66 was found between scores on this loneliness scale and the deprivation subscale of the multidimensional loneliness scale. The relationship with other variables is also rather substantial, for example, with depression ($r = .57$), with number of reported stressful life events ($r = .49$). Living arrangements were used to indicate the presence or absence of a partner in one's social network.

The person's perception of the quality of his or her network of social relationships is operationalized by means of two variables: the person's perception of the degree of intimacy as realized in his or her most-confidant relationship and the perception of the person of his or her personal network as in need of some new relationships. In determining confidant relationships, we focused on the names respondents gave in answer to a question concerning their closest relationships with others. Several characteristics of these closest relationships were asked, such as sex, type, and duration of the relationship. At the end of this series of questions, the interviewer asked for an overall indication of the degree of intimacy as realized in their relationships. The item format varied from 1, the relationship is rather superficial: "we only talk about one thing or another" to 5, the relationship is intimate: "he/she is the one I can rely on." Subsequently, the respondents were invited to rank the indicated names from 1 (most important for personal well-being) to x (least important . . .). The nature of the most important confidant relationship was determined by asking the respondent to circle a set of 20 relationship aspects with "yes, relevant in our relationship," or "no, not relevant."

The answers to each of the 20 items concerning the nature of the closest relationship were subjected to a principal component factor analysis with varimax rotation. This procedure identified three factors. We called these factors (1) emotional closeness; (2) mutual attachment; and (3) sociability. In order to conduct additional statistical analysis, items loading on a particular factor were unit weighed and summed to form an index. For example, a person who checked four out of the seven items within the emotional closeness factor received a score

of 4. For each of the most important confidant-relationship types, a mean respondent score on each of the three factors was computed. The person's perception of the quality of the network of relationships is subsequently indicated by
asking the respondents: "Do you desire new relationships with other people?"
Other questions in the interview schedule concerned background variables, social contacts, measures of self-esteem, and a measure of depression (van Rooijen, 1979).

Statistical Procedures.   Because we were interested in the effects of some
nominal or categorical variables on a dichotomous dependent variable loneliness,
an analysis based on the logit model was appropriate (Fienberg, 1977).

Results

Living Arrangements and Feelings of Loneliness.   As expected, living arrangements were significantly correlated with self-reported loneliness. People living
with a partner mentioned feelings of loneliness less frequently than people living
alone and (especially) parents without partners. In fact, about 60% of all parents
without partners mentioned feelings of loneliness, in contrast to about 13% of the
people living with a partner and 50% of the people living all alone. The differences between living arrangements were significant; the sex-differences were
of a minor order and are consequently ignored in the remainder of this chapter.
The results present a firm basis, then, for the assertion that network characteristics as measured by living arrangements, and feelings of loneliness, are two
intercorrelated conditions.

In accordance with our theoretical view, we emphasize that cognitive processes play a central role in perceiving the consequences of deficits in the social
network. Therefore, we further differentiated in the relation between living arrangements and feelings of loneliness by directing attention to the person's
perception of the degree of intimacy-as-realized in his or her most confidant
relationship and to the person's desires for new relationships.

*The Degree of Intimacy in the Most Confidant Relationship and Feelings of
Loneliness.*   As expected, there was a significant difference between the types
of most confidant relationships mentioned by people living with a partner and
people living without a partner: 89% of the men and women living with a partner
mentioned the partner; 5% a close relative; and 6% mentioned friends and neighbours. On the other hand, 3% of the men and women living without a partner
mentioned a partner; 54% a close relative; 25% a friend; 18% neighbours,

colleagues, and so on. Additionally, there was a remarkable discrepancy in the *nature* of the different types of confidant relationships. As can be seen in Table 15.1, the partner-as-confidant is characterized by a high score on emotional closeness (Factor 1). In cases where the confidant is a neighbour or colleague, the relationship is characterized by a relative high degree of sociability (Factor 3). Each of the confidant relationships scored high on mutual attachment (Factor 2).

The scores of the most confidant relationships on the overall-intimacy scale also differ according to the types of confidants mentioned (see Table 15.1). Intimacy scores were, on the whole, higher for respondents who mentioned a partner as most confidant relationship than for respondents who mentioned either a friend or a close relative. People who mentioned neighbours or colleagues scored least high on the intimacy scale. To summarize: There is a remarkable difference in perceived degree of intimacy between the partner and other most confidant relationships. As far as the intimacy component is concerned, partner and substitute relationships are not judged as comparable! This conclusion is in agreement with everyday opinions about the meaning of a partner, friend, or colleague relationship. The conclusion, however, is not in agreement with notions presented by Libby (1977) and others when they state that living alone is a positive option to marriage and other couple images in that people living alone are open to a diversity of intimate emotional relationships.

Additionally, it is important to know if differences in most-confidant-intimacy scores are related to feelings of loneliness, and the results show that this is indeed the case. People who scored less than 5 on the most-confidant-intimacy scale were more apt to be lonely than people who evaluated their most confidant relationship with a score of 5. This relation is true within each of the three categories of living arrangements distinguished in this study. Also recognizable was an (interaction) effect of living arrangement and intimacy when considered jointly: People living with a partner and considering their most confidant relationship as low in intimacy displayed a loneliness ratio that was significantly higher than could be expected when regarding living arrangements and intimacy scores independently. Consequently, the probability increases that such a person will say: "I am one of the lonely persons in our society." A "failing" (marriage) partnership notably increases the probability of loneliness.

The Desire for New Relationships and Feelings of Loneliness.   The subjective perception of one's social network as a network that needs (some) new relationship(s) is the central theme in this part of the analysis. Many respondents answered the question: "Do you desire new relationships with others?" in the affirmative (36% of all respondents). People living without a partner mentioned these desires more often than people living with a partner (42% vs. 28%). The results, presented in Table 15.2, point out that the desire for new relationships has a significant influence on feelings of loneliness. This is true within each of the

TABLE 15.1
The Most Confidant Relationship Classified by Type of Relationship
and by Mean Respondent Score on Three Factors
of Relationship Aspects and the Percent Scoring 5 ("Intimate")
on the Intimacy Scale

	Types of Most Confidant Relationship			
	Partner	*Friend*	*Close Relative*	*Neighbour, Colleague*
Mean respondent score on:				
Factor 1: emotional closeness				
(1, low → 7, high)	6.2	3.6	3.1	2.6
Factor 2: mutual attachment				
(1, low → 9, high)	7.5	6.5	6.5	6.7
Factor 3: sociability				
(1, low → 5, high)	0.6	1.6	1.7	2.7
Percent scoring 5 (intimate) on the overall intimacy scale				
(1, low → 5, intimate)	89	44	45	17

TABLE 15.2
Number of Respondents Who Labelled Themselves
as Lonely or Nonlonely and Their Desire for New Relationships,
Classified by Living Arrangements

	Living with a Partner		*Living Alone*		*Parents without Partners*		*Total*	
Desire for new relationships								
Lonely	17	*(24)*	44	*(77)*	34	*(83)*	95	*(57)*
Not lonely	53	(76)	13	(23)	7	(17)	73	(43)
		(100)		(100)		(100)		(100)
No desire for new relationships								
Lonely	16	*(9)*	32	*(34)*	18	*(40)*	66	*(21)*
Not lonely	162	(91)	61	(66)	27	(60)	250	(79)
		(100)		(100)		(100)		(100)
Total	248		150		86		484	

Statistics:
$G^2 = 2.26$, df = 2, $p = .32$.
Estimated parameters (all significant):
    ω living arrangements: − 1.414 (with partner)
                    .562 (living alone)
                    .854 (parents without partners)
    ω desire: .816

three categories of living arrangements. People who mentioned that their network needed some new relationships were, on the whole, more apt to be lonely than people who hadn't mentioned the desire for new relationships, regardless of the living arrangement considered. Interpreting this result: The subjective perception of one's social network as deficient and in need of some new relationships is an important cue for identifying oneself as lonely.

The Person's Network of Social Relationships, the Person's Perception of the Quality of the Network, and Feelings of Loneliness.   In the final section of this study, we discuss the interplay between the variables of living arrangements, the perception variables of degree of intimacy of the most confidant relationship and desire for new relationships, and labelling oneself as a lonely or nonlonely person.

The results here tended to show that the factors of living arrangements, intimacy, and the desire for new relationships each have a separate and significant influence on feelings of loneliness. People living without a partner, whose most confidant relationship has little or no intimacy, *and* who express the desire for new relationships can, as a consequence, be characterized as people with a high probability of loneliness. In contrast, people living with a partner, experiencing an intimate most confidant relationship, and expressing no desire for new relationships can be characterized as people with a low loneliness probability.

In summary: Living arrangements as well as characteristics pertaining to the subjective evaluation of one's social contacts, particularly the degree of intimacy and desires for new relationships, tend to be of crucial importance in predicting the occurrence of loneliness.

CONCLUSIONS

The study discussed here sheds light on the importance of both objective characteristics of the network of social relationships and the person's perception of the quality of the network of relationships for understanding the conditions in which the labels "lonely" or "nonlonely" are adopted by individuals.

People living without a partner are more apt to express feelings of loneliness than people living with a partner. Living arrangements as an objective feature of the social environment may then be considered an essential factor in determining the degree of well-being experienced in social relationships. The evaluations of living situations encountered in this study are in agreement with the earlier findings of Sermat (1978) and others concerning the relation between living arrangements and feelings of loneliness.

The subjective perceptions of the quality of the network of relationships-as-realized were also shown to be an important factor in the loneliness-labelling process. The subjective evaluation that one's social network is in need of new relationships proved to be a significant factor in locating loneliness under the respondents, while the perceived quality of the most confidant relationship also proved to be of great importance in evaluating the well-being in social relationships. People living alone frequently mention that their most confidant relationship is of a less intimate quality. A confidant relationship with little intimacy was related to greater occurrence of loneliness. Those people living with partners, who evaluated their most confidant relationship as less than intimate, also had a higher frequency of loneliness: A "failing" (marriage) partnership presumably increases the loneliness probability.

In regards to the cognitive process leading to the recognition of oneself as "lonely," our study has (once again) indicated the importance individuals may attribute to (1) the fact that they are living without a partner; (2) the perception that their most "confidant relationship" lacks intimacy. In order to account for this evaluative process, we should ultimately direct our attention to the dominant value orientation in our society, which places a premium on marriage and on other intimate partner relationships (see also Lopata, Heinemann, & Baum, 1982). We agree then with Rook and Peplau (1982) in asserting that society and its individual members should benefit from a change in perspectives: Let us diminish our preoccupation with amourous relationships and traditional living arrangements while opening ourselves to the possibilities (and acceptability) of other relationship arrangements.

16

Individual and Interpersonal Factors in the Etiology of Marital Distress: The Example of Remarital Couples

Janet Farrell
Howard J. Markman
University of Denver

REMARRIAGE

Remarriage is a timely topic for investigation given that 80% of divorced persons eventually marry again (Glick & Norton, 1977) and remarriages now comprise 30% of all U.S. marriages (Dean & Gurak, 1978). It is predicted that 44% of current remarriages will end in divorce, compared with 38% of current first marriages (Glick & Norton, 1976). Although the data indicate that remarriages are at higher risk for divorce, it cannot be assumed that remarital relationships are therefore more likely to be distressed than first marriages. An alternative explanation is that remarried persons are less traditional than first marrieds and more inclined to terminate unsatisfactory relationships having done so once before. The latter explanation is consistent with the fact that second divorces occur in about 2 years less time than initial divorces (Glick & Norton, 1977).

Studies comparing the subjective satisfaction levels of first marital (FM) and remarital (RM) couples have yielded equivocal results. Whereas two studies (Glenn & Weaver, 1977; Renne, 1971) found RM couples to be slightly less satisfied than FMs, White (1979) reported that RM men were slightly more happy than FM men, whereas RM women were slightly less happy than women in first marriages. Although the results of these cross-sectional comparisons seem to indicate fairly comparable levels of satisfaction between FM and RM couples, the global measures of marital satisfaction that were used may have been insensitive to true group differences.

Regardless of whether remarrieds tend to have less satisfactory relationships or are merely less traditional, remarriages form a major subgroup of all marriages about which little empirical information is available. Several hypotheses have

251

been proposed regarding the unique characteristics and needs of remarital couples. In particular, two competing hypotheses have been offered concerning RM as compared to FM couples: a deficit hypothesis suggesting that RM's are at greater risk for subsequent problems than FM's and a competing competency hypothesis suggesting they are at less risk due to positive training effects from their first marriages. Those who view divorce and remarriage from a deficit perspective cite such factors as poor mate selection and individual psychological problems as explanations for the apparent divorce proneness of remarried persons. Utilizing data from a 1970 National Fertility Survey, Dean and Gurak (1978) compared the marital homogamy (similarity to husband in age, education, and religious identification) of women in their first and second marriages as well as in the previous marriages of the remarried women. The results indicated the remarried women experienced lower homogamy in both current and first marriages than did the first-married women. Dean and Gurak concluded that the low homogamous mate selection patterns of some women made them disproportionately prone to divorce and remarry. Although individual psychological problems have also been blamed for unsuccessful first marriages (Bergler, cited by Cherlin, 1978), Overall (1971) found the remarried people reported less psychopathology on a general rating scale than did either first married or divorced persons. However, there is evidence that if remarriage occurs too soon after a previous divorce, then unresolved psychological stresses from that major life change can be carried into the new relationship (Bloom, Asher, & White, 1978). For example, Hetherington, Cox, and Cox (1977) found that it took families an average of 2 years to stabilize after a divorce.

Those who espouse a competency perspective of remarriage see remarried persons as either equally well-adjusted as first marrieds, but facing greater life stress (Cherlin, 1978), or even better adjusted, having learned from the training ground of their earlier marital experiences (Duberman, 1975). The only empirical support for the training ground model of remarriage was provided by Albrecht (1979), who found that 88% of the remarrieds sampled stated that their present marriage was "much better" than the former marriage that had ended in divorce, and 65% felt that the experience gained in the earlier marriage helped them in adjusting to the present marriage. However, in addition to the problems inherent in using post hoc self-report measures, this study made no comparisons that would support the position that remarried persons are better adjusted than their first married counterparts.

Several recent studies have supported the position that the stresses of remarriages place them at higher risk for developing relationship distress. Cherlin (1978) attributed these stresses to the incomplete institutionalization of remarriage after divorce, due to such factors as children and financial commitments from the previous marriages. Becker (cited in Cherlin, 1978) found that the presence of children from a previous marriage increased the probability of divorce, with Messinger (1976) reporting that the most frequently cited sources of remarital difficulties were children from the previous marriage, followed closely by financial problems. However, Spanier and Furstenberg (1982) found that neither marital status (remarried or not) nor the presence or absence of children were related to personal well being four years following divorce. Hetherington et al. (1977) found that remarriage of a former spouse caused renewed emotional trauma, especially for the ex-wives, adding further stress to already strained interactions surrounding children and finances. Likewise, Duberman (1975) found that remarital family integration was better if the previous spouse had died rather than been divorced. Continuing ties with the first family and extended kinship networks formed by two or more nuclear families may preclude the reconstituted family's ability to solidify its boundaries and establish clear roles within it (Walker, Rogers, & Messinger, 1977).

Cherlin further asserted that societal institutions such as language and laws do not provide clear guidelines and support for restructured families. For example, stepparents in remarriage lack appropriate labels that distinguish them from the child's natural mother or father, and they have no legal rights of guardianship, even though they may assume the lion's share of responsibility for parenting that child. Likewise, incest laws apply only to natural relatives, not to stepkin. The ambiguity that results from the absence of predetermined, legally sanctioned roles in reconstituted families may increase the number of potential problem areas between family members.

Clingempeel's (1981) finding that remarried persons in complex stepfamilies (those in which both divorced/remarried spouses had children from a previous marriage) reported significantly lower marital satisfaction and had poorer communication than those from simple stepfamilies (in which only one spouse had children from a previous marriage) would appear to support the stress hypothesis of remarriage. However, the causal direction of this finding is unclear—Do members of complex stepfamilies experience more role stress or do people with different personality characteristics form complex versus simple stepfamilies? Contrary to Cherlin's hypothesis of incomplete remarital family boundaries, Clingempeel did not find a direct negative correlation between frequency of contact with former spouses and quality of the remarital relationship. Rather, persons who maintained moderate frequencies of contact with ex-spouses exhibited better marital quality than persons with either high or low contact, suggesting that weaknesses in forming and maintaining intimate relationships predispose some remarital persons to both high and low levels of contact with former spouses.

Thus, it is unclear from the empirical studies available (1) whether remarital persons are at higher risk for marital distress than first maritals; or (2) if in fact they are, whether the higher risk is attributable to the increased stresses of remarriage or to predisposing individual characteristics that may make them prone to divorce and remarry. Farrell and Markman (1983) reasoned that since communication measures are one of the best predictors of current and future marital satisfaction, a premarital comparison of the communication of remarital and first marital couples would indicate whether or not the RM couples are at higher risk for developing subsequent marital distress. Several theories of positive marital communication focus on the importance of developing an understanding of one's spouse that is demonstrated by having accurate perceptions of the spouse's position (Gottman, Notarius, Markman, Bank, Yoppi, & Rubin, 1976; Knudson, Sommers, & Golding 1980). Specifically, we postulated that low perceptual accuracy would be a sign of poor communication and high perceptual accuracy a sign of good communication. We compared the partners' perceptual accuracy of each other on two communicational measures: communication box ratings (where couples' rate each other's communication on an ongoing basis, Markman & Poltrock, 1982) and a questionnaire tapping knowledge of partner's opinions and beliefs regarding salient marital issues and related these results to premarital satisfaction levels. We present the method and results of this study in detail since it has not been presented before.

THE PRESENT STUDY

Method

Twenty-five couples between the age of 25 and 40 who were planning marriage were recruited for the study, 12 couples in which both partners had been previously married and 13 couples in which neither partner had been previously married. All subjects were white, with the exception of one RM couple and one FM female. Each couple participated in a 2-hour experimental session in which they filled out questionnaires and engaged in two problem-oriented interaction tasks using the communication box. The Marital Preferences questionnaire, which is a modified version of the Test of Communication Between Engaged Couples (Schulman, 1974), was completed by all individuals twice, once for themselves and once in which they predicted their partner's responses to questions regarding salient marital issues such as finances, sex roles, and children. In addition, during the two 15-minute interaction tasks, the couples were instructed to rate the subjective impact of their partner's communication statements on a five-point scale and to predict the impact ratings that their partners would make in response to their communications using the communication box. The subjects' predictions of their partners' responses to the measures were then correlated with the partners' actual responses to yield perceptual accuracy correlations for each subject on the Marital Preferences questionnaire and the communication box ratings.

Results

Marital Preferences Questionnaire.   Two-way mixed (group and sex) analyses of variance on the perceptual accuracy correlations were used to analyze the data. The results for the Marital Preferences questionnaire indicated a significant group effect (F (1, 23) = 6.47, p < .02), and that the first marital (FM) couples were significantly more accurate in their predictions of their partners' responses (FM males' r (N = 13) = .55, FM females' (r (N = 13) = .58) than were the remarital (RM) couples (RM males' r (N = 12) = .38, RM females' r(N = 12) = .49). An independent t test also indicated that the FM subjects were in significantly higher agreement with their partners (t(1,12) = 2.97, p ≤ .01) than the RM subjects (FM couples' r(N = 13) = .55, RM couples' r(N = 12) = .38). Thus, on the Marital Preferences questionnaire, the FM couples had more accurate perceptions of each other's values and beliefs about marital issues and they were in higher agreement in their responses to the questionnaire items than were the RM couples.

Communication Box Ratings.   Correlating subjects' mean prediction ratings with partners' mean impact ratings resulted in significant correlations for both FM males (r(N = 13) = .59, p < .03) and FM females (r(N = 13) = .51 p < .05), and nonsignificant correlations for both the RM males (r(N = 12) = .32, p = ns) and the RM females (r(N = 12) = .28, p = ns). The FM subjects' mean impact ratings were also significantly correlated with their partners' (r(N = 13) = .76, p < .01), whereas the RM subjects' mean impact ratings did not correlate significantly with their partners' (r(N = 12) = .29, p = ns). Thus, across both the questionnaire and the interaction measures, the FM subjects were consistently more perceptually accurate and similar to their partners than the RM couples. There were no significant group differences in subjective relationship satisfaction as measured by the Locke-Wallace Premarital Adjustment Test (Locke & Wallace, 1959). However, mean prediction and impact ratings of partners' communications were significantly correlated with relationship satisfaction for the FM males and females but not for the RM group, with the exception of the RM females' impact ratings.

LINKING INDIVIDUAL AND INTERPERSONAL CHARACTERISTICS

The major findings of this study indicated that, contrary to the training ground model of remarriage and in support of the deficit model of remarriage, the RM compared to the FM couples were both less similar in marital values and beliefs and less perceptually accurate on the two communication tasks. In addition, the RM's communication box ratings were not correlated with relationship satisfaction in three of four analyses, while in all analyses the FM's communication ratings were correlated with relationship satisfaction. In discussing these findings, we focus on the potential linkages between individual characteristics and interpersonal functioning, in order to highlight the importance of examining the determinants of good communication as well as the communication process itself.

The differences in actual similarity on the comunicational measures are consistent with previous studies that suggest that RM couples may be selecting mates who are dissimilar to them. Dean and Gurak (1978) found that RM couples showed more dissimilarity in demographic characteristics such as age, education, and religious affiliation than first maritals and concluded that dissimilar mate selection put RM couples disproportionately at risk for divorce. The present study found significantly less similarity between the RM partners than the FM partners on communication variables, which have a more direct link to marital adjustment than demographic variables. Thus, the RM couples may be starting out their marriages being more dissimilar, and perhaps less compatible, than the FM subjects. The perceptual accuracy differences indicate that the RM couples may also be poorer communicators than the FM couples. Regardless of whether dissimilar mate selection led to the poorer communication of the RM couples and hence lower perceptual accuracy, or whether poor communication led to both dissimilar mate selection and low perceptual accuracy, the finding lends support to a communicational deficit perspective on remarriage.

The differences between RM and FM couples in patterns of correlations between communication ratings and relationship satisfaction mirror the differences found between those who declined and those who accepted a premarital communication program offered in our research center at the University of Denver. That is, with the exception of the RM females' impact ratings, the communication box prediction and impact ratings did not correlate with their relationship satisfaction scores, whereas the FM couples' did. Like the communication program decliners, the RM couples' relationship satisfaction appears less responsive to perceived communication quality than the FM couples' satisfaction. In view of the fact that the RM and FM mean relationship satisfaction scores did not differ, the RM couples' communication deficits do not appear to be negatively affecting their premarital relationships. We hypothesized that this was due to an unlinking of communication quality and relationship satisfaction in the RM couples, which may indicate that RM persons evaluate partners on factors other than communication during the mate selection process. These factors may also differ for the RM males and females.

Family sociologists have argued that RM females are at a disadvantage on the marriage marketplace because they tend to be older and have children. Thus they may be less selective in choosing a mate the second time around and/or select mates based on different criteria. The present study provided some support for this position. The RM females in our study may be in a less valued position socioeconomically because their mean personal incomes were significantly below those of the RM males ($t(1,10) = 3.14$, $p < .01$; RM males = $17,000/year, RM females = $9000/year), whereas the FM males and females had equal mean income levels ($12,000/year). In addition, of the 6 RM females who had children from their previous marriages, 5 had custody, whereas only 1 of the 10 RM fathers had custody of his children. Thus, not only did the RM females have lower incomes but half of them were raising children. The presence of children may have increased the mothers' motivation to remarry and provide the children with a father while simultaneously lowering the mothers' remarital marketability. This hypothesis is supported by previous studies suggesting that children reduce the marketability of RM women (Koo & Suchindran, 1980).

Although the remarital men may not suffer the economic liabilities their partners do, goals other than good communication may determine their relationship satisfaction. The major motivation for divorced men to enter quickly into remarriage seems to be loneliness. As Bell (1982) noted:

> For divorced men the replacement of the ex-wife in their lives by another woman may be a necessity. Gordon (1976) observes that traditionally many men have depended on the women they marry to be their only close friends and confidantes. When this is true the loss of their wives leaves them friendless. Often a new woman is quickly found to fill this role [p. 553].

Similarly, Rubenstein and Shaver (1980) suggest that for men, divorce leads to loneliness and the need to replace their lost relationship.

Another closely related explanation for the apparent lack of responsiveness to communication of the RM males and females is low self-esteem. That is, they may choose mates who are dissimilar either because they perceive themselves as devalued commodities on the marriage market and hence cannot afford to be choosy, or because they want a dissimilar mate who can compensate for their own shortcomings. They may also communicate poorly because they are reluctant to honestly self-disclose or make direct assertions for fear of rejection by their partners. Gilbert (1976) proposed a curvilinear relationship between self-disclosure and marital satisfaction in which self-disclosure increases to the point where: "needs for security may override needs for depth in the relationship, such that 'rocking the boat' becomes more risky than maintaining the status quo" [p. 228] and hence avoid conflicts in an effort to maintain stability in their marriages. Satir (1972) attributed inability to deal with familial conflict openly and directly to parental lack of self-esteem, which is transmitted to and adopted by the child in his/her own marital relationship as an adult. Although the study included no self-esteem measures, some evidence for low self-esteem of the RM subjects is provided by the communication box prediction ratings, which were significantly below those of the FM group. That is, they assumed that their communications would have a more negative impact on their partners than the first marital subjects did. If, in fact, the remaritals do lack self-esteem, one reason might be that they view their unsuccessful first marriages as reflections on their abilities to be satisfactory mates to anyone. An alternative explanation is that low self-esteem leads to a fear of loneliness and an inability to be content without a constant relationship (Rubenstein & Shaver, 1980). Thus, the re-maritals may be willing to settle for less satisfying relationships than the first maritals because any relationship appears preferable to being alone. There was evidence for this in the Farrell and Markman study. More than half the RM men and over one-third of the RM women had spent no time alone without serious relationships since their divorces. Although at the time of the study the mean number of months since divorce was 48 for the RM males and 44 for the RM females, many of the RM subjects had spent that entire postdivorce period in one serious relationship or another.

Their inability to be alone may reflect emotional or financial insecurity on the part of these remarital subjects that likely discourages the risk taking inherent in open communication and self-disclosure, particularly around conflict issues. Ironically, their need for the security of a committed relationship may be the very factor that compromises their ability to maintain that relationship. That is, short-term concessions to "keep the peace" may ultimately result in a more serious breach in the very relationship they so desparately want to maintain. One re-marital women, whose subjective relationship satisfaction score was high, demonstrated this conflict-avoidant style even in her participation in the experiment. She was living with her fiance and had arranged to meet him after work at the marital laboratory for their second experimental session; she was there on time but he failed to appear. The experimenter called them a week later to arrange another appointment, asked her if there had been a miscommunication about the time of the previous appointment, and she said she did not know because she had never broached the subject of the missed appointment with her partner!

To summarize, we have suggested that RM females place importance on financial security, and RM males place importance on emotional security, as compared to their FM counterparts. In addition, there is some evidence to sug-gest that the RM males and females in our sample may lack self-esteem and may feel that any relationship is preferable to being alone. Due to their focus on security-related rewards, and their apparently high motivation to enter into an-other relationship soon after divorce, the RM couples are hypothesized to be less concerned with evaluating their partners in terms of intimacy-related charac-teristics such as communication.

This interpretation fits with Kelley's recent elaborations of interdependency theory. Kelley (1983) proposes that people evaluate relationships based on direct and indirect sources of satisfaction within a relationship. Direct sources of satis-faction or rewards refer to pleasing and displeasing outcomes that people get directly from each other by being in the relationship. Indirect sources of satisfac-tion or rewards are based on the attributions people make about each other and their relationship, based on the interpersonal tendencies that people express in their interactions. To use Kelley's (1983) example, when he goes on a picnic with his wife, the satisfaction of eating a good sandwich is a direct source of reward, while the attribution that his wife is a loving, caring person based on her actions and that she is an interesting companion on the outing are indirect sources of reward. Kelley's reward typologies are comparable to Foa and Foa's (1974) direct and indirect rewards and Parson and Bales's (1955) instrumental and affective rewards. In these terms we would suggest that RM couples are more concerned with instrumental (direct) rewards available in their relationships, such as financial and emotional security, rather than with the more affective (indirect) rewards associated with how people interact with one another, such as attributions about intimacy and love. Since Kelley assumes that these attributions are made primarily based on interactions, we hypothesize that remaritals are not responsive to their relationship interactions.

There is one exception to this pattern. The communication box impact ratings for RM females were significantly correlated with relationship satisfaction. This finding suggests that the RM females may desire both security related direct rewards and intimacy related indirect rewards, but that for now their security needs may be overriding their intimacy needs. The RM females may value communication and intimacy, but may be willing to forego these because of their perceived and real lack of alternatives in the marital marketplace. However, to the extent that communication is etiologically related to subsequent relationship satisfaction, the ability to communicate well should be predictive of future satisfaction regardless of how central it currently is to these couples. Their lack of perceptual accuracy thus indicates that the RM couples are at risk for future relationship distress.

If quality of communication is predictive of subsequent marital satisfaction even in relationships that are originally based on more direct, instrumental rewards, then communication must progress over time from a less central to a more central role in these relationships. Since we believe that it does, we want to understand how this progression might occur during the course of a marriage. Using the remarital couples as our example, the interaction between communication and the more direct rewards in a relationship may be understood based on their effects on what Kelley and Thibaut (1978) term "the comparison level (CL) of the relationship."

Having set the stage for a conflict avoidant relationship during mate selection, the RM couple is then faced with having to work out the inevitable problems of domestic cohabitation in the absence of established mechanisms for negotiation. This situation is compounded by the finding that the RM couples tend to be more dissimilar than FM couples, and thus they will likely have more potential problem areas to negotiate. In addition, conflict avoidance may be particularly problematic in remarriages because of the sheer number of domestic issues involved in merging two households (Messinger, 1976). It is likely that many of these problems will not get resolved but will fester as unresolved marital sores that eat into relationship satisfaction levels causing them to diminish over time. This may occur even though the areas of desirable direct interdependence continue to exist at the same level as before. At the very least, conflict avoidance limits the areas in which relationship satisfaction can grow. In the absence of such relationship growth, the gap between the attractiveness (CL) of the marriage and that of alternative relationships (CL_{alt}) would not increase over time. Investment in and commitment to the relationship would not necessarily be reflected in its duration, and the alternative of starting over in a new relationship might compare favorable to staying in the present one. Likewise, if conflict avoidance allows unresolved marital stresses to accumulate, alternatives may begin to appear even more attractive, resulting in greater marital dissatisfaction. An exception to this outcome would be cases in which direct interdependence allowed the partners to build a secure, comfortable material base together, which even in the absence of effective communication might make the relationship continue to appear preferable to its alternatives. If this instrumental basis for the relationship is reinforcing and secure enough to the partners, it might even motivate them to overcome their unfamiliarity with and/or aversion to intimate communication in order to preserve the relationship. Another exception would be if the perceived Cl_{alt} were so unacceptable that even a greatly deteriorated marital relationship was still considered satisfactory to the partners by comparison to its alternatives.

Kelley and Thibaut's notion of comparison levels in relationships may thus provide a promising framework in which communication can be incorporated with other sources of rewards into an empirically useful theory of relationship exchange. However, the results of the remarital study that lead us to speculate about the relationship between these direct and indirect rewards must be interpreted very tentatively. Although we can safely conclude that the RM premarital couples in our small sample are poorer communicators than the FM couples, we can only infer that the reason for this difference is that they place a lower priority on communication than they do on direct instrumental rewards. This inference is based on indirect evidence such as the lack of correlation between their communication and relationship satisfaction scores and the apparent financial and emotional neediness of the remarital subjects. More direct methods of assessing an individual's direct and indirect relationship goals, rewards, and subjective comparison levels are necessary to confirm or discomfirm these inferences. Although subjective measures such as the Locke-Wallace Marital Adjustment Test (1959) have proven to be good global indices of marital satisfaction, self-report techniques seem inadequate in tapping the factors that determine those subjective ratings. Not only can it be difficult to accurately capture affective material through verbal reports (Wills, Weiss, & Patterson, 1974), but self-report is further limited by social desirability. It may be difficult for a woman to admit that her major attraction to her husband is his position as a prominent physician, affording her a comfortable, prestigious life-style. Likewise, a many may be considered shallow if he admits that his wife's appearance was a key factor in his decision to marry her, preferring to attribute the attraction to her intelligence or sensitivity. It is even more difficult to tap the subconscious emotional security needs a spouse may fill, such as replacing a parent figure in the partner's life or otherwise compensating for some real or perceived deficit in the partner. Yet in our work with couples in marital therapy, we as clinicians are made all too aware of the salience of these emotional relationship needs when they are not being met.

It seems likely that a combination of measurement techniques may be necessary in order to accurately assess the goals and needs of individuals in intimate relationships. These might include communication samples from couples about specific instrumental and affectional relationship issues, direct self-report, self-esteem measures, historical information about an individual's past relationships and family of origin, and projective techniques aimed at tapping interpersonal needs, values, and priorities.

Accurate assessment of how direct and indirect relationship goals and needs impact current relationship functioning has important implications for treatment and prevention of marital distress as well. Helping couple members to understand the needs they originally sought to meet within the relationship, how those needs may have changed over time, and the extent to which those needs have been and/or continue to be met within the relationship are major goals of marital therapy. Such an understanding helps couples take a step back from the content of their present conflicts to evaluate how those conflicts may reflect underlying needs that are not being met within the relationship. For example, a remarital woman raising young children may select a spouse who is very supportive of her parenting functions—a direct reward—but who may not be particularly self-disclosive or encouraging of her self-disclosures. As the children mature and the need for direct support lessens, the remarital female may find herself increasingly lonely and discontent and may believe that her spouse has somehow changed. Sensing her discontent, her husband might attempt to increase the level of direct rewards her provides her by an instrumental behavior such as remodeling their home, a project that may make him even less available to her emotionally. When such attempts on his part do not result in an increase in her satisfaction levels, he might feel bitter and angry because he feels caught in a no-win situation.

Careful examination of marital goals and needs in counseling may help this couple to understand the subtle changes in the wife's goals and needs over time and how the husband's present attempts to increase her satisfaction are directed at needs that were more important to her in the past. At the same time, the wife may come to realize that she still values her husband's direct rewards to her as a provider, but that she also wants to increase the exchange of indirect, affectual rewards within the relationship as well. Having placed the present conflicts into historical relationship perspective, the couple is then in a better position to evaluate the extent to which they are willing and able to change the relationship and what the costs to the relationship in terms of direct benefits might be.

It is clear that this hypothetical couple had poor communication before seeking counseling in that the wife was unable to communicate the source of her marital dissatisfaction in a way that was understandable to her husband. It is likely that she had felt some dissatisfaction over the relative lack of affectual rewards throughout the relationship. However, the previously high level of direct rewards may have compensated for what she felt was missing, and fear of losing the direct rewards made it risky for her to communicate her dissatisfaction in the past. It was only when her need for the instrumental benefits lessened that she was willing to risk "rocking the boat" by expressing her discontent to her husband. When she finally did so, her inexperience in communicating her own needs, his inexperience in actively listening to her, and the accumulation of unresolved stresses from years of poor communication made it difficult for them to effectively exchange information even when they were motivated to do so.

Thus, poor relationship communication can result from both motivational and skill deficits. The importance of motivation to communicate is demonstrated by the results from our ongoing research program in which the relatively poorer comunicators tended to decline the offer of a premarital communication enhancement program, while the better communicators were more likely to enroll in it. A couple's motivation to communicate and their perception of the risks involved in reciprocal self-disclosure should be carefully assessed and dealt with in marital therapy, in addition to providing skill training in communication.

In terms of prevention of marital distress, our premarital intervention project has demonstrated that, as in many public health programs, the persons who may need a preventive service the most tend to be those who are least inclined to voluntarily take advantage of it. Just as wellness clinics have begun to educate the public about the need for preventive medical care, it is hoped that increased public awareness and acceptance of preventive mental health will increase enrollment in such programs as premarital communication enhancement. However, the social obstacles to such utilization cannot be overlooked. While the data may be available that communication is correlated with relationship satisfaction, as long as the economic, social, and emotional climate is bleak for divorced adults, communication is likely to continue to be a lower premarital priority than the promise of direct relief from loneliness and instrumental stresses. Remarital couples may be more motivated to improve their communication a year or two after the remarriage, when their more direct needs have been met and the stresses of merging two households have brought the need for communication into sharper focus. Providing communication training to remarital couples at this relationship stage could be seen as early secondary prevention (Cowen, 1973), that is, identifying problems in communication after they have emerged but early enough that they do not further degrade the other rewarding aspects of the remarital relationship.

SUMMARY AND CONCLUSION

To summarize, in this chapter we have suggested that a combination of both individual and interactional factors influences the quality of marital communications and that the role of extracommunicational factors in marital interaction is particularly salient in studying the communication of couples planning remarriage. The nature of the marriage market, children, finances, personal loneliness, and low self-esteem may all influence both the mate selection and subsequent communication patterns of remarital couples.

In conclusion, the study of marital communication can benefit from a conceptual framework that considers both individual and interpersonal variables, such as Kelley's (1983) notion of direct and indirect relationship rewards. This framework needs to be elaborated to specify the various reward sources and how they interact with communication in determining relationship satisfaction. Using such a framework to study different identifiable subgroups within the marital population, such as remaritals, older couples, or specific cultural subgroups, may be one way of providing a window on the relationship between individual characteristics and couple's interaction in determining relationship satisfaction.

ACKNOWLEDGMENT

Research reported in this chapter supported by NIMH Grant MH RO1 35525-01, awarded to Howard Markman.

V
SUMMARY AND PERSPECTIVE

17

Mea Culpas and Lamentations: Sir Francis, Sir Isaac, and "The Slow Progress of Soft Psychology"

Ellen Berscheid
University of Minnesota

INTRODUCTION

The first international conference ever entirely devoted to the study of interpersonal relationships has presented us with an extraordinarily rich array of food for thought—so rich, in fact, that some of us, like the man in the Alka-Seltzer commercial who groans "I ate the whole thing!" may already be appreciating the limitations of the intellectual digestive system. Thus, in anticipation of successfully providing more than even gargantuan appetites can comfortably accommodate, conference organizers often arrange to conclude their procession of offerings with an antidote of sorts. Customarily, this takes the form of changing the focus from the present to the future by enjoining the final speaker to step back from the banquet to address the twin questions "Well, *now* where are we?" and, perhaps more importantly, "What lies ahead?"

In addition to providing perspective, it is eminently useful to have the answers to these questions. Those who know where they are can navigate more swiftly and safely than those who do not. These questions are also especially appropriate for those of us who have been present at the birth of the science of relationships, because cartographers of science have yet to formally position us on their maps. If asked about us, in fact, they would probably place us somewhere in those unknown and mysterious regions ancient map makers designated with pictures of serpents and dragons and the legend "Here Be Monsters!" Here be monsters, indeed. Since they most certainly inhabit the territory we aspire to occupy, I take them as the theme of my concluding comments.

A SCIENCE OF RELATIONSHIPS: "WHERE ARE WE?"
AND "WHAT LIES AHEAD?"

Where is this territory? In a general sense, this is an easy question to answer. The emerging science of relationships lies on the fringes of several of the social and behavioral sciences, including (and especially) psychology and sociology. Within my own discipline, for example, a strong interest in relationships is emerging from social, developmental, and clinical psychology, or, from what are often regarded as the "softest" areas of psychology's terrain. The nascent science of relationships, then, is clearly located on the margins of the softer areas of what are often themselves considered to be the "soft sciences." That is where we undeniably are.

The answer to the second question "What lies ahead?" is virtually defined by the answer to the first. That is, given our geographical location, we have no reason to expect that the problems that have plagued the soft sciences as a whole, and their softer portions especially acutely, will not carry over to plague the study of human relationships. These old familiar problems, in fact, are likely to assume frightening proportions as we proceed in the relationship area.

Before amplifying this forecast of toil and trouble, it should perhaps be quickly acknowledged that, whatever lies ahead, the relationship domain is eminently worthy of capture. I simply take it as a given that we are all keenly aware of the necessity of an interdisciplinary science of relationships and of the enormous contribution such a science could make to virtually all of the social, behavioral, and health sciences, and thus ultimately to human welfare. It is not, then, our future glories that need discussion, but rather some of the troubles that lie ahead. These, as I have indicated, are virtually dictated by our position in a kind of scientific "no-man's land."

Specifically, our location on the fringes of the soft sciences means that at our back (and not infrequently *on* our back, as I want to discuss) is the traditional conception of scientific activity and, most importantly, the traditional standards against which the performance of any scientific enterprise is assessed. In front of us, indeed surrounding us on the other three sides, lies our restless and impatient public constituency—because, of course, to be located on the margins of the soft sciences is also to be positioned deep into public territory. Each of us knows all too well the problems, distractions, and vulnerabilities this entails, but these problems for a science of relationships are exacerbated by the fact that the public's appetite for the answers to a thousand cosmic questions about relationships can only be described as voracious, impatient, and unrelenting.

My thesis, then, is simply that it is virtually inevitable that the infant science of relationships will get caught in heavy crossfire between the descendants of Sir Francis Bacon and the man on the street who happens to be suffering from his second divorce and wants us not only to tell him why but what he can do to avoid such disasters in the future. I wish to elaborate the nature of this crossfire, because I suspect that many of the ambushes we in the soft sciences have experienced in the past would have been less successful had we had a clearer understanding of where hostilities were likely to come from and why. At the very least, if our detractors had not so often had the advantage of surprise, the number of self-inflicted wounds their attacks have occasioned might have been reduced.

Among these wounds I count the periodic "dark nights of the soul" that have characterized almost all of the disciplines from which a science of relationships is emerging. Within my own field of experimental social psychology, lamentations about the state of the discipline began to surface at least 15 years ago (dating these from the publication of Ring's [1967] paper about the "frivolity" of social psychology). If the ensuing so-called "crisis of confidence" in social psychology now seems to have settled down to the level of a low grade fever, it remains, nonetheless, a persistent and nagging one, as is illustrated by an article that recently appeared in one of the new *European Monographs in Social Psychology* series. In the first paragraph of the paper (Potter, 1982), there appeared a footnote; turning back to the end pages, I found the author's solemn caveat: "Throughout the paper I assume that social psychology is a science" [p. 47]!

Sociologists who make social structural assumptions about the bases for social behavior have also had their doubts in recent times (e.g., Burgess & Bushell, 1969; Stryker, 1977). Ironically (considering the source of the doubts that plague the psychological social psychologists these days), some of them view, as Blank (1982) observes: ". . . experimentation and an individual orientation [as] essential palliatives to their own type's rigid reliance on extrapersonal, social structural explanations based in correlational methods of data analysis" [p. 226].

Clinical psychology and counseling psychology have not fared any better, which brings me to the confession that I poached both my title and the springboard for my comments from my colleague Paul Meehl and his 1978 *Journal of Clinical and Counseling Psychology* paper entitled "Theoretical Risks & Tabular Asterisks: Sir Karl, Sir Ronald, and the Slow Progress of Soft Psychology."

Meehl's thesis (1978) is a familiar one. It is that theory and research in the soft sciences in general, and in the soft areas of psychology in particular, lack the cumulative character of scientific knowledge. He states:

> I consider it unnecessary to persuade you that most so-called "theories" in the soft areas of psychology (clinical, counseling, social, personality, community, and school psychology) are scientifically unimpressive and technologically worthless . . . In the developed sciences, theories tend either to become widely accepted and built into the larger edifice of well-tested human knowledge or else they suffer destruction in the face of recalcitrant facts and are abandoned. . . . But in fields like personology and social psychology, this seems not to happen. There is a period of enthusiasm about a new theory, a period of attempted application to several fact domains, a period of disillusionment as the negative data come in, a growing bafflement about inconsistent and unexplicable empirical results, multiple resort to ad hoc excuses, and then finally people just sort of lose interest in the thing and pursue other endeavors [pp. 806–807].

Meehl goes on to say:

> I do not think that there is any dispute about this matter among psychologists familiar with the history of the other sciences. It is simply a sad fact that in soft psychology theories rise and decline, come and go, more as a function of baffled boredom than anything else; and the enterprise shows a disturbing absence of that *cumulative* character that is so impressive in disciplines like astronomy, molecular biology, and genetics [p. 807].

The major point of Meehl's paper is that our failure to subject our theories to grave danger of refutation (hence the reference to Sir Karl Popper) stems importantly from our reliance on null hypothesis tests of statistical significance (hence the reference to Sir Ronald Fisher). It is not, however, this argument that I wish to pursue; rather, I wish to focus on his theme that there is something desperately wrong with soft psychology.

That theme, of course, we hear in a hundred different songs sung both within science, as Meehl's paper illustrates, as well as without. To illustrate the latter, let me give an example of the public version of the concern that the study of human behavior lacks a cumulative character and the conclusion that there is, therefore, something wrong with us. In *The New York Times* of April 30, 1982, there appeared an editorial based on an article in *Psychology Today* in which several psychologists were asked to identify ''the most significant work in psychology over the last decade and a half.'' To quote the editorial: ''The results are astonishing: it would seem that there has been none.'' The editor based his conclusion on the fact that one psychologist cited teaching apes how to talk as the most significant advance, while another cited the failure of apes to learn how to talk as the most significant, yet another chose something else, and some persons asked couldn't think of anything. The editorial concludes:

> The failure of the eleven psychologists to agree on almost anything evinces a serious problem in their academic discipline. Physicists or biologists asked the same question would not concur on everything but there would be a substantial commonality in their answers.

The subheadline for the editorial was: ''If This is Consensus, Psychology Can't Be Much of a Science.''

THE DIFFICULTY OF "SCIENTIZING" THE SOFT SCIENCES . . . AND THE USUAL CONCLUSION

Leaving our public for a moment (avidly reading their *Psychology Todays*), let us return to Meehl's (1978) paper, for he goes on to observe that, lest anyone think he is unjustly beating up on psychology, he recognizes that "human psychology is hard to scientize" [p. 807]. That word "scientize" doesn't appear in my dictionary, but when Meehl asserts that human psychology is hard to scientize, I take it that he does *not* mean that it is hard to make systematic and interpersonally verifiable observations of human behavior, or even that it is all that hard to make probabilistic predictions about the likelihood of certain of those behaviors occurring in the future. Rather, I have little doubt that Meehl intended the word "scientize" to refer to science with a capital "S," implicitly preceded by the adjective "hard" with a capital "H"; or, in other words, to refer to that conception of science that is drummed into the head of every school child, that we ourselves absorbed as students, and that our graduate students in the social and behavioral sciences continue to absorb today.

We are speaking, of course, of the legacy of Sir Francis Bacon, Sir Isaac Newton, and René Descartes (who, had he been English instead of French, undoubtedly would have been knighted and thus could have been included in my title where he very much deserves to belong). The word "scientize," then, clearly refers to that model of science first provided by classical physics and its legendary triumphs, and to the Baconian–Cartesian–Newtonian view of the world it embodies. Thus, by the assertion that "human psychology is hard to scientize," and by his assumptions about the "slow progress of soft psychology," I take Meehl to mean that despite almost a century of concerted endeavor, we in psychology, along with our brethren in the other soft sciences, have yet to come up with anything faintly resembling classical physics—or astronomy or molecular biology—or, in other words, we have yet to come up with anything that satisfies most people's notions of what a science ought to look like.

Science with a Capital "S"

We are all familiar with this conception of science that most everyone, within science and without, pretty much agrees we don't measure up to. The Cartesian–Newtonian model of science is outlined in a hundred philosophy of science texts. It also has been recently and engagingly discussed by the physicist Fritjof Capra (1982) (who also, and not incidentally to ourselves, chronicles the trauma that subatomic physicists have experienced in surmounting that view in treating material phenomena that defy its assumptions). Relying on Capra's characterization, I should like to quickly recall some of its features to mind, since it is on this stage that a science of relationships must perform and it is by these standards that our performance inevitably will be judged.

From Bacon, of course, we were given the empirical method of science, or the inductive procedure of making experiments, drawing general conclusions from those experiments, and testing those conclusions through further experimentation. In addition to our passion for scientific experimentation, Capra (1982) observes that we got something else from Sir Francis:

> The "Baconian spirit" profoundly changed the nature and purpose of the scientific quest. From the time of the ancients the goals of science had been wisdom, understanding the natural order and living in harmony with it. . . . Since Bacon [however], the goal of science has been knowledge that can be used to dominate and control nature . . . [pp. 55–56].

From Bacon, then, we learned that wisdom and understanding of nature's forces is not enough; the purpose of science is to help us *change* nature, to harness it to our own ends. And that, of course, places particular emphasis on a precise knowledge of the causal dynamics of the variables involved in producing a phenomenon, as well as on the technology required for control of each. Without such knowledge, a science cannot quite measure up to Baconian standards.

Monsieur Descartes added other critical features, as we know. From him we absorbed our belief in the absolute certainty of scientific knowledge—in the possibility, indeed the necessity, of discovering absolute truth: " 'All science is certain, evident knowledge,' he wrote, and so 'We reject all knowledge which is merely probable . . .' " [quoted in Capra, p. 57]. Thus we learned that probabilistic statements about the occurrence of phenomena are not quite enough; such products of scientific activity do not really measure up to Cartesian standards.

Descartes, of course, added numerous other features to our conception of science. Most importantly he gave us the analytic method—or the procedure by which we search for the absolute truth by breaking a problem down into manageable subpieces under the assumption that all aspects of even the most complex phenomena can be understood by reducing them to their constituent parts. He gave us, in other words, reductionism, which encompasses a number of other beliefs and assumptions, among them the belief that objects have intrinsic properties that are independent of their environments. Reductionism was part and parcel of something else Descartes left us, which was the view of the world— both animate and inanimate—as a machine. Machines, of course, do not grow and evolve; they have no purposes or intent; they are governed by exact linear mathematical laws; and their single effects often have single and simple causes.

But it was Newton who, as we know, breathed life into the visions of Bacon and Descartes and who, thus, indelibly imprinted their conception of science on the world. This conception is even yet so firmly established that the word "science" barely permits of any alternative other than "hard science," or the epistemological position that has proved so useful to those whose phenomena admit of a piece of "hard" material matter, such as a particle, a gene, or a cell, as the basic unit of analysis. This, then, remains science with a capital "S," despite the fact that physics itself has had to almost completely abandon this view in order to treat certain important nonorganic phenomena. And this view still sets the standards by which any scientific enterprise is judged today, despite the fact that many problems in biology, in medicine, and, indeed, in all the sciences— both hard and soft—lie dormant and unexplored because they, too, like many subatomic phenomena, are not compatible with this approach to knowledge (see Capra, 1982). It is thus inevitable that the performance of a science of relationships will be judged against these standards. Consequently we cannot reasonably expect that the criticisms meted out to it will be any less harsh than those leveled against the soft sciences in general, particularly the areas from which a science of relationships is emerging.

The "Intrinsic Difficulties" of Our Subject Matter

The criticisms well may be, in fact, even more harsh. Let me return again to Meehl's paper and his observation that human behavior is hard to scientize, taking the work "scientize" to mean measuring up to the aforementioned standards. In addition to our excessive preoccupation with testing null hypotheses, Meehl (1978) cites what he calls "the terrible intrinsic difficulty of our subject matter" [p. 807]. Furthermore, he takes the trouble to list and describe 20 features of the phenomena in our domain that make human psychology hard to "scientize." A mention of only a few of these should quickly persuade the reader that each and every problem Meehl identifies is painfully familiar to anyone who has thought about the problem of relationships.

First, we have the dreary "openers," or those problems involved in even performing simple descriptive analyses of our phenomena. Here, we have the "response-class problem," or those problems that result from the well-known "difficulties of slicing up the raw behavioral flux into meaningful intervals identified by causally relevant attributes on the response side" [p. 808]. We also have what Meehl calls "situation-taxonomy problems," and, even aside from these, we have numerous other problems dealing with our unit of measurement.

Hair raising as our problems of descriptive analysis are, it is when we attempt to move to causal analysis that we encounter the real monsters in our domain. There is, for example, the problem of "divergent causality"; there are systems, certainly seen in relationship phenomena, in which slight differences in the exact character of the initial conditions do not statistically "wash out" or "balance" over the long run; rather, their effects are amplified over time. Waller's (1967) notion of alienation spirals in marital relationships may be an example. There is also the problem that certain very critical causal events in the history of the relationship not only are unknown, but actually may be, to all intents and purposes, simply unknowable. Then there is the problem of "nuisance variables," or that fact that within social systems often " . . . there is operative a non-negligible class of variables that are not random but systematic, that exert a sizeable influence, and are themselves also sizeably influenced by other variables, either exogenous to the system or contained in it, such that we have to worry about the influence of these variables, but we cannot always ascertain the direction of the causal arrow"; as a consequence, " . . . the system is statistically and causally indeterminate" [p. 810].

There are still other intrinsic difficulties with our subject matter. There is the problem of "feedback loops" that may be so complex that they simply cannot be decomposed, and then as all of us who have thought about relationships know, there is the problem of "random walk." With respect to this last, Meehl comments that "There is a widespread and understandable tendency to assume that the class of less-probable outcomes, given constancy of other classes of causally efficacious variables, should, in principle, be explicable by detecting a class of systematic input differences." But Meehl notes that there is an alternative possibility:

> At several points that are individually minor but collectively critical . . . , it is almost a "chance" affair whether the patient does A or not A, whether [for example] his girlfriend says she will or will not go out with him on a certain evening, or whether he happens to hit it off with the ophthalmologist that he consults about some particular vision disturbances that are making him anxious about becoming blind, and the like. If one twin becomes psychotic at the end of such a random walk, it is possible that he was suffering from what was only, so to speak, "bad luck"—not a concept that appears in any standard list of biological and social nuisance variables! [p. 811]

Even presuming that the relationship expert is able to identify the random walk that a couple has taken to disaster, one can imagine the reaction that would greet the therapist's scientific opinion that they had simply, and irrevocably, suffered from "bad luck."

Meehl goes on to list several other "intrinsic difficulties," but the one I wish to highlight, because it is the one that I believe to be at the heart of many of our other troubles, is that which Meehl calls "the sheer number of variables" problem. As he discusses, the number of variables we must deal with is large from several different viewpoints. It is large and heterogeneous on the causal side, both in terms of immediate precipitating factors and in terms of historical causal influences, and it is large on the effect side as well. Meehl goes on to say:

> It should be noted that this matter of sheer number of variables would not be so important (except as a contributor to residual 'random variation' in various kinds of outcomes) if they were each small contributors and independent, like the sources of error in the scattering of shots at a target in classical theory of errors. But in psychology this is not typically the situation. Rather, the variables, although large in number, are each nuisance variables that carry a significant amount of weight, interact with each other, and contribute to ideographic development via the divergent causality mode [p. 812].

The fact that those who think about relationship phenomena are all too familiar with the "sheer number of variables" problem has been well documented. People who focus on relationships understand that they are dealing with a very large and causally complex system. For example, in our own conceptualization of relationships (Kelley, Berscheid, Christensen, Harvey, Huston, Levinger, McClintock, Peplau, & Peterson, 1983), we classify the relevant causal factors into, first, those primarily associated with the individual; second, those primarily associated with the partner; third, those associated with the interaction of these two sets of variables with one another; fourth, variables associated with the social environment in which the relationship is embedded; fifth, variables associated with the physical environment in which the relationship is located; and, finally, of course, those represented by the interactions that take place between all of these types of variables.

This is a monster of a system, both in sheer size and in potential causal complexity, and it is, perhaps, an occasion for self-congratulation that relationship theorists and researchers have shown no unwillingness to face the fact that this is, indeed, the causal domain of relationship phenomena. But recognizing the overwhelming intrinsic difficulties of our subject matter and conquering them are something else, especially when the criteria for determining what constitutes a successful conquest are set by the traditional standards of science.

IS THERE SCIENTIFIC LIFE AFTER REDUCTIONISM?

The essential problem that confronts us, then, is that the methods and standards of our scientific activity have been set with subject matter that seems to be different from our own in at least three critical ways: First, the systems that surrounded the phenomena with which the classical physicists were concerned often had the property that the interactions between the various subparts of the system were weak or nonexistent; second, the relationship describing the behavior of these sub-parts was often linear (see von Bertalanffy, 1980, p. 19); and, third, the system itself was often much smaller. Our knowledge that it is highly unlikely that the system in which relationship phenomena are embedded possesses these properties immediately robs us of the exquisite intellectual comfort of the traditional reductionistic approach whereby the larger system is broken into smaller and more manageable subsets of variables whose relationships with each other are capable of being grasped by the human mind. That is, we are aware that the phenomena in which we are interested are surrounded by a large number of interdependent variables, which collectively and by the fact of their interdependence, constitute a *system*, and so we are also painfully aware that the reductionistic analytical method smashes that system into a thousand different fragments. And so, we know that reducing what is essentially an ''open'' system (and ''open'' if only by virtue of the sheer number of variables involved) down to a much smaller and manageable system may violently assault its integrity and, thus, compromise into uselessness anything we subsequently think we have discovered about it.

But our discomfort with the reductionistic method goes even deeper. At the time we are reducing the system down to manageable size for study, we are usually aware that the *rules* by which we are reducing it are pretty arbitrary, at least in terms of the properties of the system as a whole. Usually, our decision rules are not even stated. Although I know of no such formal set of rules, it seems conceivable that some reasonable, if loose, guidelines could be constructed. For example, the values of some variables in the system may stay so universally constant that they may be, for all practical purposes, ignored. Other variables may interact with certain others in the system only weakly, producing little diversity or magnitude of effect, and so possibly they too may be safely excluded. Such arguments for exclusion are, however, rarely mustered and it's easy to understand why; a great deal of knowledge is required to reduce a system down intelligently for careful scrutiny of its subparts. Furthermore, even if both we and our grandmother identify a variable as extremely central to the system, it may be that for ethical or technological reasons (and usually both), we cannot systematically examine its role. In any event, and for a wide variety of reasons, we in the social sciences often just pluck out of the larger system a couple of "do-able" variables that strike our fancy and hope for the best.

Unfortunately, the inevitable penalty for excluding from one's system variables that everyone, including the man in the street, knows (intuitively if not experientially) belong in the system (on the basis that they importantly affect the phenomena in question) is to have one's findings regarded as irrelevant, impractical, uninteresting, academic, and so forth. If one doubts that this is the penalty for positing an arbitrarily constricted system for the phenomenon of interest, one needs only to glance at the criticisms that have been chronically lodged against much theory and research in social psychology in recent years. The lion's share of that criticism goes something like this: "You may have, in your laboratory and with your experimentation, shown that variable X influences phenomenon Y, but this tells us little or nothing of interest about phenomenon Y as it appears in nature because, first, you have wholly ignored the role of the social and physical context in which you manipulated X (usually a laboratory experiment in an academic setting) and the interaction of these contextual variables with X to produce the Y effects; in other words, you have made the patently false assumption that you may safely ignore the context in which a behavior is embedded in your causal analysis of it. Furthermore (and especially if the context was a laboratory experiment), X may have been manipulated in the presence of variables that appear nowhere else in nature—and, in fact, X itself may only rarely appear in nature and so, of all the variables that are believed to importantly affect Y, X may be the least important of these." And so on the argument goes. The essence of the criticism, then, is that: "The system in which phenomenon Y is actually embedded in nature is most probably much larger, and possibly quite different, than the system defined by your theory or your experiment, and, therefore, your findings are of questionable interest; quite possibly, they are irrelevant.''

Regrettably, often the only response to that attack can be a well-memorized recital of the reductionistic catechism that one *can* profitably study parts of the system in isolation from the remainder, even though the remainder is suspected to importantly affect the smaller subportion under scrutiny. But *our* problem in the soft sciences, which is surely a major factor in our crises of confidence, is that we have become too sophisticated to wholeheartedly believe the reductionistic dogma any longer.

Relationship theorists and researchers, especially, seem to be reluctant to make the comfortable reductionistic assumptions. In fact, much of the interest in relationships that is emerging is the result of dissatisfaction with these assumptions that continue to underlie most theory and research in the sciences, both hard and soft. An interest in relationships has grown from the recognition that most human behavior takes place in a social context, often within the context of relatively enduring relationships with other people, and that human behavior simply cannot be well understood without reference to that context. And so, for example, relationship researchers already seem to be taking such problems as "emergent novelty" seriously, or, as Feigl puts it (1958, p. 415), "The impossibility of the derivation of the laws of the complexes ('wholes') from the laws that are sufficient to predict and explain the behavior of their constituents in relative isolation." The problem of "equifinality" within a large system is also increasingly recognized, or the fact that there may be many causal paths to the same end state and so delineating one of these paths does not exhaust the causal possibilities.

IS THE "SYSTEMS" APPROACH OUR SALVATION?

Thus, in attempting to avoid a reductionistic approach to the problem of relationships, it appears that some theorists and investigators are beginning to embrace what has been termed the "systems" approach. At least theoretically if not in practice, this approach tries to preserve the integrity of a highly interdependent system of variables for purposes of understanding it. This, in the social and behavioral sciences, virtually requires observation of the system *in vivo* and *in situ*, since by virtue of its size, as well as ethical and technological problems, it cannot be duplicated in the laboratory.

It is not surprising that relationship researchers should look eagerly toward the systems approach, for it is very much in the Zeitgeist. It is, in fact, increasingly hailed as the salvation of the social and behavioral sciences as the best candidate we have for that new "paradigm" Kuhn (1962) was talking about, a paradigm that, as our faith in reductionism grows weaker, many of us feel we desperately need. Some even regard the systems approach as the royal road to a new conception of all science. Within these growing ranks are physicists (e.g., Capra, 1982), biologists (e.g., von Bertalanffy, 1980) and others within the hard sciences, as well as those in the soft, who believe we must find an alternative to he Cartesian–Newtonian model (e.g., see Bevan, 1982a; Gergen, 1982). Perhaps most relevant to those of us interested in relationships is the burgeoning field of marital and family therapy from which much impetus for a science of relationships has been generated, and which itself has largely taken a systems position (see Berscheid & Peplau, 1983).

Unfortunately, the potential benefits of the systems approach strike me as discouragingly modest. For example, a reading of von Bertalanffy (1980) left me with only two: First, there is the possibility that different systems share the same principles, so that what is learned about one system may be transferable to another. That, indeed, would be useful; if it were to be the case, for example, that all systems evolve towards complexity (or, to the contrary, that all systems evolve toward homogeneity), that would be valuable information. In advance, however, we can speculate that this is somewhat unlikely and, at the least, very difficult to ascertain.

The second benefit held out to us by the systems approach is what von Bertalanffy (1980) calls "explanation in principle" for large and complex systems. He gives us an example:

> Theoretical economics is a highly developed system, presenting elaborate models for the processes in question. However, professors of economics, as a rule, are not millionaires. In other words, they can explain economic phenomena well "in principle" but they are not able to predict fluctuations in the stock market with respect to certain shares or dates. Explanation in principle, however, is better than none at all. If and when we are able to insert the necessary parameters, system-theoretical explanation "in principle" becomes a theory, similar in structure to those of physics [p. 36].

It is here, of course, that one becomes overcome with waves of uneasiness. "Explanation in principle" sounds dangerously like *ad hoc* explanation; it does not at *all* sound much like what Bacon and Descartes had in mind. Or, let me put this another way: In 1973 when Bill McGuire published his influential article, "The Yin and Yang of Progress in Social Psychology," he offered some opinions about what he called the "Sources of the New Social Psychology." He predicted that a "radically different" paradigm would emerge and proceeded to sketch "The Ultimate Shape of the New Paradigm." For example:

> On the creative side, it will involve theoretical models of the cognitive and social systems in their true multivariate complexity, involving a great deal of parallel processing, bidirectional relationships, and feedback circuits [p. 450].

Although McGuire cautioned that he felt somewhat "uncomfortable" detailing what this radically different paradigm would look like, its outlines were clearly "systemy." A few pages later in the same article, however, and in the context of encouraging ourselves and our students to think in terms of more complex models, he made two acute predictions. The first of these was that we would all probably "shy away from the mental strain of keeping in mind so many variables, so completely inter-related" [p. 452]. The second was that:

> . . . such complex theories allow so many degrees of freedom as to threaten the dictum that in order to be scientifically interesting, a theory must be testable, that is disprovable. These complex theories, with their free-floating parameters, seem to be adjustable to any outcome [p. 452].

In other words, in a large and complex system there are so many wild cards that it is possible for anyone with any imagination to come up with a royal flush of causal explanation—or an "explanation in principle"—every time. Predicting in *advance* what will happen so as to be able to control it, even assuming we had the ethical right and the technological means to do so, is, then, an entirely different matter with such a system. It is, perhaps, an impossibility.

This may be what Harold Rausch (1981) had in mind in his comments in his *Contemporary Psychology* review of Robyn Penman's book on *Communication Processes and Relationships* (1980), which takes a systems approach. After noting the popularity of the systems perspective within the discipline of marital and family therapy, Rausch also comments:

> When it comes to research (as we usually think of research) on interaction, however, systems theory has had far less effect. How are investigators to conduct "hard-nosed," scientific research when they are asked to reject what are assumed to be fundamental premises of science? Systems theory rejects the search for cause-effect relations; it is concerned rather with variety and constraints and with equi- and multi-finality. Rejected are notions of independent and dependent variables; emphasis is on interdependence and organization. Rather than seeking basic elements and static entities, its focus is on contextual hierarchical structures and fluctuating processes. Instead of trying to discover laws of behavior, it attempts to understand human rules of action. Systems "theory" is far less a theory than an epistemological position—a different *paradigm,* to use the currently fashionable term. As an epistemology, it has major methodological implications, and these implications are disruptive to our usual notions of research design and procedure [pp. 752–753].

To that I add my own suspicion that as an epistemology, the systems perspective not only has "major methodological implications," implications for the manner in which knowledge is obtained, but it also has implications for the "limits" (see Feigl, 1958) of knowledge, at least within our domain.

In any event, the systems approach seems to me to be more problematical than it appears at first glance. This may help explain why, despite the glowing words and enthusiasm, the visible evidence of such an approach in concrete research is a good deal less than one might expect. Its adoption presents, first of all, some very *practical* problems. With respect to descriptive analysis, for example, the investigator who truly takes the systems approach can easily drown in his or her data. Measurement of all the variables suspected to be of import over the time dimension required for later causal analysis can enervate and demoralize even the most ambitious investigator. And, with respect to causal analysis itself, neither our minds nor our statistics are equipped to deal with such a welter, particularly if the relationships between the variables are not relatively simple and linear. And then, of course, there is the deeper problem of lowering our epistemological aspirations to something like "explanation in principle" and what the consequences of that are likely to be. Leo Tolstoy provides us with an "explanation in principle" of marital infidelity in *Anna Karenina;* we ourselves aspired to something different.

In sum, it is not at all clear that there is scientific life after reductionism. The systems approach appears more to describe our problems than to provide a certain means of salavation from them.

THE FUNDAMENTAL HEADACHE A SCIENCE OF RELATIONSHIPS PRESENTS

I have tried to sketch the fundamental dilemma that will surely plague the development of a science of relationships, and it is the same hoary dilemma that has haunted the disciplines from which this science is emerging: We are caught forever between the proverbial rock and a hard place, between our knowledge that the phenomena we are trying to understand lie deeply embedded in a large and causally complex system and that, therefore, the convenient reductionistic faith that we can smash that system into a million fragments in pursuit of an understanding of the system is, for us, very difficult to maintain; and, yet, we often seem to have no choice other than to take a piece-meal approach for, first, we simply cannot cope very well with anything else and, second, we seem to be in danger of losing our legitimacy as a scientific enterprise if we cut our aspiration level down to anything we can ever hope to meet.

If this is the problem, what is the answer? Having come this far, I regret to say that I have no answer, not even the glimmerings of one. I believe this dilemma to be fundamental in the true sense of the word. It admits to no easy remedy; perhaps no remedy at all. If one truly confronts what Meehl calls the terrible "intrinsic difficulties" of our subject matter, and if one also strongly suspects that the Cartesian–Newtonian epistemology is, in some important degree, unsuited to it, then that means that to work in the relationship domain is to forever bear the tensions and ambiguities and discomforts inherent in this dilemma.

SOME SUGGESTED "ASPIRINS" WE MIGHT TAKE EN ROUTE TO A SCIENCE OF RELATIONSHIPS

Nevertheless, I think there are some things we could do that could go a long way to ease our discomfort as we proceed, and I should like to quickly list them:

First, I think we might recognize, and lead others to recognize, those intrinsic difficulties in our subject matter more than we have. These difficulties are no mere academic footnote to our scientific enterprise; they are the screaming headlines. That we have not kept them in the forefront, I attribute to at least two factors. The first is our suspicion that if we looked these bogies square in the face, we would die of fright or otherwise lose our confidence that we in the social and behavioral sciences can ever accomplish anything useful. Our past record, which is nowhere near as dismal as some seem to think, should reassure us on that score (e.g., Kiesler, 1982; Tornatsky & Solomon, 1982). For social psychologists, in particular, the successful application of basic theory and research to problems in medicine and law, as well as business, ought to be heartening.

The second major factor responsible for our not keeping the intrinsic difficulties of our subject matter in mind is surely the pervasiveness of reductionistic dogma, which minimizes and denies these difficulties. It does so not only through its emphasis on the analytic method but also through another of its facets, which is that all phenomena can ultimately be reduced to physical phenomena which, in turn, implies that the epistemology suited to the latter is equally well suited to the former.

In any event and for whatever reasons, it is clear that we tend to forget that our job is infinitely more difficult than that which confronted the classical physicists, and that to characterize our progress as "slow" is to wholly overlook the differences between our subject matter and theirs. The truth of the matter (from the perspective of God and Omniscient Jones) may well be that our progress has been incredibly rapid. But when have we heard anyone say *that*?! Despite the fact that "... none of us yet knows what the proper time scale for significant progress in psychology may turn out to be" (1982, p. 1313), as Bevan put it in his 1982 Presidential address to the American Psychological Association, few of us give ourselves the benefit of the doubt. However, from the fact that not even the most advanced of the soft sciences bears much of a resemblance to classical physics, it seems to me to be as reasonable to assume that we will *never* look like classical physics as it is to assume that such a science is our ultimate destination and that, therefore, our progress toward it has been slow.

Second, just how much a science of relationships ultimately will differ from the model of science we now accept depends on just how mean Mother Nature has been to us. That she has not been as generous as we hoped is clear. Nevertheless, it may be that certain portions of the system with which we are concerned are less interdependent than others, and so can be broken off in reductionistic fashion with good results. Identifying just exactly what subparts function relatively independently of the others is undoubtedly a matter of luck and art, as always. In any event, abandoning the reductionistic *faith* does not necessarily mean abandoning the *analytic method;* it does mean, however, that it cannot be usefully employed indiscriminantly and with abandon—that some justification is necessary, and that justification ultimately resides, not in philosophical treatises and personal preferences as some current debates seem to imply, but in the relationship of that portion of the system under scrutiny to the remainder of the system (e.g., see Baddely, 1981; Jenkins, 1974, for an illustration of the impact of this problem on cognitive psychology). And that is, essentially, an empirical question to which the current concern with "ecological validity" and "multimethod" approaches in many areas of psychology is, of course, addressed.

Third, and as this suggests, while I doubt that the so-called "systems" approach is our salvation, I do think that there are real benefits to be had from keeping the systems perspective in the forefront of our thinking. Only by taking the larger perspective can we hope to identify the variables importantly implicated in the system and their relationships with one another. Or, to put it another way, people who take a systems approach are unlikely to spend decades of their research time and effort minutely scrutinizing the elephant's toenail in the blind faith that it ultimately will tell them something important about the nature of elephants.

For example, when one adopts a systems view of a phenomenon, certain problems emerge as interesting and important and other problems are rendered insignificant. To illustrate from my own area of interest, emotion, it will be recalled that William James' "sequence problem" dominated emotion theory and research for many years. The problem was to ascertain the temporal causal order in which the various elements of emotional experience occurred. Did the perception of the "exciting" stimulus event occur first, then the internal physiological events, and then the subjective experience of emotion, or was the order different? The sequence problem assumed that there *is* an immutable linear causal order, and, also, that finding out what it was would tell us something interesting about emotion. Contemporary emotion theorists, however, have concluded that all of these occur within a continuous feedback loop such that each is both stimulus and response to the others, and that untangling the loop, or laying out the precise order of these events in a specific instance, probably isn't going to tell us anything of much importance about human emotion (e.g., see Candland, 1977). As this suggests, another benefit of the systems view is the likelihood that questions of process will receive more attention, and questions of static structure will be regarded as less interesting, than they traditionally have been.

There are still other benefits to be had from a systems perspective, and many of these have been nicely laid out in the writings of Kurt Lewin (see Deutsch, 1954). The fact that Lewin is also commonly regarded as the "founder" of experimental social psychology may help explain why experimental social psychologists could win the prize for having the most crises of confidence in social science within the shortest period of time. That is, Lewin's "systems" perspective, which forever sensitized us to the context in which behavior is embedded, was injected early into our bloodstream along with the Cartesian–Newtonian epistemology to which it is, in many ways, hostile. It is not surprising, then, that these two elements sometimes attack each other as foreign bodies, with the result that American social psychologists periodically come down with a fever. The irony, of course, is that Lewin's systems perspective can be traced to the work of Faraday and Maxwell in physics and their "field theory," which itself ultimately forced physicists to do their own painful soul searching and to drop many of their own Cartesian–Newtonian assumptions. I think it instructive, however, that the physicists blamed God and the subject matter He gave them for their troubles. *We* have blamed ourselves and have concluded that there is something wrong with us—that if we were only smart enough, or had the right tools, or if only we could create that new paradigm Kuhn was talking about, we could proudly join the ranks of "real" scientists; but, until then, elaborate statements of mea culpa, both to our brethren in the hard sciences and to our public constituency, are in order.

Fourth, I think we might be more aware than we have of how we have been encouraged to take an apologetic posture by our interested spectators. With respect to the hard sciences, we all recognize our tendency to look over our shoulder at "big brother" to make sure that we are doing what is expected of us, but, as George Mandler (1982) recently observed, we should also be aware that this influence is a two-way street—that big brother has been looking over his shoulder at "little brother" and "little sister" to make sure that we stay within the decreed realm of what is proper and permissible. (And I resist my impulse here to suggest some of the ways this influence is wielded through the National Academy [see *The APA Monitor*, June, 1982] and also through federal research funding.)

With respect to our public constituency, their demands for apology are even clearer. But what often has not been recognized is that despite the intrinsic differences in subject matter that have made it difficult for us to even approach the Cartesian–Newtonian standards, the standards that the public measures us by are even higher than these. They are, in fact, an absurd caricature of the standards to which the material sciences are held.

Consider, for example, the daily fare of the clinical or the counseling psychologist. The man on the street wants to know whether, if he goes ahead and marries this particular woman, he will suffer a divorce. The counselor may say that knowing nothing about him, about the woman, about the context in which this relationship was formed, or about the context in which it is going to evolve, the man has, on an actuarial basis, a 40% chance for divorce and 60% against. That, of course, is not what this man wants to know. What he wants to know is whether *he,* personally, is in the 60% or whether he is in the 40%. What he wants, in other words, is an individual point prediction. That is bad enough, but it is not all! He often adds, "And, by the way, if you find out I'm in the 40%, tell me how I can get into the 60%." Point predictions, knowledge of causal dynamics, *and* an understanding of means of control to change the course of events are the daily task of the clinical and counseling psychologist. But, now, I ask you to imagine the response of an expert in thermodynamics if I were to ask him or her when the pot of stew sitting on my stove is going to boil, or the response of a classical physicist if we were to ask him or her to plot the fall of a single snowflake. As the distinguished scholar E. H. Gombrich observed (1979):

> Not even Newton could have fully explained the . . . fact that the apple fell, if he had gone on to ask why it fell at that very instant. There are too many variables— the weight of the fruit, the strength of the stalk, the intensity of the wind, the elasticity of the bough—each of which would have to be subsumed under a general law of which this was an instance. Outside the laboratory, this would be a hopeless enterprise [p. 136].

Yet it is succeeding at this "hopeless enterprise" that is demanded of us by others—and, amazingly enough, it is the standard we ourselves have to a large extent internalized.

It is easy enough to see, or course, how the standard got escalated for us. Apart from the fact that our public fervently desires us to be able to perform such tasks for them (and the wish is often mother to the demand), the fact that the system in which our phenomena are embedded is both very large and that parts of it are ethically and technologically beyond our control shifts the stage upon which we must perform from the laboratory to the natural world. To illustrate, the physicist, in response to our request, is likely to say something like Mandler (1975) says to his readers when discussing the problem of human emotion; that is:

> . . . scientific systems are not designed and do not intend to predict the behavior of objects or systems, which are unique combinations of innumerable variables. Scientific systems discuss the operations of variables often in the abstract, but not the particular concatenation within an individual object or system [p. 227].

What the physicist can add to that, however, and we usually cannot, is "If you will only step inside my laboratory for a moment, I will make you a stew (or an atom bomb or whatever) using my own ingredients, my own pot, and my own stove, and I can tell you when *that* particular stew will boil; but there are many ways to arrive at a stew, and since I don't know how you arrived at yours (and probably not even you could tell me fully), all I can do is to tell you about some general laws that will help you to make sense of its behavior.'' We usually cannot perform this demonstration. But, then, how do we demonstrate that we know something? Since we can neither create nor control our variables at will (for ethical reasons, if nothing else), we are moved by default to the natural arena to make predictions about the operation of a constellation of variables created by God or someone else, *but*—and this is the problem—we are then often held to the individual point prediction standards of the laboratory.

I might add, parenthetically, that we do as well as we do is a wonder and probably somewhat attributable to the fact that while we ourselves neither have, nor ethically wish to have, the means to control the variables that affect people's lives, they themselves (as well as "fate") sometimes *do* have such control and they also have the ethical right to manipulate them. Consequently, they themselves sometimes act on such tentative wisdom and understanding as we can give them and, in turn, give us the opportunity to check our predictions. This, however, is a very different and far more unwieldly process of confirmation than is often recognized.

Fifth, it is heresy, no doubt, but I deeply believe that a true understanding of the ways in which the phenomena in which we are interested are intrinsically different from that of classical physics leads us to entertain the hypothesis that the classical conception of what science is, and what it is supposed to do, is a pernicious one to us, to our students, and to our public. I mean "pernicious" in the true sense of the word, which is "to undermine." What it undermines is our chance of developing a versatility of approaches to our phenomena that are suited to them, an epistemological stance that is realistic to them, and of recruiting researchers who want to work to understand these phenomena but, understandably, do not wish to be regarded as "second-rate" scientists. One implication of this is that we need to take a second look at philosophy of science courses (and their effect on our students) that set up the soft sciences as examples not of scientists working on intrinsically different and difficult phenomena, but of what *not* to do in science or what is *wrong* with a particular scientific enterprise.

We might, then, return to our roots, to the conception of science as the business of making systematic observations of events that are interpersonally replicable and verifiable and to the original aim of trying to make sense of those events, whether or not that sense can be converted to mathematical formulae and precision and whether it leads to changing nature or to simply appreciating it. In that effort we might, then, elevate descriptive analysis of our phenomena from its current low status and reject premature attempts at causal analysis. We might also drop our excessively simplistic, almost psychotically so, notions of what constitutes adequate causal analysis (e.g., see Mackie, 1965), and we might elevate actuarial prediction to something more than a technique used by book-keepers in insurance companies. Especially, we might accept with grace the fact that our theories never have been (any more than are most scientific theories) designed to permit individual point predictions in naturalistic situations.

And, finally and most importantly, we might simply accept that the science of relationships we are attempting to develop can no more expect to meet the Cartesian–Newtonian criteria of successful performance than have psychology, sociology, economics, or other of the social and behavioral sciences. There is little doubt, however, that we will be measured against these standards. And when, and inevitably, we come up short, we can conclude that there is something wrong with us; we can issue official mea culpas and lamentations to all external spectators; internally, we can point accusing fingers at each other while simul-taneously rushing off to seek the Holy Grail of resolution and absolution in the form of a ''new paradigm''; and we can, as always, plead our youth, even though we are getting a little long in the tooth for that. But there is another alternative: We can stop to consider not only the difficulties of the task we undertake, but its importance to the human condition. And if we do that, I doubt we will feel the need to apologize to anyone.

ACKNOWLEDGMENTS

I wish to express my appreciation to Steve Gangestad, Nancy Brekke, and Peter Glick, all of the University of Minnesota, for their helpful comments, as well as to Charles Kiesler, Carnegie-Mellon University, and Willard Day, University of Nevada.

References

Abelson, R. P. (1976). A script theory of understanding, attitude and behavior. In J. Carroll & T. Payne (Eds.), *Cognition and social behavior*. Hillsdale, NJ: Lawrence Erlbaum Associates.

Abramovitch, R., Corter, C., & Land, B. (1979). Sibling interaction in the home. *Child Development, 50,* 997–1003.

Adams, B. N. (1967). Interaction theory and the social network. *Sociometry, 30,* 64–78.

Adams, M. (1976). *Single blessedness*. London: Heinemann.

Aiello, J. R., & Jones, S. E. (1971). Field study of the proxemic behaviour of young school children in three subcultural groups. *Journal of Personality and Social Psychology, 19,* 351–356.

Ainsworth, M. A. S., & Bell, S. M. (1969). Some contemporary patterns of mother-infant interaction in the feeding situation. In A. Ambrose (Ed.), *Stimulation in early infancy*. London: Academic Press.

Ainsworth, M. A. S., & Bell, S. M. (1970). Attachment, exploration and separation: illustrated by the behaviour of one-year-olds in a strange situation. *Child Development, 11, 16 67.*

Ainsworth, M. A. S., Bell, S. M., & Stayton, D. S. (1974). Mother-infant attachment and social development. In P. M. M. Richards (Ed.), *The integration of a child into a social world*. Cambridge: Cambridge University Press.

Ainsworth, M. A. S., Blehar, M. C., Waters, E., & Wall, S. (1978). *Patterns of attachment: A psychological study of the strange situation*. Hillsdale, NJ: Lawrence Erlbaum Associates.

Albrecht, S. (1979). Correlates of marital happiness among the remarried. *Journal of Marriage and the Family. 41,* 857–867.

Alexander, R. D. (1979). Natural selection and social exchange. In R. L. Burgess & T. L. Huston (Eds.), *Social exchange in developing relationships*. New York: Academic Press.

Alfgren, S. H., Aries, E. J., & Oliver, R. R. (1979). Sex differences in the interaction of adults and preschool children. *Psychological Reports, 44,* 115–118.

Alker, H. A. (1972). Is personality situationally specific or intrapsychically consistent? *Journal of Personality, 40,* 1–16.

Allan, G. (1977). Class variation in friendship patterns. *British Journal of Sociology, 28,* 389–393.

Allen, B. P., & Potkay, C. R. (1981). On the arbitrary distinction between states and traits. *Journal of Personality and Social Psychology, 41,* 916–928.

Allison, P. D., & Liker, J. K. (1982). Analyzing sequential interaction data in two-person systems. *Psychological Bulletin, 91,* 393–403.

Altman, I., & Taylor, D. A. (1973). *Social penetration: The development of interpersonal relationships.* New York: Holt, Rinehart & Winston.

Andreyeva, G. M., & Gozman, L. J. (1981). Interpersonal relationships and social context. In S. W. Duck & R. Gilmour (Eds.), *Personal relationships 1: Studying personal relationships.* London: Academic Press.

Antill, J. K. (1983). Sex role complementarity versus similarity in married couples. *Journal of Personality and Social Psychology. 45,* 145–155.

Argyle, M., & Furnham, A. (1982). The ecology of relationships: Choice of situation as a function of relationship. *British Journal of Social Psychology, 21,* 259–262.

Argyle, M., & Furnham, A. (1983). Sources of satisfaction and conflict in different long-term relationships. *Journal of Marriage and the Family, 45,* 481–493.

Argyle, M., Furnham, A., & Graham, J. A. (1981). *Social situations.* Cambridge: Cambridge University Press.

Argyle, M., Graham, J. A., Campbell, A., & White, P. (1979). The rules of different situations. *New Zealand Psychologist, 8,* 13–22.

Argyle, M., & Henderson, M. (1984). The rules of friendship. *Journal of Social and Personal Relationships, 1,* 211–237.

Argyle, M., & Henderson, M. (1985). *The anatomy of relationships.* London: Heinemann.

Argyle, M., Henderson, M., Bond, M., Iizuka, Y., & Contarello, A. (in press) Cross cultural variations in relationship rules. *International Journal of Psychology.*

Argyle, M., Henderson, M., & Furnham, A. (*in press*). The rules of social relationships. *British Journal of Social Psychology.*

Arnold, M. (1960). *Emotion and personality.* New York: Columbia University Press.

Arundale, R. B. (1980). Studying change over time: Criteria for sampling from continuous variables. *Communication Research, 7,* (2), 227–263.

Asher, S. R., & Gottman, S. M. (1981). *The development of children's friendships.* Cambridge: Cambridge University Press.

Atkinson, J., & Huston, T. (1984). Sex-role orientation and division of labor early in marriage. *Journal of Personality and Social Psychology, 46,* 330–345.

Attili, G. (1983). *Normal children's attachment processes: Functional independence and adaptiveness to environment of child-child and child-adult relationships.* Paper presented at *The Second World Congress of Infant Psychiatry,* Cannes, France.

Attili, G., & Camaioni, L. (1981). Differenze sessuali nel comportamento sociale infantile: Problemi e richerche. *Giornale Italiano di Psicologia, VIII*(1), 55–79.

Attili, G., & Camaioni, L. (1983). I segnali non-verbali della prefezenzia lita in bambini in età prescolare. In G. Attili & P. Ricci-Bitti (Eds.), *Comunicare senza parole.* Roma: Bulzoni.

Attili, G., Hold, B., & Schleidt, M. (1982). *Relationships among peers in kindergarden: A cross-cultural study.* Paper presented at the IXth congress of the International Primatological Society, Atlanta, GA. in M. Taub and F. A. King (Eds.) Current Perspectives In Primate Social Dynamics, : van nostrand Reinhold.

Austin, J. (1980). *How to do things with words* (2nd ed.). Oxford: Oxford University Press.

Averill, J. R. (1979). Anger. In *Nebraska Symposium on Motivation, 1978.* Lincoln: University of Nebraska Press.

Backman, C. W., (1976). Explorations in psycho-ethics: The warranting of judgments. In R. Harré (Ed.) *Life sentences: Aspects of the social role of language.* New York: Wiley.

Backman, C. W. (1981). Attraction in interpersonal relationships. In M. Rosenberg & R. H. Turner (Eds.), *Social psychology: Sociological perspectives.* New York: Basic Books.

Backman, C. W. (1982). Toward an interdisciplinary social psychology: We're closer than we think. In L. Berkowitz (Ed.), *Advances in experimental social psychology* (Vol. 14). New York: Academic Press.

Backman, C. W. (1985). Identity, self presentation, and the resolution of moral dilemmas: Towards a social psychological theory of moral behaviour. In B. Schlenker (Ed.), *The self and social life.* New York: McGraw-Hill.

Baddeley, A. (1981). The cognitive psychology of everyday life. *British Journal of Psychology, 72,* 257–269.

Bakeman, R., & Ginsberg, G. P. (unpublished manuscript, Georgia State University, 1980). The use of video in the study of human action. In K. Knorr & G. P. Ginsberg (Eds.), *Methods of social research: Developments and advances.* London: Academic Press.

Barnett, D. W., & Zucker, K. B. (1980). The others-concept: Explorations into the quality of children's interpersonal relationships. In H. C. Foot, A. J. Chapman, & J. R. Smith (Eds.), *Friendship and social relations in children.* New York: Wilcy.

Bartlett, F. C. (1932). *Remembering: A study in experimental and social psychology.* Cambridge: Cambridge University Press.

Bartrop, R. W., Lazarus, L., Luckhurst, E., Kiloh, L. G., & Penny, R. (1979). Depressed lymphocyte function after bereavement. *Lancet, 97,* 834–836.

Baumeister, R. F. (1982). A self-presentational view of social phenomena. *Psychological Bulletin, 91,* 3–26.

Baumrind, D. (1967). Child care practices anteceding 3 patterns of preschool behaviour. *Genetic Psychology Monographs, 75,* 43–88.

Baumrind, D. (1971). Current patterns of parental authority. *Developmental Psychology Monographs, 4*(1, Pt. 2), 1–103.

Baxter, L. A. (1982). Towards a dialectical understanding of interpersonal relationships: Research and theory in the 1980s. Keynote address, Ninth Annual Communication Conference, California State, Fresno.

Baxter, L. A. (1983). Relationship disengagement: An examination of the reversal hypothesis. *Western Journal of Speech Communication,*

Beck, A. T. (1967). *Depression.* New York: Harper & Row.

Becker, G. S. (1976). *The economic approach to human behaviour.* Chicago: University of Chicago Press.

Bell, R. (1982). *Marriage and family interaction.* Homewood, IL: Dorsey Press.

Bem, D. J., & Allen, A. (1974). On predicting some of the people some of the time: The search for cross-situational consistencies in behavior. *Psychological Review, 81,* 506–520.

Bem, D. J., & Funder, D. C. (1978). Predicting more of the people more of the time. *Psychological Review, 85,* 485–501.

Berger, P. L., & Luckman, T. (1966). *The social construction of reality.* Garden City, NY: Doubleday-Anchor.

Berk, R. A., & Berk, S. F. (1979). *Labor and leisure at home: Content and organization of the household day.* Beverly Hills, CA: Sage.

Bernard, H. R., Killworth, K. D., & Sailor, L. (1982). Informant accuracy in social-network data. V. An experimental attempt to predict actual communication from recall data. *Social Science Research, 11,* 30–66.

Bernard, J. (1968). *The sex game.* Englewood Cliffs, NJ: Prentice-Hall.

Bernard, J. (1973). *The future of marriage.* New York: Bantam.

Berndt, T. J. (1981). Effects of friendship on prosocial intentions and behaviour. *Child Development, 52,* 636–643.

Berscheid, E. (1983). Emotion. In H. H. Kelley, E. Berscheid, A. Christensen, J. H. Harvey, T. L. Huston, G. Levinger, E. McClintock, L. A. Peplau, & D. R. Peterson (Eds.), *Close relationships.* New York and San Francisco: Freeman.

Berscheid, E. (1985). Interpersonal attraction. In G. Lindzey & E. Aronson (Eds.), *Handbook of social psychology* (3rd ed.). Reading, MA: Addison-Wesley.

Berscheid, E. (in press). *Affect in close relationships.* New York: Plenum.

Berscheid, E., & Fei, J. (1977). Romantic love and sexual jealousy. In G. Clanton & L. G. Smith (Eds.), *Jealousy.* Englewood Cliffs, NJ: Prentice-Hall.

Berscheid, E., & Peplau, L. A. (1983). The emerging science of relationships. In H. H. Kelley, E.

Berscheid, A. Christensen, J. H. Harvey, T. L. Huston, G. Levinger, E. McClintock, L. A. Peplau, & D. R. Peterson (Eds.), *Close relationships*. New York and San Francisco: W. H. Freeman.

Berscheid, E., & Walster, E. (1969). *Interpersonal attraction*. Reading, MA: Addison-Wesley.

Berscheid, E., & Walster, E. (1974). A little bit about love. In T. L. Huston (Ed.), *Foundations of interpersonal attraction*. New York: Academic Press.

von Bertalanffy, L. (1980). *General system theory: Foundations, development, applications* (rev. ed.). New York: George Braziller.

Bevan, W. (1982a). A sermon of sorts in three plus parts. *American Psychologist, 37*, 1303–1322.

Bevan, W. (1982b). William Bevan has strong words for his field. *American Psychological Association Monitor, 13*, (3), 1–7.

Bigelow, B. J. (1977). Children's friendship expectations: A cognitive developmental study. *Child Development, 48*, 246–253.

Billings, A. (1979). Conflict resolution in distressed and non-distressed couples. *Journal of Consulting and Clinical Psychology, 47*, 368–376.

Blank, T. O. (1982). *A social psychology of developing adults*. New York: Wiley.

Block, J. (1961). *The Q-sort method in personality assessment and psychiatric research*. Springfield, IL: Charles C. Thomas.

Block, J. (1977). Advancing the science of personality: Paradigmatic shift or improving the quality of research? In D. Magnusson & N. S. Endler (Eds.), *Psychology at the crossroads: Current issues in interactional psychology*. Hillsdale, NJ: Lawrence Erlbaum Associates.

Block, J., & Block, J. (1969). *Instructions for the California child Q-sort (memorandum)*. Berkeley, CA: University of California, Institute for Personality Assessment and Research.

Blood, R. O. (1972). *The family*. New York: Free Press.

Bloom, B., Asher, S., & White, S. (1978). Marital disruption as a stressor: A review and analysis. *Psychological Bulletin, 85*, 867–894.

Blurton-Jones, N. (Ed.). (1972). *Ethological studies of child behaviour*. Cambridge: Cambridge University Press.

Bochner, A. (1982). On the efficacy of openness in close relationships. In M. Burgoon (Ed.), *Communication yearbook 5*. New Brunswick, NJ: Transaction Books.

Bojanovsky, J., & Bojanovsky, A. (1976). Zur Risikozeit des Selbstmordes bei Geschiedenen und Verwitweten. *Nervenarzt, 47*, 307–309.

Booth, A. (1972). Sex and social participation. *American Sociological Review, 37*, 183–193.

Booth, A., & Hess, E. (1974). Cross-sex friendships. *Journal of Marriage and the Family, 36*, 38–47.

Bornstein, P. E., Clayton, P. J., Halikas, J. A., Maurice, W. L., & Robbins, E. (1973). The depression of widowhood after thirteen months. *British Journal of Psychiatry, 122*, 561–566.

Bott, E. (1957). *Family and social network*. London: Tavistock.

Bowers, K. S. (1973). Situationism in psychology: An analysis and a critique. *Psychological Review, 80*, 307–336.

Bowlby, J. (1969). *Attachment and loss: I attachment*. London: Hogarth Press.

Bowlby, J. (1973). *Attachment and loss: II separation: Anxiety and anger*. London: Hogarth Press.

Braiker, H. B., & Kelley, H. H. (1979). Conflict in the development of close relationships. In R. L. Burgess & T. L. Huston (Eds.), *Social exchange in developing relationships*. New York: Academic Press.

Brazelton, T. B., Koslowski, B., & Main, M. (1974). The origins of reciprocity: The early mother-infant interaction. In M. Lewis & L. A. Rosenbaum (Eds.), *The effects of the infants on its caregiver*. New York: Wiley.

Bringle, R. G. (1981a). Conceptualizing jealousy as a disposition. *Alternative Lifestyles, 4*(3), 274–290.

Bringle, R. G. (1981b). Viewing jealousy from a personality perspective. In E. Aronson (Chair),

Exploring sexual jealousy: An interdisciplinary approach. Symposium presentation at the meeting of the American Psychological Association, Los Angeles.

Bringle, R. G. (1982). *Preliminary report on the revised Self-Report Jealousy Scale.* Unpublished manuscript.

Bringle, R. G., Evenbeck, S., & Schmedel, K. (1977). *The role of jealousy in marriage.* Paper presented at the meeting of the American Psychological Association.

Bringle, R. G., Renner, P., Terry, R. L., & Davis, S. (1983). An analysis of situation and person components of jealousy. *Journal of Research in Personality, 17,* 354–368.

Bringle, R. G., Roach, S., Andler, C., & Evenbeck, S. (1977). *Correlates of Jealousy.* Paper presented at the meeting of the Midwestern Psychological Association, Chicago.

Bringle, R. G., & Williams, L. J. (1979). Parental-offspring similarity on jealousy and related personality dimensions. *Motivation and Emotion, 3,* 265–286.

Brinkgreve, C., & Korzec, M. (1978). *"Margriet weet raad," gevoel, gedrag, moraal in Nederland 1938–1978.* Utrecht: Spectrum.

Briscoe, C. W., & Smith, J. R. (1975). Depression in bereavement and divorce: Relationship to primary depressive illness: A study of 128 subjects. *Archives of General Psychiatry, 32,* 439–443.

Brodzinsky, D. M., Messer, S. B., & Tew, J. D. (1979). Sex differences in children's expression and control of fantasy and overt aggression, *Child Development, 50,* 372–379.

Bronson, W. C. (1975a). Developments in behaviour with agemates during the second year of life. In M. Lewis & L. Rosenblum (Eds.), *Friendship and peer relations.* New York: Wiley.

Bronson, W. C. (1975b). *Toddlers' behaviours with agemates.* Norwood: Ablex.

Brown, G. W. (1982). Early loss and depression. In C. M. Parkes & J. Stevenson-Hinde (Eds.), *The place of attachment in human behavior.* New York: Basic Books.

Brown, G. W., Bhrolchain, M. N., & Harris, T. (1975). Social class and psychiatric disturbance among women in an urban population. *Sociology, 9,* 225–254.

Brown, G. W., & Harris, T. (1978). *Social origins of depression: A study of psychiatric disorders in women.* London: Tavistock/New York: Free Press.

Bruner, J. S. (1975). The ontogenesis of speech acts. *Journal of Child Language, 2,* 1–19.

Bryson, J. B. (1976). *The nature of sexual jealousy: An exploratory study.* Paper presented at the meeting of the American Psychological Association, Washington, DC.

Bryson, J. B. (1977). *Situational determinants of the expression of jealousy.* Paper presented at the meeting of the American Psychological Association, San Fransisco.

Bunch, J. (1972). Recent bereavement in relation to suicide. *Journal of Psychosomatic Research, 16,* 361–366.

Burgess, R. L. (1981). Relationships in marriage and the family. In S. W. Duck & R. Gilmour (Eds.), *Personal relationships 1: Studying personal relationships.* London: Academic Press.

Burgess, R. L., & Bushell, D. (Eds.). (1969). *Behavioral sociology.* New York: Columbia University Press.

Burgess, R. L., & Huston, T. L. (Eds.). (1979). *Social exchange in developing relationships.* New York: Academic Press.

Buunk, B. (1978). Jaleozie 2: Ervaringen van 250 Nederlanders. *Intermediair, 14,* (12), 45–51.

Buunk, B. (1980a). *Intieme relaties met derden. Eeen sociaal psychologische studie.* Alphen aan de Rign: Samson.

Buunk, B. (1980b). *Attribution and jealousy.* Paper presented at the meeting of the 82nd International Congress of Psychology, Leipzig.

Buunk, B. (1980c). Extramarital sex in the Netherlands. Motivations in social and marital context. *Alternative Lifestyles, 3,* 11–39.

Buunk, B. (1982a). Anticipated sexual jealousy: Its relationship to self-esteem, dependency and reciprocity. *Personality and Social Psychology Bulletin, 8,* 310–316.

Buunk, B. (1982b). *Jealousy: Some recent findings and issues.* Paper presented at the International Conference on Personal Relationships, Madison, WI.

Buunk, B., & Hupka, R. (1984). *Cross-cultural differences in the elicitation of sexual jealousy.* Unpublished manuscript.

Byrne, D. (1961). The repression-sensitization scale: Rationale, reliability, validity. *Journal of Personality, 29,* 334–339.

Byrne, D., Barry, J., & Nelson, D. (1963). The relation of revised repression-sensitization scale to measures of self-description. *Psychological Reports, 13,* 323–334.

Cairns, R. B. (1979). *Social development: The origins and plasticity of interchanges.* San Francisco: W. H. Freeman.

Caldwell, B. M. (1969). A new "APPROACH" to behavioral ecology. In I. P. Hill (Ed.), *Minnesota symposia on child psychology* (Vol. 2). Minneapolis: University of Minnesota Press.

Caldwell, M. A., & Peplau, L. A. (1982). Sex differences in same-sex friendship. *Sex Roles, 8,* 721–732.

Campbell, A. Converse, P. E., & Rodgers, W. L. (1976). *The quality of American life.* New York: Russell Sage.

Candland, D. K. (1977). The persistent problems of emotion. In D. K. Candland, J. P. Fell, E. Keen, A. I. Leshner, R. Plutchik, & R. M. Tarpy (Eds.), *Emotion.* Monterey, CA: Brooks/Cole.

Caporael, L. R. (1981a). The paralanguage of giving: Baby talk to the institutionalized aged. *Journal of Personality and Social Psychology, 40,* 876–884.

Caporael, L. R. (1981b). *Baby talk messages and non-baby talk messages to the institutionalized aged: Complexity and content.* Unpublished manuscript.

Capra, F. (1982). *The turning point: Science, society and the rising culture.* New York: Simon & Schuster.

Carey, R. G. (1977). The widowed: A year later. *Journal of Counseling Psychology, 24,* 125–131.

Carson, R. C. (1979). Personality and exchange in developing relationships. In R. L. Burgess & T. L. Huston (Eds.), *Social exchange in developing relationships.* New York: Academic Press.

Carter, H., & Glick, P. C. (1976). *Marriage and Divorce: A social and economic study* (rev. ed.). Cambridge: Harvard University Press.

Cattell, R. B., Eber, H. W., & Tatsuoka, M. M. (1970). *Handbook for the 16 Personality Factor Questionnaire.* Champaign, IL: Institute for Personality and Ability Testing.

Chapman, A. J., Smith, J. R., & Foot, H. C. (1980). Humour, laughter and social interaction. In P. E. McGhee & A. J. Chapman (Eds.), *Children's humour.* Chichester: Wiley.

Charlesworth, R., & Hartup, W. W. (1967). Positive social reinforcement in a nursery school peer group. *Child Development, 38,* 993–1002.

Cherlin, A. (1978). Remarriage as an incomplete institution. *American Journal of Sociology, 3,* 634–650.

Cherlin, A. (1981). *Marriage, divorce, remarriage.* Cambridge, MA: Harvard University Press.

Chester, R. (1983). *Step-relations.* Social Psychology Seminar, University of Oxford.

Christensen, A., & King, C. E. (1982). Telephone survey of daily marital behavior. *Behavioral Assessment, 4,* 327–338.

Clanton, G. (1981). Frontiers of jealousy research. *Alternative Lifestyles, 4*(3), 259–273.

Clanton, G., & Smith, L. G. (1977). *Jealousy.* Englewood Cliffs, NJ: Prentice-Hall.

Clark, H. H. (1985). Language use and language users. In G. Lindzey & E. Aronson (Eds.), *Handbook of social psychology* (3rd ed.). Reading, MA: Addison-Wesley.

Clark, M. S., & Mills, J. (1979). Interpersonal attraction in exchange and communal relationships. *Journal of Personality and Social Psychology, 37,* 12–24.

Clarke-Stewart, K. A. (1973). Interaction between mother and their young children: Characteristics and consequences. *Monographs of the Society for Research in Child Development, 38,* 153.

Clayton, P. J. (1974). Mortality and morbidity in the first year of bereavement. *Archives of General Psychiatry, 30,* 747–750.

Clayton, P. J., Halikas, J. A., & Maurice, W. L. (1972). The depression of widowhood. *British Journal of Psychiatry, 120,* 71–78.

Clayton, R. R., & Voss, H. L. (1977). Shacking up: Cohabitation in the 1970s. *Journal of Marriage and the Family, 39,* 273–283.

Clingempeel, W. G. (1981). Quasi-kin relationships and marital quality in stepfather families. *Journal of Personality and Social Psychology, 41,* 890–901.

Cook, T. D., & Campbell, D. T. (1979). *Quasi-Experimentation: Design and Analysis Issues for Field Settings.* Chicago: Rand-McNally.

Cottington, E. M., Matthews, K. A., Talbott, E., & Kuller, L. H. (1980). Environment events preceding sudden death in women. *Psychosomatic Medicine, 42,* 567–574.

Cousins, P. C., & Vincent, J. P. (1983). Supportive and aversive behavior following spousal complaints. *Journal of Marriage and the Family, 45,* 679–682.

Cowan, C., Cowan, L., Coie, L., & Coie, J. (1978). Becoming a family: The impact of the first child's birth on the couple's relationship. In W. B. Miller & L. F. Newman (Eds.), *The first child and family formation.* Chapel Hill, NC: Population Center.

Cowen, E. L. (1973). Social and community intervention. *Annual Review of Psychology, 24,* 423–472.

Crago, M. A. (1972). Psychopathology in married couples. *Psychological Bulletin, 77,* 114–128.

Cranach, M. von, Kalbermatten, U., Intermuhle, K., & Gugler, B. (1982). *Goal-directed action.* London: Academic Press.

Crawford, M. (1977). What is a friend? *New Society, 42,* 116–117.

Davis, K. E., & Todd, M. (1983). Friendship and love relationships. In K. E. Davis (Ed.), *Advances in descriptive psychology,* (Vol. 2). Greenwich, CT: JAI Press.

Davis, K. K., & Lee, J. W. (1980). Time series models for communication research. In P. R. Monge & J. N. Capella (Eds.), *Multivariate techniques in human communication research.* New York: Academic Press.

Dean, G., & Gurak, D. (1978). Marital homogamy the second time around. *Journal of Marriage and the Family, 40,* 559–570.

Dembrowski, T. M., Weiss, S. M., Shields, J. L., Haynes, S. G., & Feinleib, M. (Eds.). (1978). *Coronary prone behaviour.* New York: Springer.

Denfield, D. (1974). Dropouts from swinging: The marriage counselor as informant. In J. R. Smith & L. G. Smith (Eds.), *Beyond monogamy.* Baltimore: Johns Hopkins University Press.

Derlega, V. J., & Margulis, S. T. (1982). Why loneliness occurs: The interrelationship of social-psychological and privacy concepts. In L. A. Peplau & D. Perlman (Eds.), *Loneliness: A sourcebook of current theory, research and therapy.* New York: Wiley.

Deutsch, M. (1949). An experimental study of the effects of co-operation and competition upon group process. *Human Relations, 2,* 199–232.

Deutsch, M. (1954). Field theory in social psychology. In G. Lindzey (Ed.), *Handbook of social psychology* (Vol. 1). Reading, MA: Addison-Wesley.

de Waal, F. (1982). *Chimpanzee politics.* London: Jonathan Cape.

De Waele, J.-P., & Harré, R. (1979). Autobiography as psychological method. In G. P. Ginsburg (Ed.), *Emerging strategies in social psychological research.* Chichester: Wiley.

Dickens, W. J., & Perlman, D. (1981). Friendship over the life-cycle. In S. W. Duck & R. Gilmour (Eds.), *Personal relationships 2: Developing personal relationships.* London: Academic Press.

Dominian, J. (1976). *Depression.* London: Fontana.

Duberman, L. (1975). *The reconstituted family: A study of remarried couples and their children.* Chicago: Nelson-Hall.

Duck, S. W. (1977a). Inquiry, hypothesis and the quest for validation: Personal construct systems in the development of acquaintance. In S. W. Duck (Ed.), *Theory and practice in interpersonal attraction.* London: Academic Press.

Duck, S. W. (1977b). *The study of acquaintance.* Farnborough: Saxon House Ltd.

Duck, S. W. (1977c). *Theory and practice in interpersonal attraction.* London: Academic Press.

Duck, S. W. (1980). Personal relationships research in the 1980s: Towards an understanding of complex human sociality. *Western Journal of Speech Communication, 44,* 114–119.

Duck, S. W. (1982). A topography of relationship disengagement and dissolution. In S. W. Duck (Ed.), *Personal relationships 4: Dissolving personal relationships.* London: Academic Press.

Duck, S. W. (Ed.). (1984). *Personal relationships 5: Repairing personal relationships.* London: Academic Press.

Duck, S. W., & Gilmour, R. (Eds.). (1981a). *Personal relationships 1: Studying personal relationships.* London: Academic Press.

Duck, S. W., & Gilmour, R. (Eds.). (1981b). *Personal relationships 2: Developing personal relationships.* New York: Academic Press.

Duck, S. W., & Gilmour, R. (Eds.). (1981c). *Personal relationships 3: Personal relationships in disorder.* London: Academic Press.

Duck, S., Miell, D. K., & Gaebler, H. (1980). Attraction and communication in children's interactions. In H. C. Foot, A. J. Chapman, & J. R. Smith (Eds.), *Friendship and social relations in children.* New York: Wiley.

Duck, S. W., & Sants, H. K. A. (1983). On the origin of the specious: Are personal relationships really interpersonal states? *Journal of Social and Clinical Psychology, 1,* 27–41.

Duncan, S., & Fiske, D. W. (1977). *Face-to-face interaction: Research, methods and theory.* Hillsdale, NJ: Lawrence Erlbaum Associates.

Dunn, J., & Kendrick, C. (1980). The arrival of a sibling: Changes in patterns of interaction between mother and first-born child. *Journal of Child Psychology and Psychiatry, 21,* 119–132.

Dunn, J. B., & Richards, M. P. M. (1977). Observations on the developing relationship between mother and baby in the neonatal period. In H. R. Schaffer (Ed.), *Studies in mother-infant interaction.* London: Academic Press.

Dunphy, D. C. (1963). The social structures of urban adolescent peer groups. *Sociometry, 26,* 230–246.

Durkheim, E. (1951). *Suicide: A study in sociology.* Glencoe, IL.: The Free Press.

Eakins, B., & Eakins, R. G. (1978). *Sex differences in human communication.* Boston: Houghton Mifflin.

Eaton, W. (1978). Life events, social support, and psychiatric symptoms: A reanalysis of the New Haven data. *Journal of Health and Social Behaviour, 19,* 230–234.

Ekblom, B. (1964). Significance of psychological factors with regard to risk of death among elderly persons. *Acta Psychiatrica Scandinavica, 39,* 627–633.

Elms, A. C. (1975). The crisis of confidence in social psychology. *American Psychologist, 30,* 967–976.

Emler, N. P. (1981, September). Gossip and social participation. Paper presented at Annual Conference of BPS Social Section, Oxford.

Emmerich, W. (1971). Structure and development of personal-social behaviours in preschool settings, Educational Testing Service, Head Start Longitudinal Study.

Endler, N. S. (1966). Estimating variance components from mean squares for random and fixed effects analysis of variance models. *Perceptual and Motor Skills, 22,* 559–570.

Endler, N. S., & Hunt, J. McV. (1968). S-R Inventories of Hostility and comparisons of the proportion of variance from persons, responses, and situations for hostility and anxiousness. *Journal of Personality and Social Psychology, 9,* 309–315.

Endler, N. S., & Hunt, J. McV. (1969). Generalizability of contributions from sources of variance in the S-R Inventories of Anxiousness. *Journal of Personality, 37,* 1–24.

Endler, N. S., & Magnusson, D. (1976a). Toward an interactional psychology of personality. *Psychological Bulletin, 83,* 956–974.

Endler, N. S., & Magnusson, D. (1976b). *Interactional psychology and personality.* New York: Wiley.

Engel, G. L. (1978). Psychologic stress, vasodepressor (vasovagal) syncope, and sudden death. *Annals of Internal Medicine, 89*, 403–412.

Erikson, E. H. (1963). *Childhood and society.* New York: Norton.

Farrell, J., & Markman, H. (1983). *A test of the training ground model with couples planning remarriage.* Manuscript in preparation.

Feighner, J. P., Robins, E., Guze, S. B., Woodruff, R. A., & Winokur, G. (1972). Diagnostic criteria for use in psychiatric research. *Archives of General Psychiatry, 26*, 56–73.

Feigl, H. (1958). The "mental" and the "physical." In H. Feigl, M. Scriven, & G. Maxwell (Eds.), *Minnesota studies in the philosophy of science, Vol. II: Concepts, theories, and the mind-body problem.* Minneapolis: University of Minnesota Press.

Feirstein, B. (1982). Breaking up. *New York, 24*, 38–48.

Feldman, P., & Orford, J. (Eds.). (1980). *Psychological problem: The social context.* Chichester: Wiley.

Felson, R. B., & Ribner, S. A. (1981). An attributional approach to accounts and sanctions for criminal violence. *Social Psychology Quarterly, 44*, 137–142.

Festinger, L. (1954). A theory of social comparison processes. *Human Relations, 7*, 117–140.

Fienberg, S. E. (1977). *The analysis of cross-classified categorical data.* Cambridge, MA; The MIT Press.

Fischer, C. S., & Phillips, S. L. (1982). Who is alone? Social characteristics of people with small networks. In L. A. Peplau & D. Perlman (Eds.), *Loneliness: A sourcebook of current theory, research and therapy.* New York: Wiley.

Fishbein, M., & Ajzen, I. (1975). *Belief, attitude, intention, and behaviour: An introduction to theory and research.* Reading, MA: Addison-Wesley.

Fishman, P. (1978). Interaction: The work women do. *Social Problems, 25*, 397–406.

Fiske, S. T. (1980). Social cognition and affect. In J. Harvey (Ed.), *Cognition, social behavior and the environment.* Hillsdale, NJ: Lawrence Erlbaum Associates.

Flavell, J. (1974). The development of inferences about others. In T. Mischel (Ed.), *Understanding other persons.* Oxford: Blackwell.

Fletcher, G. J. O. (1983). The analysis of verbal explanations for marital separation: Implications for attribution theory. *Journal of Applied Social Psychology, 13*, 245–258.

Foa, U. G., & Foa, E. B. (1974). *Societal structures of the mind.* Springfield, IL: Charles C. Thomas.

Foot, H. C., Chapman, A. J., & Smith, J. R. (1977). Friendship and social responsiveness in boys and girls. *Journal of Personality and Social Psychology, 35*, 401–411.

Foot, H. C., Chapman, A. J., & Smith, J. R. (1980). *Friendship and social relations in children.* New York: Wiley.

Ford, M. E. (1982). *Androgyny as self-assertion and integration: Implications for psychological and social competence.* Unpublished manuscript, Stanford University School of Education.

Forgas, J. P. (1979). *Social episodes: The study of interaction routines.* New York: Academic Press.

Francis, J. L. (1977). Toward the management of heterosexual jealousy. *Journal of Marriage and Family Counseling, 3*, 61–69.

Frederick, J. F. (1971). Physiological reactions induced by grief. *Omega, 2*, 71–75.

Frentz, T., & Rushing, J. (1979). *Fulfilling closeness and distance needs through consensual relationship definitions and communicative vibration.* Paper presented to Western Speech Communication Association Convention.

Freud, S. (1959). Mourning and melancholia. In *Collected papers* (Vol. 4, pp. 152–170). New York: Basic Books. (Original work published 1917)

Friedman, M., Byers, S. O., & Brown, A. E. (1967). Plasma lipid responses of rats to an auditory stimulus. *American Journal of Physiology, 212*, 1174–1178.

Funder, D. C. (1982). On the accuracy of dispositional versus situational attributions. *Social Cognition, 1,* 205–222.

Galejs, L. (1974). Social interaction of pre-school children. *Home Economics Research Journal, 2,* 153–159.

Garside, R. F., Birch, H., Scott, D. McI., et al. (1975). Dimensions of temperament in infant school children. *Journal of Child Psychology, Psychiatry and Allied Disciplines, 16,* 219–231.

Gelman, R., & Shatz, M. (1977). Speech adjustments in talk to 2-year olds. In M. Lewis and L. A. Rosenblum (Eds.), *Interaction, conversation and the development of language.* New York: Academic Press.

Gergen, K. J. (1982). Psychology without history and society. *Contemporary Psychology, 27,* May, 360–361.

Gergen, K. J., & Gergen, M. M. (1981). *Social psychology.* New York: Harcourt Brace Jovanovich.

Gilbert, S. (1976). Self disclosure, intimacy and communication in families. *The Family Coordination, 25,* 221–231.

Gilford, R., & Bengtson, V. (1979). Measuring marital satisfaction in three generations: positive and negative dimensions. *Journal of Marriage and the Family, 41,* 387–398.

Gilligan, C. (1982). *In a different voice.* Cambridge, MA: Harvard University Press.

Gilmartin, B. G. (1977). Jealousy among the swingers. In G. Clanton & L. G. Smith (Eds.), *Jealousy.* Englewood Cliffs, NJ: Prentice-Hall.

Ginsburg, G. P. (1979). The effective use of role-playing in social psychological research. In G. P. Ginsburg (Ed.), *Emerging strategies in social psychological research.* Chichester: Wiley.

Ginsburg, G. P. (1980a). Epilogue: A conception of situated action. In M. Brenner (Ed.), *The structure of action.* Oxford, Blackwell.

Ginsburg, G. P. (1980b). Situated action: An emerging paradigm. In L. Wheeler, (Ed.), *Review of personality and social psychology,* (Vol. 1). Beverly Hills, CA: Sage.

Ginsburg, G. P. (1981, November). *Closing remarks.* Paper presented at the One Day Conference on Long Term Relationships. Oxford.

Glass, D. C. (1977). *Behaviour patterns, stress and coronary disease.* Hillsdale, NJ: Lawrence Erlbaum Associates.

Glenn, N., & Weaver, C. (1977). The marital happiness of remarried divorced persons. *Journal of Marriage and the Family, 39,* 331–337.

Glick, I., Weiss, R. S., & Parkes, C. M. (1974). *The first year of bereavement.* New York: Wiley.

Glick, P., & Norton, A. (1976). Marital instability: Past, present and future. *Journal of Social Issues, 32,* 5–20.

Glick, P., & Norton, G. (1977). Marrying, divorcing and living together in the US today. *Population Bulletin, 39,* 461–478.

Goffman, E. (1959). *The presentation of self in everyday life.* New York: Doubleday/Anchor.

Goffman, E. (1971). *Relations in public.* New York: Basic Books.

Goldberg, D. P. (1972). *The detection of psychiatric illness by questionnaire.* London: Oxford University Press, Maudsley Monograph No. 21.

Gombrich, E. H. (1979). *Ideals and idols: Essays on values in history and in art.* Oxford: Phaidon Press.

Goodwin, J. S., Bromberg, S., Taszak, C., Kazubowski, P. A., Messner, R. P., & Neal, J. F. (1981). Effects of physical stress on sensitivity of lymphocytes to inhibition by prostgland in E$_2$. *Journal of Immunology, 127,* 518–522.

Gorer, G. D. (1965). *Death, grief and mourning.* New York: Doubleday.

Gottlieb, B. H. (Ed.). (1981). *Social networks and social support.* Beverly Hill, CA: Sage.

Gottman, J. M. (1979a). Detecting cyclicity in social interaction. *Psychological Bulletin, 86,* 338–348.

Gottman, J. M. (1979b). *Marital interaction: Experimental investigations.* New York: Academic Press.

Gottman, J. M. (1981). *Time-Series Analysis: A Comprehensive Introduction for Social Scientists.* Cambridge: Cambridge University Press.

Gottman, J., Notarius, C., Markman, H., Bank, S., Yoppi, S., & Rubin, M. (1976). Behavior exchange theory and marital decision making. *Journal of Personal and Social Psychology, 34,* 14–23.

Gove, W. R. (1972a). The relationship between sex roles, marital roles and mental illness. *Social Forces, 51,* 34–44.

Gove, W. R. (1972b). Sex, marital status and suicide. *Journal of Health and Social Behaviour, 13,* 204–213.

Gove, W. R., & Hughes, M. (1980). Reexamining the ecological fallacy: A study in which aggregate data are critical in investigating the pathological effects of living alone. *Social Forces, 57,* (No. 4), 1157–1177.

Gove, W. R., Hughes, M., & Style, C. B. (1983). Does marriage have positive effects on the psychological well-being of the individual? *Journal of Health and Social Behavior, 24,* 122–131.

Graham, J. A., Argyle, M., & Furnham, A. (1980). The goals and goal structure of social situations. *European Journal of Social Psychology, 10,* 345–366.

Guntrip, H. (1961). *Personality structure and human interaction: The developing synthesis of psychodynamic theory.* London: Hogarth Press.

Haan, N. (1982). Can research on "morality" be scientific? *American Psychologist, 37,* 1096–1104.

Hahn, B. (1933). Jealousy as a neurosis. *Forschrifte der Medizen, 51,* 336–344.

Hansen, G. L. (1980). *Jealousy: Toward a comprehensive model.* Paper presented at the Annual Meeting of the National Council on Family Relations, Portland, OR.

Harré, R. (1977). Friendship as an accomplishment: An ethogenic approach to social relationships. In S. W. Duck (Ed.), *Theory and practice in interpersonal attraction.* London: Academic Press.

Harré, R. (1981). Expressive aspects of descriptions of others. In C. Antaki (Ed.), *The psychology of ordinary explanations of social behaviour.* London: Academic Press.

Harré, R., & Secord, P. F. (1972). *The explanation of social behaviour.* Oxford: Blackwell.

Harris, M. (1975). *Cows, pigs, wars and witches.* London: Hutchinson.

Hartup, W. W. (1975). The origins of friendship. In M. L. Lewis & L. A. Rosenblum (Eds.), *Friendship and peer relations.* New York: Wiley.

Hartup, W. W. (1978a). Children and their friends. In H. McGurk (Eds.), *Issues in childhood social development.* London: Methuen.

Hartup, W. W. (1978b). Peer relations and the growth of social competence. In M. W. Kent & J. E. Rolf (Eds.), *The primary prevention of psychopathology,* (Vol. 3). Hanover, NH: University Press of New England.

Harvey, J. H., Town, J. P., & Yarkin, K. L. (1981). How fundamental is "The fundamental attribution error?" *Journal of Personality and Social Psychology, 40,* 346–349.

Harvey, J. H., Weber, A. L., Yarkin, K. L., & Stewart, B. (1982). Attribution and breakdown in close relationships. In S. W. Duck (Ed.), *Personal relationships 4: Dissolving personal relationships.* London: Academic Press.

Harvey, J. H., Wells, G. L., & Alvarez, M. D. (1978). Attribution in the context of conflict and separation in close relationships. In J. H. Harvey, W. Ickes, & R. F. Kidd (Eds.), *New directions in attribution research* (Vol. 2). Hillsdale, NJ: Lawrence Erlbaum Associates.

Harvey, J. H., Yarkin, K. L., Lightner, J. M., & Town, J. P. (1980). Unsolicited interpretation and recall of interpersonal events. *Journal of Personality and Social Psychology, 38,* 551–568.

Helsing, K. J., & Szklo, M. (1981). Mortality after bereavement. *American Journal of Epidemiology, 114,* 41–52.

Henderson, M., & Argyle, M. (1985). Social support by five categories of work colleagues: Relationships between activities, stress and satisfaction. *Journal of Occupational Behavior, 6,* 229–239.

Henderson, S., Byrne, D. G., & Duncan-Jones, P. (1981). *Neurosis and the social environment.* Sydney: Academic Press.

Hendrix, L. (1979). Kinship, social class and migration. *Journal of Marriage and the Family, 41,* 399–407.

Henley, N. M. (1977). *Body politics: Power, sex and nonverbal communication* Englewood Cliffs, NJ: Prentice-Hall.

Hetherington, E., Cox, M., & Cox, R. (1977). The aftermath of divorce. In J. J. Stevens & M. Mathews (Eds.), *Mother-child, father-child relations.* Washington, DC: NAEYC.

Hewstone, M., Argyle, M., & Furnham, A. (1982). Favouritism, fairness and joint profit in long-term relationships. *European Journal of Social Psychology, 12,* 283–95.

Heyman, D. K., & Gianturco, D. T. (1973). Long-term adaptation by the elderly to bereavement. *Journal of Gerontology, 28,* 359–362.

Hill, R. (1970). *Family development in three generations.* Cambridge, MA: Schenkman.

Hinde, R. A. (1969). Analysing the roles of the partners in a behavioural interaction—mother–infant relations in rhesus macaques. *Annals of the New York Acadamy of Science, 159,* 651–667.

Hinde, R. A. (1976). Interactions, relationships and social structures. *Man, 11,*(No. 1), 1–17.

Hinde, R. A. (1979). *Towards understanding relationships.* London: Academic Press.

Hinde, R. A. (1981). The bases of a science of interpersonal relationships. In S. W. Duck & R. Gilmour (Eds.), *Personal relationships 1: Studying personal relationships.* London: Academic Press.

Hinde, R. A. (1982). *Ethology.* Oxford: Oxford University Press.

Hinde, R. A., Easton, D. F., Meller, R. E., & Tamplin, A. M. (1982). Temperamental characteristics of 3–4 year-olds and mother–child interaction. *Ciba Foundation Symposium, 89,* 66–85.

Hinde, R. A., Easton, D. F., Meller, R. E., & Tamplin, A. M. (1983). Nature and determinants of preschoolers' differential behaviour to adults and peers. *British Journal of Developmental Psychology, 1,* 3–19.

Hinde, R. A., & Roper, R. (1982). Social behaviour in a play group: The incidence of peer-peer relationships. *Bulletin de Psychologie.*

Hinde, R. A., & Tamplin, A. M. (1983). Relations between mother-child interaction and behaviour in preschool. *British Journal of Developmental Psychology, 1,* 231–257.

Hinde, R. A., Titmus, G., Easton, D. F., & Tamplin, A. M. (1985). Incidence of 'friendship' and behaviour towards strong associates versus non-associates in preschoolers. *Child Development.*

Hollingshead, A. B., & Redlich, F. C. (1958). *Social class and mental illness.* New York: Wiley.

Holmes, T. H., & Rahe, R. H. (1967). The social readjustment scale. *Journal of Psychosomatic Research, 11,* 213–218.

House, J. S. (1981). *Work stress and social support.* Reading, MA: Addison-Wesley.

Hunt, M. (1969). The affair. Cleveland: World Publishing.

Hupka, R. B. (1981). Cultural determinants of jealousy. *Alternative Lifestyles, 4*(3), 310–356.

Huston, T. L. (Ed.). (1974). *Foundations of interpersonal attraction.* New York: Academic Press.

Huston, T. L., & Levinger, G. (1978). Interpersonal attraction and relationships. In M. R. Rosenzweig & L. W. Porter (Eds.), *Annual review of psychology,* (Vol. 29). Palo Alto, CA: Annual Reviews.

Huston, T. L., & Robins, E. (1982). Conceptual and methodological issues in studying close relationships. *Journal of Marriage and the Family, 44,* 901–925.

Huston, T. L., Surra, C. A., Fitzgerald, N. M., & Cate, R. M. (1981). From courtship to marriage: Mate selection as an interpersonal process. In S. W. Duck & R. Gilmour (Eds.), *Personal relationships 2: Developing personal relationships.* London: Academic Press.

Ickes, W. A. (1983). A basic paradigm for the study of unstructured dyadic interaction. In H. T. Reis (Ed.), *Naturalistic approaches to studying social interaction.* San Francisco: Jossey-Bass.

Jacob, T., Feiring, C., & Anderson, C. (1980). Factor analysis of data on the Barrett-Lennard relationships inventory from married couples. *Psychological Reports, 47,* 619–626.

Jacobson, N. S., & Margolin, G. (1979). *Marital therapy.* New York: Brunner/Mazel.

Jaremko, M. E., & Lindsey, R. (1979). Stress coping abilities of individuals high and low in jealousy. *Psychological Reports, 44,* 547–553.

Jenkins, J. J. (1974). Remember that old theory of memory? Well, forget it! *American Psychologist, 29,* 785–795.

Johnson, J. H., & Sarason, I. G. (1978). Life stress, depression and anxiety: Internal-external control as a moderator variable. *Journal of Psychosomatic Research, 22,* 205–208.

Johnson, M. P., & Leslie, L. (1982). Couple involvement and network structure: A test of the dyadic withdrawal hypothesis. *Social Psychology Quarterly, 45,* 34–43.

Jones, E. E., & Pittman, T. S. (1982). Toward a general theory of strategic self presentation. In J. Suls (Ed.), *Psychological perspective on the self.* Hillsdale, NJ: Lawrence Erlbaum Associates.

Jones, W. H., Chernovetz, M. E., & Hansson, R. O. (1978). The enigma of androgyny: Differential implications for males and females? *Journal of Personality and Social Psychology, 46,* 298–313.

de Jong-Gierveld, J. (1978). The construct of loneliness: Components and measurement. *Essence, 2*(No. 4), 221–237.

de Jong-Gierveld, J. (1980). *Het begrip eenzaamheid in theorie en praktijk.* Deventer: Van Loghum Slaterus.

de Jong-Gierveld, J., & Aalberts, M. (1980). Singlehood, a creative or a lonely experience? *Alternative Lifestyles, 3,*(No. 3), 350–368.

de Jong-Gierveld, J., & Aalberts, M. (1982). De alleenstaanden. In B. Buunk (Ed.), *Andere leefvormen.* Deventer: Van Loghum Slaterus.

de Jong-Gierveld, J., & Raadschelders, J. (1982). Types of loneliness. In L. A. Peplau & D. Perlman (Eds.), *Loneliness: A sourcebook of current theory, research and therapy,* New York: Wiley.

Kaprio, J., & Koskenvuo, M. (1983). *Mortality after bereavement: A prospective study.* Unpublished manuscript, Department of Public Health Science, University of Helsinki, Finland.

Katz, E., & Lazarsfeld, P. F. (1955). *Personal influences.* Glencoe, IL: Free Press.

Katz, I. (1981). *Stigma: A social psychological analysis.* Hillsdale, NJ: Lawrence Erlbaum Associates.

Kay, C. L., & McKinney, I. P. (1967). Friendship fluctuation in normal and retarded children. *Journal of Genetic Psychology, 110,* 233–241.

Kay, K. (1977). Toward the origin of dialogue. In H. R. Schaffer (Ed.), *Studies in mother–infant interaction.* New York: Academic Press.

Keiser, G. J., & Altman, I. (1976). Relationship of nonverbal behavior to the social penetration process. *Human Communications Research, 2,* 147–161.

Kelley, H. H. (1979). *Personal relationships: Their structures and processes.* Hillsdale, NJ: Lawrence Erlbaum Associates.

Kelley, H. H. (1983). The situational origins of human tendencies: A further reason for the formal analysis of human structure. *Personality and Social Psychology Bulletin, 9,* 8–30.

Kelley, H. H., Berscheid, E. S., Christensen, A., Harvey, J., Huston, T. L., Levinger, G., McClintock, E., Peplau, A., & Peterson, D. R. (Eds.), (1983). *Close relationships.* New York and San Francisco: W. H. Freeman.

Kelley, H. H., & Thibaut, J. W. (1978). *Interpersonal relations: A theory of interdependence.* New York: Wiley-Interscience.

Kelly, C., Huston, T. L., & Cate, R. (1985). Premarital relationship correlates of the erosion of satisfaction in marriage. *Journal of Social and Personal Relationships, 2,* 167–178.

Kenrick, D. T., & Stringfield, D. O. (1980). Personality traits and the eye of the beholder. *Psychological Review, 87,* 88–104.

Kiesler, C. A. (1982). Testimony before the Subcommittee on Sciences, Research and Technology, United States House of Representatives.

Kline, F. G. (1978). Time in communication research. In P. M. Hirsch, P. V. Miller, & F. G. Kline (Eds.), *Strategies for communication research.* Beverly Hills, CA: Sage.

Knapp, M. (1978). *Social intercourse: From greeting to goodbye.* Boston: Allyn & Bacon.

Knapp, M., Ellis, D., & Williams, B. (1980). Perceptions of communication behavior associated with relationship terms. *Communication Monographs, 47,* 262–278.

Knudson, R. M., Sommers, A. A., & Golding, S. L. (1980). Interpersonal perception and mode of resolution in marital conflict. *Journal of Personality and Social Psychology, 38,* 751–763.

Kobrin, F., & Hendershot, G. (1977). Do family ties reduce mortality? Evidence from the US, 1966–68. *Journal of Marriage and the Family, 39,* 737–747.

Komarovsky, M. (1964). *Blue collar marriage.* New York: Random House.

Kon, I. S. (1981). Adolescent friendship. In S. W. Duck & R. Gilmour (Eds.), *Personal relationships 2: Developing personal relationships.* London: Academic Press.

Koo, H. P., & Suchindran, C. M. (1980). Effects of children on women's remarriage prospects. *Journal of Family Issues, 1,* 497–515.

Kosloski, K., Ginsburg, G., & Backman, C. (1982, September). *Retirement as a process of active role transition.* Paper presented at the NATO symposium on Role Transitions, University of Wisconsin, Madison.

Kraus, A. S., & Lilienfeld, A. M. (1959). Some epidemiological aspects of the high mortality rate in the young widowed group. *Journal of Chronic Diseases, 10,* 207–217.

Kreckel, M. (1982). Communicative acts and extralinguistic knowledge. In M. von Cranach & R. Harré (Eds.), *The analysis of action: Recent theoretical and empirical advances.* Cambridge: Cambridge University Press.

Kressel, K., & Deutsch, M. (1977). Divorce therapy: An in-depth survey of therapists' views. *Family Process, 16,* 413–443.

Kuhn, T. S. (1962). *The structure of scientific revolutions.* Chicago: University of Chicago Press.

La Gaipa, J. J. (1977). Testing a multidimensional approach to friendship. In S. W. Duck (Ed.), *Theory and practice in interpersonal attraction.* London: Academic Press.

La Gaipa, J. J. (1981). A systems approach to personal relationships. In S. W. Duck & R. Gilmour (Eds.), *Personal relationships 1: Studying personal relationships.* London: Academic Press.

Lau, R. R., & Russell, D. (1980). Attributions in the sports pages. *Journal of Personality and Social Psychology, 39,* 29–38.

Lazarus, R. (1968). Emotions and adaptation: Conceptual and empirical relations. In W. J. Arnold (Ed.), *Nebraska Symposium on Motivation.* Lincoln: University of Nebraska Press.

Lazarus, R. S., Averill, J. R., & Opton Jr., E. M. (1970). Towards a cognitive theory of emotion. In M. B. Arnold (Ed.), *Feelings and emotions.* New York: Academic Press.

Lazarus, R. S., & Launier, R. (1978). Stress-related transactions between person and environment. In L. A. Pervin & M. Lewis (Eds.), *Perspectives in interactional psychology.* New York: Plenum.

Leigh, G. K. (1982). Kinship interaction over the family life span. *Journal of Marriage and the Family, 44,* 197–208.

Lerner, R. (1979). A dynamic interactional concept of individual and social relationship development. In R. L. Burgess & T. L. Huston (Eds.), *Social exchange in developing relationships.* New York: Academic Press.

Lerner, M. J., Miller, D. T., & Holmes, J. G. (1976). Deserving and the emergence of forms of justice. In L. Berkowitz & E. Walster (Eds.), *Advances in experimental social psychology* (Vol. 9). New York: Academic Press.

Leventhal, H. (1980). Toward a comprehensive theory of emotion. In L. Berkowitz (Ed.), *Advances in experimental social psychology,* (VOl. 13). New York: Academic Press.

Levinger, G. (1977). Re-viewing the close relationship. In G. Levinger & H. L. Raush (Eds.), *Close relationships.* Amherst, MA: University of Massachusetts Press.

Levinger, G. (1983). Development and change. In H. H. Kelley et al., *Close relationships.* New York and San Francisco: W. H. Freeman.

Levinger, G., & Breedlove, J. (1966). Interpersonal attraction and agreement: a study of marriage partners. *Journal of Personality and Social Psychology, 3,* 367–372.

Levinger, G., & Raush, H. L. (Eds.). (1977). *Close relationships: Perspectives on the meaning of intimacy.* Amherst, MA: University of Massachusetts Press.

Levinger, G., & Snoek, J. D. (1972). *Attraction in relationship: A new look at interpersonal attraction.* New York: General Learning Corporation.

Lewis, R. A. (1978). Emotional intimacy among men. *Journal of Social Issues. 38,* 108–121.

Lewis, R. A., & Spanier, G. B. (1979). Theorizing about the quality and stability of marriage. In W. R. Burr, R. Hill, F. I. Nye, & I. L. Reiss (Eds.), *Contemporary theories about the family* (Vol. 1). New York: Free Press.

Libby, R. W. (1977). Creative singlehood as a sexual life-style: Beyond marriage as a rite of passage. In R. W. Libby & R. N. Whitehurst (Eds.), *Marriage and alternatives: Exploring intimate relationships.* Glenview, IL: Scott, Foresman & Co.

Litwak, E., & Szelenyi, I. (1973). Primaire groepsstructuren en hun functies: familie, buren en vrienden. In *Hulpverlenen en Veranderen, Handboek Psych. Gezondheid & Welzijnswerk, 4*(9), 26.

Livesley, W. J., & Bromley, D. B. (1973). *Person perception in childhood and adolescence.* Chichester: Wiley.

Llewellyn, K. (1962). *Jurisprudence.* Chicago: Chicago University Press.

Lobsenz, N. M. (1977). Taming the green-eyed monster. In G. Clanton & L. G. Smith (Eds.), *Jealousy* Englewood Cliffs: NJ: Prentice-Hall.

Locke, H., & Wallace, K. (1959). Short marital adjustment and prediction tests: Their reliability and validity. *Marriage and Family Living, 21,* 251–255.

Lopata, H. Z. (1973). Self-identity in marriage and widowhood. *Sociological Quarterly, 14,* 407–418.

Lopata, H. Z. (1975). On widowhood: Grief work and identity reconstruction. *Journal of Geriatric Psychiatry, 8,* 41–55.

Lopata, H. Z. (1979). *Women as widows: Support systems.* New York: Elsevier.

Lopata, H. Z., Heinemann, G. D., & Baum, J. (1982). Loneliness: antecedents and coping strategies in the lives of widows. In L. A. Peplau & D. Perlman (Eds.), *Loneliness: A sourcebook of current theory, research and therapy.* New York: Wiley.

Lott, A., & Lott, B. (1974). The role of reward in the formation of positive interpersonal attitudes. In T. L. Huston (Ed.), *Foundations of interpersonal attraction.* New York: Academic Press.

Lott, B. (1974). Behavioural concordance with sex role ideology related to play areas, creativity, and parental sex typing of children. *Journal of Personality and Social Psychology, 36,* 1087–1100.

Lowenthal, M. F., Thurnher, M., & Chiriboga, D. (1975). *Four stages of life: A comparative study of women and men facing transition.* San Francisco: Jossey-Bass.

Lubinski, D., Tellegen, A., & Butcher, J. N. (1981). The relationship between androgyny and subjective indicators of emotional well-being. *Journal of Personality and Social Psychology, 40,* 722–730.

Ludwig, S. A. (1982). *An investigation of jealousy among homosexuals and heterosexuals.* Paper presented at the meeting of the Midwestern Psychological Association, Minneapolis.

Lynch, J. J. (1977). *The broken heart: The medical consequences of loneliness.* New York: Basic Books.

Lytton, H. (1973). Three approaches to the study of parent-child interaction: Ethological, interview and experimental. *Journal of Child Psychology, Psychiatry & Allied Disciplines, 14,* 1–17.

McCall, G. J. (1970). The social organization of relationships. In G. J. McCall, M. McCall, N. K. Denzin, G. D. Suttles, & S. B. Kurth (Eds.), *Social relationships.* Chicago: Aldine.

McCall, G. J. (1974). A symbolic interactionist approach to attraction. In T. L. Huston (Ed.), *Foundations of interpersonal attraction.* New York: Academic Press.

McCall, G. J., & Simmons, J. L. (1978). *Identities and interactions* (rev. ed.). New York: Free Press.

McCall, G. J., & Simmons, J. L. (1982). *Social psychology: A sociological approach.* New York: Free Press.

McGuire, W. J. (1973). The yin and yang of progress in social psychology: Seven Koan. *Journal of Personality and Social Psychology, 26,* 446–456.

McIntyre, A. (1972). Sex differences in children's aggression. *Proceedings of the 80th Annual Convention of the American Psychological Association, 7,* 93–94.

MacMahon, B., & Pugh, T. F. (1965). Suicide in the widowed. *American Journal of Epidemiology, 81,* 23–31.

McNeill, D. N. (1973). *Mortality among the widowed in Connecticut.* New Haven: Yale University.

Maccoby, E. E., & Jacklin, C. N. (1974). *The psychology of sex differences.* Stanford: Stanford University Press.

Mackie, J. L. I. (1965). Causes and conditions. *American Philosophical Quarterly, 2,* 245–264.

Maddison, D. C., & Viola, A. (1968). The health of widows in the year following bereavement. *Journal of Psychosomatic Research, 12,* 297–306.

Maddison, D. C., & Walker, W. L. (1967). Factors affecting the outcome of conjugal bereavement. *British Journal of Psychiatry, 113,* 1057–1067.

Main, M., & Weston, D. R. (1981). The quality of the toddler's relationship to mother and to father: Related to conflict behaviour and the readiness to establish new relationships. *Child Development, 52,* 932–940.

Mandler, G. (1975). *Mind and emotion.* New York: Wiley.

Mandler, G. (1982). Emotion and stress: A view from cognitive psychology. *Symposium on Emotions in health and illness: Foundations of clinical practice,* University of California, San Francisco.

Manges, K., & Evenbeck, S. (1980). *Social power, jealousy, and dependency in the intimate dyad.* Paper presented at the meeting of the Midwestern Psychological Association, St. Louis.

Markman, H. J., & Poltrock, S. (1982). A computerized system for recording and analysis of self-observations of couples' interactions. *Behavior Research Methods and Instrumentation, 14,* 186–190.

Margolin, G., & Wampold, B. E. (1981). Sequential analysis of conflict and accord in distressed and nondistressed marital partners. *Journal of Consulting and Clinical Psychology, 49,* 554–567.

Marsh, P., Rosser, E., & Harré, R. (1978). *The rules of disorder.* London: Routledge & Kegan Paul.

Mathes, E. E., Phillips, J. T., Skowran, J., & Dick, W. E. (1982a). Behavioral correlates of the interpersonal jealousy scale. *Educational and Psychological Measurements. 42,* 1227–1231.

Mathes, E. E., Roter, P. M. & Joerger, S. M. (1982b). A convergent validity study of six jealousy scales. *Psychological Reports, 50,* 1143–1147.

Mead, G. H. (1934). *Mind, self and society, from the standpoint of a social behaviorist.* Chicago: Chicago University Press.

Mead, M. (1970). Jealousy: Primitive and civilised. In F. Lindenfield (Ed.), *Radical perspectives on social problems. Readings in critical sociology.* London: Macmillan.

Mechanic, D. (1978). *Medical sociology* (2nd ed.). New York: Free Press.

Meehl, P. E. (1978). Theoretical risks and tabular asterisks: Sir Karl, Sir Ronald, and the slow progress of soft psychology. *Journal of Consulting and Clinical Psychology, 46,* 806–834.

Mehrabian, A. (1976). *Manual for the questionnaire measure of stimulus screening and arousability.* Los Angeles: University of California Press.

Messinger, L. (1976). Remarriage between divorced people with children from previouse marriages: A proposal for preparation for remarriage. *Journal of Marriage and Family Counseling. 38,* 273–281.

Miell, D. E. (1985). *Strategies and skills in developing relationships*. Unpublished doctoral dissertation, University of Lancaster, England.

Miell, D. E., & Duck, S. W. (1985). Strategies in developing friendships. In V. Derlega & B. Winstead (Eds.), *Friendship and Social Interaction*. New York: Springer Verlag.

Mikula, G., & Stroebe, W. (Eds.). (1977). *Sympathie, Freundschaft and Ehe: Psychologische Grundlagen zwischenmenschlicher Beziehungen*. Bern: Huber.

Milardo, R. M., Johnson, M. P., & Huston, T. L. (1983). Developing close relationships: Changing patterns of interaction between pair members and social networks. *Journal of Personality and Social Psychology, 44,* 964–976.

Miller, N., & Maruyama, G. (1976). Ordinal position and peer popularity. *Journal of Personality and Social Psychology, 33,* 123–131.

Mills, J., & Clark, M. S. (1983). Exchange and communal relationships. In L. Wheeler (Ed.), *Review of Personality and Social Psychology,* (Vol. 3). Beverly Hills, CA: Sage.

Minde, K. (1983). Some determinants of parenting premature singletons and twins. In *Infancy in a Changing World* (Vol. 2). Abstracts of the 2nd World Congress of Infant Psychiatry, Cannes, p. 122.

Mischel, W. (1968). *Personality and assessment*. New York: Wiley.

Mischel, W. (1973). Toward a cognitive social learning reconceptualization of personality. *Psychological Review, 80,* 252–283.

Mischel, W. (1977). The interactions of person and situation. In D. Magnusson & N. S. Endler (Eds.), *Personality at the crossroads*. Hillsdale, NJ: Lawrence Erlbaum Associates.

Mooney, H. B. (1965). Pathological jealousy and psycho-chemotherapy. *British Journal of Psychiatry, 111,* 1023–1042.

Moore, S. G., & Updegraff, R. (1964). Sociometric status of preschool children as related to age, sex, nurturance-giving and dependence. *Child Development, 35,* 519–524.

Morris, D. (1977). *Manwatching: A field guide to human behaviour*. London: Jonathan Cape.

Morton, T. L. (1978). Intimacy and reciprocity of exchange: A comparison of spouses and strangers. *Journal of Personality and Social Psychology, 36,* 72–81.

Morton, T. L., & Douglas, M. A. (1981). Growth of relationships. In S. W. Duck & R. Gilmour (Eds.), *Personal relationships 2: Developing personal relationships*. London: Academic Press.

Mowatt, R. R. (1966). *Morbid jealousy and murder: A psychiatric study of morbidly jealous murderers at Broadmoor*. London: Tavistock.

Nahemow, L., & Lawton, M. P. (1975). Similarity and propinquity in friendship formation. *Journal of Personality and Social Psychology, 32,* 205–213.

National Center for Health Statistics. (1970). Mortality from selected causes by marital status. *Vital and Health Statistics,* Series 20, No. 8.

National Center for Health Statistics. (1976). Differentials in health characteristics by marital status: United States, 1971–1972. *Vital and Health Statistics,* Series 19, No. 104.

Newcomb, T. M. (1961). *The acquaintance process*. New York: Holt, Rinehart & Winston.

Nezlek, J. B., Wheeler, L., & Reis, H. T. (1983). Studies of social participation. In H. T. Reis (Ed.), *Naturalistic approaches to studying social interaction*. San Francisco: Jossey-Bass.

Niemi, T. (1979). The mortality of male old-age pensioners following spouse's death. *Scandinavian Journal of Social Medicine, 7,* 115–117.

Nisbett, R., & Ross, L. (1980). *Human inference: Strategies and shortcomings of social judgment*. Englewood Cliffs, NJ: Prentice-Hall.

Norton, R. (1983). Measuring marital quality: A critical look at the dependent variable. *Journal of Marriage and the Family, 45,* 141–151.

Nucci, L. P., & Turiel, E. (1978). Social interactions and the development of social concepts in preschool children. *Child Development, 49,* 400–407.

Olweus, D. (1976). *Modern interactionism in personality psychology and the analysis of variance components approach: A critical examination.* Reports from the Institute of Psychology, University of Bergen, Norway.

Olweus, D. (1977). A critical analysis of the "modern" interactionist position. In E. Magnusson & N. S. Endler (Eds.), *Personality at the crossroads.* Hillsdale, NJ: Lawrence Erlbaum Associates.

O'Neill, G., & O'Neill, N. (1972). *Open marriage.* New York: Evans.

Orthner, D. K. (1975). Leisure activity patterns and marital satisfaction over the marital career. *Journal of Marriage and the Family, 37,* 91–102.

Orvis, B. R., Kelley, H. H., & Butler, D. (1976). Attributional conflict in young couples. In J. H. Harvey, W. J. Ickes, & R. F. Kidd (Eds.), *New directions in attribution research,* (Vol. 1). Hillsdale, NJ: Lawrence Erlbaum Associates.

Osofsky, J. D., & Danzger, B. (1974). Relationships between neonatal characteristics and mother-infant interaction. *Developmental Psychology, 10,* 124–130.

Ossorio, P. (1978). *What actually happens: The representation of real-world phenomena.* Columbia, SC: University of South Carolina Press.

Overall, J. E. (1971). Associations between marital history and the nature of manifest psychopathology. *Journal of Abnormal Psychology, 2,* 213–221.

Palys, T. S. (1979). *Personal project systems and perceived life satisfaction.* Unpublished doctoral dissertation, Carleton University. Northfied, MN.

Paré, W. P., Rothfeld, B., Isom, K. E., & Varardy, A. (1973). Cholesterol synthesis and metabolism as a function of unpredictable shock stimulation. *Physiology and Behaviour, 11,* 107–110.

Parke, R. D., Power, T. G., & Gottman, J. (1979). Conceptualizing and quantifying influence patterns in the family triad. In M. E. Lamb, S. J. Suomi, & G. R. Stephensen (Eds.), *The study of social interaction: Methodological issues.* Madison: University of Wisconsin Press.

Parkes, C. M. (1964a). The effects of bereavement on physical and mental health: A study of the medical records of widows. *British Medical Journal, 2,* 274–279.

Parkes, C. M. (1964b). Recent bereavement as a cause of mental illness. *British Medical Journal of Psychiatry, 110,* 198–204.

Parkes, C. M. (1970). The first year of bereavement: A longitudinal study of the reaction of London widows to the death of their husbands. *Psychiatry, 33,* 444–467.

Parkes, C. M. (1972). *Bereavement: Studies of grief in adult life.* London: Tavistock Publications.

Parkes, C. M., Benjamin, B., & Fitzgerald, (1969).

Parkes, C. M., & Stevenson-Hinde, J. (Eds.). (1982). *The place of attachment in human behaviour.* New York: Basic Books Inc.

Parks, M. R. (1982). Ideology in interpersonal communication. In M. Burgoon (Ed.), *Communications yearbook 5.* New Brunswick, NJ: Transaction Books.

Parson, T., & Bales, R. (1955). *Family socialization and interaction process.* Glencoe: Free Press.

Patterson, G. R. (1982). *Coercive family process, volume 3.* Eugene, OR: Castalia Publishing Co.

Payne, R. F. (1980). Organizational stress and social support. In C. L. Cooper and R. Payne (Eds.), *Current concerns in occupational stress.* Chichester: Wiley.

Peevers, B. H., & Secord, P. F. (1973). Developmental changes in attribution of descriptive concepts to persons. *Journal of Personality and Social Psychology, 27,* 120–128.

Pennebaker, J. W. (1982). *The psychology of physical symptoms.* New York: Springer-Verlag.

Peplau, L. A. (1983). Roles and gender. In H. H. Kelley, E. Berscheid, A. Christensen, J. H. Harvey, T. L. Huston, G. Levinger, E. McClintock, L. A. Peplau, & D. R. Peterson (Eds.), *Close relationships.* New York and San Francisco: W. H. Freeman.

Peplau, L. A., Cochran, S., Rook, K., & Padesky, C. (1978). Loving women: Attachment and autonomy in lesbian relationships. *Journal of Social Issues, 34,* 7–27.

Peplau, L. A., & Gordon, S. L. (1983). The intimate relationships of lesbians and gay men. In E. R. Allgeier & N. B. McCormick (Eds.), *The changing boundaries: Gender roles and sexual behavior.* Palo Alto, CA: Mayfield.

Peplau, L. A., & Perlman, D. (1982). Perspectives on loneliness. In L. A. Peplau & D. Perlman (Eds.), *Loneliness: A sourcebook of current theory, research and therapy*. New York: Wiley.

Perlman, D., & Peplau, L. A. (1981). Toward a social psychology of loneliness. In S. W. Duck & R. Gilmour (Eds.), *Personal relationships 3: Personal relationships in disorder*. London: Academic Press.

Pervin, L. A. (1983). The stasis and flow of behaviour: Toward a theory of goals. *Nebraska Symposium on Motivation*. Lincoln: University of Nebraska Press.

Peterson, C. (1980). Memory and the "dispositional shift." *Social Psychology Quarterly, 43*, 372–380.

Piaget, J. (1977). *The moral judgement of the child*. Harmondsworth: Penguin Education Books.

Plomin, R. (1982). Childhood temperament. In B. Lakey & A. Kazdin (Eds.), *Advances in clinical child psychology*, (Vol. 6). New York: Plenum.

Potter, J. (1982). ". . . Nothing so practical as a good theory." The problematic application of social psychology. In P. Stringer (Ed.), *Confronting social issues: Some applications of social psychology* (Vol. 1). London: Academic Press.

Price, R. H., & Bouffard, D. L. (1974). Behavioral appropriateness and situational constraint as dimensions of social behaviour. *Journal of Personality and Social Psychology, 30*, 579–586.

Psarska, A. D. (1970). Jealousy: Factor in homicide in forensic psychiatric material. *Polish Medical Journal, 9*, 1504–1510.

Radloff, L. (1975). Sex differences in depression: the effects of occupation and marital status. *Sex Roles, 1*, 249–265.

Rahe, R. H., Rubin, R. T., & Arthur, R. J. (1974). The three investigators study: Serum uric acid, cholesterol, and cortisol variability during stresses of everyday life. *Psychosomatic Medicine, 36*, 258–268.

Ramey, J. W. (1975). Intimate groups and networks: Frequent consequences of sexually open marriage. *Family Coordinator, 24*, 515–530.

Rands, M., & Levinger, G. (1979). Implicit theories of relationship: An intergenerational study. *Journal of Personality and Social Psychology, 37*, 649–661.

Rausch, H. L. (1965). Interaction sequences. *Journal of Personality and Social Psychology, 2*, 487–499.

Rausch, H. L. (October 1981). A hard look at systems. *Contemporary Psychology, 26*, 752–753.

Reeder, G. D. (1982). Let's give the fundamental attribution error another chance. *Journal of Personality and Social Psychology, 43*, 340–344.

Reis, H. T. (1984). Social interaction and well-being. In S. W. Duck (Ed.), *Personal relationships 5: Reparing personal relationships*. London: Academic Press.

Reis, H. T., Nezlek, J., & Wheeler, L. (1980). Physical attractiveness in social interaction. *Journal of Personality and Social Psychology, 38*, 604–617.

Reis, H. T., Senchak, M., & Solomon, B. (1985). Sex differences in the intimacy of social interaction. *Journal of Personality and Social Psychology, 48*, 1204–1217.

Reisman, J. M. (1981). Adult friendships. In S. W. Duck & R. Gilmour (Eds.), *Personal relationships 2: Developing personal relationships*. London: Academic Press.

Renne, K. S. (1971). Health and marital experience in an urban population. *Journal of Marriage and the Family, 33*, 338–350.

Ring, K. (1967). Experimental social psychology: Some sober questions about some frivolous values. *Journal of Experimental Psychology, 3*, 113–123.

Ringer, R. J. (1976). *Winning through intimidation*. Greenwich, CT: Fawcett.

Rogers, C. (1968). The significance of the self-regarding attitudes and perceptions In C. Gordon & K. Gergen (Eds.), *The self in social interaction*. New York: Wiley.

Rokeach, M. (1960). *The open and closed mind*. New York: Basic Books.

Rommetveit, R. (1980). On "meanings" of acts and what is meant and made known by what is said in a pluralistic social world. In M. Brenner (Ed.), *The structure of action*. Oxford: Blackwell.

van Rooijen, L. (1979). Widows' bereavement: Stress and depression after one-and-a-half years. In I. G. Sarason & C. D. Spielberger (Eds.), *Stress and anxiety*, (Vol. 6). Washington, DC: Hemisphere.

Ross, L. (1977). The intuitive psychologist and his short-comings: Distortions in the attribution process. In L. Berkowitz (Ed.), *Advances in experimental social psychology* (Vol. 10). New York: Academic Press.

Rossi, A. (1968). Transition to parenthood. *Journal of Marriage and the Family, 30*, 26–39.

Roussy de Sales, R. de (May 1938). Love in America. *Atlantic Monthly,*

Rubin, Z. (1970). Measurement of romantic love. *Journal of Personality and Social Psychology, 16*, 265–273.

Rubin, Z. (1973). *Liking and loving: An invitation to social psychology*. New York: Holt, Rinehart & Winston.

Rubenstein, C., & Shaver, P. (1980). *In search of intimacy*. New York: Delacorte Press.

Rushton, J. P., Jackson, D. N., & Paunonen, S. V. (1981). Personality: homothetic or idiographic? *Psychological Review, 88*, 582–589.

Russell, D. (1982). The measurement of loneliness. In L. A. Peplau & D. Perlman (Eds.), *Loneliness: A sourcebook of current theory, research and therapy*, New York: Wiley.

Russell, D., Peplau, L. A., & Cutrona, C. E. (1980). The revised UCLA loneliness scale: Concurrent and discriminant validity evidence. *Journal of Personality and Social Psychology, 39*, 472–480.

Russell, G. (1978). The father role and its relation to masculinity, femininity, and androgyny. *Child Development, 49*, 1174–1181.

Russianoff, P. (1982). *Why do I think I am nothing without a man?* New York: Bantam Books.

Ryder, R., Kafka, J. S., & Olson, D. H. (1971). Separating and joining influences in courtship and early marriage. *American Journal of Orthopsychiatry, 41*, 450–464.

Sabini, J., & Silver, M. (1982). *The moralities of everyday life*. New York: Oxford University Press.

Satir, V. (1972). *Peoplemaking*. Palo Alto, CA: Science and Behavior Books.

Scanzoni, J. (1979). Social exchange and behavioral interdependence. In R. L. Burgess & T. L. Huston (Eds.), *Social Exchange in developing relationships*. New York: Academic Press.

Scarf, M. (1980). *Unfinished business*. New York: Ballantine.

Schachter, S. (1959). *The psychology of affiliation*. Stanford, CA: Stanford University Press.

Schachter, S. (1964). The interaction of cognitive and physiological determinants of emotional states. In L. Berkowitz (Ed.), *Advances in experimental social psychology* (Vol. 1). New York: Academic Press.

Schlenker, B. R. (1980). *Impression management: The self-concept, social identity, and interpersonal relations*. Monterey, CA: Brooks/Cole.

Schlenker, B. R. (1982). Translating actions into attitudes: An identity-analytic approach to the explanation of social conduct. In L. Berkowitz (Ed.), *Advances in experimental social psychology* (Vol. 14). New York: Academic Press.

Schlenker, B. R. (1985). Identities and identifications. In B. R. Schlenker (Ed.), *The self and social life*. New York: McGraw-Hill.

Schneider, D. J., Hastorf, A. H., & Ellsworth, P. C. (1979). *Person perception*. Reading, MA: Addison Wesley.

Schulman, M. L. (1974). Idealization in engaged couples. *Journal of Marriage and the Family, 36*, 139–147.

Schuster, S., O'Donnell, Murray, S. A. & Cook, W. A. (1980). Person, setting and interaction contributions to nursery school social behaviour patterns. *Journal of Personality, 48*, 24–37.

Schwarz, N., & Clore, G. L. (1982). *Mood, misattribution, and judgements of well-being: Informative and directive functions of affective states*. Unpublished manuscript, University of Illinois.

Scott, M. B., & Lyman, S. M. (1968). Accounts. *American Sociological Review, 33*, 46–62.

Sears, R. R. (1977). Sources of life satisfactions of the Terman gifted men. *American Psychologist*, *32*, 119–128.

Sears, R. R., Maccoby, E. E., & Levin, R. (1957). *Patterns of child rearing*. New York: Harper & Row.

Selman, R. L. (1976). Towards a structural analysis of developing interpersonal relations concepts: Research with normal and disturbed pre-adolescents. In A. D. Pick (Ed.), *Minnesota symposia on child psychology* (Vol. 10). Minneapolis: University of Minnesota Press.

Selman, R. L. (1981). The child as a friendship philosopher. In S. R. Asher & J. M. Gottman (Eds.), *The development of children's friendships*. New York: Cambridge University Press.

Selye, H. (1946). The general adaptation syndrome and the diseases of adaptation. *Journal of Clinical Endocrinology*, *6*, 117–230.

Sennett, R. (1977). *The fall of public man*. New York: Vintage Books.

Sermat, V. (1978). Sources of loneliness. *Essence*, *2*,(4), 271–276.

Shanas, E., Townsend, P. et al. (1968). *Old people in three industrial societies*. New York: Atherton.

Shatz, M., & Gelman, R. (1973). The development of communication skills: Modifications in the speech of young children as a function of the listener. *Monographs of the Society for Research in Child Development*, *38*,(5).

Shettel-Neuber, J., Bryson, J. B., & Young, L. E. (1978). Physical attractiveness of the "other person" and jealousy. *Personality and Social Psychology Bulletin*, *4*, 612–615.

Shotter, J. (1980). Action, joint action, and intentionality. In M. Brenner (Ed.), *The structure of action*. Oxford: Blackwell.

Simpson, A. E., & Stevenson-Hinde, J. (1985). Temperamental characteristics of three- to four-year-old boys and girls and child-family interactions. *Journal of Child Psychology and Psychiatry*, *26* (No. 1), 43–53.

Sklar, L. S., & Anisman, H. (1981). Stress and cancer. *Psychological Bulletin*, *89*, 369–406.

Smith, J. L. (1982). A structuralist interpretation of the Fishbein model of intention. *Journal for the Theory of Social Behaviour*, *12*, 29–46.

Smith, P. K., & Green, M. (1975). Aggressive behaviour in English nurseries and play groups: Sex differences and response of adults. *Child Development*, *46*, 211–214.

Smith, R. B. III, Tedeschi, J. T., Brown, R. C. Jr., & Linskold, S. (1973). Correlations between trust, self esteem, sociometric choice and internal-external control. *Psychological Reports*, *32*, 739–743.

Smith, R. E., Johnson, J. H., & Sarason, I. G. (1978). Life change, the sensation seeking motive, and psychological distress. *Journal of Consulting and Clinical Psychology*, *46*, 348–249.

Snaith, R. P., Constantopoulos, A. A., Jardine, M. Y., & McGuffin, P. (1978). A clinical scale for the self-assessment of irritability. *British Journal of Psychiatry*, *132*, 164–171.

Shneidman, E., & Farberow, N. (1965). Statistical comparisons between attempted and committed suicides. In N. Farberow & E. Shneidman (Eds.), *The cry for help*. New York: McGraw-Hill.

Snow, C. (1972). Mother's speech to children learning language. *Child Development*, *43*, 549–564.

Snyder, M. (1979). Self-monitoring process. In L. Berkowitz (Ed.), *Advances in experimental social psychology* (Vol. 12). New York: Academic Press.

Snyder, M. (1982). Understanding individuals and their social worlds. Invited address to the annual meetings of the American Psychological Association, Washington, DC.

Solomon, G. E. (1969). Emotions, stress, the CNS and immunity. *Annals of the New York Academy of Sciences*, *164*, 335–343.

Spanier, G. B. (1983). Married and unmarried cohabitation in the United States: 1980. *Journal of Marriage and the Family*, *45*, 277–288.

Spanier, G. B., & Furstenberg, F. F. (1982). Remarriage after divorce: A longitudinal analysis of well being. *Journal of Marriage and the Family*, *44*, 709–720.

Spence, J. T., & Helmreich, R. L. (1978). *Masculinity and femininity*. Austin, TX: University of Texas Press.

Spencer-Booth, Y. (1968). The behaviour of twin rhesus monkeys and comparisons with the behaviour of single infants. *Primates, 9,* 75–84.

Stark, R., & McEvoy, J. (1970). Middle class violence. *Psychology Today, 4,* 52–65.

Starr, J., & Carnes, D. (1972). Singles in the city. *Society, 9,* 43–48. *Statistisches jahrbuch fur die Bundesrepublik Deutschland*. Kohlhammer: Stuttgart und Mainz.

Stein, Z., & Susser, M. W. (1969). Widowhood and mental illness. *British Journal of Preventive and Social Medicine, 23,* 106–110.

Steiner, I. D. (1972). *Group process and productivity*. New York: Academic Press.

Steiner, I. D. (1974). *Benevolent vs malevolent views of the environment*. Unpublished manuscript, Psychology Department, University of Massachusetts, Amherst, MA.

Stevenson-Hinde, J., & Simpson, A. E. (1982). Temperament and relationships. In *Temperamental Differences in Infants and Young Children*. Ciba Foundation Symposium 89. London: Pitman Books.

Stevenson-Hinde, J., & Simpson, A. E. (in prep.). Maternal reports of interactions in families with preschool children.

Stroebe, M. S., & Stroebe, W. (1983). Who suffers more? Sex differences in health risks of the widowed. *Psychological Bulletin, 93,* 279–301.

Stroebe, M. S., Stroebe, W., Gergen, K. J., & Gergen, M. (1981). The broken heart reality or myth? *Omega: The Journal of Death and Dying, 12,* 87–105.

Stroebe, W., Stroebe, M. S., Gergen, K. J., & Gergen, M. (1980). Der Kummer-Effekt: psychologische Aspekte der Sterblichkeit von Verwitweten. *Psychologische Beitrage, 12,* 87–106.

Stroebe, W., Stroebe, M. S., Gergen, K. J., & Gergen, M. (1982). The effects of bereavement on mortality: A social psychological analysis. In J. R. Eiser (Ed.), *Social psychology and behavioral medicine*. Chichester: Wiley.

Stryker, S. (1977). Developments in "two social psychologies": Toward an appreciation of mutual relevance. *Sociometry, 40,* 145–160.

Stueve, C. A., & Gerson, K. (1977). Personal relations across the life cycle. In C. S. Fischer (Ed.), *Networks and places: Social relations in the urban setting*. New York: Face Press.

Sullivan, H. S. (1953). *The interpersonal theory of psychiatry*. New York: Norton:

Surtees, P. G. (1980). Social support, residual adversity and depressive outcome. *Social Psychiatry, 15,* 71–80.

Swann, W. B. Jr. (1985). The self as an architect of social reality. In B. R. Schlenker (Ed.), *The self and social life*. New York: McGraw-Hill.

Swenson, C. H. Jr. (1973). *Introduction to interpersonal relations*. Glenview, IL: Scott, Foresman.

Tajfel, H. (Ed.). (1978). *Differentiation between social groups: Studies in the social psychology of intergroup relations*. London: Academic Press.

Tessler, R., Mechanic, D., & Diamond, M. (1976). The effect of psychological distress on physician utilization: A prospective study. *Journal of Health and Social Behavior, 17,* 353–364.

Thibaut, J. W., & Kelley, H. H. (1959). *The social psychology of groups*. New York: Wiley.

Thomas, A., & Chess, S. (1977). *Temperament and development*. New York: Brunner/Mazel.

Thornton, A., & Freedman, D. (1979). Changes in the sex role attitudes of women, 1962–1977: Evidence from a panel study. *American Sociological Review, 44,* 831–843.

Toffler, A. (1970). *Future shock*. New York: Random House.

Tornatsky, L. G., & Solomon, T. (1982). Contributions of social science to innovation and productivity. *American Psychologist, 37,* 737–746.

Triandis, H. C. (1977). *Interpersonal behavior*. Monterey, CA: Brooks/Cole.

Twining, W., & Miers, D. (1976). *How to do things with rules*. London: Weidenfeld and Nicholson.

Vacchiano, R. B. (1977). Dogmatism. In T. Blass (Ed.), *Personality variables in social behavior.* Hillsdale, NJ: Lawrence Erlbaum Associates.

Vachon, M. L. S., Sheldon, A. R., Lancee, W. J., Lyall, W. A. L., Rogers, J., & Freeman, S. J. J. (1982). Correlates of enduring distress patterns following bereavement: Social network, life situation and personality. *Psychological Medicine, 12,* 783–788.

Vandell, D. L., & Mueller, E. C. (1980). Peer play and friendships during the first two years. In H. C. Foot, A. J. Chapman, & J. R. Smith, (Eds.), *Friendship and social relations in children.* New York: Wiley.

Vaughn, C. E., & Leff, J. P. (1976). The influence of family and social factors on the course of psychiatric illness. A comparison of schizophrenic and depressed neurotic patients. *British Journal of Psychiatry, 129,* 125–137.

Vaukhonen, K. (1968). On the pathogenesis of morbid jealousy. *Acta Scandinavia Psychiatrica* (Suppl. 202).

Verbrugge, L. M. (1977). The structure of adult friendship choices. *Social Forces, 56,* 579–597.

Waite, L. J. (1981). U.S. women at work [specialist issue]. *Population Bulletin, 26*(2).

Walker, C. (1977). Some variations in marital satisfaction. In R. Chester & J. Peel (Eds.), *Equalities and inequalities in family life.* London: Academic Press. .

Walker, K. N., MacBride, A., & Vachon, M. L. (1977). Social support networks and the crisis of bereavement. *Social Science and Medicine, 2,* 35–41.

Walker, K. N., Rogers, J., & Messinger, L. (1977). Remarriage and divorce: A review. *Social Casework, 23,* 276–283.

Walker, K. & Woods, M. (1976). *Time Use: A measure of household production of family goods and services.* Washington, DC: Home Economics Association.

Wallach, M. A., & Leggett, M. I. (1972). Testing the hypothesis that a person will be consistent: Stylistic consistency versus situational specificity in size of children's drawings. *Journal of Personality, 40,* 309–330.

Waller, W. (1938). *The family: A dynamic interpretation.* New York: Cordon.

Waller, W. (1967). *The old love and the new: Divorce and readjustment.* Carbondale, IL: Southern Illinois University Press. (Orginal work published 1930).

Walster, E., Walster, G. W., & Traupmann, J. (1978). Equity and premarital sex. *Journal of Personality and Social Psychology, 36,* 82–92.

Ward, S., Wackman, D. B., & Wortella, E. (1977). *How children learn to buy: The development of consumer information-processing skills.* Beverly Hills, CA: Sage.

Weiner, B., Graham, S., & Chandler, C. (1982). Pity, anger and guilt: An attributional analysis. *Personality and Social Psychology Bulletin, 8,* 226–232.

Weiss, R. S. (1973). *Loneliness: The experience of emotional and social isolation.* Cambridge, MA: The MIT Press.

Weiss, R. S. (1975). *Marital separation.* New York: Basic Books.

Wellman, B. (1979). The community question: the intimate networks of East Yorkers. *American Journal of Sociology, 84,* 1201–1231.

Wheeler, L., & Nezlek, J. (1977). Sex differences in social participation. *Journal of Personality and Social Psychology, 35,* 742–754.

White, G. L. (1977). *Inequity of emotional involvement and jealousy in romantic couples.* Paper presented at the meeting of the American Psychological Association, San Francisco.

White, G. L. (1981a). A model of romantic jealousy. *Motivation and Emotion, 5,* 295–310.

White, G. L. (1981b). Relative involvement, inadequacy and jealousy: A test of a causal model. *Alternative Lifestyles, 4,* (3), 291–309.

White, G. L. (1981c). *Construct validity of four jealousy scales.* Unpublished manuscript. (Available from Palo Alto Veterans Hospital, Palo Alto, CA 94305.)

White, G. L. (1981d). Jealousy and partner's perceived motives for attraction to a rival. *Social Psychology Quarterly, 44,* 24–30.

White, L. (1979). Sex differentials in the effect of remarriage on global happiness. *Journal of Marriage and the Family, 41*, 869–876.

Whiting, B., & Edwards, C. P. (1973). A cross cultural analysis of sex differences in the behaviour of children aged three to eleven. *Journal of Social Psychology, 21*, 171–188.

Wiggins, J. S. (1979). A psychological taxonomy of trait-descriptive terms: The interpersonal domain. *Journal of Personality and Social Psychology, 37*, 395–412.

Wilkinson, L. (1975). Response variable hypotheses in the multivariate analysis of variance. *Psychological Bulletin, 82*, 408–412.

Wills, T. A., Weiss, R. L., & Patterson, G. R. (1974). A behavioral analysis of the determinants of marital satisfaction. *Journal of Consulting and Clinical Psychology, 42*, 802–811.

Wilmot, W., & Baxter, L. (1983). Reciprocal framing of relationship definitions and episodic interaction. *Western Journal of Speech Communication.*

Winch, P. (1958). *The idea of a social science.* London: Routledge & Kegan Paul.

Wish, M., Deutsch, M., & Kaplan, S. J. (1976). Perceived dimensions of interpersonal relations. *Journal of Personality and Social Psychology, 33*, 409–420.

Wong, P. T. P., & Weiner, B. (1981). When people ask "why" questions, and the heuristics of attributional search. *Journal of Personality and Social Psychology, 40*, 650–663.

Yarrow, L. J. (1963). Research in dimensions of early maternal care. *Merrill-Palmer Quarterly, 9*, 101–114.

Young, M., Benjamin, B., & Wallis, C. (1963). Mortality of widowers. *Lancet, 2*, 454–456.

Youniss, J. (1980). *Parents and peers in social development: A Sullivan-Piaget perspective.* Chicago: University of Chicago Press.

Zajonc, R. B. (1980). Feeling and thinking: Preferences need no inferences. *American Psychologist, 35*, 151–175.

Zedeck, S. (1971). Problems with the use of "moderator" variables. *Psychological Bulletin, 76*, 295–310.

Author Index

Subject Index

321